THE COUNSELING

OF

COLLEGE STUDENTS

The Counseling of College Students

Function, Practice, and Technique

EDITED BY MAX SIEGEL

Brooklyn College of the City University of New York

FOREWORD BY HARRY D. GIDEONSE

THE FREE PRESS, *New York*

COLLIER MACMILLAN LIMITED, *London*

Printed in the United States of America

Collier-Macmillan Canada, Ltd., Toronto, Ontario

Library of Congress Catalog Card Number: 68–10368

First Printing

To

President Harry D. Gideonse

Whose vision, perceptiveness, and support
brought about the application
of the techniques and principles
described in this book

and

To

Fritzi, Shelley, Ellen, and Ozzie
My Family Group at Home

Whose interest, patience, and support
made possible the completion
of the book.

Contributors

NAME	BROOKLYN COLLEGE TITLE
Roberta Baker	*Assistant Professor, Department of Student Services; and Assistant Dean of Students (Career Counseling and Placement Center)*
Myron E. Berrick	*Assistant Professor, Department of Education; and Coordinator, Teacher Counseling and Placement Center*
Richard Fitzpatrick	*Assistant Professor, Department of Student Services; and Administrator of School of General Studies Services in the Office of the Dean of Students*
Ruth R. Frankel	*Associate Professor, Department of Health and Physical Education (Women)*
Harry D. Gideonse	*President-Emeritus, Brooklyn College; Chancellor, New School for Social Research*
Richard E. Gruen	*Assistant Professor, Department of Student Services*
Murray M. Horowitz	*Associate Dean of the College*
Irene Impellizzeri	*Associate Dean of Teacher Education*
Norman Kiell	*Associate Professor, Department of Student Services; and Counselor to the Physically Handicapped*
Ernst Koch	*Professor, Department of Student Services; Associate Dean of Students; and formerly, Disciplinary Counselor and Professor of German*

NAME	BROOKLYN COLLEGE TITLE
Irving Krongelb	*Assistant Professor, Department of Student Services; and Assistant Director of Admissions*
Archie Mac Gregor	*Assistant Professor, Department of Student Services; and Assistant Dean of Students (Student Activities Program)*
John J. O'Sullivan	*Newman Chaplain*
Samuel Pearlman	*Associate Professor, Department of Student Services; and Coordinator of the Specialized Counseling Program*
Phillip B. Shaw	*Professor, Department of English; and formerly, Coordinator, Reading and Study Program*
Max Siegel	*Professor, Department of Education; Coordinator, School Psychologist Training Program; and formerly, Associate Dean of Students*
Herbert Stroup	*Dean of Students; Chairman, Department of Student Services.*
Max Weiner	*Associate Professor, Department of Education; and Coordinator, Guidance and School Counseling Program*

Foreword

HARRY D. GIDEONSE

Students have "problems." They are not necessarily deep-seated disturbances in the treatment of which a psychologist's professional skill is required. They are "problems" because a course of action that has been undertaken is blocked and it is not clear what the student should do next. The essence is that the individual's circumstances must be evaluated and a new plan of action formulated.

The old reliance on parents and teachers is frequently—or even typically—no longer available. The tension line between contemporary parents and their children is highly charged. The Berkeley slogan, "never trust an adult" or "don't listen to anyone over thirty," is not only a reflection of the gap between the generations, but is also an unplanned by-product of the shift of the actual teaching responsibility from regular members of the college faculty to a multitude of teaching assistants who have their own "problems," and whose major concerns are related to their own progress as graduate students. Even in cases where the relations with the parents are healthy and supportive, the fact that the present student generation is likely to be the first in the family to receive "higher" education tends to throw the students back on the advice of others; and even if we should succeed in the course of the next ten or twenty years in our efforts to find fully qualified and mature members of the faculty, we would still have to cope with the change in the professional orientation of the faculty itself.

The new member of the faculty is not primarily a contributor to a

Harry D. Gideonse is President-Emeritus, Brooklyn College; Chancellor, New School for Social Research.

college community or a teacher—he is first of all a statistician or a biologist with loyalties and commitments to his profession. He is interested "in his own work." Responsibility and concern for the individual student compete with his absorption in "research." The student—apart from the classroom—distracts the new teacher from his principal interest; and even if office hours are conscientiously observed, the student senses a type of specialized intellectual interest that is not easily related to his own sense of frustration.

Teaching is essentially a human concern. It is an activity that arrives at learning through the development of intellectual integrity, capacity for individual judgment, and the clarification of identity. Counseling, which is frequently confused with "administration," is more frequently concerned than the average teacher in the typical contemporary classroom with these as professional issues.

Specialized scholarship is concerned with ever-narrowing fields of interest which do not "add up" in a sense of direction and of meaning in the education of a student, even if they do "add up" to a bachelor's degree in the Registrar's office. All these factors are intensified as the acceleration of change affects career plans, as the enormous expansion of higher education breeds impersonality, and as the new recruits to the teaching profession reflect the specialized scholarship of the graduate faculties and a consequent lack of interest and lack of professional ability to give meaning and relevance to the "general education" which remains the basic theoretical core of the average student's college education.

All over the United States counseling and guidance programs have developed in a groping and pragmatic effort to cope with these weaknesses in the formal educational program. At times the movement is itself a reflection of the need for specialization which condemns an amateur effort to futility. This is true of the skills and information which are essential to the success of an effective placement or career counseling program or to a program for the physically handicapped. Sometimes it is a process of interpretation of tests and curricular options, which are the fruit of the regular faculty's action but which the ordinary member of that faculty is frequently unable to interpret effectively for the student. Everywhere the process of counseling is concerned with the restoration of some perspective for the individual student and with the impact of the educational process as a whole.

In the competition for status and recognition on the campus, the new counseling "profession" at times shows some symptoms of developing the disease for which it was supposed to provide an effective therapy. I shall never forget an address by a college psychologist at a leading university who, on the basis of carefully improvised tests and other criteria, defined two-thirds of the students at his university as "unhappy," supplementing this with the additional fact that over 27% were so "unhappy" as to require what he called "counseling." Another "professional" in the field—who has achieved the status of a "professor" in counseling—announced that "psychological safety" required that the individual must be accepted "as of unconditional worth," and that counseling must provide "a climate in which external evaluation is absent" in order "to foster creativity." When the counselor, he continued, "permits the individual to, a complete freedom of symbolic expression, creativity is fostered. This permissiveness gives the individual complete freedom to think, to feel, to be, whatever is most inward within himself."

This rejection of norms of any type, which amounts to advocacy of cultural anarchy (sociologically termed *anomie* since the days of Durkheim), is, of course, subversive of freedom under any definition of the term. It is also alien to the idea of education in any society, whether in Soviet Russia, Communist China, Jewish Israel, or pluralist New York City. I think it would be safe to say that there is not one example in human history of an educational institution that did not have a normative concern, and in this case specialization has itself produced, in the pursuit of "psychological safety in the counseling process," a norm exactly opposite to the historic objective of the counseling movement as a whole.

The authors who have contributed to Dr. Siegel's volume are all concerned with the solid, earthy, everyday realities of the counselor's world. It is clear from their contributions that their professional concerns are not metaphysical. Their concerns are deeply interwoven with the state of our culture as a whole, outside of the college and on the campus. The counseling is interstitial in the sense that it depends for its creative contribution to the work of the college—and of the community which it serves—on a sensitive and alert awareness of the impact of the college as a whole, and on the evaluation of change in any of its aspects. If there are changes in the culture in which the college operates—think, for example, of the impact of integration in a community such as New York City—or if there are changes in the peer-group student culture on the campus (and today these major formative factors change critically and deeply every few years), or if there are changes in the college's own curriculum or in the country's evaluation of its educational product, these factors all have a bearing on the quality of an effective counseling program.

No one planned it that way, but the trend toward impersonality and abdiction, either voluntary or involuntary, by others have created the circumstances in which professional initiative and imagination have made the concern of counseling today a concern with the human core of the educational enterprise.

Preface

This book represents a collaborative effort on the part of a group of Brooklyn College colleagues. Early in 1965, the Editor invited a number of distinguished members of the faculty, all educators who were specialists in their respective areas, to prepare an original contribution to a book on the counseling of college students. Each contributor was asked to write a chapter, based on his experience, but geared to the growing needs of college administrators and student services personnel throughout the country. As conceived, therefore, the book was to be written *by* Brooklyn College faculty members, but was not to be *about* Brooklyn College.

The charge to each author was twofold: first, to cover the assigned area so that graduate students preparing to enter the field of counseling, guidance, or student personnel administration might have an up-to-date text or guide which would cover the most significant aspects of working with students; second, to provide the growing army of workers in this field with the kind of manual which might help them to offer the much-needed counseling services required by the mushrooming college population. With these general goals in mind, the Editor made clear that this was *not* to be a book which would provide a theoretical or conceptual framework for counseling. The intent was rather to create a book which would focus largely on function, practice, and technique. As a final concern, the book was to serve as a resource for those readers seeking more detailed elaboration of any of the subject areas covered. The Editor, with the cooperation of each author, therefore made it a point to provide as extensive a reference bibliography as possible for the benefit of neophytes in the field as well as senior members of the profession.

The Editor has made every effort to permit each author to retain his own particular style and flavor of writing, while exercising the editorial privilege granted to him of modifying chapter structures and references.* Needless to say, wherever opinions are expressed, they are the opinions of the writer and not necessarily those of the Editor. Such virtues as the book may possess belong, of course, to the contributors. The Editor must assume responsibility for any limitations, prepared as he is for the fact that no book is without certain limitations.

In one way or another, many colleagues have helped this book to become a reality. Members of the faculty and administrative staff, too numerous to mention by name, were helpful in a variety of ways. Mrs. Thelma Abelew, who was a Fellow in the Department of Student Services during the preparation of the book, provided invaluable assistance in her examination of the manuscript, preparation of the Appendices, and compilation of references which are acknowledged elsewhere in this volume. Miss Margaret Nesselhauf provided her usual expert typing and related secretarial skills throughout the project. In the background, but ever present, the supportive figures of President Harry D. Gideonse, and his successor President Francis P. Kilcoyne, loomed large, helping the Editor to maintain an unflagging interest in bringing the book to completion. To all of these friends and colleagues and to the publishers and professional societies who granted permission for reprinting, the Editor extends his deep appreciation. Thanks go also to Mr. John Richard Parrack, the Production Editor assigned to this writer by the Free Press. Always patient and understanding of delays and recurring bottlenecks, Mr. Parrack was helpful in too many ways to detail here. Finally, the personal thanks of the writer to his personal secretary for over twenty-five years—his wife—who again provided help, as she has throughout the years, in so many ways.

Max Siegel, *Editor*

Brooklyn College of
the City University of New York

* In general, the 1957 Revision of the Publication Manual of the American Psychological Association, Washington, D.C., has been followed.

Contents

Part IV Function and Practice: Specialized

Part V Serving the Student

Appendices

Introduction

MAX SIEGEL

In his 1963 State of the Union Message to the Congress, John F. Kennedy expressed his concern for the youth of America in the following words:

> The future of any country which is dependent on the will and wisdom of its citizens is damaged, and irreparably damaged, whenever any of its children is not educated to the fullest extent of his capacity, from grade school through graduate school.

Educators are acutely aware of the recent unprecedented upsurge of interest in expanding educational facilities and in making maximum use of these facilities so that students may utilize their skills to their fullest capabilities. The attack upon the problem of identifying and educating gifted and talented students who do not utilize their abilities effectively is a direct result of the often-reported challenge facing contemporary education in the flood of students threatening to engulf the colleges of this country. A staggering and impressive literature has poured forth related to this problem.

As this book goes to press, one-half of the United States population is under twenty-five, and slick public relations activities have been set in motion, directed toward the nation's youth, which offer statistics on the fabulous income return that education, as an investment, brings in over a lifetime. It is sad that the established and significantly high correlation between education and earnings is used as the major incentive for youngsters to keep on an "education kick." No case need be made here for the

Max Siegel is Professor, Department of Education; Coordinator, School Psychologist Training Program; and formerly, Associate Dean of Students, Brooklyn College of the City University of New York.

inextricable interdependence, interaction, and interrelatedness of education and society. The writer has elsewhere pointed out that education is a function and reflection of society (Siegel, 1958). People in the contemporary American scene are part of a social matrix which has a variety of interdependent relationships, each of which may support them, but frequently does not. Harold Taylor (1952), while at Sarah Lawrence, defined education as the formal means a society takes to submit its members to a common set of intellectual and social experiences. He pointed out that educational systems mirror the political, economic, psychological, social, and moral forces of society. Erich Fromm (1959) has described us as a nation ruled by things and suffering from what the French long ago called *la malaise du siecle*—the illness of the century. Fromm says we have much, but we are little, an attitude leading to defeatism, conscious or unconscious. Since we really are preoccupied with having, rather than being, in Fromm's terms, we lose sleep about health, money, family problems—but not about problems of society because we have cut ourselves off from the experiences of social concern, from the relatedness to others as part of our lives.

Harry D. Gideonse (1966), addressing himself to what he called "a compensatory concept of education," emphasizes that the exclusive pursuit of material security will not provide fitness for the responsibilities of a free society. Gideonse notes that maturity is anchored in the capacity to cope with tension and with polar values, a capacity "recognized as the criterion of a free man by social philosophers as widely divergent as Alexis de Tocqueville and Martin Buber," and that "education can play a positive rather than a passive role." (1966, pp. 43–44)

Rollo May (1955), accepting the Annual Award of the New York Society of Clinical Psychologists over ten years ago, commented on how much we know about bodily chemistry, but how little about why people hate, why they cannot love, why they suffer anxiety and guilt, and why they destroy each other. It does not appear that man has changed much since then.

John W. Gardner (1961) urges a national commitment to an authentic national preoccupation with concern for individual fulfillment, with our schools and colleges the heart of a national endeavor. Gardner asks whether the lack of excellence in our society, the slackness, slovenliness, and bad workmanship in our national life, are not the distractions of a well-heeled society under the narcotic of easy living. Educating everyone up to the limit of his ability does not mean sending everyone to college, as Gardner points out (1961, p. 78). The principle of equality and democracy, pushed to its extreme, will lead us to the establishment, at its present rate, of colleges at about the intellectual level of summer day camps—but colleges they will be called! The key to happiness, self-respect, and inner confidence is not the unique province of the magical word *college,* but rather of the word *excellence.*

It is in these terms that the present book has been conceived, created, and now shared with the reader. Ultimately, the counseling process in colleges and universities is not material or fact or skill oriented, but rather directed toward self-understanding, self-direction, and self-fulfillment. Thus, the effort has been made to gear the book to the overall needs of the student, rather than to any one part of these needs. The reader undoubtedly will note a certain amount of overlapping from chapter to chapter. The Editor chose to retain some overlapping, preferring not to emasculate the author's material while excising sections that would require excessive cross references.

The book is divided into five major parts. Part I provides a background for an understanding of the history of college counseling and the personality of college students. Part II includes the essential tools with which to work: interviewing, testing, and group techniques. In Part III those counseling and student personnel services which may involve *all* students are reviewed: admissions, general and academic or curricular counseling, student activities, and placement services are covered here. Part IV deals with specialized functions and practices, including vocational counseling; mental health services; counseling the physically handicapped; health, religious, and disciplinary counseling; and academic improvement services. Part V presents an overview of the teacher and the counselor with a philosophical discussion of freedom and responsibility in students and a chapter on administrative matters. A list of journals related to student personnel work and a list of audio-visual aids are included in the Appendices.

The contributors to this volume share the hope that improvement in counseling and related advisement services to students will contribute to the true purposes of higher education. The Editor, in turn, would hope that through these services in combination with formal college curricula students may leave the campus with what President Lyndon B. Johnson, in his address to the White House Conference on Education on July 21, 1965, called "the educated mind." The President spoke then of "a mind—not simply a repository of information and skills—but a source of creative skepticism, characterized by a willingness to challenge old assumptions, and to be challenged—a spaciousness of outlook—and convictions deeply held, but which new facts and experience can modify." Perhaps Harry D. Gideonse had a similar thought in mind when, as President of Brooklyn College, he addressed the faculty, urging against what he called "the euphoria of entrenched inertia." The authors and this Editor hold to the fantasy that they may help both students and faculty avoid this euphoria and, hopefully, help them to achieve the maturity of free men and women.

REFERENCES

Fromm, E. Freedom in the work situation. In M. Harrington & P. Jacobs (Eds.), *Labor in a free society*. Los Angeles: Univ. of Calif. Press, 1959.

Gardner, J. W. *Excellence*. New York: Harper, 1961.

Gideonse, H. D. The purpose of higher education: a re-examination. In L. E. Dennis & J. F. Kauffman (Eds.), *The college and the student*. Washington: Amer. Council on Educ., 1966. Pp. 23–46.

May, R. Toward a science of man. Address at the New York Academy of Sciences, May 13, 1955.

Siegel, M. Compulsory education and adolescent personality. In M. Krugman (Ed.), *Orthopsychiatry and the school*. New York: Amer. Orthopsychiatric Assoc., 1958. Pp. 235–244.

Taylor, H. The philosophical foundations of education. In *The fifty-first year-book of the National Society for the Study of Education*. Part I. *General education*. Chicago: Univ. of Chicago Press, 1952. Ch. 2.

Part I

Background

Chapter 1

The History of College Counseling

RICHARD FITZPATRICK

Today

In California college students and their associates riot, stage sit-in strikes, force the Chancellor of the University of California to tender his resignation. Across the country, students protesting United States policy in Viet Nam block entrance to a Navy Reserve Officers Training Corps commissioning ceremony, and Columbia University cancels the program lest there be bloodshed.

Comments come from all sides: the students are at last shedding their apathy and self-centeredness; the students are showing what dangerous radicals they really are. What kind of training, or lack of training, led to these campus revolutions? Why is it the colleges cannot control their students?

The last two questions are aimed directly at the area of student personnel services. They require determination as to whether the disturbances are something unprecedented in American higher education and as to just what type of structure the colleges have evolved to guide their students.

Yesterday

Are student protest riots at American universities a new phenomenon? History says not. Butts (1947, p. 304), for example, points out that in the

Richard Fitzpatrick is Assistant Professor, Department of Student Services; and Administrator of School of General Studies Services in the Office of the Dean of Students, Brooklyn College of the City University of New York.

seventeenth century at Harvard "riots were frequent." Bevis (1936) documents a whole series of disorders at the same respected institution, culminating in the expulsion of an entire class in 1810. Among those dropped for assembling under the "Rebellion Tree" in defiance of a school order was George Washington Adams, grandson of a former president and son of a future president. At the same time, President Ebenezer Fitch of Williams was forced to state, "Three classes in succession were in a state of insurrection against the government of the college. For ten days we had a great deal of difficulty, but the faculty stood firm, and determined to give up no right." (Durfee, 1860, pp. 85–86) At the University of South Carolina, "Disorders . . . beginning in 1812 and increasing during the following year culminated on the night of February 8, 1814 in a riot, which the militia of the town was called out to quell. One of the professor's houses was stoned, and his family driven out; Tutor Reid's windows were smashed with brickbats; Prof. B was burned in effigy." (Green, 1916, p. 28) In this case the faculty did not "stand firm"; the upheaval ended only when Professor B resigned. Thus the riot was not unknown on American campuses.

How, then, have the colleges sought to regulate the conduct of their students, to prevent actions such as the above? Briefly stated, the authority and responsibility rested generally with the president when the institution had few students. Then, with growth in numbers came a delegation, first to tutors or teachers, then to specialists with an increasing degree of training and competence. Most recently has come recognition that overspecialization can defeat the very ends it seeks to attain. Increasingly, it is apparent that the most effective way to guide students is through the integrated efforts of officers of administration, committees of the teaching faculty, the student personnel specialists, and even representatives of the students themselves.

As with all evolutionary processes, there have been countless mutations and sub-species. Hence, to acquire perspective on the areas treated in subsequent chapters, it is advisable to consider some characteristics of American higher education and the development of the specialized areas which have now become the province of student personnel administration.

American Higher Education

As Flexner (1930) has pointed out, the American college student is considered an immature adolescent, in need of constant supervision and guidance, whereas his European counterpart is recognized as an adult, quite capable of making his own decisions and conducting his own life. Leonard (1956, p. 3) carries this theme further: "Any conduct on the part of a student that is considered a breach of morals reflects as much on the institution as on the student. In Europe, on the other hand, such conduct is not thought to be the concern of the institution, nor does it reflect adversely upon the university's reputation." She points to the youth of early American students and the desire of colonial governments to strengthen family life as precursors of the *in loco parentis* attitude assumed by the colleges.

These early colleges felt it was their prime obligation to perpetuate the values of the community, political or religious, which had founded them. This, too, was a mandate to mould the character as well as the intellect of the student. In later centuries men would wonder whether the schools should seek to remake their society; but in the colonial period, when the pattern for the American college was being formed, there was no such revisionist thinking.

Era of the Patriarch

If the early college was *alma mater* to her students, clearly the president was *pater familiae*. There is an oft-quoted aphorism that a college is but the lengthened shadow of a man. Certainly this was no exaggeration in early America. The president taught a full schedule of classes, administered the financial affairs of the institution, and saw to the hiring and dismissal of faculty and supporting staff. President Dunster of Harvard, for example, complained of the extra work he had to do for his students: in addition to his teaching duties, he was compelled to "be their Steward and to direct their brewer, baker, cook, how to prepare their commons." (Bevis, 1936, p. 15) It was the rule rather than the exception that the college president also maintained immediate and direct supervision of the conduct of the students.

If the scholars did not live under the same roof as the president, they roomed with professors or carefully chosen friends of the president. It was understood that any misconduct was to be brought promptly to his attention. The reason cited for the dismissal of Increase Mather as president of Harvard was his refusal to move with his family to Cambridge where he could exercise continuous supervision over the students. Nor did the close proximity of student and president end with the eighteenth century: The archives of Mount Saint Mary's College contain a letter from the former Empress of Mexico, dated April 20, 1829, wherein Senora de Iturbide expressed regret that her son Salvador no longer slept in President McGerry's room. (Meline & McSweeney, 1911)

The same files contain a myriad of similar parental letters, always addressed to the president of the college. The parents clearly expected the president to be their surrogate. Leonard (1956) has cited some dozen; a few others may serve to convey the numerous student personnel chores the patriarch was expected to perform in the first third of the nineteenth century:

> Please make my son write to me. (Meline & McSweeney, 1911, p. 202)
> [My son] must not sit with the driver of the stage when coming home lest he fall in front of the wheels. (p. 203)
>
> If it be a rule at your seminary for boys to have guns you may procure him one, as he desires, tho' when I was at a lycee in Paris we were not allowed to have them. (p. 237)
>
> John must be curtailed in part of his extravagance. (p. 249)
>
> [A father in Mobile asked the president to collect $115.47 rent due from a tenant in Baltimore and apply it to his son's bill.] (p. 237)
>
> [Another father has] no objection to whatever is required by your discipline in the treatment of my son, and if you think you will have to expel him I wish you to retain in part payment of his bill his books and clothes, except what he may wear. (p. 317)

Rise of the Specialist

As the colleges grew in size, the president could no longer simply echo Dunster's complaint about being "Steward to the students" and carry on bravely, nor serve as rent collector as Purcell was asked to do. If he was to have any time at all for leadership of the school, his peripheral duties would have to be delegated. Some responsibilities went to the man known today as the business manager but called bursar in those days to preserve the academic atmosphere. Other duties went to today's student personnel specialists, who bore the ancient title of rector or proctor.

Cowley (1940) claims that the rector was not a newcomer at all, but had a venerable ancestry going back to those staff members charged with overseeing the students in the medieval university. Butts (1947) supports this point of view in tracing the development of the "college," first a boarding house for young scholars. "Masters" were assigned initially to keep discipline in the college, and only later took on teaching or tutorial functions.

No matter what theory of ancestry is accepted, however, the first personnel services in American colleges developed around the purely physical needs of the students. With dining facilities in the college town often limited in scope, and perhaps posing temptations to the sobriety of the young student, the schools sought to develop a "common" eating place for the academic community. As today, the students were seldom satisfied with the fare or the manner in which it was served. There may have been some basis for objections on the latter score; Harvard, for example, did not "bind the cooks to keep or cleanse any particular scholar's spoons, cups, or such like, but at their own discretion." (Bevis, 1936, p. 30) Clearly, supervision by a specialist was needed.

In America, just as in the case of the ancient European colleges, as soon as the student body had overflowed the president's home, and those of the faculty members and the town minister, special provisions for student housing were required; and, just as there had been a master in charge of the medieval school, a supervisor was needed here. At first the school added this task to the teaching duties of its regular faculty members or tutors in exchange for free lodging. The teachers, understandably, resented this intrusion on their scholarly reveries, and the constant pranks of their charges. Here, too, the specialist, called the proctor or prefect, entered the college scene.

Some of the housing, while comparable to the ordinary living accommodations of the times, seems to have tested the mettle of student and proctor, as the following report, *circa* 1818, indicates:

> The school buildings . . . were all constructed of hewn logs and two stories high. We were awakened at a very early hour by one of the prefects walking up and down the dormitory, smacking his hands together with a noise that could be heard all over the house—and if any fellow was observed playing possum, his cot was tilted to one side and he was unceremoniously dumped out on the floor. Each boy . . . went down to take his morning ablutions at the pump . . . a long trough dug out of a single log pierced at both sides with a dozen or more holes through which water flowed continually day and night, summer and winter. In winter . . . the splashing water formed a mound of ice just where we had to get in order to catch the water—and it was an every-day occurrence for some of us to get a fall and slip into the pool which formed by the frozen spray—and many a time we found . . . icicles formed on our hair. (Meline & McSweeney, 1911, pp. 78–79)

Housing and food of whatever degree of luxury required money, or at least something which could be bartered for education and sustenance. While the colonial colleges were primarily for the sons of gentlemen or prosperous tradesmen or artisans, there was always the chance for one not so favored by birth to gain an education. Scholarships existed, although usually only for ministerial aspirants. The working student was known as early as 1657, when it is recorded that Zacariah Bridgen had worked his way through Harvard "by ringinge the bell and waytinge in the hall." (Sharpe, 1946, p. 2)

As the curricula of the colleges began to include subjects more closely related to earning a living than were those of the classical education, more and more worthy but poor students sought ways to further their education by scholarship or labor. As usual, the president first determined who would receive such aid. In most schools he later delegated this responsibility to the bursar, who in time found the need for a specialist within his own office who could evaluate people and potential as well as dollars. Thus, the position of financial counselor began.

Just as the first services provided for students answered such concrete physical needs as food and shelter, punishment existed at the physical level. When Master Nathaniel Eaton was discharged by Harvard, one of the more serious indictments was that he frequently administered twenty or thirty stripes to students for breach of discipline. (MacRae, 1951) Yet his successor, President Dunster, was praised for personally administering floggings for blasphemy as a feature of Commencement Day activities. (Bevis, 1936, p. 30) As time passed, canings and birchings gave way to fines, fines to revocations of privileges; but even with these less strenuous measures the president needed a helper, and so the Prefect of Discipline joined the college team.

Countertrends

By the middle of the nineteenth century there were some personnel specialists in American colleges, but, as already noted, they labored principally in areas relating to immediate physical needs of the student. Less tangible aspects of counseling were either covered indirectly or totally ignored. Decisions were simple and clearcut: the student passed or failed, obeyed the rules or was expelled. There was little formal interest as to why he failed or rebelled.

Several causative factors for this attitude can be identified. First, there was tradition: colleges had always operated this way, so why change? Second, while sound psychological principles had often been used by educational leaders, psychology as a separate discipline had not yet emerged. Third and perhaps most important, at this point in its history the American college came more and more under the influence of the German university. As Lloyd-Jones (1940) states,

> After the Civil War . . . American higher education was vastly affected by German intellectualism and attendant impersonalization, and professors' interests became more and more exclusively centered on scholarship *per se*. . . . Increase in numbers in turn made it advantageous for leaders in higher education to narrow the definition of such education in order to render their task a possible one. This narrowing of the definition was attempted primarily by focusing attention on intellectual development to the deliberate neglect of other aspects of development. (pp. 10–11)

Brouwer (1949) agrees, stating that theory was felt somehow to be better than practice, knowing better than doing, and mind better than body (p. 217). The colleges came to consider only the mind and its functions as within their province.

Support for this pattern was to prevail for three quarters of a century. Woodrow Wilson, during his Princeton years, complained, "The side shows are so numerous, so diverting, so important that they have swallowed up the circus." (Weidner, 1929, p. 249) Flexner (1930, p. 28) stated in his monumental study, "It is not the business of education to avoid every break, every jolt, every crisis." Today Robert Maynard Hutchins is perhaps the most vocal exponent of the college where all effort and emphasis is on intellectual development, but he speaks for a decreasing minority.

Still More Specialists

Even as the colleges were stressing intellectual content, however, they were sowing the seeds for yet greater varieties of guidance personnel. The first factor historically was the advent of elective subjects. Francis Wayland at Brown, Henry Tappan at the University of Michigan, and—most influential of all—Charles William Elliot of Harvard led the way in offering a wide variety of courses. White at Cornell, Barnard at Columbia, Gilman at Johns Hopkins, Jordan at Stanford, and Harper at Chicago furthered the trend. (Butts, 1947)

If the student had choices to make and was to make them wisely, then it followed that he could profit from the experience of others. At first, this informal counseling came from friends or from the general faculty. Gradually, as each college came to have a dean, the dean assumed guidance responsibilities. In recent years most colleges have acquired not one but several deans, typically, at least a Dean of Instruction and a Dean of Students. (Bragdon, 1939) The latter devoted increasing interest to the curricular choices of his students. In small schools he carried the entire workload himself; in the larger institutions of necessity he acquired assistants, at times drawn from the teaching faculty, at times from non-teaching college personnel.

Closely related to the development of curricular guidance was the development of vocational advisory services and, one step beyond, graduate employment services. While in the colonial and federal period students attended college to prepare for a specific profession, in the latter half of the nineteenth century the colleges prepared men for a far wider range of choices. Here, too, advice was needed in relation not only to academic requirements but to personal qualifications. The latter area, of course, was not to acquire a scientific basis until well into the twentieth century; nevertheless, another area of specialization had appeared.

The last specialty to be recognized, yet one which underlay all the others, was that dealing with mental health. G. Stanley Hall pioneered in this area during both his teaching career at Johns Hopkins and his tenure as President of Clark University. (Butts, 1947) The development of testing, with varying degrees of scientific accuracy, at the start of the twentieth century brought a new type of activity to the campus. With it came a new specialist in tests and measurement, originally recruited from the staff of the infant department of psychology but later in increasing numbers from personnel trained for precisely that role.

Rounding out the sphere of personal counseling has been the provision of psychiatric services. As the Group for the Advancement of Psychiatry (1957) observed,

> The presentation of a course in mental hygiene and the establishment of a counseling system in Washburn College, Topeka, Kansas, by Dr. Karl Menninger in 1920 was one of the earliest efforts in the field. In the same year, a psychiatrist, Dr. H. M. Kearns, was appointed to the staff of the United States Military Academy at West Point. In rapid succession, Dartmouth (1921), Vassar (1923), and Yale (1925) established psychiatric services as part of their health programs. . . . Five hundred and fifty psychiatrists in the United States do some consulting for colleges, though only about twenty-five devote themselves full-time to educational institutions. (p. 1)

Kiell (1963) points out that "there have been strong and frequent resistances expressed to such academic facilities." Even the schools which offer extensive services refer to them in their college bulletins only in the most general and euphemistic terms. In this area the old prejudices still must be overcome.

The Situation Today

The college student personnel specialist has become a permanent part of the college scene. Even in those institutions which consider theirs a solely intellectual mission, there is recognition that learning can best take place if disruptive factors are removed. Such factors may arise within the individual himself, creating a need for the personal counselor or mental hygienist. Or they may come from groups of students interacting with each other or acting with or against the school; here is a task for the disciplinary officer, be he the dean of students or residence hall counselor. Or the disruption may be related to monetary concerns, in which case help comes from the financial counselor or placement specialist. Each of the many services has a contribution to make toward assuring that learning takes place under optimum conditions and that the rights of others to teach and learn are not damaged by the actions of an individual or group of individuals.

Training for personnel to meet these needs is no longer solely a matter of trial and error; courses and programs exist, almost in overabundance, to prepare for any specialty. Rather, the need today is for a unification of effort on the part of personnel specialists, teaching faculty, and, increasingly, the student body itself. The competence and diversity of the personnel worker does not imply that he should do the entire job himself. The experience of the college teacher, and his demonstrated intellectual capacity, certainly qualify him to make a major contribution in guiding students. He must, however, really want to serve in this area if he is to do an even adequate job. There are understandable reasons why he may wish to stay out of counseling: it reduces the time available for teaching or research; it may also diminish opportunities for advancement. Woodburne (1950) advises, "Administrative duties as a qualification for promotion are looked on with suspicion by many faculty members. This arises, in part, . . . from the fact that administration has been a part-time and casual occupation of scholars." (pp. 36–37)

And what of the student? Can he be trusted to participate in his own government? The college-age student is considered mature enough to serve in the armed forces; he can vote in some states and marry in all. He has demonstrated capacity to work in the current civil rights movement; he conducts radio programs for the general public; he assists in community improvement projects. He can run a business or, for a further example, a responsible newspaper: "*The Daily Sun,* the official Cornell University newspaper is a private, profit-making company with a salaried staff; it is, in fact the only morning newspaper in Ithaca and usually runs to 12 pages." (American National Red Cross, 1961, p. 11) The evidence would indicate that students, given the chance, can do rather well in self-management.

There must, of course, be a balance. Faculty members wish assurance that they will not lose too much of their traditional autonomy. Eggertsen (1950) says, paraphrasing a colleague, "The college teaching staff resembled the middle class in that it was being squeezed from two sides. Administrators are often successful in guarding their power, or even in extending it, while, at the same time, a more active and mature student population is demanding that the regulation of student affairs be taken from the faculty." (pp. 107–108)

Finally, there is that nebulous, sometimes ominous element known as *The Administration*. It does not matter that 99% of college administrators were teachers initially. The fact that they have left the classroom for the boardroom brands them somewhat lower than Benedict Arnold in the eyes of former colleagues. Students, too, find The Administration an excellent whipping boy. A teacher must be respected; after all he does assign grades, and he may be consulted about a graduate school recommendation. Verbal assault on The Administration, on the other hand, always finds a sympathetic audience, and is sufficiently non-specific to assure safety from reprisal.

What does the chief administrator really do? First, he operates within the legal framework set by his community and the college charter. He also serves as middleman between the Board of Trustees and the operating institution. Finally, his is the ultimate responsibility for assuring that the rest of the college is paid as well and as promptly as possible, has space in which to teach qualified students on a specific schedule, and that the college as a whole is respected in the academic world. In short, today he carries a load which might make President Dunster feel that being "steward to the scholars" was really not too onerous.

In the area of student personnel, the president is the person who will determine the quality of service provided. His philosophy of education will dictate whether counseling is to be omitted, tolerated, or supported. His choice of dean or deans will determine the action or inaction of the personnel program. His recognition of the worth of counseling services performed by both specialists and teaching faculty will do much to influence the caliber of person attracted and degree of enthusiasm that person shows in his work.

If the president sets the policy, however, it is the dean, in any but the smallest college, who must carry it out. The dean must be the hub of the wheel, binding all the specialists together in a common enterprise. His concept of democracy will determine whether or not decisions are to be the result of shared deliberation, and whether or not the students are to be offered an opportunity to participate in forming the policies aimed at their welfare.

This, then, would seem to be the picture of student personnel services emerging in the sixties: a clearly defined framework within which the officers of the administration afford their staff members, both teachers and student personnel specialists, a chance to use their experience and training to help participating students grow and profit to the highest degree from all phases of college life.

REFERENCES

American National Red Cross. *Profile of a college student—by college students.* Washington: Author, 1961.

Arbuckle, D. S. *Student personnel services in higher education.* New York: McGraw-Hill, 1953.

Bellman, S. I. (Ed.) *The college experience.* San Francisco: Chandler, 1962.

Bevis, A. M. *Diets and riots.* Boston: Marshall Jones, 1936.

Bragdon, Helen D. *Educational counseling of college students.* Washington: Amer. Council on Educ., 1939.

Brouwer, P. J. *Student personnel services in general education.* Washington: Amer. Council on Educ., 1949.

Butts, R. F. *A cultural history of education.* New York: McGraw-Hill, 1947.

Cowley, W. H. History and philosophy of student personnel work. *J. nat. Assoc. Deans Women,* 1940, 3, 152–162.

Donovan, G. F. *College and university student personnel services.* Washington: Catholic Univ. Press, 1962.

Durfee, C. *A history of Williams College.* Boston: A. Williams, 1860.

Eggertsen, C. Some practices in faculty organization. *Yearb. John Dewey Soc.,* 1950, 10, 105–116.

Flexner, A. *Universities, English, German, American.* New York: Oxford, 1930.

Green, E. *A history of the University of South Carolina.* Columbia, S.C.: State Company, 1916.

Group for the Advancement of Psychiatry. *The role of psychiatrists in colleges and universities.* New York: Author, 1957, 17.

Hand, H. C. Studying the students and their communities. *Yearb. John Dewey Soc.,* 1950, 10, 165–180.

Kiell, N. Mental health and the college bulletin. *Improv. Coll. Univ. Teach.,* 1963, 11, 92–96.

Leonard, Eugenia A. *Origins of personnel services in American higher education.* Minneapolis: Univ. of Minn. Press, 1956.

Lloyd-Jones, Esther M. D. *Social competence and college students.* Washington: Amer. Council on Educ., 1940.

Lloyd-Jones, Esther M. D. Personnel work and general education. *Yearb. nat. Soc. Stud. Educ.*, 1952, 51, Part I.

Lloyd-Jones, Esther M. D. & Smith, Margaret R. *A student personnel program for higher education.* New York: McGraw-Hill, 1938.

MacRae, J. G. Responsibility of the college for the welfare of the student. In R. W. McDonald (Ed.), *Current issues in higher education 1950.* Washington: Dept. of Higher Educ., Nat. Educational Assoc., 1951.

Meline, Mary & McSweeney, F. *The story of the mountain.* Emmitsburg, Md.: The Weekly Chronicle, 1911. 2 vols.

Morison, S. *The founding of Harvard University.* Cambridge: Harvard Univ. Press, 1935.

Mueller, Kate H. *Counseling for mental health.* Washington: Amer. Council on Educ., 1947.

Murphy, G. The cultural context of guidance. *Personnel Guid. J.*, 1955, 33, 4–9.

Sharpe, R. T. *Financial assistance for college students.* Washington: Amer. Council on Educ., 1946.

Strang, Ruth. *Counseling technics in college and secondary school.* (Rev. ed.) New York: Harper, 1949.

U.S. President's Commission on Higher Education. *Higher education for American democracy.* New York: Harper, 1947.

Weidner, Maude. *The college of tomorrow. Students speak out.* New York: New Republic, 1929.

Williamson, E. G. *The student personnel point of view.* Washington: Amer. Council on Educ., 1949.

Williamson, E. G. *Student personnel services in colleges and universities.* New York: McGraw-Hill, 1961.

Woodburne, L. S. *Faculty personnel policies on higher education.* New York: Harper, 1950.

Chapter 2

The Personality of the College Student

IRENE IMPELLIZZERI

The College Education Explosion

One of the new practical intuitions among researchers in the physical sciences is that a leap from one order of magnitude to another may be much more than a quantitative change. It may introduce new principles, new relations, and entirely new phenomenology. In the fall of 1966, the number of students in the nation's colleges and universities rose to over six million. The demographic pressures behind this trend assure that it will continue upward. Shifts in the level of conventional aspiration, together with the progressive degradation of all alternatives to college, suggest that the increase in the post high school educational population will continue monotonically but with explosive acceleration. More than one half of all high school graduates use the higher educational facilities of the country, and a striking qualitative change in the ethical and emotional texture of higher education—in the values that form the context of intellection—seems to be occurring in consequence.

One problem is that, with so large a fraction of an age group enrolled in educational institutions, the diversity of students is necessarily very great; but the institutions, true as they should be to traditions which date from decades in which they engaged a much smaller segment of the population, have been slow to seek means for compassionate and respectful treatment of diversity and, instead, have tended to seek for analytical

Irene Impellizzeri is Associate Dean of Teacher Education, Brooklyn College of the City University of New York.

techniques which in effect deny the diversity by postulating common factors and manageable categories.

It is easy to accuse administrators of depersonalizing their institutions for the sake of economy or executive comfort; it is tempting to believe that they resort to the eerie rhetoric of the computer in order to evade the responsibilities of dealing with human students in human terms. Yet there is scarcely an academic administrator who does not subscribe to the view that the idiosyncrasy of every person—his individuality as it eats and yawns and rages in the here and now—is preeminently significant and perhaps sacred. Everyone knows that, however prolific we are, we cannot be prodigal with human resources, and everyone feels that human resources are unlike all other commodities; people are not fungible, and that which is common to many minds is somehow lifeless and small compared with what is peculiar to one mind. Creation is a private act, and a society should be a great swarm of privacies, not a sterile aggregate. It is hard to find a dean or a counselor who does not feel and fear the entropy of personality.

Campus insurrections—examples of the "Berkeley Syndrome"—are at least in part expressions of the uneasiness of students who sense that their schools are not fully recognizing them as individuals. It is as if society as a whole has seen that it needs intelligence in large quantities, but has improvised only a very crude engine to locate and filter the stuff. As yet the filter is so ill designed that the raw material has backed up behind it. And, by its very nature, this raw material is aware of the crudity and improvidence of the arrangements in which it is caught. Aware that the university is more of a filter than a creative process—aware also that the filter itself is designed with mesh of extremely conventional size and shape —students, even those who can easily slip through the mesh, are rebelling.

It is perhaps a sign of our national love of expertise that our colleges attempt to make up for the seeming indifference of large-scale administration by an almost adhesive therapeutic concern with that fraction of the student body which misbehaves. In some institutions it must almost seem to the student that he has the choice of being a statistic or a case. The average intensity of personal counseling is perhaps quite sensible, but averages are deceptive. We cannot say that a man with his head in the refrigerator and his rear in the oven is, on the average, comfortable. What is needed is a diffusion or dispersion of the personal concern and the technique of guidance to the whole congeries of students.

To achieve this we would have to abandon our over-reliance on technology. We say we would like to know much more about the "personalities" of our college students, but we rely on technology to help us do so.

We use the terms of restrictive statistics and "objective" tests which "validate" each other and which "predict" events in a world modeled on themselves; we depend on instruments which conceal prototypic premises derived from social Darwinism, and which disserve the objectivity they ostensibly implement.

The Student, Education, and Society

To know more about our students, whatever our intentions may be, we must grasp a few distinctions—primarily that between Bertillon measurements and a portrait. Similarly, we shall have to retain a picture of education as it should be, a loving and opportunistic process of human cultivation careful of integrity and careless of logical boundaries, rather than accept what has become a formalistic and frequently tiresome set of exercises.

To be sure, there are practical difficulties in the personalist's view of education, but these practical difficulties turn out to adhere to precisely those matters in which personality goes beyond simple behavioral specifications susceptible to group handling. The obvious solution to the conflict of imperatives, as between the practical and the personal, is to say that if a school is in itself healthy it is up to the student to develop himself within this ambience. The argument is neat but not persuasive. It involves a *petitio principii*, for if teaching were really individual, if institutions were oriented towards the student's record of learning rather than the young instructor's record of teaching, and if the incentives to education were more than the factitious association of a bachelor's degree with a non-menial job, then the college "ambience" might favor the personal development of students.

But we cannot assume that the college milieu exists which would fully reward the high expectations most students bring to the beginning, at least, of their experience in college. For most students do have high expectations of what they will become, aspirations that are immemorial if not inborn. Each seems to cherish as his own secret, wrapped in embarrassments and learned humilities, the belief that he could be great. Although this hope may be corrupted into a desire for notoriety, it is not in itself invalid; for it is grounded in a realistic appraisal of the potential of youth in a revolutionary and well-fed society. Today's technology and the cultural rejection of prescriptive order provide opportunities that never before existed for personal teleology, for each person to choose what person he will become.

Yet the college student, deeply committed to being true to the self he secretly believes can be great, faces the world from inside a persona which has already been formed by his interaction with a wide range of social influences, and the features of which he has compiled—rather than conceived—from a narrow range of observed possibilities. The new technology, the population explosion, culture through mass media, the mechanized and automated cities that insulate us from the nonhuman world, and the liberal and permissive upbringing of a people whose whole economy is geared to serving the young: all these are perpetuated through the young dependents they produce.

As a consequence, life styles, themselves formed by the rapidly changing technologies, are altered so fast that a *generational gap* is maintained. The young continue to set the pace even though Mom and Dad are more apt today than ever before to be wearing "collegiate" clothes, essaying a "teen beat" dance step or two at adult parties, and appropriating the casual manners and styles associated with adolescent entertainment and advertisements. We might see in this the reverse of the thesis of Friedenberg (1959) in *The Vanishing Adolescent:* far from vanishing, at least in this regard, the adolescent not only maintains his lead but imposes his personality to influence the life styles of adults and preteens alike.

Lacking impressive adult models, young people in and out of college habitually look to mass media, directly and via their contemporaries, for the values and attitudes that will comprise their identities. In Marshall McLuhan's (1964) phrase which the world so soon made trite. "The medium is the message." Media offer the young person irresistible instruction in the superficial values of what is perhaps the first synthetically homogeneous culture in history. So motile is the process that the talks become teachers, the aligned members of the group reinforcing each others' values and ideas. Thus we note similar media tastes and attitudes in college students of different regions and backgrounds.

But it would be a mistake to regard mass media as purveyors only of the inherently trivial. They also cast abroad versions of "the best that has been thought and said," often, to be sure, trivializing them in the process. But, even though at the cost of vulgarization, they do achieve one curious result: they provide for the average college freshman an overlay of intellectual and moral sophistication which he assumes all the more easily because the rote curriculum of high school has given him little of comparable appeal and even less in the way of critical standards to use in assimilating ideas and attitudes. As a result, American college freshmen have an ostensible range of reference and an apparent sophistication far beyond their actual experience or solid knowledge; they have been trained to refer to intellectual things; and, as long as this training in effective reference stands them in good stead, they tend to be incurious about those things.

Student Attitudes and Creativity

One might expect that a generation of young people oriented towards college, from homes where *education* is a value, would also be oriented towards the creative process of individual learning and would be aware of and perhaps use methods of inquiry and scholarship. This is not necessarily the case. An examination of children's art reveals that with the onset of puberty (and the concomitant seeking of self-identity through the peer group and accommodating of the self's structure to the structures of the mass media and technology), the inventiveness of children is suddenly replaced by superficiality and self-conscious imitation. On this basis we might well speculate that a parallel diminution occurs in the impulses of the college student toward imaginative inquiry.

With such powerful internal and external pressures to account for, pressures releasing, blocking, forming, and prodding, what position shall one take with respect to the student's capacity for personal development, a capacity which we have not (and *a fortiori* he has not) yet learned to develop fully? We may believe that those movements from within that constitute the personal teleology can be nurtured to respond discriminatingly to the external pressures; or we may acquiesce in the belief that we are all essentially and solely the creatures of predetermining influences, cultural, biological, or socio-economic. Such is the tacit philosophy behind the fashionable verb *to predict*.

Psychology offers a compromise between these two positions by recognizing man's need to make free choices in a universe which his intuition tells him he does not control. Though he may regard the world as chaos, he can still find in himself a method of perceiving and bringing about within the chaos small arrangements of order, one of which is his own personality. He can make sense out of what he sees within himself as well as out of what his predecessors have generated in the arts and science.

At the college age as at no other stage in life there is great urgency for physical fulfillment, for freedom of address towards the great ideas, for new footings and confluences with adults and with contemporaries, and for competence in significant work. At no other period of development, then, is there such need to cope with varied and conflicting pressures and to make tentative order of both the inner and outer realities. The main task of the postadolescent period is to develop that personal quality which brings about order among these forces. What is required of the student, therefore, is to effect a metamorphosis, perhaps the most significant of his life, one which forecasts the future with remarkable accuracy, one which is critical for fulfilling the personal odyssey toward maturity.

Maturity

Almost everyone has some concept of the maturity which is his objective, even though it eludes him as he tries to define it and even though it changes form (ideally, from amorphousness to clarity) as he proceeds uncertainly toward it. Counselors, scrambling for safe ground, typically combine and expand the statements of the great thinkers on this matter. Among these, Rogers (1958) describes as mature persons

> . . . who: are able to take self-initiated action and to be responsible to those actions; are capable of intelligent choice and self-direction; are critical learners, able to evaluate the contributions made by others; have acquired knowledge relevant to the solution of problems; are able to adapt flexibly and intelligently to new problem situations; have internalized an adaptive mode of approach to problems, utilizing all pertinent experience freely and creatively; are able to cooperate effectively with others in these various activities; and, finally, who work, not for the approval of others, but in terms of their own socialized purposes. (p. 387)

Rogers (1958) himself questioned "Whether this goal is appropriate to our current culture. . . . Since our culture to a very large degree is organized on an authoritarian and hierarchical basis and only partially upon a democratic basis, it may seem to some that education should reflect this ambivalence." (p. 387) But in the last criterion of his list Rogers has apparently provided for this ambiguity. What are a person's "own socialized purposes" if they are not his personal compromise between self-assertion and conformity, the mark of his stage in what William James (1892) called "the progress of the social self" from an incontinent appetite for applause towards the approbation of an ideally knowing and austere tribunal *in petto*?

The danger of such a prescription as Roger's is, of course, that it places perilously great demands upon any college faculty. Students themselves are telic; they approach maturity, or what they think is maturity, in much the same way in which a writer creates a story. They begin with the general effect they wish to achieve and work out the details. In a sense, the young write their autobiographies in their heads before they live them. William James writes that when we contemplate great choices or great acts, we make our decisions with a view to the kinds of persons we will thereby become and the joy we may take in being such persons. This is particularly true among college-age boys and girls. Most students who write for college literary magazines do so not because they are driven by the desire to express some particular thing; they write because they wish to be writers. Students will sometimes tell you that they love to write but do not wish to publish; but they are careful to emphasize that they wish to write. Similarly, a student matures by referring to an image of the mature person, an inchoate image and one subject to change on short notice, but a telic image nonetheless. What are the available sources of such images?—literature, one hopes; the mass media, inevitably; the student's father or mother, even today; but also the succession of individuals elevated by chance and the Board of Trustees to positions of tutelage and authority. A teacher, then, teaches by what he is as well as by what he says. If a faculty abounds with arrivistes, intellectual prima donnas, verbal sadists, petty men who cannot distinguish between denigration and criticism, derivative non-conformists, and would-be Socratics who keep wondering why Socrates always won *his* arguments and they *never* do, the counselor has a task beyond the capacity of psychology.

It is, therefore, not enough for the counselor to formulate in his own mind the image of a mature person or any other ideal of adjustment or personality development and to encourage a student to move toward this ideal image. The ideal image may not correspond to one or more ideal images which the student harbors in his own breast. One cannot assume that the student accepts any conventional definition of maturity or constructive personality; the student may harbor the ambition to be dangerous, or formidable, or outrageous, or unpredictable, or slippery. Instead of trying to get the student's practice to conform to the counselor's principles, the counselor had best work with the student's hopes and improve those. He can, in fact, safely ignore the fact that the student's behavior may fall far short of the student's own hopes, so long as the hopes remain alive. The redoubtable battery of "instruments" by which counselors sometimes try to discover what a student is could well be laid aside in favor of a sympathetic inquiry into what the student wished he were.

Choice of College

The guidance staff of a college usually encounters the student too late to influence his basic attitudes towards and expectations of college. He will have chosen the college on the basis of these attitudes and expectations (which he often does not clearly recognize), and the events of the application process—the tensions, the invidious commentary of his friends and rivals, the precautionary pieties of admissions interviewers, etc.—may cause him to see the college in relation to his external, social milieu rather than to his internal hopes and needs. This may then distort his perception of his hopes and needs.

Douvan and Kaye (1962, pp. 222–223) point out, however, that the adolescent usually is not pressed or assisted (and in practice cannot realistically attempt) to make a very refined selection in choosing a school; he chooses the *type* of school to which he will apply. This is as far as his limited knowledge of his own talents will take him. But even this unspecific kind of choice may imply much and influence much. McArthur (1960) found that young men from public secondary schools tend to be more utilitarian in their approach to college and more vocation-minded, while those from private schools are less scientifically and technically oriented, apt to be underachievers with respect to grades, and inclined to see their highest college goals as personal enrichment rather than attainment of teacher-selected objectives. This spectrum of dispositions apparently is perpetuated in the college themselves. Stern (1962) sees the range of colleges (and their populations) as extending from an "elite" group where a highly intellectual climate prevails and where learning is prized for its own sake to colleges where utilitarian ambitions are dominant. In the latter, the students are more practical and also more repressed; unlike the youths in the "high intellectual climate," Stern notes, they "accept authority and like to assume it."

But even within these collective climates, and particularly in the huge urban and state universities, there is heterogeneity, since students of similar values or background find each other early in their college careers, forming cliques and "nesting boxes"—groupings which express the need for reinforcement of the personalities and personality-aspirations they had formed (or had had formed for them) before college.

Physique and Development

The student, then, in a manner of speaking, chooses his college; and he gravitates toward his friends. There is at least one area, however, in which he has still less choice: he does not choose his body. Although as guidance people we can consider with some expertise the voluminous literature about the influences of family and society on personality, when we look at some of the presumed consequences of the growth and relative health of the body, we must retreat to the position of informed laymen.

We may suspect that there is a relationship between all aspects of the physical constitution and personality; but although there has been a great deal of research in this area, its findings have been suggestive rather than conclusive; and we still lack the one-to-one correspondences so convenient for categorizing. We do know that no reliable instant deductions concerning a student's over-all personal maturity can be drawn from the fact that he appears fully grown. Tanner's (1962) analysis of physiological as compared with anthropometric changes at adolescence clearly suggests that determining a college student's level of maturation requires more sophisticated procedures than are commonly employed. Yet general experience shows that although adult bodily proportions do not guarantee mature emotional development, they do undoubtedly aid it or, by their absence, retard it.

Studies on adolescent concerns with physique and physical appearance and on psychological correlates of different rates of maturation offer persuasive evidence of the intensity with which the student observes and measures his own physical development. An inadequate masculine physique and deficient secondary sex characteristics tend to trouble otherwise normal boys and can result in serious personality conflicts or psychosomatic complaints. Equally obviously, girls, too, experience deep concern lest abnormal physical development complicate their social and emotional life. We can expect, therefore, that the late-maturing student in general, and the male in particular, will have difficulties in adjustment and in psychological development far exceeding those of the normal young person. (Tanner, 1962, pp. 207–222)

So interrelated do we assume all aspects of the physical constitution and personality to be, that positive correlations (albeit of varying degree) do not surprise us; indeed, we expect them. In one of the important older studies, Schoeppe and Havighurst (1952), report that 1. performance on developmental tasks is positively interrelated at any given age, and, 2. performance in a given task area at one age is positively related to subsequent performance in that area. This interrelationship is currently the subject of much research. Recent investigations, such as those by Escalona (1960, 1965), have sought a relationship between early physiological characteristics encompassing a wide range of behaviors and subsequent functioning. This work will contribute significantly to the understanding of the physiological bases of the personality.

We also know little about the subtler effects of environment on physical growth and maturation and on psychological functioning, particularly the effects on concentration and sustained intellectual performance under anxiety or tension. The experimental subjects in the Ford Foundation Project (Fund, 1957) were on the average two years younger than a control group of students. We would like to know, for example, what role the actual physical and psychological fact of the prestigious college and its campus played in stimulating them; for the data show that, while there was a greater incidence of initial adjustment difficulty among the younger students than among the control students, problems were soon resolved. These experimental students not only showed no ill effects psychologically, but exceeded the control group scholastically as well.

Just as we are unsure of specific effects of the inadequate physique on the personality, so we have little precise knowledge of the correlation between normal maturation of the secondary sex characteristics and the emergence from adolescent coveting of sexual objects into a mature and responsible tenderness between the sexes. Profound personality changes must still occur before the student is able to emerge from a primarily anatomical and physiological conception of sex into mature, self-controlled psychosexuality.

Although sexual development can (but does not necessarily) indicate maturity, sex disturbances do seem to be inextricably bound up with general psychological disturbances. Several detailed reports (Blaine & McArthur, 1961; Wedge, 1958; Whittington, 1963; Group, 1965) deal with students experiencing extreme difficulty in normal sexual development and a concomitant disruption of functioning in other aspects of their personalities. However, the cases reported comprise students who come to or are referred to the mental health services on the campus. The incidence and description of sexual behavior disorders, such as persistent homosexuality, among non-clinic cases on any campus cannot be determined, since most data on this subject are obtained in polls like those conducted by Kinsey (1948) and are not dependable.

A recurring cause for an obvious sexual component in personality disturbances is the abrupt release of the student from strict parental supervision when he arrives at college. Since the counselor can neither restore parental supervision and its restrictive but sometimes supportive pressures on students nor undertake to deal in depth with the residues of guilt and shame by a therapeutic reconstruction of the student's recollected experience, the counselor can only deal with the symptoms rather than with the causes of anxiety, of the boisterous denial of anxiety, and of retributive behavior by the manumitted adolescent.

Tanner (1962, p. 217), discussing the difficulty of penetrating to the source of personality problems which show up in the college years, notes that whether drives such as aggressiveness or social dominance can be satisfied directly or must find compromised or sublimated outlet depends on factors ranging from the cultural to the biological. Among the biological factors he includes the possible influence of sex hormones on the brain, which may be neurologically different where there is easy access to sexual intercourse as compared with situations where there must be repression. The action of these hormones may determine the threshold of discharge of certain neurones that establish a particular behavior pattern in an individual, thus giving rise to characteristic modes of response which would not otherwise emerge.

Such physiological effects may well be occurring among growing numbers of college students as a result of changes in patterns of actual sexual experience and in the social attitudes that cause repression. The permissive and "enlightened" parental response to the changing times has alleviated certain tensions and repressions in the homes where college aspirations are found, although it has perhaps created other problems of identity and responsibility. The fact that less guilt is involved in the sexual experience has created a climate for the increase in the reporting of premarital sexual experiences. There are also more married students on the campus today, evidencing a socially acceptable response to the needs for sex and love.

Interpreting recent college questionnaires and interviews, *Newsweek* (March 22, 1965) states,

> two-thirds of the boys and girls polled believe that prevailing campus standards encourage promiscuity; and more than four out of five said that their experiences in college had made them take a more tolerant attitude toward those who defy traditional sexual morality. Fifty-eight percent of the girls feel that current attitudes make it harder for them to say no. Presumably the same permissive climate encourages the boys to ask the question more frequently.

The advisability of employing the term *promiscuity* must be considered in the light of the at least temporarily monogamous nature of many college sexual relationships both in and out of legal wedlock. The old ideal of romantic love—though without the connotation of permanence—is still *the* criterion for male-female relationships. Goldsen (1960) observes, "virtually everyone said they [sic] considered loving and being loved [very important on their (sic) scale of values] . . . This is one of the greatest points of unanimity in the opinions reported by the college students." (p. 91)

Still, college students bring their pragmatism to bear even on their emotional needs. Farnsworth (1965) describes three general points of view regarding sexual behavior, which can be characterized as 1. the traditional morality, 2. the new morality, and 3. amorality. The traditional morality is based upon respect for authority and voluntary renunciation in line with traditional ideals. Amorality, as defined by Farnsworth, is "the central belief that no restrictions are needed." It appears that there are no significant numbers of students caught up in this belief. What some observers see in this age group as ostentatious manifestations of amorality are usually temporary and can be interpreted as the self-conscious floutings of the resentful and rebellious. The *new morality*, however, is very much a part of today's college personality mainstream and stands for many varying moralities: ethical, rational, and personal codes to fit a situation created by, and between, young people for whom "fidelity and consideration of others occupy a very high place" and for whom sexual experience follows naturally from friendship and love.

Farnsworth (1965) observes, "Not only is there thought to be a qualitative change in sexual practices but also an acceleration in the onset of such behavior. What was thought to be characteristic behavior at 18 or 20 years of age may now be observed in persons 16 to 18 or even younger." (p. 1) Such casual campus morality as Farnsworth reports is undoubtedly an expression of the intense emotional hunger found at this age level, and there is reason to suspect that what is true of the incidence of the new morality also pertains to other departures from traditional morality, which themselves may have intense emotional hunger as their base.

Emotional Disturbance Among Students[1]

We do not know whether this emotional hunger approaches pathology, since, except for the persons actually referred or presenting themselves to the clinic, information on "campus marriage," homosexuality, and other emotional displacement and nontraditional variants of sexual behavior is scattered and indefinite. But case histories compiled from *clinic* data suggest that, at least for the clinic cases, some of these "variants" are symptoms of serious and pervasive ego dysfunction.

1. See also, Chapter 11.

It is worth repeating at this point that we have little basis for generalizing about the "emotionally disturbed" and the "normal" or "adjusted" portions of college population. What we have are rich and varied data on those who come to the health, mental health, or guidance staffs of colleges for help on emotional problems, and a paucity of data on those who do not. The two populations possibly are differentiated, not because they fall on either side of a line between pathology and health, but because they fall on either side of a threshold of self-revelation. The level of this threshold is a public one, determined, among other things, by confidence, acceptance of, or awareness of the attitudes of counselors to such problems. If this threshold were higher because of a greater general feeling that it is weak or self-damaging to go to a counseling service, we would have fewer data on emotional disturbance among students. If it were lower because of increased acceptance and social approval by students, we would have more data.

We do, however, have some data. For example, from the few colleges and universities which have comprehensive health services,

> For every 10,000 students,
> 1000 will have emotional conflicts of sufficient severity to warrant professional help;
> 300 to 400 will have feelings of depression severe enough to impair their efficiency;
> 100 to 200 will be apathetic and unable to organize their efforts—"I can't make myself want to work";
> 20 to 50 will be so adversely affected by past family experiences that they will be unable to control their impulses (character disorders);
> 15 to 25 will become ill enough to require treatment in a mental hospital;
> 5 to 20 will attempt suicide, and 1 to 3 will succeed. (Farnsworth, 1964)

Such statistics become more meaningful when subjected to demographic analysis, such as the following, reported by Cornell University: of 639 cases seen in one year, 70 per cent were males and 30 per cent females, 63 per cent were between 18 and 21 years of age; 9 per cent were 17 years or younger, while 28 per cent were 22 years or older. Forty-seven per cent lived in dormitories; 19 per cent lived in rooms; 18 per cent lived in apartments; 12 per cent were members of fraternities or sororities; 6 per cent lived in their own homes, in cooperatives, or in other lodgings; 9 per cent were married. It should be noted that married students are significantly unrepresented in these statistics, as are students living in apartments and fraternities. Those living in dormitories and rooms are overrepresented.

It should also be noted that 40 per cent of Cornell's patients were freshmen. (Braaten & Darling, 1961, pp. 239–240)

A well-known study (Terman & Oden, 1959) of mentally superior persons seems to indicate that all types of pathology occur less frequently in the gifted than in the average group. But this inference has been criticized as begging the question. It is argued that by selecting subjects only among those with demonstrated capacity for success, Terman eliminated many students whose abilities were inhibited by poor emotional or physical health. Moreover, Terman's category of the gifted was very broadly defined; there is no evidence that the more unusually gifted the student is, the less likely he is to manifest pathology. But the fact that severe emotional disturbance *does* occur in the functioning (college-accepted) gifted group confronts the counselor daily in the clinic's appointment book.

Whittington's (1963, p. 84) casebook on the mental health services at the University of Kansas lists the following symptoms seen in 232 cases handled at the clinic during the academic year 1960–1961: neurotic reactions, 81; personality disorders, 81; transient situational personality disturbance, 44; schizophrenic reactions, 32; psychophysiological reactions, 11; organic brain disease, 3; affective psychosis, 1; mental deficiency, 1. There were 11 cases without mental disorder.

There is every indication that Whittington's listing represents the range of symptoms appearing at other colleges. Selzer (1960) of the University of Michigan Health Services reports, "of 506 students interviewed by the psychiatrists on the clinic staff, 35.4 per cent were psychoneurotics, 24.5 per cent had personality disorders, and 21.7 per cent were schizophrenes. Adjustment reactions comprised only 8.3 per cent of the disorders noted. Thus, 81.6 per cent of the patient group fell into the three major psychodiagnostic categories." (p. 136)

Few suicidal cases were reported. The incidence doubtless is higher than reported, since the incidence of depression is high; however, depression among students is not usually conspicuous to college administrators and guidance personnel except where there is thought to be an actual possibility of suicide; it is the suicidal or suicide-threatening form of depression that gets the most attention and documentation. But there seems to be an even less adventitious link between depression and suicide. Braaten (1963) and Braaten and Darling (1962) report that the response on the Minnesota Multiphasic Personality Inventory of suicidal college students indicated that not only were they more depressed but more obsessive-compulsive and more schizoid than were non-suicidal students. Whether this combination of symptoms has a necessary connection with the academic performance of the student and would on that account come to the attention of the counselor, we do not know. One study of college mental health patients states, "Patients with such tendencies [suicide] were, as a group, good or very good students, as measured by their cumulative average, while the non-suicidal mental health division patients on the average did poorer academic work." (Braaten & Darling, 1962, p. 690)

Narcotics addiction (or psychic dependence on drugs) is one of the more recent phenomena coming increasingly to the attention of the clinician, and much of it can be considered a manifestation of character disorder. The motivation for indulging in drugs is far beyond the conceivable scope of a counselor's inquiry. Although the example and encouragement of the peer group weigh heavily, there seems to be another, more pathetic explanation for students' taking some varieties of the drugs. The high value currently set on the creative and novel intellectual product is apparently encouraging students to experiment with drugs capable of drastically altering their perceptions. Particularly in some of the higher-intellectual colleges, colleges where College Entrance Examination Board scores cluster about the 700's, there seems to be strong temptation to use clinical means to bring about new perceptions which, it is hoped, will emerge as novel and "creative," eliciting the commendation of the instructor.

It is ironic that the groups that experiment with hallucinogenic drugs, characteristically feel in other matters that what can be technologically mass-produced is of little value; for nothing could be more assembly-line than their descriptions of their awarenesses, perceptions, and other apocalyptic expansions. That these drugs should be essential to that very area of biochemistry to which we look with increasing hope for advances in mental health and therapy is a further irony. At any rate, it is clear that the epidemic nature of the hallucinogenic experience does not distress those participants who reject with scorn the group activities described by simpler souls as wholesome. Further, for the sake of the new "awareness," they slowly risk the loss of the college experience whose flaccidity must be cited as one of the factors that drove them to experimentation in the first place.

Etiological Factors in Emotional Disturbance

Of the etiology and prognosis of psychiatric disorders in college age and younger adolescent patients, we await more positive information. A progress report of ongoing research by Masterson, Tucker, and Berk (1963) indicates that thinking disorder in adolescents is related to early age of onset and to a family history of psychosis, suggesting constitutional or genetic concepts of etiology. That emotional disorder in adolescence frequently does have pathological antecedents is also reported by Whittington (1963, p. 76), who found that a large number of his patients at the University of Kansas had shown personality deviations or symptoms in childhood. Erikson (1959) provides a theoretical model in which pathology in postadolescence rests on a history of failure to achieve prerequisite personality qualities at previous stages of development. He uses the term ego *identity* "to denote certain comprehensive gains which the individual, at the end of adolescence, must have derived from all his preadult experience in order to be ready for the tasks of adulthood." (p. 101)

Of psychopathology in the college-age person, Erikson (1959) writes that many patients break down in the postadolescent period as a result of "an inability to establish an identity: . . . they all suffer from acute identity diffusion . . . manifest at a time when the young individual finds himself exposed to a combination of experiences which demand his simultaneous commitment to physical intimacy (not by any means overtly sexual), to decisive occupational choice, to energetic competition, and to psychosocial self-definition." (pp. 122–123) The lack of a sense of self is revealed nowhere more strongly than when the young person attempts to achieve significant social contacts, and it is manifested by such behavior as tension and flight into stereotyped and formalized interpersonal relationships, peculiar strains in early efforts at achieving intimacy, and inability to rescue a developing value structure from those who would subvert it. (p. 125)

To attend college is to journey from the known social, geographic, and familial confines to emancipation and responsibility within a larger psychological society than has previously been experienced. The most dramatic of the social changes in today's colleges are quantitative: there are more students from lower-income families, more married students, more students from minority and nonwhite groups. What impact these new groups of the student population have on college personality through their roles, reactions and influence, no one yet has satisfactorily defined. In particular, it may be that the gross changes in the population attending institutions of higher education relate to one set of institutions—community colleges, normal schools turned liberal arts colleges, etc.—while certain of the psychological problems which we have described as increasingly frequent relate to another set of institutions—the high intellectual ones—in which the proportion of first-generation-in-college students may actually be on the decline.

Influences on College Students

Research over the past two decades describes the college student as self-interested, group dependent, and peer-group oriented; rationalistic and utilitarian in his approach to morality, religion, and relations with others, yet needing love; concerned with interpersonal experiences rather than scholarship in school. But these characterizations must be more closely related than they have been thus far to a social taxonomy of colleges.

Of the peer-group's power over individual members, Newcomb (1962, pp. 469–470) observed that the preceptions of reality to which students respond in all but the simplest situations are conditioned not only by physiological make-up, but by perception patterns that have been learned as a result of successes and failures. Noting powerful, complex interrelationships between individuals' notions of success and failure and groups' influences on these perceptual habits, he traced this power of the group to its ability to reward or punish by according applause or shame. Governed by standards that might appear arbitrary to outsiders, groups create a social reality that has the psychological impact of ineluctability.

But the empirical grounds are "not as solid as many of us would like to believe" for concluding that substantial peer-group effects *in fact* occur in contemporary colleges. Student peer-group studies (Newcomb, 1962) seem to justify the following conclusions:

> 1. Under certain conditions there have been several demonstrations of marked changes in attitude, of consensual nature.
> 2. A much larger set of studies fails to show significant amounts of such changes. . . . Almost without exception, however, these studies have made no attempt to study differentiated peer-groups . . . [but have assumed that] . . . entire classes, or even entire student bodies, constitute membership groups.
> 3. Many and probably most of this larger body of studies have, quite understandably concentrated upon the kinds of attitude changes that educators consider desirable.

We cannot expect that group pressures will be relieved by the influence of the teacher. "Teachers' influence, if it is to be effective, must be caught up in the norms of student groups, and the degree to which this occurs bears no necessary relationship to the frequency of their direct contact with students. It can operate at a distance, mediated by some students so as to affect others." (Newcomb, 1962, p. 485)

What would be needed in order to heighten the influence of the faculty would be moderately-sized college groupings, considerable overlapping between memberships of instruction groups and living groups, and overlapping between both these areas and areas of faculty contact. In a situation so structured, student groups could experience simultaneous excitation from the "same lecture, the same book, or the same seminar, with resulting reverberations in their peer-group life, so that they re-enforce and sustain one another's excitement." In the typical large university such an outcome is only a chance occurrence. But unless the college structure is changed to make this desirable outcome possible, what can be expected is the continuation of the present trend in which "increasingly (in this country, at any rate) the social-psychological motors of student life are racing, disconnected from the wheels of intellectual development." Under these conditions, "the means of exploiting the power delivered by these motors are at [anyone's] command." (Newcomb, 1962, pp. 486–487)

Ten years ago, Wise (1958) thought he detected a trend away from mindless passivity and a gradual change among the agents capable of exerting power over student life. "The shift in control of student behavior has shown consistent change; from a strict regimentation imposed by the college administration, the control passed to faculty-student and then to student groups, and the current trend seems to be toward an even more individualistic system, wherein the outside controls are minimal." (p. 38) But it is difficult to see how the student's passage through the earlier stages of this process would leave him so unmarked by each of the agents that its imprint would not be visible even when external controls have been shed.

Students and Values[2]

There are reports that students who remain in college are likely to become more skeptical and tolerant and less ethnocentric than they were as freshmen (Plant, 1962; Webster, Freedman, & Heist, 1962) and that seniors show greater liberalism and sophistication in political, social, and religious outlook than freshmen. Yet other reports view the college student as "self-confident, self-satisfied, and self-centered," divorced from involvement in any issues larger than the immediate world of friends, relatives, and hometown. (Jacob, 1957, pp. 14–15) Is the one collective student responding to adult attitudes by reaction and the other responding by reflection? And would the small minority of students, estimated at one to two per cent across the land, aroused to demonstration by the Vietnam war be characterized as sophisticated or naive? How do we know what correspondence, if any, exists between the written or oral responses to polls and questionnaires and the students' actual outlooks? From their respective

2. See Chapter 18.

positions, several researchers (Jacob, 1957; Reisman, 1958; Wise, 1958) agree that there is little efficacy in value questionnaires and such tests in which students respond to questions based on testers' assumptions couched in outdated cliches and begging to be answered in kind. One wonders, for example, if the questions given the Vassar student were not perceived in just this way. In great numbers these students appeared to shun the intellectual and social extremes of the bohemians and the debutantes in favor of moderation, collective harmony, long-range security, and a "smoothly-moving collegiate experience." (Bushnell, 1962, p. 507–508)

We should also examine Jacob's (1957) picture of college as a cocoon in which new value orientations can mature and solidify. Is he referring to the pleasures of being dormant and secure, or to the risks of metamorphosis? Wise (1958) suggests the former: "To sum up, many of today's college students may be described as rather cautious seekers after an inner security in an outwardly secure world." (p. 31)

Perhaps because of the extraordinary increase in the number of applicants for each available place, there *is* a great desire to conform to the requirements of the educational system, not so much to accept the discipline without which scholastic achievement is impossible as to reap whatever benefits, economic or otherwise, may come with a college degree. There is no question that the tone of college education has become increasingly jaded. There seems to be less eager doubt, less hopeful searching, less constructive intellectual boldness, less playfulness, less childlike wonder in the classroom than ever before. The great questions have given way to mere questioning, the quest has given way to restlessness. And there is an extraordinary air of disappointment on most campuses. A large number of students, demonstrably of high intellectual ability, who very clearly intend ultimately to enter learned or skilled fields, do drop out of college, sometimes for a year or two, sometimes forever, because college is not what they expected or wanted.

The opposite side of the coin shows the constructive, creative, and often heroic enthusiasms of students dedicated to internally developed ideals of justice or liberty, confident in their convictions and not attracted by rabble-rousing or marching for marching's sake. These students use techniques of passive or quite active resistance to traditional forms which they believe unfair or unworkable. They comprise a group of social activists and pacifists well publicized lately, perhaps beyond their actual force and number. Whether this minority, eager to demonstrate its beliefs as well as its discontents, will grow far beyond the traditional percentage of student dissenters we do not know. We do know that the effectiveness of student demonstration is not as great in this country as it once was and that our students, in contrast with students in the rest of the world, have relatively little hope of changing things. That they are socially and politically impotent is seen by all but the most vigorous and naive students, and this awareness may have some bearing on the coolness and indifference attributed to the student population by various researchers. The only real power adolescent college students have is economic; but as they are dependent on others for their money, and as that money is quickly used up, this economic power cannot be effectively harnessed to radical or long range objectives.

Is it the tendency of today's students to be glib, to follow lines of least resistance, and to avoid responsibility? Eddy (158, pp. 9–20) found the verbalized ideas of students on their achievement in college to be "If pushed, inspired, or led, we would achieve more at college and get more out of the college experience." But glibness is fostered by the rewards which multiple-choice tests offer to those who respond rapidly, who tolerate intellectual approximation, and who dismiss subtleties and doubts with the formula that the correct answer is "the answer you can tell they want." If this glibness should come to characterize the personality of the young, the consequences to society could be serious. For, as Riesman (1950) shows in *The Lonely Crowd,* and more recently Arendt (1963) in her study of Eichmann, the lack of deeply felt and deeply understood personal values creates a neutral and malleable quality much favored by both the totalitarian personality and the businessman.

When asked directly about college effectiveness, Cornell students express satisfaction. The majority of the students, far from being rebellious, are conservative (Goldsen, 1960). This is by now a familiar note; and it is no surprise that, while a vast majority of students declare allegiance to traditional democratic rights, few become deeply moved by anything political. Perhaps college students are still too young to translate ideals into an adequate response; or perhaps they are mouthing words they assume interviewers want to hear, and confusion or emptiness lies beneath; so they remain inert and conservative until they are pushed, inspired or led.

The Cornell students said that they were virtually all believers, in some ethico-religious sense, but there seemed to be striking incongruities in the subjects' statements about their beliefs and their actions. The religious values actually held by students were, according to the investigator, "secular, vague, and personal." And a majority of these "believers" held that "goals which serve highly individual and personal ends" would be essential to their ideal belief system. (Goldsen, 1960, pp. 201–202) With such an amorphous view of religion prevalent on the campus, it is no surprise that a sizeable majority of the National Merit Scholars, especially men, expressed a decreasing need for religious faith and an indifference to the teaching of religious values in colleges (Webster, Freedman, & Heist, 1962).

Academic Performance and Personality

Scarcely a report on the college student or his college fails to suggest ways of strengthening the existing college system in which the ripening personality is caught up. Since only the strong student takes care of himself and can meet effectively what so many others experience as the "shock of averageness" (Whitla, 1962), many critics call for intensive and significant guidance to nourish and develop students who might otherwise be lost in the press of college. Others urge a sharper contrast between high school and college approaches to instruction; and, to vary the climate, the establishment of satellite colleges within monolithic universities. (Riesman, 1958) Still others suggest a change from an intellectually-centered curriculum to an experientially-centered one, placing greater demands on liberal arts students for personal decisions.

It is entirely possible that such a reorientation of the liberal arts college could create a situation in which liberal arts colleges could be used as a "glory hole" for adolescents of mediocre intelligence whose parents can not accept their children's limitations. The keener intelligences might gather in the more vocationally-oriented universities and institutes of technology where the elegances of cognition are on open display. The supposition, however, that keen intelligence is accompanied by a keen ambition to use it is not clearly supported by data; indeed we know little about the relationship between measured intelligence and measured achievement except that it is less than stable and is suggestively fractional. This may mean that academic achievement calls for traits unrelated to the special kinds of intelligence which largely determine the over-all global IQ. Or it may mean that academic achievement is dependent in large but varying measure on adventitious factors in the domain of personality. There is extensive literature on certain of these extra-intellectual factors as they relate to academic achievement. Demographic, psychosocial, institutional variables have been studied. Stein (1963) classifies current effort to determine the relationship between academic performance and antecedent personality factors. His conclusions bear out those of Sexton (1965), who reviews twenty-five years of research on attrition in college.

With all this investigation there is no clear evidence of the role played by any specific variable in scholastic achievement.

For this inconclusiveness a basic defect of methodology may be responsible. The tacit premise of statistical research in such questions is that individual idiosyncrasies cancel out in the mass; but, in fact, the dynamics of the college classroom are by no means so diverse as to assure that institutional styles and even styles within subject-matter departments are not highly significant in determining the grades of students at a given level of academic achievement. It is entirely possible, for example, that certain kinds of voluble and disputatious personality might be considered highly acceptable in humanistic disciplines and wholly unacceptable in engineering or in mathematics. In other words, there has been inadequate research on the effect of institutionalized personality-expectations upon the measures of academic performance themselves.

But if research is lacking on the effect of personality on academic performance, it is even more conspicuously lacking on the effect of academic performance on personality. In classical ages and throughout the Middle Ages, the persistent assumption was that the intellectual apprehension of moral and ethical truths would in fact affect the personal practice of morality and ethics. With the discovery of the immense force which unconscious and subconscious drives and reactions exert upon conduct, however, the development of personality began to be regarded as determined exclusively by pre-intellectual and sub-intellectual experience. Among psychologists, there are few who believe that conduct can be altered from the pulpit and many who believe that it can be altered only on the couch. Yet there are suspiciously few data on this point. There is no data-backed reason to believe that what a student learns about psychology, about ethical theory, about the history of philosophy, and about biology is without effect upon his personality.

There is, again, no reason to believe that the experience of success does not change a student's self-image. Certainly the converse is a familiar occurrence in colleges. Every college counselor knows the effect upon a boy of moving from a high school where (without extraordinary effort) he has been conspicuously able to a college where only the most strenuous effort will keep him in the running. But there is very little research on the effect of college experiences on a student's self-ranking on intellectual scales.

The actual abilities of students are, moreover, almost certainly affected by the challenge of college work. Not only do the mentally superior hold their own over a period of years, but they actually become more intelligent as they exercise their intelligence. The most noteworthy studies in mental growth (Bayley, 1956; Bayley, 1957; Bayley & Oden, 1955; Florence, 1947; McConnell, 1934; Pinneau & Jones, 1958; Silvey, 1951; Terman & Oden, 1959) indicate that students' mental ability can be expected to increase significantly during the college years. It is entirely possible that these increases are a statistical artifact: they may be the result of the highly selective purview of the tests and the focusing of abilities by practice. Nevertheless, recent work in genetic psychology and in molecular biology suggests that experience improves one's receptivity to further experience. The effect upon the adolescent personality of an awareness of growing intellectual powers constitutes a neglected but important field for research.

Needed Research

There are two studies which suggest lines for investigating the relation of institutional styles and procedures to the development of intellectual capacities of students. Pepinsky (1960) notes the invariable presence of a supportive person in the lives of bright high achievers. The role of this sponsor or patron is conceived of as in no way conflicting with the desirability of a loosely structured program, such as was preferred by the highly gifted and creative subjects of Drehvdal's study (1962). The preference of gifted students for a less authoritarian educational structure is also suggested by Warren and Heist (1960). One important line of investigation would be an extended longitudinal study of such preferences as they are viewed retrospectively by the subjects. The list of teachers to whom a college senior feels beholden may not be the same list that he would construct ten or fifteen years later when he has begun to assume managerial responsibilities in his economic life and paternal responsibilities in his domestic life.

Because college students are very accessible as subjects for psychological investigation, the volume of research on student aptitudes and attitudes is great. That the yield in significance is comparatively small is noted by Sanford (1962) and by Wise (1964), among many others. The available studies are incomplete and circumscribed, and one cannot avoid the suspicion that they are atypically distributed over the college population. The most sophisticated campuses have been the most studied, but they are not the most populated. There is, therefore, no reliable description of American college students as a broad group; moreover, time-changes in students are virtually impossible to describe.

So prestigious is theoretical science and so complete is our assumption that science precedes and produces technology that the paucity of research may inhibit many practicing counselors. It is a fact, however, that design and efficient use often precedes theoretical abstraction. Steam engines, for example, preceded even the most rudimentary theories of thermodynamics, and indeed the basic discoveries of thermodynamic theory proceeded from steam-engine technology. It would be a disservice to psychological theory as well as to the college student were the practicing college counselor to withhold his counsel pending systematic investigation.

In addition, the theoretical bases of all applied psychology, including guidance, will almost certainly be revolutionized within the next decade by the rapid development of instrumentation and by information yielding new insights into the bio-physical mechanisms of thought and feeling. Molecular biology begins to furnish nearly adequate models of the processes by which protoplasm makes more protoplasm and cell transmits to cell an immense variety of potentialities and a rich lexicon for translating the demands of the environment into cues for individual growth and change. The significance of molecular biology for psychologists is pointed out by Schmitt (1965):

> In the context of their application in the rapidly expanding fields of molecular neurology and molecular neuropsychology, recent techniques and concepts of neuro- and psychopharmacology offer much promise. Affective behavior, involving mood and coloring of normal behavior or various degrees of abnormal behavior, is thought to be conditioned by small molecular modulators, such as the potent biogenic amines and a wide variety of pharmacological agents, including tranquilizers. Such compounds may affect not only axons and synapses in the central nervous system but also the nerve cell bodies, possibly by influencing synthetic processes through their biogenetic controls. Such experiments may lead to better understanding of the nature of brain and behavioral abnormalities and, hopefully, to methods of improving normal memory processing and learning. (p. 935)

The revolution, Schmitt points out, may be the most far reaching in human history: "Whether one likes it or not, man has embarked on the greatest of human experiments, probably far overshadowing in potentialities the exploration of outer space—namely, that of determining whether, by taking thought, man can discover the mechanism of thinking and whether, by so doing, he can achieve new orders of understanding not excluding certain aspects of his inner personal nature." (p. 935)

The social and political risks of such a revolution in our knowledge and control of our own process of knowledge and control are obvious; the philosophical consequences may be immediate and deadly. The mere hope that molecular biology, assisted by the analytical techniques made possible by the digital computer, can set up a complete physical description of mental events, may entice psychologists into taking a view of the mind even more reductive than that which has tended to grow up under the supposed auspices of behaviorism and experimental psychology. It is a persistent tendency of scientists to delimit their inquiries according to their available methodology and then implicitly to deny the reality of all phenomena and problems outside the scope of their inquiries: *rem metiri posse, rem esse putare*. Pending the clear success of the revolution in psychology, those who accept the responsibility of easing and guiding the educational experiences of human beings—and we must remember that of all human beings, the college student is distinctively the archetype of the culture, and that what happens to him happens, in a sense, to us all—must resist the temptation to discard insights based upon less microscopically precise data and implying a less exclusively physical model of experience. They should ignore the Damoclean electron microscope hanging over their heads. It is, after all, by no means certain that when the revolutionary expansion of our knowledge of the physical characteristics of psychological events is pushed to a new level of precision we shall be any closer to the formulation of a world without mysteries, a world without opacities.

The finest instrument now at the disposal of the counselor is his own head, equipped with ears, eyes, and tongue. For the time being, at any rate, the best use of this instrument demands that it correspond in its mode of action more closely to the subject it is used to studying, not to a computer with a capacious but coarsely categorizing memory and rigid procedures of inference. For the time being, it is humanistic research rather than reductive research that is useful for guidance.

REFERENCES

Arendt, Hannah. *Eichmann in Jerusalem: a report on the banality of evil.* New York: Viking Press, 1963.

Bayley, Nancy. Individual patterns of development. *Child Develpm.*, 1956, 27, 45–75.

Bayley, Nancy. Data on the growth of intelligence between 16 and 21 years as measured by the Wechsler-Bellevue Scale. *J. genet. Psychol.*, 1957, 90, 3–5.

Bayley, Nancy & Oden, Melita H. The maintenance of intellectual ability in gifted adults. *J. Geront.*, 1955, 10, 91–107.

Blaine, G. B. & McArthur, C. C. *Emotional problems of the student*. New York: Appleton-Century-Crofts, 1961.

Braaten, L. J. Some reflections on suicidal tendencies among college students. *Ment. Hyg., N.Y.*, 1963, 47, 562–568.

Braaten, L. J. & Darling, C. D. Mental health services in college: some statistical analyses. *Student Med.*, 1961, 10, 235–253.

Braaten, L. J. & Darling, C. D. Suicidal tendencies among college students. *Psychiat. quart.*, 1962, 36, 665–691.

Bushnell, J. Student culture at Vassar. In N. Sanford (Ed.), *The American college*. New York: Wiley, 1962. Pp. 489–514.

Department of Commerce, Bureau of the Census. *Statistical abstracts of the United States*. Washington: Author, 1966.

Douvan, Elizabeth & Kaye, Carol. Motivational factors in college entrance. In N. Sanford (Ed.), *The American college*. New York: Wiley, 1962. Pp. 199–224.

Drevdahl, J. E. Educational etiology of creativity. *Gifted child quart.*, 1962, 6 (3), 91–94.

Eddy, E. *The college influence on student character*. Washington: Amer. Council on Educ., 1959.

Erikson, E. H. Identity and the life cycle. *Psychol. Issues*, 1959, 1 (1).

Escalona, Sibylle K. Some determinants of individual difference. *Trans. N.Y. Acad. Sci.*, 1965, 27 (7), 802–816.

Escalona, Sibylle K. & Heider, Grace M. *Prediction and outcome: a study in child development*. New York: Basic Books, 1960.

Farnsworth, D. L. Emotional problems of college students. Feelings and their medical significance. *Ross Laboratories*, 1964, 6 (10), No. 43216.

Farnsworth, D. L. Sexual morality and the dilemma of the colleges. Paper read at Amer. Orthopsychiat. Assoc., Cambridge, Mass., March, 1965.

Farnsworth, D. L. *Psychiatry, education, and the young adult*. Springfield, Ill.: Charles C Thomas, 1966.

Florence, Louise M. Mental growth and development at the college level. *J. educ. Psychol.*, 1947, 38, 65–82.

Freedman, M. B. Studies of college alumni. In N. Sanford (Ed.), *The American college*. New York: Wiley, 1962. Pp. 847–886.

Freedman, M. B. Personality growth in the college years. *Coll. Bd. Rev.*, 1965, 56, 25–32.

Freedman, M. B. The passage through college. *J. soc. Issues*, 1956, 12, 13–28.

Friedenberg, E. Z. *The vanishing adolescent*. Boston: Beacon Press, 1959.

Fund for the Advancement of Education. *They went to college early*. New York: Author, 1957.

Group for the Advancement of Psychiatry. *Considerations on personality development in college students*. New York: Author, 1955. No. 32.

Group for the Advancement of Psychiatry. *Sex and the college student*. New York: Author, 1965. No. 60.

Golden, Rose. *What college students think*. Princeton: Van Nostrand, 1960.

Habein, Margaret L. (Ed.) *Spotlight on the college student*. Washington: Amer. Council on Educ., 1959.

Havighurst, R. J. *American education in the 1960's*. Columbus: Ohio State Univ. Press, 1960.

Impellizzeri, Irene. The nature and scope of the problem. In L. M. Miller (Ed.), *Guidance for the underachiever with superior ability*. Washington: Govt. Print. Off., 1961, No. 25.

Jacob, P. E. *Changing values in college: an exploratory study of the impact of college teaching*. New York: Harper, 1957.

James, W. *Psychology: briefer course*. New York: Holt, 1892.

Kinsey, A. C., Pomeroy, W. B., & Martin, C. E. *Sexual behavior in the human male*. Philadelphia: W. B. Saunders, 1948.

McArthur, C. Sub-culture and personality during the college years. *J. educ. Sociol.*, 1960, 33, 260–268.

McConnell, T. R. Changes in scores on the psychological examination of the American Council on Education from the freshman to the senior year. *J. educ. Psychol.*, 1934, 25, 66–69.

McConnell, T. R., & Heist, P. The diverse college student population. In N. Sanford (Ed.), *The American college*. New York: Wiley, 1962. Pp. 225–252.

McLuhan, M. *Understanding media*. New York: McGraw-Hill, 1964.

Masterson, J. F., Tucker, K., & Berk, Gloria. Psychopathology in adolescence, IV: clinical and dynamic characteristics. *Amer. J. Psychiat.*, 1963, 120, 357–366.

Murphy, L. B. & Raushenbush, E. (Eds.). *Achievement in the college years: a record of intellectual and personal growth*. New York: Harper, 1960.

Newcomb, T. M. Student peer-group influence. In N. Sanford (Ed.), *The American college*. New York: Wiley, 1962. Pp. 469–488.

Pepinsky, Pauline N. A study of productive nonconformity. *Gifted child quart.*, 1960, 4 (4), 81–85.

Pinneau, S. R. & Jones, H. E. Development of mental abilities. *Rev. educ. Res.*, 1958, 28, 392–400.

Plant, W. T. *Personality changes associated with a college education*. California: San Jose State Coll., 1962.

Riesman, D. *The lonely crowd*. New Haven: Yale Univ. Press, 1950.

Riesman, D. The Jacob report. *Amer. sociol. Rev.*, 1958, 23, 732–739.

Rogers, C. *Client-centered therapy*. New York: Houghton-Mifflin, 1958.

Russell, B. Reconciliation of individuality and citizenship. In R. E. Egner and L. Denon (Eds.), *The basic writings of Bertrand Russell*. New York: Simon and Schuster, 1961. Pp. 449–451.

Sanford, N. Research and policy in higher education. In N. Sanford (Ed.), *The American college*. New York: Wiley, 1962. Pp. 1009–1034.

Schmitt, Francis O. The physical basis of life and learning. *Science*, 1965, 149 (3687), 931–936.

Schoeppe, Aileen, & Havighurst, R. J. A validation of development and adjustment hypotheses of adolescence. *J. educ. Psychol.*, 1952, 43, 339–353.

Selzer, M. L. The happy college student myth: psychiatric implications. *Arch. gen. Psychiat.*, 1960, 2, 131–136.

Sexton, Virginia S. Factors contributing to attrition in college populations: twenty-five years of research. *J. gen. Psychol.*, 1965, 72, 301–326.

Stern, G. G. Environments for learning. In N. Sanford (Ed.), *The American college*. New York: Wiley, 1962. Pp. 690–730.

Silvey, H. M. Changes in test scores after two years in college. *Educ. psychol. Measmt.*, 1951, 11, 494–502.

Stein, M. I. *Personality measures in admissions.* New York: Coll. Entr. Examin. Bd., 1963.

Strodtbeck, F. L. Family interaction, values and achievement. In D. C. McClelland (Ed.), *Talent and Society.* New York: D. Van Nostrand, 1958.

Tanner, J. M. *Growth at adolescence.* Springfield, Ill.: Charles C Thomas, 1962.

Terman, L. M., & Oden, Melita H. *The gifted group at mid-life.* Stanford, Calif.: Stanford Univ. Press, 1959.

U.S. Department of Labor, Bureau of Labor Statistics. *Special labor force report: interim revised projections of U.S. labor force. 1965–1975.*

Warren, J. R., & Heist, P. A. Personality attributes of gifted students. *Science*, 1960, 132, 330–337.

Webster, H. Changes in attitudes during college. *J. educ. Psychol.* 1958, 49, 109–117.

Webster, H., Freedman, M., & Heist, P. Personality changes in college students. In N. Sanford (Ed.), *The American college.* New York: Wiley, 1962. Pp. 811–846.

Wedge, B. M. (Ed.). *Psychological problems of college men.* New Haven: Yale Univ. Press, 1958.

Whitla, D. K. Guidance in the university setting. *Harvard educ. Rev.*, 1962, 32 (4), 450–462.

Whittington, H. G. *Psychiatry on the college campus.* New York: Int. Univ. Press, 1963.

Wise, W. M *They came for the best of reasons—college students today.* Washington: Amer. Council on Educ., 1958.

Wise, W. M. The American student and his college. In *From high school to college.* New York: Coll. Entr. Examin. Bd., 1964. Pp. 8–14.

Part II

Tools

Chapter 3

The Counseling Interview

RICHARD E. GRUEN

Introduction

The interview is an artful tool or method used for many purposes, for a variety of reasons, and as a result of different professional motivations. The interview is used in many settings both academic and nonacademic. It crosses disciplinary lines; it is used widely in research of all varieties. It is fundamental to all of the "helping professions" and the social and behavioral sciences. It is well known to the consumer, has become involved with our political life, and is indispensable to the mass communication media. Most people like to interview; most of us like to be interviewed. It is no wonder that the interview has been called a conversation with a purpose! It must be stated initially that there is no one correct way to interview.

The aim of the present chapter is to scrutinize the role of the counseling interview in higher education. We will focus in part on the research interview in the college and university. While the essentials of interviewing, the basic ingredients, are the same in most settings and for most purposes, there are, of course, variations for the approximation of specific goals, and use of the interview is often tailored to specific settings. Counseling interviews, whatever the specific nature of the counseling, differ mostly in terms of goals. Some of the variations are concerned with the nature of the population involved.

Richard E. Gruen is Assistant Professor, Department of Student Services, Brooklyn College of the City University of New York.

When one becomes concerned about interviewing in a given population, one necessarily becomes concerned about the characteristics of that population. The college and university population, in the writer's opinion, is in many ways a distinctive group. College counseling personnel, moreover, have a distinction of their own, and research with a college student population has its unique qualities. These assumptions have many implications for the counseling process and hence for interviewing. The college and university population, composed of persons in actuality and potentiality, is usually and for the most part late adolescent. These students are often extremely verbal and articulate and are in a process of rapid development and change. They are seeking identities in a variety of areas and are responding to the stress of the developmental process and to college life. They are moving forward in large forward and small backward strides and reacting to transitional phenomena. This population in the process of becoming is often dogmatic, absolute in its thinking, concerned with the problems of striving for personal emancipation and independence, and is full of conflicting emotions. These students are resident in an atmosphere of searching intellectual stimulation and demands in which compensatory defenses are at work.

As admission standards to colleges and universities spiral upward and the transient subcultural characteristics of each college generation change with increasing rapidity in response to the pressures of a changing culture and society, the implications for the counseling of college students become equally complex. Fundamental to the professional interviewing of college students is an understanding of the personality characteristics of late adolescence and early adulthood and, more specifically, an understanding of the developmental tasks of this transitional period and of the nature, especially in a personal and cultural context, of the changes themselves.

The counseling services available to students in colleges and universities today include some combination of the following, variation of nomenclatures notwithstanding: psychological or therapeutic, vocational or career, departmental and preprofessional, educational, and placement. Also included are general-curricular or faculty advisement and cocurricular or extracurricular or student activities advisement, including advisement to social groups and academic societies, advisement to students in publication endeavors, veterans counseling, financial aid counseling, and advisement through health services. The interview is used as a tool in the advisement and counseling processes in all of these areas in higher education, differing in each case, of course, in its specific goals, depth, and duration.

It should be realized at the outset that interviewing is a subjective art; this, however, makes it no less useful. Evidence suggests that agreement among interviewers while significantly better than chance, is relatively low. The "correctness" of the interview is based on a consensus of interviewer judgment and estimates of predictive validity are difficult. Good interviewing is concerned with variation and spontaneity, and its specific content cannot be reduced to rules and formulae. Because of this, many inexperienced people in the counseling field think that it is easy to interview or that little training is needed. Often, faculty in colleges and universities feel that anyone can interview. They assume that, because of its spontaneity and lack of rigid rules and techniques, the interview is simpler and more natural than it really is.

Essentials of the Interview

The professional counseling interview is a purposeful goal-directed tool, a method of communication between two (or more) people interacting with each other with varying degrees of structure, and directed toward a meaningful exchange of ideas. The interview is focused on a specific content area for the purpose of helping in some form of adjustment. Its specific characteristics depend on the purpose and nature of the interview.

In order for there to be understanding, there must be communication, a basic necessity in professional interviewing. The counseling interview is the environmental field in which motivated perception, understanding, and communication take place. It is the fundamental tool in counseling that will determine the direction and success or failure of the counseling goal. The interview, however, is more than a tool, technique, method, or process. It is all at the same time, the foundation of counseling, the milieu of counseling; and it establishes the psychological climate for communication and interaction. It is in the interview, or the sequence of interviews, that the relationship between counselor and counselee begins, develops, and ends. Without the interview there can be no give and take, no dialogue, no communication, no expression of feelings, no meaningful movement toward goals, and, therefore, no counseling.

Garrett (1942, p. 8) calls interviewing "a skilled technique that can be improved and eventually perfected primarily through continued practice." Fenlason, Ferguson, and Abrahamson (1962) remark, "Its skillful use has made it an art as well as a method." This writer believes that professional interviewing is both an art and a science inextricably linked.

Fenlason et al. (1962, p. 3) state,

> A good interview represents both a verbal and non-verbal interaction between two or more people working toward a common goal. The interview is a purposeful conversation. When the conversation is aimed at furnishing insight and gaining information, or furthering understanding, or aiming at some form of help or counsel, its purpose is truly a professional one. . . . The word *professional* implies that the interviewer has had special preparation for his work; that his training, based on transmissable knowledge and skills has been acquired formally.

Bingham, Moore, and Gustad (1959, p. 3) state,

> An interview is a conversation directed toward a definite purpose other than satisfaction in the conversation itself. . . . much of the interaction between these two [interviewer and interviewee] is carried on by gestures, postures, facial expressions, and other communicative behavior. Even the words acquire varieties of meanings and values as they are spoken with different inflections or in different contexts. All of these means of communication—the spoken words, the gestures, the expressions, the inflections—contribute to the purposeful *exchange* of meanings, which is the interview.

There is no orthodox way of interviewing on any occasion, no specific rigid sequential rules to be consistently followed without pause. There are, however, general principles and purposes. The principal general goals of the interview are to obtain information, to give information, or to attempt to influence the development of greater self-awareness which may result in some change of attitudes, modification in behavior, or attending reduction in anxiety. An interview can have as its components, one, two, or all of the above functional attributes.

The need to provide a climate for effective communication is a common denominator of all counseling interviews, as are the corollary needs for effective listening, observation, the establishment of rapport, and appropriate counselor attitudes. These will be covered more fully in a later section of this chapter. The formulation and phrasing of questions in the interview, the development of tentative hypotheses on the part of the interviewer as the interview progresses, and the development of the counseling relationship are central in all counseling interviews.

Hahn and MacLean (1955) point out some of the many and varied purposes of the counseling interview. Included are the following:

1. To establish rapport between the counselor and the counselee;

2. To collect new information and amplify or interpret information already gathered;

3. To permit the counselee to "think aloud" in the presence of a sympathetic listener;

4. To convey necessary information to the counselee;

5. To find socially acceptable and personally satisfying alternatives with and for the counselee.

Garrett (1942, p. 26) considers,

> The aim [in the interview] is to obtain knowledge of the problem to be solved and sufficient understanding of the person troubled and of the situation so that the problem can be solved effectively. Whether the two functions of understanding and helping are combined in one agency or interviewer or divided among several will modify the detail of the methods used but not their essentials.

According to Tyler, research has been making an emphasis on any one kind of orthodox interview procedure less and less justifiable. She remarks (1961, p. 39),

> It seems clear that each counselor develops his own style and that he varies it as circumstances demand. Warmth and responsiveness are important and increasing skill comes with experience. Counselors seem to be making a distinction between cases and between parts of the same case on the basis of whether affective or cognitive communication predominates. Comparisons of referred with voluntary cases remind us that the attitude a client brings to a situation as well as the counselor's own attitude must be considered. Individual differences of all sorts are apparent. A procedure that works well with one counselee may antagonize others. . . .

Tyler's remark is important because a review of counseling literature and of recent research demonstrates that perceptions, rather than responses, and understanding, rather than techniques, need to be emphasized.

Fenlason et al. (1962, p. 129) state that the major components of the professional interview are "*purpose, structure,* the dynamic *processes* inherent in the interaction of individuals, *technical procedures, attitudes* and *predisposing elements*." They state further (1962, p. 130), "The purpose of the interview should be intellectually formulated. Some workers insist that the interviewer who cannot formulate the objective or objectives of his interview before he undertakes it has neither reason nor right to conduct it."

Since the interview is focused on a specific content area, planning for the encounter with the counselee is necessary, although it should not be too rigid. The control of the interview must always remain with the interviewer. If this is not the case, the interview can develop into simply an aimless conversation.

Theoretical Considerations

Even though today it is recognized that the interview, in a general sense, has similar objectives whatever the goals and the setting, there are varied theoretical considerations dependent upon counseling formulations or points of view held by groups of professionals in the field. These points of view generally grow out of training, experience, personal or institutional bias, the demands of the setting, personal identification, or a combination of several of these variables.

In earlier years, according to the Minnesota point of view, whose main protagonist was Paterson, the principal concern was with occupational adjustment and the objective measurement of traits. The use of tests and the use of the case history interview were pivotal in this approach. A more intellectualized type of interview was stressed. Client feelings and interaction were not initially considered as very important, although more recent modifications in this formulation have included more dynamic factors. Basic here is the trait-factor theory, a formulation which grew rapidly from the testing movement between 1930–1945 and is concerned basically with intelligence, interests, and academic aptitudes. It is fundamentally methodological in nature.

The Rogerian approach was based on the major themes of psychoanalysis. According to this theoretical formulation, counseling and the interview are seen in terms of emotional interchange and modification of the self-concept of the interviewee. Here the interviewer assists the client in recognizing and dealing with his own feelings as mirrored by the counselor.

In spite of some recent modifications in both of these points of view, each incorporating in eclectic fashion some of the features of the other, the balance has shifted from the major emphasis on the objectivity and reality factors of the Minnesota point of view toward the expression of feelings of the Rogerian point of view. Nonetheless, there are and will continue to be problem-centered interviews, relationship-centered interviews, and interviewers who are successful in both. The difficult task is to make something happen.

Bingham et al. (1962) point out that, despite individual differences, considerable agreement about the counseling interview has now developed. They state that most counselors embrace the purposes of the counseling interview as one in which information is obtained, information is given, and attitudes are changed.

Outgrowths of counseling and interviewing approaches from the field of psychotherapy and psychoanalysis can be seen in the following chart based on Wolberg (1954, p. 88).

FORMULATION OR APPROACH	FOCUS	OBJECTIVE
Guidance	existent work, social-interpersonal difficulties	correcting these as expediently as possible
Persuasion	faulty attitudes and values	inculcating a correct philosophy of life
Emotional catharsis	suppressed and repressed feelings and experiences	release of pent-up emotions
Reassurance	irrational fears and attitudes	correcting misconceptions and mistaken attitudes
Reeducative	distortions in interpersonal operations	enhancing character assets and minimizing liabilities
Semantic	language and communication disturbances	clarifying concepts, values, and goals
Non-directive	feelings behind verbalizations	releasing spontaneous growth processes
Freudian	past life experiences	development of mature genitality
Adlerian	present *life style*	resolve feelings of inferiority and compensatory power mechanisms
Jungian	exploration of elements in collective unconscious	release individual from crippling influence of *archetypes*
Rankian	union and separation strivings	resolving ubiquitous birth trauma
Horney	contradictions of character structure	dissipation of character disturbances and of unrealistic self-image
Sullivan	individual's relationship with people	restoration of self esteem and good interpersonal relationships

In scrutinizing theoretical formulations relevant to the counseling interview, the importance of communication theory and, relatedly, perception theory cannot be underestimated. Bingham et al. (pp. 9–11) state generally,

> The interview is basically a communications system. The interview, involving as it does two persons who must communicate their feelings and ideas to one another, is enormously complicated, subject to difficulties at various points. If interviewing is to be improved, it is essential that attention be paid to all similar points at which trouble occurs. . . . The same message will not mean the same thing to two different people. Each interprets what he hears in terms of his unique history. . . . People attach different values to words as signals. . . .

From the standpoint of the interviewer, they state the problem thus:

> the interviewer must help the client to find and apply words which actually describe the situation. . . . Many interviewers find it difficult to select the words which convey what they want to. The overworked "uh-huh" is probably, in many cases, a non-committal substitute for the interviewer unable to select words to convey his understanding of a statement. . . . (p. 10)

It can readily be seen that one of the great problems of good professional interviewing is perceiving properly the meaning of what the interviewee is saying. The interviewer must perceive the interviewee's world as the interviewee sees it. There must be the greatest possible freedom of communication in the interview. Nevertheless, in the interviewer's effort to approximate the purposes that he has set for himself, he must be knowledgeable of what to ignore. On this point, Cannell and Kahn (1957, p. 15) remark,

> The interviewer's problem is to bring about a much smaller stream of communications, consisting almost solely of the relevant items. The irrelevant topics must be avoided, and the relevant bits of information must be communicated in rapid succession over a short space of time. . . . To the extent that the interviewer is not able to eliminate irrelevancies, the interviewing process becomes costly and inefficient. To the extent that the interviewer fails to obtain full communication of the relevant items, the interview content becomes biased and the conclusions inaccurate.

Sullivan (1954) sees the interview as an "interpersonal phenomenon." According to Sullivan, the term *interview* does not apply to a fixed period of time, but rather to "a course of interpersonal events." He observes about the interview, ". . . the data for its study and comprehension are to be derived from the observation of what goes on between the participants—or, to phrase it another way, from an observation of the field of their interaction. . . ." (p. ix) In addition, he has pointed out (p. xi) that "the processes in the interview are kept obscure by the mutual anxiety of the participants." The counselor and the client, "while strongly motivated to meet, are also driven by anxiety to withdraw from each other."

> The understanding of such blocks to communication, reflecting underlying anxiety anticipation of hurt from another human being, is a major goal of the interview. The interview itself may be looked upon as a miniature of all communicative processes, containing within it the essential qualities of all human relationships, and much data relevant to the getting along of people in any social setting (Sullivan, 1954, p. xvii).

With reference to interview goals, Sullivan (1954, p. xii) states,

> This interplay of movements—multiple variations of advance and retreat—is characteristic of the field of the interview. . . . the goal of interviewing is not to do away with these movements, but to recognize them, explore their origins, and come to an understanding of their significance in the current situation. . . .

A general principle that the writer believes to be of great importance is that the interviewer should not be a stranger to the principle of genuine sincerity. Interviewing is not an effort in gamesmanship or gimmickry. The interviewer should not resort to clever or subtle questioning to accomplish his purpose. Such interview behavior is usually ineffectual and always unprofessional. This is especially true with a late adolescent population that usually has high sensitivity where sincerity is concerned, and is quick to point up hypocrisy wherever it is found. Needless to say, a good counseling relationship cannot be built on such a foundation. Procedures of this sort violate the right of an individual to his own course of action. The interviewer has no ethical right to decide what is best for the client.

One important function of the interview is to attempt to work through distortions of thinking and the discrepancies between how the person sees himself and how he would like to be. Frequently, objective information alone helps students on the road to reorganizing their thinking or adjusting their self-concepts. Although in many instances distortions and self-concept reorganization necessitate more than simple information, we must remember that in college counseling we are dealing, for the most part, with a normative population in which objective facts do often make their mark.

Caplow (1956, p. 167) posits the following as basic principles of interviewing most generally agreed upon:

> 1. The interviewer should not inject his own attitudes or experiences into the conversation or express value judgments. . . .

2. Because any sequence of questions structures the subject matter, the interview should have the minimum number of questions in the simplest form adaptable to the problem. . . .

3. The response which can be anticipated from a question is often quite different from the logical complement of the question. . . .

4. All interview questions entail certain unpredictable effects. . . .

5. The attitude of the interviewer toward the respondent should always be extremely attentive and concentrated. . . .

6. The expert interviewer is much more than a recording device. No matter what the form of the interview, he should pursue his questioning to the point where no significant ambiguities exist for *him*. . . .

In the college or university, interviewing and counseling irrespective of the goals—academic, vocational, personal, or other—should facilitate work in the academic classroom as well as adjustment. It should help the counselee initiate a rational problem-solving method that may be helpful to the student in all of his undertakings, academic and otherwise.

Counseling interviews differ to a great extent from other interviews in that during the counseling interview decisions and choices are made. A general goal of all counseling and thus a pivotal aim in the counseling interview process is decision making. The tasks of late adolescence and early adulthood center around decision making in many areas and are inextricably linked to the problems of identity. This fact alone adds considerable stress to the developmental process at this stage. Life in the university and constant exposure to ideas and varying philosophies add other stresses. During the course of interviews, the counselor in effect teaches the skills of decision making while attempting at the same time to reduce anxiety. The paucity of research into what actually occurs in the decision-making process complicates the counselor's task. Much more work is needed in this area.

Tyler (1961, p. 189) points out, "We cannot really single out certain types of interviews and say that they and they alone fall in this category of decision-making interviews since any interview may involve some decision making, regardless of its main purpose. . . ." In order for the student to have the opportunity for an optimum decision-making experience, there must be a psychological climate for the decision-making process apparent in the sequence of interviews. To foster such experience, says Tyler (1961, p. 196),

> there should be an atmosphere completely free of any sort of threat to his [the student's] self-esteem, an atmosphere of genuine respect and liking. Attitudes should be given the same status as facts. They should be recognized, clarified, accepted, and understood. Dependable informa-

tion should be readily available and freely used. It should be clear from the beginning that decision is in the student's hands. The counselor will help to put things together but will not attempt to decide for him.

It is interesting to note that one of the negative or critical student reactions to counseling is "the counselor did not tell me what to do." The acoustics being what they are, it must be carefully stated that the student always makes his own decisions. It may be necessary to repeat this fact in different ways during the course of several interviews. In the initial interview it is incumbent upon the interviewer to take the opportunity to define what counseling is, expressing it in terms of the student's symbols. The interviewer should be constantly watchful for the appearance of pseudo-decisions. His desire, conscious or unconscious, to close the case hastily, realistic reasons notwithstanding, may motivate him to conclude that pseudo-decisions are in fact actual decisions. The interviewer should also be aware of his own need, whatever the reason, to complete a case and the consequent inclination to rationalize wrongly that a decision has been reached by the student. The interviewer must also be alert to instances in which indecisiveness is part of the character structure of the student and to the resultant possibility that therapeutic services may be needed before specific educational, vocational, or other reality decisions can be made. Present knowledge and emerging research is leading more and more professional counselors to the point of view that decision making is closely allied to personality development. As Tyler (1961, p. 203) has indicated, "research on developmental stages in choices promises to be very useful to counselors. A good beginning has been made in the study of vocational development." Recent analytic studies involving content analyses and decision-making processes demonstrate promise and provide new insight into the interview process.

The Educational Counseling Interview

Many high school graduates enter college or university life with a major misconception as to the role of the counselor or faculty advisor. Many college freshman believe as a result of their high school experience, that the counselor or advisor sees students only if they are in academic or disciplinary trouble. This false notion must be dispelled immediately in freshman interviews in order for effective educational counseling to ensue. It is of great importance for the interviewer to state what counseling is and what it is not. Educational counseling includes program planning, the choice of courses in line with the characteristics and needs of the student insofar as the curriculum permits, with some insight into the stresses of the individual. As in other counseling interviews, decision making is a salient feature. The interview in educational counseling is fundamentally centered around obtaining information and giving information. It does not stop there, however. The basic general characteristics of effective professional interviewing are as applicable here as they are in those more specialized counseling efforts to which they are more absolutely necessary.

The entering freshman, for example, is beginning a new life in a relatively strange milieu. He needs to be assessed developmentally. He needs information; he needs to be accepted; he needs to feel that someone cares. He is now in a different range of students, and some reorganization of relative self-image needs to take place. The range of intellectual abilities and other scholastic characteristics is usually now more homogeneous; on the other hand, the social and cultural horizons now are usually much broader. The college population frequently comes from a wider geographical area and represents many different cultures and sub-cultures. It is less encapsulated and encapsulating. The counselor may have to attempt to work out some of the entering freshman's acculturation problems in addition to orienting him to the university and planning his program. Some estimation of potential perhaps is necessary. A great deal of information needs to be disseminated either in individual counseling interviews or group orientation procedures or both. Special problems need to be identified.

At the sophomore level, educational counseling is linked with precareer counseling. It is a crucial time, especially since the college student is normally at the point of choosing his major department or broader area of concentration. If the student is enrolled in a liberal arts curriculum, the aims of a liberal arts education should again be discussed and interpreted. This point is a matter of great confusion among many students and some counselors.

Educational counseling at the junior level (in four year programs) becomes involved with preplacement or pregraduate school or preprofessional school information. Educational counseling at the senior level is still more demanding in this respect, and the psychological element of separation anxiety coupled with the realistic demands and cultural expectations make educational counseling at this level an extremely important matter. In the counseling of seniors, educational counseling interviews are inseparably linked to the placement function as to the dynamics of independence strivings and to emancipation problems. What is beginning to emerge is that the college counselor perhaps needs to be the "compleat" counselor.

The Career Counseling Interview

There has been much change in the conduct of career counseling over the years. The first approach was that of Frank Parsons, in whose book, *Choosing a Vocation* (1909), the steps necessary in helping an individual locate a job in consonance with his skills, interest, and abilities were outlined. These steps were:

1. Analyze the individual; find out about his abilities, interests, experience;
2. Analyze the job in terms of its requirements;
3. Match the information about the individual with the information about job requirements.

The emphasis today is no longer in terms of a mechanical matching. In the half century since Parsons' book the experience of vocational counselors, psychologists, and researchers has altered the perspective of the field. This is not to say that specific objective information about the individual and occupations are not important; these are necessary and indispensable. There can be no career counseling without information.

Philosophically, however, certain changes have emerged. The choice of career is now looked at and studied from the point of view of developmental stakes in a life-long process: Career choice is continuous and is inextricably linked to the psychological development of the individual and his needs. Research into the mechanism of vocational development has made it necessary to look at the counselee in a more dynamic way. While the need of college students for occupational information is imperative, and in many instances the counseling interview remains the proper setting in which such information is given, evaluated, questioned, and discussed in terms of the counselee's needs and preferences; the personal concomitants of career choice are no less important. Career counseling has become more complex and specialized as a result of the increased number of variables to be considered. Career development among college students is viewed more in terms of personal development and as a part of seeking identity and satisfying needs. The interview in career counseling is no longer a data collection-and-matching process or a sequence of techniques alone. Career development as a continuous process means, as Bingham et al. (1959, p.

226) say, that "Counseling is now seen as a process whereby the individual learns a set of skills that will enable him not only to solve the problems of the moment but, more important, similar problems as they may occur later. . . ."

The college population involved in career counseling is, on the whole, a normative population. While it is true that career counseling emphasizes such reality factors as abilities, achievements, aptitudes, and qualifications and prerequisites for job requirements, it is also concerned with the need satisfaction of the student. Exploration of the self-concept of the counselee has many implications for the counseling interview. Unconscious as well as conscious material becomes involved; moreover, Erikson's (1963) constructs of normative crises during late adolescence and the little knowledge available from decision-making theory emphasize the need for a better understanding of the personality configuration of the college student appropriate to his stage of personal development. While career counseling is not psychotherapy, and should not be, the forces that shape the choice and development of a career are dynamic and often subtle. The exploration demanded needs time, and it is in the interview that this exploration best occurs. Many colleges and universities are remiss in not providing the more professionalized and specialized counseling in this area. Many career counseling facilities, moreover, are still at the matching-process or information-giving stage, and many college vocational counselors are woefully unprepared to deal with the complex problems of career choice and development.

The Clinical Interview

Clinical, psychological, or therapeutic services for students in colleges and universities have grown in recent years. With the knowledge that is now available about stresses of college, the crises in later adolescence and early adulthood, and the other dynamic pressures of development during the college years, the need for mental health services has become more apparent and, at long last, more acceptable to administrators and faculties.

The major goals of the clinical interview are the development of self-awareness, alteration of attitudes, modification of behavior, and reduction of anxiety. As Bingham et al. (1959, p. 246) state, "fundamentally, the clinical interview is employed to assist an individual to regain emotional composure or control, to overcome distressing or debilitating symptoms which have interfered with his being able to lead a normal happy life. . . ." These goals are not unlike the aims of other types of counseling interviews, nor are they independent of the major goals of higher education.

Earlier it was stated that without communication there is no professional interview, but it is listening that is so important to the clinical interview. Listening—that ability to listen is a skill basic to good communication. Various authorities have described it:

> The voice that speaks in him [in this instance the counselee] speaks low, but he who listens with the third ear hears also what is expressed almost noiselessly, what is said *pianissimo*. . . . Men speak to us and we speak to them not only in words but also with the little signs and expressions we unconsciously send and receive. . . . (Reik, 1948, p. 149)

> Effective listening demands not only that the interviewer hear and understand what is being said, but that he also hear and understand what is communicated through silence. . . . (Fenlason et al., 1962, p. 143)

Barbara (1958, pp. 1–6) stresses the following in artful listening:

> *concentration, active participation,* and *objectivity.*
>
> *Concentration* allows for patience with ourselves and our removal of distractions in the paths of our listening. *Active participation* involves keeping our minds in a state of relaxed alertness, open and flexible to all relevant changes in a given situation. *Comprehension* is the understanding and grasp of the true idea or meaning of what is heard objectively or hearing the other person out without imposing our preconceived notions or opinions.

Barbara points out also that in order to listen well one must have the capacity and the desire to examine critically, to evaluate and reshape values and aptitudes and relationships to oneself and to others. Garrett (1942) states that it is essential for the interviewer to accustom himself to listening to what his client means as to what he says.

It is important for the interviewer to continuously ask himself, "What is the student really saying?" The answer to this question is often frightening to the interviewer, which is probably one reason why the question is sometimes not asked.

Observation is another basic ingredient of the interview, described by Fenlason et al. (1962, p. 145) as follows:

> *Observation* is a process operative in an interview from its inception to its close. The interviewer does not *observe* in the scientific sense of observing and noting phenomena in controlled experiments. Because he works with a human being in a fluid situation, his observation consists of noticing what he sees, hears and apprehends in the interview. The interviewer with all his senses depends primarily on his eyes and ears for his information. . . .

The facial expressions, voice volume, gestures, physical movements, and general appearance give clues to the extent of anxiety, degree of control, and other observable manifestations of behavior, on which hypotheses and inferences may be formed, however tentative. Rollo May (1939) has stated that a good counselor sees few wounds that are not his own.

Establishing the Relationship

Establishing rapport and providing the climate for the relationship between the participants in counseling is another important function of the interview. Above all, the relationship must be genuine. This growth-provoking component of effective counseling is inherent in the interview and more specifically must commence in the initial interview.

Rapport between counselor and student is a vital and primary consideration, whether a continuing counseling relationship develops from the initial interview, or whether its purpose is limited to obtaining information. This rapport reflects the client's relations with other people throughout his life, his feelings about them, and his methods of dealing with them. According to Fenlason et al. (1962, p. 157), the "word *rapport* is used to denote a relationship characterized by harmony and accord." Darley (1946) defines rapport as the prevailing climate achieved and maintained throughout the interview. *Rapport* is concerned with what goes on between the participants in multidimensional ways, according to Sullivan (1954), who further stipulates that processes are kept obscure by the mutual anxiety of the participants.

Darley (1946, p. 13) lists the requirements of rapport as follows:

1. The interviewer should be friendly and interested.
2. The interview room should be comfortable and have the appearance of privacy.
3. The interviewer should appear unhurried, even though many people are waiting to see him.
4. The interviewer should accept whatever hesitant and halting attitudes and ideas the client puts forth and should express neither moral or ethical judgment, nor approval or disapproval of these attitudes and ideas.
5. The interviewer should accept the client as a conversational equal during the interview.
6. The interviewer must always make clear to the client the limitations of his agency so that the client will not expect too much.
7. The interviewer must always make clear that the responsibility for planning and final action rests with the client.

Bingham et al. (1959, p. 37) rightly point out,

> The interviewer and the interviewee both bring into the interview their own characteristics, their own life histories, their own personalities. What happens in the interview, however, cannot be understood merely by studying these two participants as separate entities. Rather it is essential to realize that they relate, that they interact, that this relationship, this interaction, a product of their two personalities, is what determines the outcome of the interview.

Cannell and Kahn (1957, pp. 79–80) have noted,

> 1. The interviewer must create and maintain an atmosphere in which the respondent feels that he is fully understood and in which he is safe to communicate fully without fear of being judged or criticized.
> 2. Such a relationship frees the respondent for further communication . . . the respondent is encouraged to consider the topic more deeply and to explore more fully and frankly his own position.
> 3. This type of interaction also keeps the communication sharply focused on the topic in which the interviewer is interested.

Hamilton (1951) points out that the counselor's attitude of acceptance is of essential importance. He defines it thus:

> This means acceptance of the other person as he is—in whatever situation, no matter how unpleasant or uncongenial to the interviewer, with whatever behavior, aggressiveness, hostility, dependence, or lack of frankness he may manifest. This attitude can come only from a respect for people and a genuine desire to help anyone who is in need or trouble. It is translated through courtesy, patience, willingness to listen, and not being critical or disapproving of whatever the client may complain of, request, or reveal about himself. The first requisite in any interview is to make the person feel welcome and comfortable, and for this the interviewer himself must be relaxed and friendly. (p. 52)

In Tyler's (1961, p. 25) words, "Acceptance involves primarily two things. First—a willingness to allow individuals to differ from one another in all sorts of ways, and second, a realization that the on-going experience of each person is a complex pattern of striving, thinking, and feeling."

One of the best descriptions of rapport as an element of college counseling is that of Hahn and MacLean (1955, p. 83):

> Rapport . . . means sustained interest and mutual understanding and respect between two human beings who are analyzing together, and seeking solutions for, a problem important to the one because it is his problem and to the other because it is his job to help. Expenditure of whatever time is necessary to establish this relationship in a preliminary interview or interviews is justified. On the part of the counselee it involves developing a feeling of ease, born of growing confidence in the

counselor's competence, interest, knowledge, and skill, and a feeling of freedom to reveal both facts and emotions. On the part of the counselor it entails treating the student as a responsible adult, being considerate of all attitudes and feelings, resistant to shock whatever may be said. He must be patient in the face of repetition, indecision, or inconsistency and sensitive to the timing of his questions and comments. He must use sharp retorts and critical comments or warm and tender sympathetic ones only as tools, not as expressions of his own emotions, temper, judgments, or morals. He must remember that counseling is perhaps the most ideal kind of teaching, with the student on one end of the log and himself on the other in relaxed discussion. While it is not necessary for him to win a student's liking, he must capture his respect and avoid dislike. And throughout the series of interviews this rapport must be maintained.

The interviewer must also have the ability to empathize. *Empathy* is a rather difficult term to define; it has subtle shades of meaning. Bingham, Moore, and Gustad (1959, p. 46) state that empathy "refers to the ability of one individual to respond sensitively and imaginatively to another's feelings." According to Fenlason et al. (1962, p. 204), "*empathy* is the capacity of an individual to identify himself with another in terms of the way another would feel and act. It is the essence of understanding the *why* of another's attitudes and behavior." It is important, however, for the interviewer to realize that pity has no place in the interview.

Rogers (1962, p. 416) stresses the importance of the empathetic relationship:

> I believe the quality of my encounter is more important in the long run than is my scholarly knowledge, my professional training, my counseling orientation, the techniques I use in the interviews. In keeping with this line of thought, I suspect that for a guidance worker also the relationship he forms with each student—in brief or continuing—is more important than his knowledge of tests and measurements, the adequacy of his record keeping, the theories he holds, the accuracy with which he is able to predict academic success, or the school in which he received his training.

And Rollo May (1939, p. 77) points out the bond between empathy and understanding, saying, "[Empathy] . . . is the feeling, or the thinking of one personality into another until some state of identification is achieved. In this identification real understanding between people can take place; without it in fact, no understanding is possible. . . ."

Most of what is written today and most of today's research stress rapport, relationship, and the interaction of the participants in the interview rather than specific interview schedules or rigidly held rules of interviewing.

Kelly (1955, p. 954), representative of this trend, admonishes, ". . . what the clinician should always bear in mind is that, regardless of whether he is accepting or rejecting, active or non-committal, perceptive or obtuse, he creates a professional obligation for himself whenever he lets a person confide in him. . . ."

The Appraisal Interview

The appraisal, evaluation, selection, or assessment interview in the college or university setting is basically an information-getting, and to some extent an information-giving, interview. This type of interview is found in the areas of admission, readmission, evaluation of need in financial aid advisement, selection for scholarships, special programs, placement, and personnel recruitment. The goal here is to assess a college student's qualifications, background, and readiness for a specific purpose where competition with others is usually involved. Basically it is not a counseling interview in the true sense of that term. It is a close relative of the personnel interview in business and industry as well as in the interview in other openly evaluative, judgmental, and competitive situations.

It has been this writer's experience that college students have some apprehension about interviews of this nature, perhaps because they are largely judgmental. It is astonishing how many students get through college with a minimum experience of appraisal interviews, so that by the time they are seniors the recruitment, job placement, or personnel interview sometimes becomes a source of great anxiety. The students' knowledge that they are competing in an open market either for a job or admission to graduate or professional school creates some measure of resistance and indecision as to just how much they should reveal about themselves. An ethics-need conflict often comes into play, with certain kinds of open-ended questions presenting a problem to many students, especially those who are inexperienced.

Recently, this writer had occasion to screen a large number of college dropouts who desired admission as nonmatriculated students at Hunter College of the City University of New York. The interview was the basic tool in this assessment. In planning for these interviews, basically selection interviews, the writer established the following criteria of assesment:

1. Motivation and evidence of change.
2. Present ability to cope with an academic situation intellectually and personally.

3. Evaluation of student's activities since being dropped and the constructiveness of these activities.

4. Evidence of applicant's ability to organize his life with regard to employment, situational problems, etc.

5. Evidence of growth in ability of applicant to see himself realistically.

6. Assessment of attitudes relevant to his developmental period.

7. Assessment of reasonable assurance of success.

8. Extent of resolution of adolescent difficulties and crises in identity (where applicable).

9. Extent of applicant's jeopardy, and assessment of possible forfeiture of higher education were the applicant to return to college at this time.

10. Interval of time elapsed since being dropped.

Techniques of Interviewing

Again it must be emphasized that there is no one way to interview, no consecutive set of rules to follow in proper sequence. There are, however, general principles to be kept in mind, to be used as reference points upon which modifications and innovations are made according to the circumstances, the goals of the interview, and the personal characteristics of the interviewer. Tyler (1961, p. 39) supports this view:

> Research . . . has been making less and less justifiable an emphasis on any one kind of orthodox interview procedure. It seems clear that each counselor develops his own style and that he varies it as circumstances demand. Warmth and responsiveness are important and an increasing skill comes with experience. Counselors seem to be making a distinction between cases and between parts of some cases on the basis of whether affective or cognitive communication predominates. Comparisons of referred with voluntary cases remind us that the attitude a client brings to a situation as well as the counselors' own attitude must be considered. Individual differences of all sorts are apparent. A procedure that works well with one client may antagonize others. The emphasis of research findings are . . . on perceptions rather than responses, on understanding rather than techniques.

Darley (1946, pp. 12–13) suggests the following guidelines:

> 1. Do not lecture or talk down to the client.
>
> 2. Use simple words and confine the information you give the client to a few ideas.
>
> 3. Make sure you know what the client really wants to talk about before giving any information or answering any questions.
>
> 4. Make sure that you feel or sense his attitudes because, if hostile, these will either block the discussion or keep out the main problems.

Hinkley and Fenlason (1942, pp. 314–315) suggest:

> 1. Any show of . . . superiority on the part of the interviewer should be avoided. . . .
> 2. Any show of haste is to be avoided. . . .
> 3. Reference to the interviewer and his private affairs is to be avoided. . . .
> 4. The use of an illustration from another case history should ordinarily be avoided. . . .
> 5. It is unwise to make a statement that the patient is understood or offer any explanation of why he is in his present condition. . . .
> 6. It is usually necessary to supply the client's need for immediate assistance with some bit of information or definite statement that will make him feel that the interviewer, too, is not blundering along in a thick fog. These statements can usually be specific and confined to matters of fact. Compatible with this principle is the rule of avoiding any facile explanation of the patient's condition or any statement that he is completely understood.
> 7. The explanation of a mechanism can be made safely when it is obvious and sure, or when the explanation is not too far from ordinary rational thinking, as when the problems themselves are on a conscious level. The method of putting facts in juxtaposition so that the client is able to draw the obvious conclusion, is the preferable and usual one, and avoids the need of explanation. . . .

The initial interview may sometimes be very difficult for the student. It is here that he in some fashion presents the problem as he sees it. During this and subsequent interviews, the experienced interviewer will continuously be formulating hypotheses as to the fundamental factors in the case, testing these hypotheses, rejecting some, and tentatively seeking further corroboration. Without such a process, techniques will have little value. In the formulation of questions the interviewer should strive for clarity of meaning by using words or terms that are, insofar as is possible, connected with the student's experience. The interviewer should avoid professional jargon.

Some students are unusually reticent in the first interview. Confidence and trust take time to develop, and the first step is to establish rapport. The student needs some structure and some statement as to what the counseling process is all about. Sometimes it might be helpful to say something like this: "Counseling is a give and take relationship, a collaboration between us. We have to work together, as I'm sure you know. There's not much I can do for you unless you tell me something of your problem, unless you tell me something about yourself." The interviewer should be able from time to time to be reassuring and to render support to the client.

He should, however, avoid such platitudes as "Everything will be all right." or "There's really nothing to worry about." or "In another couple of years, you will look back and laugh at this." What is happening to the student is happening now, and in his perception it may be very painful. This is hardly unusual during adolescence. Remarks such as those just cited only tend to arouse unnecessary anger in the student, cause him to doubt the counselor's understanding of the situation, and make him wonder if the counselor can help him at all.

Listening and observation initially help the counselor develop the much needed hypotheses. As Garrett (1942, p. 36) states, "even when our primary interest in a given interview is to obtain answers to a set of questions, we can profit much from letting the client talk rather freely at first." The primary technique of interviewing is the formulation of the questions. Most interviewers either ask too many or too few questions. In the asking of leading questions, or open-ended questions rather than questions that elicit a *yes* or *no* response, the interviewer is encouraging the student to talk freely. Frequently, the attitude of the interviewer in his questions, the tone of voice, and inflection, as well as the nonverbal communication, are involved in the formulation of the question. From time to time it may be helpful to lean forward and to say, "go ahead," or "I'd like to hear some more about that." The interviewer might say, "What happened then?," "surely," "naturally," "of course." A sequence of "uh-huh's" can be and usually is very much overworked in interviewing. The interviewer must provide structure if the interview is not to become tangential. When digression occurs, it may be helpful to say, "Perhaps later we can come back to that. Could you tell me more about so and so."

It is often necessary to redirect the student's trend of thought when he resists or attempts to evade the point. The interviewer or the information resulting from free expression on the part of the student may have hit a sore point. Here, timing is of extreme importance: One cannot move forward more rapidly than the student is ready to move. It may be helpful on such occasions to say, "Something makes it hard for you to talk to me about so and so. Can you tell me what it is? Perhaps you are afraid of what I will think of you." There are fine shades of individual differences, not only among different students but with the same student on different interview occasions. It must be remembered that a student goes on living between interviews. What conceivably was a sore point in the initial interview may be handled with less resistance as the relationship develops. The student may begin to feel more comfortable in the interview situation, or his life outside the interview situation may equally militate toward lesser comfort.

Occasional silence will not disturb the secure interviewer. Silences frequently accompany periods of insight and crystallization of ideas. The student may be thinking of something to say, or he may be in the process of introducing another theme into the counseling process. On the other hand, he may be reticent or with his silence he may be asking for more direction from the counselor. If the silence becomes very frequent, the counselor should perhaps ask some specific leading questions based on the motifs that have already become apparent. It falls to the skill of the counselor, however, to assess by means of tentative hypotheses the meaning of the silences. In many instances, especially with a college population, it may be that the student is apprehensive about displaying anger. If the situation warrants, it may be well to say, "It may be that I am mistaken, but perhaps most people would be very annoyed if that happened to them." Inexperienced interviewers often in their desire to help the student in increasing his self awareness, will attempt to confront him with an interpretation for which the student is not ready. This confrontation may result in anxiety, anger, and extended silence. When interpretations are offered it is frequently helpful to offer them in question form. The student should be given the opportunity to agree or disagree—to modify as well as accept or reject. The student should be encouraged to be curious about something. Supervision through the medium of a practicum or colleague can help the inexperienced interviewer deal more effectively with both silence and timing and with ascertaining the validity of his interpretations.

Many interviewers, and innumerable college officials, deans, and faculty members are dismayed that, when information is given to students, they come back at some future time and say they "didn't know" or were "never given" that information. Often counselors, administrators, and faculty members throw up their hands at such statements; but it must be remembered that perception as well as attention is involved in the process of giving information and that perception is motivated. Bingham et al. (1959, p. 260) point out, "Students may not believe what they have heard. They may not understand. They may not wish to believe what they have heard." To combat this problem, the interviewer should be in large measure creative; he should constantly seek new approaches to information giving as well as understanding. He should be aware of the role that perception plays in the interview.

Most errors due to faulty technique in interviewing center around the failure to facilitate communication and poor focus, such as the introduction of material that is irrelevant to the student's problem. Awkwardness, which frequently manifests itself in long speeches, frequent silences on the part of the interviewee, and abruptness on the part of the interviewer, is a result of poor technique. Failure to respond or not knowing how to respond to significant cues is another error of technique, as is the guessing at rather than the ascertaining of facts. Suggestiveness toward the student, either verbally or otherwise, may contaminate the responses.

The professional interviewer will know himself well enough to assess his own competence with certain types of students. He will know those informational areas with which he is not familiar, will be aware of his own biases, and will know when it is in the student's best interest to refer that student to another interviewer. The professional interviewer will know where to find out what he doesn't know; and, as counseling is centered upon the problems and needs of the counselee, the professional interviewer does not use the interview to satisfy his own needs. There should be something in the manner of the interviewer which stimulates the student to feel, "Here is a professional adult I can trust."

Personal and Professional Qualifications for Interviewers

There is no one set of optimal interviewer qualifications. The many kinds of interview situations and the differing goals of interviews, the variety of forms and styles and purposes of interviews, necessitate a wide range of skills and personal characteristics. There probably is a difference between the qualifications for interviewers who are mainly engaged in research and those who are mainly engaged in counseling. One characteristic is certain, the effective interviewer is able to comprehend the client's reality. He must be primarily an understander.

It is this writer's impression that interviewers who are primarily engaged in counseling should have the personal and professional qualifications required of college-level counselors and clinical or counseling psychologists. Interviewing and counseling cannot be separated. Fenlason et al. (1962, p. 3–4) state,

> Professional service means more than a fortuitous meeting of the individual's needs. It presupposes an understanding on the interviewer's part of the forces in the environment as well as of the attitudes and standards of the individual in relation to his particular need. It utilizes the skills which professional training affords and it emphasizes the principle that the trained individual, as the medium for meeting such needs, is also a person whose attitudes and background affect in no small measure the reactions of the individual seeking professional services.

Cannell and Kahn (1957, p. 233) hold that "the successful interviewer is one who has developed the skill necessary to put principles into practice."

Many other authorities in the field have dealt with the problem. Richardson, Dohrenwend, and Klein (1965, p. 269) point out,

> A number of obstacles stand in the way of a clear-cut definition of the characteristics desirable in an interviewer, the measurement of his performance, and the development of techniques for selecting interviewers or for predicting the success of a candidate's training as an interviewer. Because of these obstacles, relatively little research has been done on the problem; and, as a consequence, much of our existing information is based upon the impressions of experienced interviewers. Information relevant to certain kinds of interviewers is sometimes unjustifiably applied to other kinds of interviewers or generalized as applicable to "the interviewer."

Perhaps Rogers (1942, p. 254) stated it best when he wrote,

> The person who is quite obtuse to the reactions of others, who does not realize that his remarks have caused another pleasure or distress, who does not sense the hostility or friendliness which exists between himself and others or between two of his acquaintances, is not likely to become a satisfactory counselor. There is no doubt that this quality can be developed, but unless an individual has a considerable degree of social sensitivity, it is doubtful that counseling is his most promising field of effort. On the other hand, the individual who is naturally observant to the reactions of others, who can pick out of the schoolroom group the unhappy child, who can sense the personal antagonism which underlies casual argument, who is alert to the subtle differences in actions which show that one parent has a comfortable relationship with his child, another a relationship full of tensions—such a person has a good natural foundation upon which to build counseling skills.

In addition, Tyler (1961, p. 247) admonishes,

> One particular personality trait is generally considered to be more of a handicap than any other in counseling. It is the one we characterize as *rigidity*, although we are not able to define it very precisely. A person who has strong convictions about many things and feels compelled to win others over to his point of view often has difficulty in comprehending what clients are trying to express. This does not mean, of course, that counselors should have no convictions of their own. But they must be able to distinguish between more and less important values and to recognize the validity of different value systems. They must be able to shift points of view so as to see things as others see them.

It must also be remembered that, as Richardson et al. (1965, p. 271) point out, "Little systematic research has been done to isolate the personal variables that contribute to interviewers' effectiveness in different forms of interviewing or the variables that contribute to their potentialities for becoming effective through a program of training. . . ." Cannell and Kahn (1957, p. 234) point out that an important qualification for interviewers is "behavior that increases the probability of the interviewer's being perceived as within communicative range. . . . Its components have been identified as permissiveness, receptivity, and empathy." They continue,

> some people are more likely to be successful interviewers than others, partly because of their personality traits, but more because they somehow have learned how to create the psychological atmosphere in which respondent communication flourishes. The essential quality required to establish such an atmosphere is a sensitivity to human relationships, especially the relationships characteristic of the interview.

In addition to courses centered around the theoretical material needed to understand the dynamics and process of the interview, interviewing under supervision, role-playing, and the evaluation of tape-recorded interviews are indispensable to the training of interviewers. Richardson et al. (1965) discovered that the interviewer's account of how he conducted the interview bore little resemblance to the actual recorded interview. Student evaluations of the interview process can also be helpful.

Bordin's (1955) study is of special interest with respect to student evaluations. He reports that the characteristics the client deemed desirable for a counselor were related to the kind of problem the client presented in the interview situation. He found that counselees who felt that personal characteristics were desirable tended to seek counseling that involved personal-social concerns. Clients who felt that impersonal characteristics were more important than personal characteristics most frequently sought help with educational-vocational difficulties. Bordin's study supports the assumption that the characteristics the counselee considers significant in the counselor are indicative of the type of problem the counselee will discuss.

The interviewing process is inseparable from counseling. Interviewers trained for counseling in college and universities should, in this writer's opinion, be trained as counseling or clinical psychologists and should hold doctorates. Counseling psychologists working in the university setting should have completed an internship program under supervision. Effective training of the interviewer augments the validity and reliability of the interviews he conducts. The interviewer must be concerned with making his interviewing as reliable as possible. In order to develop valid and meaningful hypotheses, he must know how to secure dependable data. Persons coming from the field of social work and the other behavioral sciences, moreover, should not be excluded from counseling. Social psychologists, sociologists, and cultural anthropologists should be involved in interviewing college students for the purposes of research.

The writer has compiled the following list of *professional* attributes that an interviewer should have:

1. Ability to transcend his own culture and subcultures.
2. Analytical orientation.
3. Ability to keep from probing into problems that the interviewer or interviewee cannot handle adequately.
4. Ability to think ahead of the client.
5. Ability not to impose an unsuitable conceptual framework.
6. Ability to keep the ultimate objectives of the counseling in mind while interviewing as well as short-term objectives.
7. Ability to structure one's role in a realistic nonthreatening way.
8. Ability to establish rapport and make the client feel at ease.
9. Ability to analyze feelings.
10. Ability to write cogent and meaningful summaries.
11. Ability for oral expression.
12. Ability to communicate ideas and feelings.
13. Ability to change attitudes.
14. Ability to revise tentative hypotheses about the client.
15. Ability to listen and observe closely.
16. Ability to inspire confidence.
17. Critical judgment.
18. Capacity for suspended judgment.
19. Capacity to correlate case factors.
20. Capacity for emotional detachment from client.
21. Effective technical competence by which the client's comfort is assured.
22. Educative influence.
23. Integrative prowess.
24. Intuitive insight.
25. Keen psychological insight.
26. Knowledge of theoretical formulations.
27. Memory for names and events.
28. Objectivity.
29. Professional orientation, including professional attitudes, integrity, and ethics.
30. Reflective orientation.

31. Sense of timing.
32. Synthesizing orientation.
33. Verbal skills.

The writer has compiled the following list of *personal* attributes that an interviewer should have:

1. Ability to relate to others, especially late adolescents and young adults.
2. Basic orientation toward others.
3. Desire for personal interaction.
4. Empathy.
5. Emotional stability.
6. Freedom from annoying mannerisms.
7. Flexibility.
8. Interest in the well-being of adolescents and young adults.
9. Nondominative disposition.
10. Nonrigid personality structure.
11. Patience, poise, pleasing appearance, pleasing voice, receptivity, and sympathetic demeanor.
12. Sense of humor.
13. Sense of personal well-being.
14. Tact, tolerance, sincerity, understanding, and warmth.
15. Wide life experience.
16. Willingness to learn new techniques and concepts.
17. Humility, modesty, integrity, respect, curiosity, wonder, and non-encapsulation.
18. Sincere appreciation of late adolescents and young adults.

Richardson et al. (1965, p. 333–34) point out the many important characteristics of effective interviewers. Those that seem particularly important to this writer are the following:

1. Ability to include data that contradict hypotheses in order to modify, revise, or reject initial hypotheses.
2. Ability to respond to feelings as well as words.
3. Ability to find satisfaction in being with, listening to, and trying to understand people and society.
4. Ability to keep wondering what is going on.
5. Ability to empathize with others, but not to the point of losing oneself.

6. Does not take a markedly moralistic view of the world.
7. Does not have to use people and exert power over them.

Research Interviews at the College or University

In recent years there has been considerable research utilizing the interview as a research instrument focused on college students. Sanford (1962, p. 1020) states that when, for example,

> students are interviewed intensively during their four years of college, being asked searching questions about their past experiences and their current attitudes, feelings, and intention, these students become more aware of themselves, see themselves in different perspectives, entertain ideas that would not otherwise have entered into their scheme of things. . . .

It has only been in the past two or three decades, however, that social science methods have been used on college student populations in an effort to test hypotheses in a number of important areas. There is still a great need for a systematic and comprehensive design for conceptualizing the whole process of personality development during the college years. More than nose counting is necessary. Well-trained and adroit interviewers are needed to provide data in depth for more accurate theoretical formulations of the developmental period of late adolescence and early adulthood.

It is the writer's belief that the most effective counseling psychologists in colleges and universities are those who are constantly involved in research with college students—especially those within their own setting. A great deal of healthy cross-fertilization can occur that will help counseling psychologists, clinical psychologists, and others in their work with students, and that at the same time will aid the faculty and the administration in their understanding of the characteristics of the student population. (The same research, of course, helps to supply the data needed for systematic theoretical formulation.) The counseling psychologist, the clinical psychologist and the faculty in counseling need to know the student culture and the sub-cultures extant on their campuses. Knowledge of environmental pressures and the stresses of college is invaluable, as is the knowledge of data relevant to changes of attitudes, values, and personality during the college years. Often there are subtle changes in the foregoing areas from one college generation to another. With our ever-growing college and university population it is increasingly important to know what happens to the college student while he is in college. The clinical and counseling psychologists should be experts in communication par excellence and should turn their interviewing and other skills to research on students, faculty, and on administration-faculty, faculty-student, and administration-student relationships. The need for this type of research has become most apparent in the very recent times. Through such research, utilizing the interview, research-minded counseling personnel can be of great help in creating understanding among the factions in the university.

The insight and crystallization of ideas gained by the subjects in research is little different from that which takes place in the counseling interview. This is frequently true even when assessment procedures other than interviews are used for the purpose of research. Every researcher working with college students has heard something like this: "Gee, I never thought about that before, it gets you to thinking about yourself." This writer has had the experience of holding reaction sessions after research instruments were administered to large numbers of college students. The stimulation of reflective thinking, the increase in self-awareness, and the consolidation of thoughts and feelings among the students were very apparent. And is not greater self-awareness, after all, one of the aims of higher education? Self-understanding allays anxiety; and whether this understanding results from a classroom situation, a counseling interview, or a research interview makes little difference.

The principal point to be made is that the well-trained, effective college counselor has great opportunity to use his interviewing skills meaningfully both in counseling and other areas. While the purposes and goals of research differ somewhat from those of counseling, the basic essentials of interviewing, the general principles, are the same. Although it is not appropriate in this chapter to explore in detail the uses of the interview in research, interested readers may find Richardson, Dohrenwend, and Klein (1965) most comprehensive, helpful, and informative.

REFERENCES

Balinsky, B., & Burger, Ruth. *The executive interview*. New York: Harper, 1959.

Barbara, D. A. *The art of listening*. Springfield, Ill.: Charles C Thomas, 1958.

Bellows, R. M., & Estep, Frances M. *Employment psychology: the interview*. New York: Rinehart, 1954.

Berdie, R. F. A program of counseling interview research. *Educ. psychol. Measmt*, 1958, 18, 255–274.

Bingham, W. V., Moore, B. V., & Gustad, J. W. *How to interview*. (4th rev. ed.) New York: Harper, 1959.

Bordin, E. S. *Psychological counseling.* New York: Appleton-Century-Crofts, 1955.

Cannell, C. F., & Kahn, R. L. *The dynamics of interviewing.* New York: Wiley, 1957.

Caplow, T. The dynamics of information interviewing. *Amer. J. Social.*, 1956, 62, 165–171.

Danskin, D. G. Roles played by counselors in their interviews. *J. counsel. Psychol.*, 1955, 2, 22–27.

Darley, J. *The interview in counseling.* Washington: U.S. Dept. of Labor, 1946.

Erikson, E. H. *Childhood and society.* (2nd ed.) New York: W. W. Norton, 1963.

Fenlason, Anne F., Ferguson, Grace B., & Abrahamson, A. C. *Essentials in interviewing.* (2nd ed.) New York: Harper, 1962.

Frieke, B. G. The evaluation of assessment procedures. *Superior Student*, 7 (2), 3–9.

Garrett, Annette. *Interviewing: its principles and methods.* New York: Fam. Serv. Assoc. of Amer., 1942.

Group for the Advancement of Psychiatry. *Reports in psychotherapy: initial interviews.* New York: Author, 1959. No. 49.

Hahn, M. E., & MacLean, M. S. *Counseling psychology.* (2nd ed.) New York: McGraw-Hill, 1955.

Hamilton, G. *Theory and practice of social casework.* (2nd ed.) New York: Columbia Univ. Press, 1951.

Hinkley, R., & Fenlason, Anne F. Mental hygiene interviewing: a therapeutic approach. *Amer. J. Orthopsychiat.*, 1942, 12, 313–314.

Kelly, G. A. *The psychology of personal constructs.* New York: W. W. Norton, 1955. 2 vols.

Krishnamurti, J. *The first and last personal freedom.* New York: Harper, 1954.

Magee, R. H. The employment interview: techniques of questioning. *Personnel J.*, 1962, 41, 241–245.

Matarozzo, Ruth G., Phillips, Jeanne S., Wiens, A. N., & Saslow, G. Learning the art of interviewing: a study of what beginning students do and their pattern of change. *Psychother.: Theor., Res. Pract.*, 1965, 2 (2), 49–60.

May, R. *The art of counseling.* New York: Abington-Cokesbury Press, 1939.

May, R. *The meaning of anxiety.* New York: Ronald Press, 1950.

Muthard, J. E. The relative effectiveness of larger units used in interview analysis. *J. consult. Psychol.*, 1953, 18, 184–188.

Oldfield, R. C. *The psychology of the interview.* (3rd ed.) Pacorma, Calif.: Sherwood Press, 1947.

Reik, T. *Listening with the third ear.* New York: Farrar Strauss, 1949.

Richardson, S. A., Dohrenwend, Barbara S., & Klein, D. *Interviewing: its forms and functions.* New York: Basic Books, 1965.

Rogers, C. R. *Counseling and psychotherapy.* Boston: Houghton-Mifflin, 1942.

Rogers, C. R. *Client-centered therapy.* Boston: Houghton-Mifflin, 1951.

Rogers, C. R. The interpersonal relationship: the core of guidance. *Harvard educ. Rev.*, 1962, 32, 416–429.

Sanford, N. (Ed.) *The American college.* New York: Wiley, 1962.

Stevenson, I. The psychiatric interview. In S. Arieti (Ed.), *American handbook of psychiatry*. Vol. I. New York: Basic Books, 1959. Pp. 197–214.

Sullivan, H. S. *The psychiatric interview*. New York: W. W. Norton, 1954.

Super, D. E. *The psychology of careers*. New York: Harper, 1957.

Tyler, Leona E. The initial interview. *Personnel Guid. J.*, 24 (8), 466–473.

Tyler, Leona E. *The work of the counselor*. (2nd ed.) New York: Appleton-Century-Crofts, 1961.

U.S. Civil Service Commission. *Employment interviewing*. Washington: Author, 1956. No. 5.

Weinland, J. D., & Gross, Margaret V. *Personnel interviewing*. New York: Ronald Press, 1952.

Wolberg, L. R. *The technique of psychotherapy*. New York: Grune & Stratton, 1954.

Chapter 4

Psychological Testing and the College Counselor

MAX WEINER

Introduction

Nearly every college counselor uses in his work some type of standardized group test to measure various mental factors of counselees. What is often overlooked is the fact that standardized group data present rather complex problems when the individual scores derived from group tests are interpreted. Since, moreover, very few test manuals offer necessary information on the limitations of group tests when used to counsel individuals, the problems are increased. Even when information is offered, the reader must often study the manual thoroughly and have a sophisticated knowledge of measurement theory in order to identify the possible shortcomings of the test. A further complication results from the fact that texts on tests and measurements tend to emphasize the basic theory necessary to evaluate test manuals and tests. It is assumed the user will, after working with such a text, be able to determine for himself any important limitations.

In practice, however, the counselor usually does not have adequate time to study test manuals and must rely on the general statements given by the publishers regarding appropriate usage. Such reliance may or may not be warranted. What the college counselor requires is a paper containing information concerned with the interpretation of test scores. More spe-

Max Weiner is Associate Professor, Department of Education; and Coordinator, Guidance and School Counseling Program, Brooklyn College of the City University of New York.

cifically, the information should be of the type not generally included in a test manual or tests-and-measurements text.

A chapter such as this cannot begin to be encyclopedic. It is not the intention of the writer, therefore, to attempt to include in the few pages allotted all that may be found in a tests-and-measurements text. It is assumed that the reader is familiar with the basic information needed to interpret tests and has already read a general text on the subject. Rather, what is attempted here is to bring together in one place the type of information a counselor requires in the interpretation of individual scores earned on group standardized tests. The information emphasized in this chapter is that which is (1) generally not clearly identified by test publishers in their manuals and (2) not easily gleaned from tests-and-measurements texts or literature. All of the topics covered are presented in such a way as to provide an overview of the types of problems with which a counselor must be able to cope in order to use tests effectively. The bibliography contains books and periodicals intended to help the reader gain a more sophisticated understanding of the many topics covered in the chapter.

Tests Used by College Counselors

The college counselor uses a variety of standardized tests in his work. Achievement, scholastic aptitude, and special abilities tests are among those commonly relied on. Interest and personality inventories are often also administered. The counselor should not use any single test result as the criterion of success or failure but should recognize the additional information a test score provides about the counselee. It should always be kept in mind that any brief sample of behavior as measured by an hour or so testing situation is merely one more source of information about the counselee.

How Tests Are Used

One major function of tests in college counseling is as a predictor. The counselor is interested in knowing whether the scores earned by an individual adequately predict the counselee's readiness for college study. Was there some evidence of readiness and ability for college, for example, which could have been gleaned from tests administered as early as grades 7 or 8? How well the student is prepared to study in a given college curriculum is another frequent question. Whether a test is a good predictor of any future achievement is often determined by a correlation analysis. The validity of the instrument is then a function of the degree to which there is a high relationship of test score with a future criterion score. Since there never is a perfect correlation between two variables, one must assume that some individuals who do poorly on the predictor variable may, if given an opportunity, do well on the criterion, or vice versa. It is this issue which requires the skill of the test interpreter. Test scores for groups are relatively easy to interpret: one can rely on group statistics. What is much more difficult is to be able to determine which individual might succeed or fail on the basis of the score or scores of a single test.

Norms

When standardized tests are administered, the college counselor must decide to what extent the norm group used in the construction of the instrument is comparable to the population that he himself has in mind in connection with the students he sees. The adequacy of scores compared to the normative group, moreover, is dependent on the use to which the score is put. Here the counselor must make a decision which should be based on previous study of his college population. The average score, for example, of the national norms could be either too high or too low for the achievement required in his own college. Even though an individual may have earned a score which places him at the 80th percentile of the normative group, when compared to the students with whom he will be competing his score may be average or below average.

Another point to be remembered is that even if the test manuals report elsewhere a high correlation between the test scores and a given college curriculum (i.e. engineering, medicine, etc.) it is quite possible that there is a low and non-significant correlation between the test scores and the achievement in his college. That is, the standardization group may be quite different from the local population; for the former the test may be a good predictor yet not so good for the latter. In short, local norms must be set up before any test is used for individual counseling. A student is entitled to know that when he is counseled on the basis of tests, the counselor has compared the earned scores of the various appropriate local groups as well as with national groups.

Sex Norms

A recurring problem raised with the use of norms is related to the correct sex norms. It is not always appropriate to use male norms when a male is the counselee or female norms when a female is counselee. When a test manual offers norms grouped according to sex, the counselor must take into account the curriculum or vocation to which the student aspires or is assigned. Simply stated, almost every college curriculum or vocation may be categorized in any one of the following areas:

1. Male oriented.
2. Female oriented.
3. Neither sex dominant.

Recognizing this categorization, were a female student interested in becoming an engineer (a male-oriented vocational choice in our culture), the counselor should compare her test scores as well as her school grades with males, not females. The reverse comparison would be necessary were a male interested in nursing: His scores and school grades would have to be compared with female norms. Tests such as the Differential Aptitude Tests, whose manual provides norms according to sex, illustrate the importance of the curriculum or career orientation as a standard for appropriate norm usage.

Age Norms

The chronologically youngest student in a group, all other things being equal, will tend to earn the highest score on tests whose scores are based on age norms. This consideration is especially important where group intelligence test scores are used. An example is the Otis Quick-Scoring Test of Mental Ability. The test has 80 items. A ten year old who answered all 80 items correctly could earn an Otis I.Q. score of approximately 170. A student 18 years or older could not earn higher than an Otis I.Q. of 123 if he were to earn a raw score of 80. Consequently, two students whose I.Q. scores are identical on the same intelligence test are not necessarily equal in ability. Even if one were to assume that the scores were not subject to error in measurement, the younger of the two students would have answered fewer items correctly in order to earn the same I.Q. as the older student. This factor could be an explanation for students with similar I.Q.s earning different school and college marks.

Stated somewhat differently, if two students, one 18 and the other 15, took the same intelligence test on the same day and earned the identical I.Q. of, say, 110, the older student would have earned a higher raw score than the younger one. Such is generally the case. But in evaluating students at the same stage of scholastic development, the assumption should be made that a majority of items on any intelligence test require underlying skills—either learned or innate—in order to respond correctly to them. Further, it may be assumed that these skills are necessary for success in typical school and college courses. The student, therefore, who earns the higher raw score is the one who has more skills at the given stage of development.

In order to earn a given class mark, all students, regardless of age are graded according to raw score on a teacher-made test. The oldest student in a class could conceivably earn the highest class mark and have an I.Q. not different from the youngest student. It is the raw score, therefore, which may be the more appropriate indicator of classroom achievement than the converted I.Q. When group intelligence test scores are to be a part of decision making, the age norms should be carefully checked in order to determine whether critical differences may be attributable to the chronological age of the counselee rather than his measured ability.

Grade Equivalents

A grade equivalent, for individual counseling, is a meaningless score. The use of a grade equivalent is so deceptively simple, yet it is a quite complex measure when used to interpret individual scores. First, learning throughout a school year is not equal from month to month. Second, the grade equivalent earned by a student, even though higher than his actual grade placement, need not reflect his actual achievement level. For example, on an 8th grade arithmetic achievement test a student can earn a grade equivalent score of 12.3. This score has no interpretable meaning. Examination of the test's content would reveal no arithmetic problems on a content level above early 9th grade; therefore, a grade equivalent score of 12.3 does not mean the pupil is achieving at the 12th grade, 3rd month, in arithmetic. Most manuals do state that any score above the grade and content level for which the test was constructed is extrapolated, yet such scores are consistently and incorrectly used by counselors.

To further illustrate the dubious value of a grade equivalent, the most correct interpretation of a 12.3 earned by a student in the 8th grade should be as follows: The typical student in grade 12.3 who took the 8th grade achievement test, would earn the score the 8th grader earned. That is, if the same 8th grade achievement test had been administered to a student in grade 12.3, he would have earned approximately the same raw score as the child in grade 8. An additional complication is the fact that grade equivalent scores are extrapolated statistically above the content level of the test. What is equally important, is the unevenness of the relationship of raw scores to grade equivalent. In some areas of the conversion tables, a difference of one raw score point represents a supposed difference of as much as 5 months on the grade equivalent score.

Effects of Guessing

On many tests chance may operate to yield a higher or lower score than would be expected. This issue is especially crucial where cut-off scores are to be used for selection and decision making. The test-taking behavior of a student should always be taken into account when individuals are counseled. In order to determine the extent to which chance has influenced a given score, the answer sheet must be available to the counselor. He should be able to tell at a glance what percentage a counselee's earned score is of the total items attempted. Obviously, a student who has correctly answered all of the attempted items is a different achiever from another with the same raw score but a smaller percentage of correct items out of the total attempted.

Many tests do not include a penalty for wild guessing. Those which do have a penalty rarely affect the student adversely. In fact, scores earned on multiple-choice standardized tests are often to the advantage of the non-timid test taker who responds to all items even where his response is a wild guess. It has been shown (Weiner & Tobias, 1963) that rather respectable scores can be earned on certain achievement and intelligence tests by chance alone. The counselor can learn a great deal about a student's test-taking behavior through close examination of his answer sheet. The number of items attempted, whether difficult questions were answered correctly, the pattern of response, and the estimated number of pure guesses all are helpful adjuncts to the interpretation of an individual's score.

Floor and Ceiling

There are times when scores earned on the same type of test are compared. One may, for example, have two intelligence test scores expressed in terms of I.Q.s or two achievement test scores expressed in terms of grade equivalents. First, it must be remembered that scores earned on different tests are not comparable even when the tests purport to measure the same mental factors. In addition to the difference in norm groups used by different publishers, there is the added difficulty of differences in floor and ceiling scores attainable. One intelligence test, for instance, may have a ceiling I.Q. of 170 while another has a ceiling of 150.

What is more important, however, is the problem which occurs when individuals earn scores near the top or bottom of a given test. For them the appropriateness of the test as a whole comes into question. The individual's ability is seriously under or over estimated if the floor or ceiling of the test prevented him from showing what he could really achieve. A chief purpose of a test is to help the interpreter learn what the counselee knows, as well as what he doesn't know. A perfect raw score or a zero raw score precludes any such interpretation.

Speededness

Speed is another factor, like willingness to guess, that affects the individual scores according to the premiums the test places on it. There are some counselees whose test-taking behavior is such that for almost every response they make they check and recheck. Where a test is timed and speed is important, the individual who is a slow, careful worker is penalized if he does not complete the items. As with guessing, the counselor can make some tentative interpretations which take speed into account by examining the answer sheet to determine the number of items completed in the time allotted.

Interest Inventories

Interests measured by interest inventories may not be the interests they purport to measure. The counselor must know whether the interests of the normative group, as measured by the inventory he uses, are those of people already in the given occupations or those of people prior to their entering the occupations. The important question which must be kept in mind is whether the interests of people in an occupation who served as the normative group were the same before they entered the occupation. It could well be that career choice and the colleagues with whom an individual works have an influence on his behavior and interests. The effect may be strong enough to elicit a change in interest patterns as measured by a standardized inventory. The college counselor, therefore, should have developmental interest profiles available from high school through college and finally in various occupations. For certain occupations, however, the interest changes are so pronounced as to render interest inventories invalid. Increased use of follow-up studies would seem in this case to be most important and necessary.

Personality Tests

Something should be said about group personality tests. Where there is a need for the administration and use of such an instrument, it should be employed with considerable caution. The evidence for the validity of this type of test shows them to be of dubious value. When individuals are to be counseled on the basis of scores earned on a group personality inventory, lack of validity is even more pronounced. One major problem is centered around the definition of *normal*. A competent clinical psychologist or psychiatrist could, with considerable clinical knowledge of the individual, make some reliable judgment concerning the validity of a group personality inventory score. The judgment as measured by the standardized instrument can be no more valid than the clinical competence of the test user. In fact, there is considerable doubt concerning the value of a group personality inventory in general.

There is, however, one group personality inventory, namely, the Minnesota Multiphasic Personality Inventory, which has gained for itself a very good reputation among clinical psychologists. The use and interpretation of this inventory, however, is not within the competence of most college counselors. Considerable training and experience as a clinician are prerequisites.

Where the college counselor finds it necessary to make some evaluation of personality, rather than use a group personality test, he should try to make a sound judgment of his own about the student's personality. This judgment may then be checked against other competent opinion. Without question, the counselor should be skeptical about group "measures" of personality.

Special Ability Tests

There are times when the college counselor wishes to test for some nonacademic ability or aptitude, such as art or music. The tests which purport to be measures of these attributes are of questionable validity. It would seem from a review of the literature that the college counselor would be on more secure ground were he to use the judgment of the instructors of such specialties concerning the student's aptitude.

Equivalent Forms of Tests

Often there is a need to determine whether remedial treatment of learning deficiencies has resulted in an increment in learning. A generally accepted technique is the use of a pretests and posttests. Where standardized achievement tests are used, equivalent forms of the same test are generally available. Equivalent forms have the advantage of controlling for practice effect but have many disadvantages which may be entirely overlooked. No two forms of a test are ever totally equivalent. The correlations between different forms of the same test may be high, but this relationship is based on samples of subjects who in many cases are not even drawn from the normative population upon which the test was originally standardized. Added to this is the very real possibility that, for any given group or individual, one form may be more difficult than another. It is even possible that the differences between forms will result in a systematic error; that is, for some subjects the mean score earned on one form may yield lower scores than another form of the same test. This difference was shown in at least one study (Howell and Weiner, 1961) to be as high, in terms of grade equivalents, as one year.

Without question, the counselor should be somewhat skeptical of publishers' assertions that alternate forms are equivalent, if any important decisions depend on their use. Where alternate forms must be administered, local studies should be undertaken to determine the degree of difference between forms. A simple technique is to test a group twice, approximately 24 hours apart. On the first day administer one form of the test to half the group and the other form to the remaining half. The next day give each half group the form not taken the previous day. If the forms are equivalent, there will be no significant difference between the scores earned in the two forms of the test. It is a good idea, also, to note differences in scores gained by individuals from one day to the next. Where large score differences occur, even for one student in a 24 hour period, the counselor will have evidence for use of extreme caution in interpreting the results.

Error of Measurement

Since it is quite likely that a student's score could go down as easily as up on any subsequent testing, the counselor must have a thorough knowledge of the standard error of measurement for any score earned by an individual. Test manuals provide a standard error of measurement for the norm group or for representative samples. Often neglected, however, is a definitive statement regarding the confidence a counselor can place in an individual's earned score.

The standard error of measurement is a quantity which is needed to obtain an estimate of the *true* score. If one could be sure that the score a student earned on a first trial would be the same on any other trials, we would have a *true* score. For example, it is possible that on a first attempt at bowling one ball could knock all the pins down. This obviously does not mean the bowler is a perfect scorer; other tries would be necessary to establish an average over a period of games. The average is a closer estimate of the bowler's *true* bowling score. When a standardized test is administered only once, the resulting score may or may not be near the true score the individual could earn over a series of trials. The more unreliable the measure, the farther will the obtained score be from the true score. If the counselor must make a decision based on a single test score for an individual, the error of measurement of the test should be taken into account. Since the error of measurement is a type of standard deviation, it would seem to be good practice to use plus and minus two standard deviations when estimating a true score. If, for example, a student earns a score of 84 on a test with a standard error of measurement of 5, the true score will lie between 74 (84 minus 10) and 94 (84 plus 10) at a confidence level of 95 per cent.

Although the statistics just cited are not necessarily appropriate for individual test interpretation, they can be considered a fair estimate of an individual's score. The reader should refer to a more detailed description for this type of interpretation in a text on tests and measurements.

Growth Scores

Growth in learning as measured by standardized tests is a most difficult factor to identify. It is a relatively simple matter to measure growth, say, in reading if one begins with a group with little or no reading ability and then tests them again after a year's instruction. The increment is large enough to be measured by a standardized achievement test. On the other hand, the increment in reading ability between grades 11 and 12 or the freshman and sophomore college years is not so easily measured. In fact, the increment is such that the difference in scores could equally be attributed to such variables as the instrument, chance, unreliability, and even test-taking behavior, as well as growth. The college counselor who uses achievement tests to determine whether an individual has improved in his general academic achievement from year to year would be very hard pressed to identify the cause of the change in scores. A general rule to solve this problem would be that changes of more than two standard deviations represent a significant increment.

A distinction needs to be made here between scores of groups as compared to individuals. It is quite simple to show that two scores are significantly different from a statistical viewpoint. If the difference is large enough, it might be possible to attribute it to growth. When it comes to individual scores, however, it is quite another matter. There are too many variables which may operate to contribute to an individual's earning different scores on tests which purport to measure growth. It would be almost impossible, in fact, to specifically attribute score changes in any individual case to any single variable. For any given student it is possible for a score to show a gain or a loss without measuring the true gain or loss for that individual. Perhaps any tenable statement made regarding growth-score interpretation for an individual would have to take into account clinical evidence of change as well as test achievement.

Advanced Placement Tests

An Advanced Placement test is an achievement test used to determine whether college credit can be given for an advanced course taken in the 12th grade of high school. It is a college level test and is sponsored by the College Entrance Examination Board. The unique contribution of this type of achievement test is that the papers are graded on a five point scale from 5—high honors, to 1—no credit. In addition, each college which receives a candidate's scores determines for itself how it will use the results. Some have given credit for courses offered in their schools while others have permitted students to take advanced courses in their colleges. The validity of the test is based on local requirements, each college receiving the student's essay booklet and essay questions as well as rating. Importantly, it is recognized that valid interpretations cannot be made by a college without its having access to the entire work sample of the candidate. Scores alone do not provide enough information for an objective evaluation.

Test Selection

Perhaps the most important problem which must be faced by the college counselor is whether to use a standardized test and, if so, which test. A test should not be used unless the counselor knows exactly which questions concerning the counselee he wishes answered by the instrument. It may well be that the counselor has all the information he requires regarding the student in the transcripts and instructor reports. The standardized test scores he might add could conceivably contribute little or nothing to his information. If the counselor were to spend some thought to the question, "What significant information will the test or tests add?" he would very likely help himself select more appropriate instruments. He might even decide not to use any tests with a particular student. Even though individual instructor grades are often labelled as invalid predictors of future academic success, the average of four years' high school work is a much more valid predictor than the one hour or so sample of achievement the student performs on a standardized test.

With these considerations in mind, the counselor should first review all the data he has regarding the student and then list those questions which still remain unanswered. The questions should be those which require a knowledgeable response in order to be able to counsel the student more effectively. One question may be, for example, how well the student compares with the general population of engineering students in interests, aptitude and reading ability. Once the counselor has in mind the specific purpose for which he plans to use a test, he will be better able to make an appropriate selection. He also will be able to evaluate the test content and norms more realistically. That is, he will be selecting and using an instrument which will, hopefully, answer specific questions related to the individual he is counseling, rather than merely adding information without knowing what weight it should have in the overall picture of the individual.

Decision Making and the Test

The questions to be answered, care in selection of tests, and the subsequent interpretation of scores earned on the tests are very closely related. If the questions can be answered in general terms, such as above average, average, or below average, rather than in terms of specific cut-off scores, test selection and interpretation are not difficult. The more specific the cut-off score and the more permanent the resultant decision, the more difficult is the task of test selection and score interpretation. Since a single score for a single individual is more subject to unreliability, more than one test should be administered in order to assure a more accurate estimate of the individual's ability. The cost of retesting and multiple testing should not be a factor if the counselor will be called upon to make important decisions with his counselee on the basis of specific test scores.

The Mental Cut-off Score

When one reads a thermometer as 70 degrees, it could be evaluated as warm. Another individual might perceive the temperature as cool. The same problem is involved in test interpretation: Some counselors may consider a given reading score as good; others may consider the identical score as poor. Every counselor, based on his previous experience with various tests and student populations, has in mind an evaluation of scores earned on standardized tests. This evaluation is frequently independent of the norm group upon which the test is based.

The counselor must become aware of his own mental cut-off scores for the tests he uses. He should make use of appropriate norms and attempt to be guided by objective findings for individuals. He should make use of contingency tables rather than subjective interpretations of scores. Contingency tables, when properly constructed, provide the counselor and his counselee with a useful interpretation of scores earned.

Who Should Use Tests

One cause of continuous criticisms levelled against tests is the ever-present example of their misuse. The layman has become increasingly aware of the importance of tests in decision-making processes. Too often, he feels, they are incorrectly used in deciding what curriculum he will follow, what courses he will be permitted to take, what college will accept him, what job he will receive, what promotion will be his—and much more. Who can blame the layman, therefore, if he shows so much concern with tests and the people who use them?

Critics of tests encounter very little difficulty in finding an audience, since, all too often, these nonprofessional critics act as the "protectors" of the individuals who perceive themselves as unsuccessful because of poor test performance. Almost all test takers have a feeling that they could have done better. The critic who finds fault with tests used to make educational and vocational decisions is considered a hero of sorts. It is not enough for the test publisher or user to come to the defense of tests with remarks such as "Tests are only as good as the interpreter," and a technical explanation in terms not easily understood by the test consumer. What is needed is a careful look at how tests are used and by whom.

Test publishers, in their zeal to produce instruments which are economical, easy to administer, score, and interpret, must accept some of the responsibility for the criticisms. It is known that a large number of schools in the nation do not have qualified staff members involved in test administration. More control over who uses tests should therefore be exerted by the test publishers. It is not appropriate to assume that any administrator of a school or college can order any tests of achievement or aptitude. Nor should publishers assume that all school administrators can order certain types of tests because they are themselves qualified to use them or will assign the task to qualified personnel within their building. No test order from a school or college should be filled unless the person who will use the tests has been certified as a qualified user. Such certification could be accomplished through the American Psychological Association or the American Personnel and Guidance Association. Certification should also entail more than mere achievement of formal degree and experience requirements: The use of group tests necessitates continuous validation studies. Certifying agencies along with publishers have an obligation to police the usage of tests. There is the precedence for control of usage by the College Entrance Examination Board and by the professional organizations and publishers who administer the medical and law aptitude tests.

One other condition must also be met by the test publishers. It is not enough to include in a test manual references to limitations; the limitations must be spelled out clearly, if warranted, on the face sheet of the manual rather than buried in an obscure section. The degree of accuracy of a single score, the content emphasis of an achievement test, the type of population for which the test is appropriate are, for example, the types of information which should be readily available and visible to the user.

Again, many may be qualified to use tests, but no tests should be considered for use if there is no opportunity for continuous validation studies. Those schools and colleges which rely on the published norms are very likely to find many invalid decisions made at the local level. Follow up studies, although sometimes admittedly expensive, are a necessary method for providing a justified basis for interpretation of test scores. There is very little skill required in the use of national norms per se. What is more difficult and more important is the ability to identify groups and individuals whose scores are not within the sphere of the normative data.

For each type of test certain counselor qualifications are necessary in order to interpret correctly. The average college counselor who has had a minimum of two or three courses in tests and measurements (including statistics) could, with a moderate amount of effort, be able to understand and interpret a majority of achievement and aptitude tests by studying the test manuals and related literature. Tests, however, such as the Minnesota Multiphasic Inventory and even the Strong Vocational Inventory require long and thorough study. It is not enough to know the manuals. What is also required is supervised experiences in administering and in interpreting the results for individuals.

There is, furthermore, a group of tests which purport to measure abstract concepts (e.g., intrapunitiveness, achievement motivation, intellectual assertiveness, ideational fluency) and which require still another level of competency beyond the two or three basic courses; and there are some tests which should only be used by clinical or counseling psychologists (e.g. Rorschach, Thematic Apperception, Bender-Gestalt) who have completed a doctorate program in a college approved by the American Psychological Association. In short, the college counselor should be aware of his own limitations. The tests he uses must be those with which he is thoroughly familiar and professionally competent.

Needed Research

Finally, those who use tests have many opportunities as well as a professional obligation to contribute through research to the increased effectiveness of test usage. A large number of college counselors have made significant findings in this area; unfortunately, not enough is reported in the appropriate journals. Among the more relevant topics which should be studied are the concept of average and critical cut-off scores.

The Concept of Average

Counselors would do well to study *average* as a concept. Each instructor tends to grade students on the basis of those he teaches: The standard of a given grade is most often determined by the population being taught. Although a given grade may be determined by many factors, too often, grades are the result of comparison with others in the class. Teachers tend to grade according to local norms; that is, the ability of the group determines what individuals may earn. If all of the students were valedictorians in their respective high schools and have approximately the same ability, say, in freshman college chemistry, it is highly unlikely that all will receive As. The instructor will administer tests which will result in a fairly "normal" distribution. Had some of the C recipients, for example, been in other classes, either within the college or elsewhere, they might have earned higher grades. The A students might, in other classes, have earned Cs, and so on.

Teachers, therefore, tend to mark on a local norm basis, and their counselors use the local information to counsel on a national basis. Standardized tests must be used to yield additional (more national) information. Average scores on an achievement test may be predictive of high grades in one school, average grades in another, or below average in still another. The problems raised by the use of these differently based scores require considerable research.

Critical Cut-off Scores

A closely related area for further research is the critical cut-off score. A large number of students who apply to colleges and are rejected would have been accepted had they been eligible to apply, say, a year earlier. It is known, moreover, that those who succeed in reaching a certain test score are not the only ones qualified, that many who earned lower scores may be equally qualified for college work. There is a need for carefully designed studies to determine the relationship between actual success on a job or in a college and the related minimum scores on various tests needed to assure success. And inasmuch as the predictive value of a test is usually determined by using as the criterion group only those admitted to a college or position, the college counselor could use research in this area to help him determine which variables should not be eliminated from consideration just because of some arbitrary cut-off score in some program or institution.

Summary and Conclusion

In discussing the types of group tests and the problems encountered in interpretation of scores earned by individuals, it is to be emphasized that a superficial knowledge of group tests and their manuals is not sufficient for a college counselor. The chief purpose of the present chapter is to provide guidelines for the interpretation of individual scores and to show that these scores, when earned on group tests, are not amenable to simple interpretation. Errors and limitations of tests are more pronounced when only the individual is counseled; and the counselor, therefore, must be highly capable in the area of tests and measurements.

In some ways the publishers could be held responsible for much of the misuse of tests. It is suggested that they exercise more control over the distribution of their tests. The chief responsibility, however, lies with the test user. In this instance it is the college counselor who must assure himself that he is able to recognize his own limitations as well as strengths. No instrument, no matter how high its validity and reliability, is any better than its user. All tests should be used with extreme caution where important decisions are to be made concerning an individual.

REFERENCES[1]

The bibliography which follows is intended to provide (1) a list of representative books in the field of tests and measurements which would be helpful to the college counselor and (2) articles which report research on problems of interest to the college counselor who uses group tests. Annotation has been provided for the reader where titles are not self-explanatory.

Books

American Psychological Association. *Standards for educational and psychological tests and manuals.* Washington: Author, 1966.

Anastasi, Anne. *Psychological testing.* (2nd ed.) New York: Macmillan, 1961.
A good basic text with an excellent bibliography of tests and related information.

Anderson, P. R. *College testing. A guide to practices and programs.* Washington: Amer. Council on Educ., 1959.
Written by the Committee on Measurement and Evaluation of the American Council on Education. A good overview of test usage in colleges. Does not require a statistical background in order to gain from its pages. Should be quite helpful to the beginning college test user or those who wish to learn more about tests at the college level.

Bauernfeind, R. H. *Building a school testing program.* Boston: Houghton Mifflin, 1963.
Although written for school people rather than college, this is an excellent text for those readers who wish to have a clear, concise text which is not difficult and does not assume a thorough background in statistics. It contains a rather complete set of references at the end of each chapter, a list of test publishers and useful statements regarding the entries.

Bloom, B. S., & Peters, F. R. *The use of academic prediction scales for counseling and selecting college entrants.* New York: Free Press, 1961.

Buros, O. K. *The sixth mental measurements yearbook.* Highland Park, N.J.: Gryphon Press, 1965.
The latest of the series of yearbooks with which every college counselor should be acquainted. It contains critical reviews of tests used in the United States. It should be referred to by the college counselor as a first step in becoming knowledgeable about a test or tests he plans to use. Many reviews, it must be remembered, may not be helpful to the counselor interested in interpretation of individual scores.

Cronbach, L. J. *Essentials of psychological testing.* (2nd ed.) New York: Harper, 1960.
Of the basic tests-and-measurements texts listed in this bibliography, Cronbach's book is probably the most difficult and also most comprehensive. It can serve as an introduction to as well as a reference for the college counselor.

1. The assistance of Ruth Mechaneck of the William Alanson White Institute in compiling this bibliography is acknowledged with thanks.

Goldman, L. *Using tests in counseling.* New York: Appleton-Century-Crofts, 1961.

A most useful basic tool for elementary and secondary school as well as college counselors.

Harris, C. W. (Ed.) *Problems in measuring change.* Madison, Wisc.: Univ. of Wisc. Press, 1963.

Papers presented at a conference at the University of Wisconsin by experts in measurement who discuss the problem of measuring change.

Havighurst, R. J. *The coming crisis in the selection of students for college entrance.* Washington: Amer. Educational Res. Assoc., 1960.

A symposium addressed by seven educators dealing with the topic of selecting college students. Both intellective and nonintellective factors are discussed.

Thorndike, R. I., & Hagen, E. *Measurement and evaluation in psychology and education.* (2nd ed.) New York: Wiley, 1961.

A very good basic text.

Periodicals

Aiken, L. R., Jr. College dropouts and difference scores. *Psychol. Rep.*, 1963, 13, 905–906.

Anderson, L. B., & Spencer, P. A. Personal adjustment and academic predictability among college freshmen. *J. appl. Psychol.*, 1963, 47, 97–100.

Prediction of achievement not found to be influenced by personal adjustment.

Bachman, J. G. Prediction of academic achievement using the Edwards need achievement scale. *J. appl. Psychol.*, 1964, 48, 16–19.

Berger, B., & Hall, E. Personality patterns and achievement in college. *Educ. psychol. Measmt.*, 1964, 24, 339–346.

Brown, W. F., & Abeles, N. Facade orientation and academic achievement. *Personnel Guid. J.*, 1960, 39, 283–286.

Faking scores significantly and negatively related to achievement in college.

Calia, V. F. The use of discriminant analysis in prediction of scholastic performance. *Personnel Guid. J.*, 1960, 39, 184–185.

Campbell, D. P. The 1966 revision of the Strong Vocational Inventory Blank, *Personnel Guid. J.*, 1966, 44, 744–749.

A good statement regarding the strengths of the revised inventory.

Casserly, P. L. What's really happening in advanced placement?—Part II. *Coll. Bd. Rev.*, 1966, 16–22, No. 59.

A good review of the advanced placement program.

Chahbazi, P. Use of projective tests in predicting college achievement. *Educ. psychol. Measmt.*, 1960, 20, 839–842.

Though need-achievement scores on 2 projective tests demonstrated *rs* of .35 and .46 with first semester grades as criterion, *rs* were lower for later college grades.

College Entrance Examination Board. A statement on personality testing. *Coll. Bd. Rev.*, 1963, 11–13, No. 54.

"No existing personality test known to the board seems to have been sufficiently studied to warrant the acceptance of very serious risks that would attend the actual use of such tests in making admissions decisions."

Copeman, J., Pascoe, R., & Ward, G. The Edwards Personal Preference Scale and revised cooperative English test as predictors of academic achievement. *Proc. W. Va. Acad. Sci.*, 1961, 33, 24–216.

Demos, G. D., & Spolgor, L. J. Academic achievement of college freshmen in relation to the Edwards Personal Preference Schedule. *Educ. psychol. Measmt.*, 1961, 21, 473–479.

Though admitting the methodology employed may be questioned, the authors conclude that the EPPS is of little use in predicting or diagnosing academic achievement.

Fishman, J. A., & Pasanella, A. K. College admission selection studies. *Rev. educ. Res.*, 1960, 30, 298–310.

Studies of mass testing and routinization of selection and admission have outrun consideration of criteria or goals on which selection and guided admission must rest.

Frederickson, N., & Gilbert, A. C. F. Replication of a study of differential predictability. *Educ. psychol. Measmt.*, 1960, 20, 759–767.

Replicates a study showing that *S*s classified as noncompulsive were characterized by higher correlations between Strong Vocational Inventory scores and freshman grades in engineering than compulsive students.

French, J. W. Aptitude and interest score patterns related to satisfaction with college major field. *Educ. psychol. Measmt.*, 1961, 21, 287–294.

French, J. W. New tests for predicting the performance of college students with high-level aptitude. *J. educ. Psychol.*, 1964, 55, 185–194.

Gough, H. G., & Hall, W. B. Prediction of performance in medical school from California Psychological Inventory. *J. appl. Psychol.*, 1964, 48, 218–226.

Hansmeier, T. W. The Iowa Tests of Educational Development as predictors of college achievement. *Educ. psychol. Measmt.*, 1960, 20, 843–845.

Correlations given of ITED with college grades.

Harris, Y. Y., & Dole, A. A. A pilot study in local research with the Differential Aptitude Test Battery. *Personnel Guid. J.*, 1960, 39, 128–132.

DAT can be helpful in predicting early in high school acceptance or rejection in college and approximate college performance.

Heilbrun, A. B., Jr. Prediction of first year college dropouts using ACL Need Scales. *J. counsel. Psychol.*, 1962, 9, 58–63.

On the Adjective Check List dropouts score higher on Heterosexuality and Change, lower on Achievement, Order, and Endurance.

An improvement in prediction over ability measures is indicated.

Hills, J. R., Emory, L. B., Franz, G., & Growder, D. G. Admissions and guidance research in the university system of Georgia. *Personnel Guid. J.*, 1961, 39, 452–457.

Study evaluated the validity of College Board scores and high school records for predicting grades in the 19 colleges of the university system.

Holland, J. L. The prediction of college grades from the California Psychological Inventory and the Scholastic Aptitude Test. *J. educ. Psychol.*, 1959, 50, 135–142.

The CPI and SAT are useful in predicting college freshman grades for sample of high aptitude high school seniors. At a high level of scholastic aptitude, personality variables may yield validity coefficients which are almost three times as great as those obtained using aptitude measures alone.

Holland, J. L., & Nichols, R. C. Prediction of academic and extracurricular achievement in college. *J. educ. Psychol.*, 1964, 55, 55–65.

Records of past achievement and potential achievement scales developed from everyday activities and interests were generally superior to other kinds of variables and equalled the efficiency of the best multiple-regression equations.

Howell, J. J., & Weiner, M. Note on the equivalence of alternate forms of an achievement test. *Educ. psychol. Measmt.*, 1961, 21, 309–313.

Johnson, R. W. Interpretation of ACT difference scores. *J. Coll. Stud. Personnel*, 1966, 7, 109–112.

Discusses results of American College Tests (ACT) administered to 600,000 students in approximately 900 colleges.

Juola, A. E. Predictive validity of five college-level academic aptitude tests at one institution. *Personnel Guid. J.*, 1960, 38, 637–641.

Tests (CQT, SCAT, SAT, Ohio State Psychological Exam and Amer. Counsel. on Educ. Psychol. Exam) used on freshman found to differ slightly in predictive validity.

Kirk, B. A., Cummings, R. W., & Goodstein, L. D. College qualification tests and differential guidance with university freshmen. *Personnel Guid. J.*, 1963, 42, 47–51.

Long, J. M. Sex differences in academic prediction based on scholastic personality and interest factors. *J. exp. Educ.*, 1964, 32, 239–248.

Mann, M. J. The prediction of achievement in a liberal arts college. *Educ. Psychol. Measmt.*, 1961, 21, 481–483.

SAT and SCAT equally effective in predicting first year grades in a small women's liberal arts college.

Merwin, J. C., & Gardner, E. F. Development and application of tests of educational achievement. *Rev. educ. Res.*, 1962, 32, 40–50.

During the period under review, noticeable progress was made in understanding the use of achievement tests as predictors and the relationship between anxiety and achievement test performance.

Michael, W. B. Higher school record and college board scores as predictors of success in a liberal arts program during the freshman year of college. *Educ. Psychol. Measmt.*, 1962, 22, 399–400.

Michael, W. B. Short evaluation of the research reviewed in educational and psychological testing; advances in achievement testing. *Rev. educ. Res.*, 1965, 35, 95.

Michael, W. B., & Jones, R. A. Stability of predictive validities of high school grades and of scores on the Scholastic Aptitude Test of the College

Entrance Examination Board for liberal arts students. *Educ. psychol. Measmt.*, 1963, 23, 375–378.

Record of academic achievement in high school consistently more predictive of college grades than either part or total scores of the CEEB's SAT.

Michael, W. B., Jones, R. A., Cox, A., Gershon, A., Hoover, M., Katz, K., & Smith, D. High school record and college board scores as predictors of success in a liberal arts program during the freshman year of college. *Educ. psychol. Measmt.*, 1962, 22, 399–400.

For 432 liberal arts freshmen, high school average was more predictive of success in college than either part or total scores of the CEEB.

Miller, A. General ability and interest measures as differential predictors of academic achievement. *Educ. psychol. Measmt.*, 1964, 24, 357–362.

Six samples of freshmen given Ohio Psychological Test, Knowledge Interest Test, Special Keys Interest Agreement. Criterion was grade received in psychology course. Found that abilities usually, but not always, superior to interests. Which measure was superior depended on whether general or special scoring keys were considered and whether original or cross validation samples were considered.

Nunnery, M. Y., & Aldmon, H. F. Undergraduate grades as indicators of success in master's degree programs in education. *Personnel Guid. J.*, 1964, 43, 280–286.

Pierson, L. R. High school teacher prediction of college success. *Personnel Guid. J.*, 1958, 37, 142–145.

Best predictors in this study were high school grades.

Rinsland, H. D. Actuarial predictions in guidance. *J. educ. Res.*, 1961, 54, 168–172.

Actuarial prediction is the prediction between an individual's abilities and his achievements. Real problem in predictive studies is the low validity of the criterion, typically college grades. Aptitude tests themselves already exceed reliability of college grades and have about reached limit of reliability and predictability.

Rosen, N. A. A validation study of the College Entrance Examination Boards and other predictors at Purdue University. *Stud. Higher Educ.*, 1960, 1–22, No. 90.

Formal selection devices not as likely to be useful unless criterion (in this case first semester grade-point index) can be substantially improved.

Rusten, E. M., & Gilbert, A. C. F. The discriminant analysis technique in assigning freshmen to college chemistry courses. *J. psychol. Stud.*, 1960, 11, 253–255.

By the use of discriminant analysis technique, it was discovered that students who were successful in the four different chemistry courses could be successfully differentiated on the basis of the three variables used.

Seegard, J. E., Jr. Further investigation of an MMPI scale for predicting college achievement. *Personnel Guid. J.*, 1962, 41, 251–253.

Tempero, H. E., & Ivanoff, J. M. The Cooperative School and College Ability

Test as a predictor of achievement in selected high school subjects. *Educ. psychol. Measmt.*, 1960, 20, 835–838.

Wagner, E. E., & Sober, K. A. Effectiveness of the Guilford-Zimmerman Temperament Survey as a predictor of scholastic success in college. *J. counsel. Psychol.*, 1964, 11, 94–95.

Weiner, M., & Howell, J. J. Difficulties in the use of achievement test gains as measures of growth. *Personnel Guid. J.*, 1963, 41, 781–786.

Weiner, M., & Tobias, S. Chance factors in the interpretation of group administered multiple choice tests. *Personnel Guid. J.*, 1963, 41, 435–437.

Willingham, W. W. Erroneous assumptions in predicting college grades. *J. counsel. Psychol.*, 1963, 10, 389–394.

Worell, L. Level of aspiration and academic success. *J. educ. Psychol.*, 1959, 50, 47–54.

Aspiration measures were correlated with total grade average and decile ranks, as were high school grades, ACE scores and CEEB scores. *S*s in college. Aspiration measure differentiated graduates from nongraduates.

Chapter 5

Group Techniques in Education, Counseling, and Psychotherapy

MAX SIEGEL

The Group Explosion

Throughout this book on the counseling of college students, there are repeated references to the word *group* and to the use of *group techniques* of one kind or another. Colleagues who have contributed chapters to this volume describe or recommend the use of groups in admissions counseling; freshman orientation; academic improvement; psychological testing; curriculum advisement; student adviser leadership and other student activities; placement, career, and psychological counseling; health services; and religious counseling. This is indeed a significant sign of the times and not the sign of anything unique to the college campus. More than likely, it is quite the reverse, in that the dramatic developments of an emerging scientific discipline have begun to burst forth in colleges and universities in explosive fashion.

A review of these developments would seem appropriate in order that the reader may understand better the historical background, the nature of group process and the various techniques that employ this process, and some definitions of terms currently in use (and misuse) in the literature. In this review, the writer hopes to convey some understanding regarding *the group* in a variety of settings. The focus, however, will be largely on the application of group therapeutic techniques in working with college-

Max Siegel is Professor, Department of Education; Coordinator, School Psychologist Training Program; and formerly, Associate Dean of Students, Brooklyn College of the City University of New York.

age students, and, therefore, will be applicable to high-school and graduate students, as well as to young adults.

Historical Background

The maturation of group psychotherapy, which appears on the surface to be of relatively recent vintage, actually has been a slow process which goes back to the beginning of recorded time. The historical roots of group therapy may be considered to go back to every religious movement which has ever reached masses of people, to the Greek dramatists of the Hellenic era who were deeply interested in family relationships, to the dramas of Shakespeare, and to the group hypnotic sessions of Mesmer in the early 1700s.

Modern group pyschotherapy, as we know it, is uniquely American. Most observers credit Dr. Joseph Hersey Pratt, a Boston internist, with the beginning of group psychotherapy in 1905. Pratt (1907), as a young physician treating discouraged and disheartened tubercular patients, organized what he called *tuberculosis classes*. He conducted weekly meetings with indigent patients, admittedly as a timesaving device, initially, and gave brief inspirational talks to help them repress pessimistic thoughts and to keep them in treatment. A completely empirical development, these *classes* included lectures by Pratt on sound hygiene practices, group discussions, and exhortation to help patients overcome their pessimism, and develop increasing self-confidence and self-esteem. There were 25 patients in a class, though more often than not there were only 15 to 20 present. Pratt reported the class as having a common bond in a common disease, and described the class meeting as "a pleasant social hour for the members." While it is evident that Pratt was proceeding intuitively with little understanding of his own impact upon his patients and their impact upon each other, he began to comprehend the full implications of his work, and so indicated in his later writings (1946).

The rich, human, and fascinating heritage of group psychotherapy followed no single track or growth process. The pioneers in the wilderness include medical and nonmedical colleagues with highly varied orientations, background, and training. Controversy, theoretical differences, and claims and counterclaims have been present. Tradition, so difficult to change in the present, was no less hard to modify from the beginning of Pratt's work. Growth and development, nevertheless, moved inexorably ahead. Excellent and detailed historical accounts are provided by Moreno (1966); Mullan

& Rosenbaum (1962); Rosenbaum & Berger (1963); and Rosenbaum (1965). The interested reader may learn from these publications of the later work of Pratt; of the significant contributions of L. Cody Marsh, a former minister who turned psychiatrist; of Moreno, who claims to have coined the term *group therapy* in 1931 and who later came to be identified primarily with psychodrama, which he introduced into the United States in 1925; of Adler, who introduced group guidance concepts in Europe; of Freud, who wrote about group psychology in the 1920s; of Trigant Burrow, who used the term *group analysis* in 1925; and of other pioneers, such as Schilder, Slavson, Wender, Foulkes, Wolf, and so many others. World War II contributed heavily to the growth of group therapy, in one form or another, perhaps in large part because of personnel shortages and large-scale treatment needs. Rosenbaum (1965) points out that in a psychiatric climate which necessarily became more receptive to modifications of technique, "every school of analytic theory and psychological counseling was using some technique which was called *group psychotherapy*." (p. 1256)

During the first 35 years after Pratt's (1907) first published report, there were approximately 125 professional papers devoted to group therapy. During the next two decades, there were over 2,000 such papers. The rising crescendo in publications has been capped, very recently, with the near-simultaneous publication of a half dozen basic texts on group therapy. When the American Group Psychotherapy Association was formed in 1942, the membership was less than 20. It now numbers over 1,700, with affiliated regional societies throughout the country, and continues to grow by leaps and bounds.

Today, group psychotherapy is firmly established as a method of treatment in the mental health field. Group treatment is provided in hospitals, schools and colleges, child care institutions, child and adult guidance and mental hygiene clinics, social agencies, speech clinics, religious centers, labor unions, industry, settlement houses, military services, rehabilitation programs, and countless other settings. Indeed, the extent to which group therapy and its counterparts (by whatever titular modification) have invaded and become pervasive in contemporary society is troubling, if not dangerous. Group therapeutic methods are being employed to help choose careers; lose weight; give up smoking, gambling, or drinking; obtain sex education; find an "ideal" mate; and for other purposes far too numerous to mention. The activity, the vigor, the popularity of this old yet so-new field is both frightening and exhilarating, exciting and depressing, supportive and overwhelming. It is indeed time to give pause, take stock, and reexamine what is being done.

Problems of Semantics: Controversy

Most workers in this field are agreed that group psychotherapy is currently in the mainstream of professional practice because the world is in fact group oriented. Our tradition stressing the ethic of individual responsibility notwithstanding, it has become fundamental in modern society to solve problems in a group rather than individually. Murphy (1963) makes this point and emphasizes the making and breaking function of society as a therapeutic community. He helps to clear the air which has been polluted with attempts to keep group dynamics and group therapy on parallel, but necessarily separate, tracks. It is true, nonetheless, that these two tracks have been running parallel to each other. Following World War II, the study of group dynamics—the study of the unique ways in which a work group or recreation group or family group functions—enjoyed an impressive and growing amount of attention in universities, social service agencies, and other settings. Group psychotherapy—the meeting of individual patients with emotional difficulties to clarify their personal problems in living while experiencing their problems in this group setting—enjoyed a parallel period of growth. Inevitably, the streams of thought began to converge. Workers in each field began to share and profit from one another's experiences. Efforts to maintain a parallelism or to avoid convergence were as fruitless and as unrealistic as the attempt to teach skills alone, without regard to other problems of group living. This is anecdotally illustrated by the teacher who sent a note home with a child urging the parents to bathe him occasionally, to which the irate parents replied, "Learn him, don't smell him."

Similarly, *advising, counseling, guidance,* and *psychotherapy* are terms used interchangeably by some workers, whereas other delineate very sharply the differences among them. Even the word *group,* so seemingly clear, is used to refer to more than one, six to ten, or to increasingly higher numbers approximating the size of large lecture hall classes. All of these terms require clarification. Indeed, the very individuals being served, by whatever technique, are variously called *clients* or *patients;* and controversy rages widely regarding preference for one or the other (or some new) term. Workers in schools, of course, are able to avoid this dispute by using the word *children, pupils,* or *students,* according to age. In colleges and universities there would seem to be no problem, since all clients or patients are referred to as *students.*

The dissension, disagreement, and general feelings on the part of the advocates of one point of view or another are so intense as to render it unlikely that *any* proposed definitions can be accepted by *all* practitioners at this time. Perhaps this is all to the good, since open-mindedness is thereby encouraged and experimental efforts may be continued with terminology until consensus is agreed upon. In the opinion of the writer, much of the controversy surrounding various points of view will dissipate itself as our professional tools are sharpened by the maturation process. So long as disagreements persist, however, attention and deliberation will be devoted to vexing problems, leading inevitably to greater insights and added knowledge.

Some Definitions and Ground Rules

The Group

For purpose of this chapter, and in connection with the application of group techniques in school and college settings, the term *group* may be employed when students assemble on a volitional basis, develop relationships, interact, become interdependent, and seek to achieve common goals because of individual needs. Thus, a lynch mob, theater audience, parent-teachers meeting, freshman orientation meeting, or the usual instructional or classroom situation would *not* be regarded as a group. Similarly, every aggregate or collection or mass of individuals would *not* be regarded as a group. In these terms, however, students who assemble on a systematic, voluntary basis for help of some kind because of underachievement, uncertainty about choice of major, or any other personal problem in living, *would* be a group. In this sense, moreover, the use of the term *group* refers to what Kadis (1965) has called the *group method* to refer to utilization of the group situation as a medium of change or a growth stimulant.

Techniques

With the above understanding of what we mean by a group, it begins to matter very little, beyond compulsive semantics, whether certain programs are identified as group therapy, group counseling, group guidance, group discussion, group education, group orientation, group analysis, group work, or whatever. We would differentiate, here, between the group process and the group-oriented approach. It is apparent that the majority of educators are child-oriented or student-oriented in their approach to teaching. Others, and in increasing numbers, are proponents of group-oriented classrooms in which group-centered techniques are advocated in instruction (Bany & Johnson, 1964). As indicated earlier, this is within expectancy in a group-oriented world. We must distinguish, therefore, between the use of the group method in a process geared to helping individuals (through a group), and the application to educational processes of principles learned from group dynamics (Wolf & Schwartz, 1955).

In the present chapter, counseling and psychotherapy are used interchangeably, with the writer accepting the general agreement that these terms are not exactly synonymous. Recent publication of national conference reports which survey the training of psychologists in these areas sheds much light on the differences, as well as the similarities and overlapping (Thompson & Super, 1964; Hoch, Ross, & Winder, 1966). Definitions of clinical and counseling psychology, for example, tend to overlap strongly, but are couched in terms of severity of disturbance and degree of psychopathology. Counseling tends to be thought of in terms of focus upon particular problem areas (e.g., educational, marital, personal adjustment) within so-called "normal" limits, while psychotherapy is thought of in a deeper, intrapsychic, more pathological framework. This writer would prefer to leave the arena of trade union, guild-type defensiveness in which each discipline (or sub-discipline) argues for its autonomy. It is no longer possible to operate on the normal-abnormal track, just as we must begin to revise our historical biases surrounding what Szasz (1964) has called "the myth of mental illness."

The term *group psychotherapy*, in the author's present thinking, may be used interchangeably with group counseling, and indeed with group guidance. It should be stressed, of course, that where the service provided is that of an information center, of a clearly advisory nature, this *not* counseling or therapy or guidance. Services, therefore, which provide advice to students regarding curriculum planning, selective service registration, applications to graduate schools, and the like are not really counseling services and would more properly be called advisement programs. The writer's position in this formulation is not to be deemed xenophobic, obsessed with the idea of keeping academic "foreigners" out of the hallowed therapeutic or counseling fields. The dimensions of the problem are far more subtle than pride, status, or hierarchy. Students who seek help of any kind should obtain what they seek, but should certainly not be exposed to psychotherapy which is being attempted by a well-meaning adviser who is not clear on the delineation of roles. In order that we may see these dimensions somewhat better, and within the limits of available space, the nature of group psychotherapy will be described and illustrated.

Group Psychotherapy: The Experience

The therapy group owes its therapeutic potential to the ready identification of the inherent creativity and constructiveness present in each person. The philosophy of collective responsibility relates to the growth of group psychotherapy. The vital element in group therapy is the social interaction among patients and with the group psychotherapist. The group process is not a conforming force, but rather an impelling force that exposes the person to his responsibility as a member of the human society. In intensive group psychotherapy, the uniqueness frequently hidden in each member is emphasized, and a reliving of past experiences is entailed. Intrapsychic change induces interpersonal or social change, and conversely the interpersonal induces the intrapsychic. Martin Buber (1958) has pointed out that "all real living is meeting," and the therapy group is always a meeting in this sense, a meeting in the present.

In this connection, the potential in group psychotherapy for counteracting the growing scourge of mediocrity in our society may well be associated with the problem of creativity and its relative absence in our contemporary culture. Some of the recent work in this area indicates the sad but harsh reality that as a developmental process from infancy throughout the entire life span, creativity is universal in early childhood and, among adults, almost nonexistent! How sad is a system in which the infant is free, expressive, creative, but gradually encounters a complicated network of environmental demands, taboos, and socializing and acculturating processes which require conformity and contraindicate creativity. In our society, people are obliged to behave in restricted ways and to reveal only so much as it is safe to reveal of oneself. Anderson (1959) has stated that inspired moments reported by creative adults have come only at moments when the person can cast off the trappings of sham, the irrelevancies of the culture with which he is obliged to live and which color conscious thinking. He sees creativity as the truth within the self, in the unconscious. To live creatively is to live truthfully; it is to live truthfully as one himself sees the truth. To live merely according to the truth as anyone but himself sees the truth is not creativity, but conformity.

Those who have been able to experience being in a therapy group will best *feel* these words. Expressions of thoughts and feelings are uncensored. Sham and façade and taboos are stripped bare, with honesty, straightforwardness, and truth the order of each group session. Patients are encouraged to observe their own irrational, compulsive, repetitive, and disturbing reactions toward the other members of the group that have little or nothing to do with external reality factors or actual outer provocation. In the process of *becoming*, as that term is used by Martin Buber (1958), the patient can begin to live truthfully as he sees the truth. Through the study, modification, and resolution of projected and inappropriate responses to members of the group (including the therapist) personal action, social integration, and significant change become possible. Wolf (1963) has stated that group therapy is a balance between self-study and social study and that the dynamic interrelation of the two studies reveals and promotes the whole man.

The essence of group psychotherapy is a recognition pointed out by Frieda Fromm-Reichmann (1950, p. 190), that "no one living in this era and culture is expected either to be or to remain consistently free from any inklings of anxiety after the termination of treatment . . . but former patients should potentially be able, after treatment, to solve their conflicts and to spot and resolve their anxiety" without professional help. Thus, a patient comes into a therapy group, relates to its members, freely describes himself, his innermost feelings, and his past and present experiences. As he interacts with the others, transferences are established with behavior that is based upon his evolving personality. The therapist and the other group members react to him, interpreting his behavior. As distorted behavior gradually lessens, individuality emerges, and he more truly belongs to his group. The ultimate decision regarding termination only the patient can make, although the therapist and the others share their feelings and make patently clear what is being chosen. In the final analysis, help in the future must come from the collective and cooperative effort of peers, the extended group-society and the culture (Mullan & Rosenbaum, 1962, p. 296).

Many other questions and problems are worth considering very seriously, though space does not permit detailed examination at this point. The alternate session, open and closed groups, preparation for the group, termination, nonverbal communication, examples of resistance, transference and countertransference, crises and emergencies, would all be matters of great import in the organization of group programs. For more detailed discussion of these and other related matters, the reader is referred to the excellent recent literature (e.g., Durkin, 1964; Mullan & Rosenbaum, 1962; Wolf & Schwartz, 1962).

Group Psychotherapy: Composition and Structure

Most workers in this field are agreed that the optimal number of individuals in a group is from six to ten, with a mean of seven or eight. The treatment group differs from other groups in its unconventionality. Sitting in a circle, face-to-face, in a judgment-free climate, a member reveals his likes, dislikes, memories, experiences, present activities, hopes, dreams, fantasies, and whatever with no holds barred. Individuals may be grouped according to age, sex, or symptomatology, with no present evidence suggesting that homogeneity is superior to heterogeneity in the group process. Thus, there are groups of young adults in their early twenties, alcoholic groups, married couple groups, or mixed groups of all ages. Most workers seem to prefer some degree of homogeneity, and tend to avoid placement of children or adolescents into adult groups. Some therapists work almost entirely on a group basis, with individual sessions scheduled only as necessary. Others prefer combined individual and group therapy, a procedure which the writer's experience over the past 15 years would tend to support. Most groups meet for 90-minute sessions, once weekly. In more intensive analytic groups, two and even three such sessions may be arranged per week. Schedular considerations, especially in institutions and agencies, may limit groups to one meeting a week, often for only 45 to 60 minutes at a time. The writer's practice in private work is to have groups meet once a week for 90 minutes with most members of the group having one or two individual hours weekly, according to their time and progress in treatment.

Many attempts have been made empirically to establish criteria and standards for group suitability. Leopold (1957) has indicated the following requirements: that the patient (1) has contact with reality, (2) can be related to interpersonally, (3) has sufficient flexibility so that he may reduce or heighten intragroup tensions, and (4) can serve at times as a catalyst for the group. Patients who show destructive, impulse-motivated, antisocial behavior, who are in a constant state of acute anxiety, who cannot be reached by other group members because of constant chaotic behavior, or who paralyze group interaction over an extended period of time, should probably not be placed in a group. In general, the mentally retarded do not do well in group, although differential diagnosis in terms of emotional blocking and intellectual dysfunctioning is critical here. Within college settings, of course, this clinical population is not to be expected.

Adaptations in Schools and Colleges

As indicated earlier, the group process may be applied in a variety of ways. The writer has done this in connection with placement and career counseling (Siegel, 1960), and with underachievers (Siegel, 1965). The former was called group orientation, since these groups numbered from 10 to 70 in size and had a manifestly nontherapeutic common goal. The latter was identified as group psychotherapy, was consistent with the composition and structure described earlier, and had a clearly therapeutic purpose. Working with a similar population of college underachievers in a somewhat less clinically intensive study, Dickenson and Truax (1966) provide evidence that underachievers receiving group counseling show greater positive change in academic performance than do students in a matched control group. The writer's inference (Siegel, 1965) is similar, suggesting that the value of short-term group psychotherapy should not be underrated.

In addition to adaptations and modifications involving briefer psychotherapy, it seems clear that knowledge of group therapy and its techniques can be of help to educators in coping with problems of authority, prejudice, and dependency (Kadis, 1965, p. 247). The consultative role of the group therapist is stressed here. The implications for education and for society are striking when one considers that the student attrition rate, and staff turnover as well, may be significantly reduced through the application of these group procedures.

Training of the Group Therapist

Standards for practice and criteria for the certification of group therapists have not yet been established. All too many psychotherapists have the mistaken notion that if they are trained to do individual therapy, they are free to move ahead to organize a therapy group and "see what happens." Throughout the country, but for the most part in the largest metropolitan areas, training programs of a highly commendable quality have been developing. The American Group Psychotherapy Association, for example, conducts an annual Training Institute in January of each year. Yet large numbers of individual psychotherapists continue to initiate group work without the necessary training. Mullan and Rosenbaum (1962) devote a chapter to the matter of training, and set forth sample programs which may be followed. Minimally, the group psychotherapist should have didactic course work, clinical workshops, personal treatment as a patient in a group, and systematic supervision—all of this subsequent to sound basic training in one of the mental health disciplines (psychiatry, psychology, psychiatric social work) and intensive training in individual psychotherapy.

Discussion

A major problem confronting workers interested in group techniques is the absence of adequate conceptualization, organized research, and thorough training (Rosenbaum, 1965). The group explosion described earlier in this chapter has been reverberating around the world, with enthusiasm largely replacing the realities of an organized body of knowledge. The promise of group therapy is perhaps limitless, but has yet to be realized. Perhaps the largest need is for an explosion in systematic research, so that clinical experience and intuitive hunches may be validated. Schools and colleges represent a prime source for such research. It is the college counselor who has the resources to test structure, process, and technique. Caught up in clinical services, the counselor does not really make his greatest contribution if he simply renders services without evaluating carefully the rationale for what is being done.

Innovations in group procedures have been developing strongly during the past decade, concomitant with dynamic changes in individual approaches to psychotherapy. The literature abounds with recent references to family therapy, conjoint family therapy, cooperative psychotherapy, joint interviews, marathon groups, use of multiple therapists, married couple therapy, and a variety of related developments (Ackerman, 1958; Bach, 1966; Rosenbaum & Berger, 1963; Satir, 1964). Psychotherapists, who have so long concentrated on illness of the individual, have perforce been pressed to give attention to the psychopathology of the group. It is in these terms that Murphy (1963) has urged that group psychotherapy research begin to attempt to evaluate the kinds of personality changes that occur in therapy, as contrasted with studies of group dynamics, group cohesion, and effective learning in group situations. Other workers have begun increasingly to indicate the need for more systematic investigation of various aspects of group psychotherapy which have all too often been taken for granted in recent years. For example, the use of the group format for guidance, education, and orientation is undoubtedly rich in potential value to the members of the group, but is fraught with potential danger if it is not handled very carefully and within the limits of the training and experience of group leaders.

Redl (1963) has commented upon the analogy between the peculiar developmental phases that newly emerging scientific disciplines go through, and those which children experience in the process of growing up. In these terms, we might expect, in the growth and development of group therapy, a prolonged infancy, a stormy adolescence, and then maturity of some order or degree. The growing pains and cramps which are all too apparent in the field of group psychotherapy mark us as being still in the throes of adolescence. Perhaps we are in the period of turmoil, ambivalence, upheaval, rebelliousness, role diffusion, and identity crisis which are so often characteristic of adolescence; or perhaps we are still involved in a period of visibility limited by a fog resulting from the condensation of our professional preadolescent problems. If this be true, there is, nonetheless, much hope for us as a helping profession, since clinical experience indicates that most adolescents do manage to survive and indeed to achieve some measure of maturity.

REFERENCES

Ackerman, N. *The psychodynamics of family life.* New York: Basic Books, 1958.

Anderson, H. H. (Ed.) *Creativity and its cultivation.* New York: Harper, 1959.

Armentrout, W. W. Group counseling: misnomer of consequence? Letter to the editor. *J. counsel. Psychol.*, 1958, 5 (1), 71–72.

Bach, G. R. *Intensive group psychotherapy.* New York: Ronald Press, 1954.

Bach, G. R. The marathon group: intensive practice of intimate interaction. *Psychol. Reports*, 1966, 18, 995–1002.

Bany, Mary A., & Johnson, Lois V. *Classroom group behavior: group dynamics in education.* New York: Macmillan, 1964.

Barry, R., & Wolf, Beverly. *Modern issues in guidance-personnel work.* New York: Bureau of Publ., Teachers Coll., Columbia Univ., 1957.

Bennett, Margaret E. *Guidance and counseling in groups* (2nd ed.) New York: McGraw-Hill, 1963.

Billings, Mildred L. *Group methods of studying occupations.* Scranton, Pa.: Int. Textbook, 1941.

Bilovsky, D., McMasters, W., Shorr, J. E., & Singer, S. L. Individual and group counseling. *Personnel Guid. J.*, 1953, 31, 363–365

Broedel, J., Ohlsen, M., Proff, F., & Southard, C. The effects of group counseling on gifted underachieving adolescents. *J. counsel. Psychol.*, 1960, 7 (3), 163–170.

Brunson, May A. *Guidance: an integrating process in higher education.* New York: Bureau of Publ., Teachers Coll., Columbia Univ., 1959.

Buber, M. *I and thou*, tr. Ronald Gregor Smith. New York: Charles Scribner's, 1958.

Burrow, T. The group method of analysis. *Psychoanal. Rev.*, 1927, 14 (3), 268–280.

Calia, V. F. A group guidance program in action. *Jr. Coll. J.*, 1957, 27, 437–442.

Carter, E., & Hoppock, R. College courses in careers. *Personnel Guid. J.*, 1961, 39, 373–375.

Cohn, B., Ohlsen, M., & Proff, F. Roles played by adolescents in an unproductive counseling group. *Personnel Guid. J.*, 1960, 38, 724–731.

Corsini, R. J. Historic background of group psychotherapy: a critique. *Group Psychother.*, 1955, 3, 213–219.

Dickenson, W. A., & Truax, C. B. Group counseling with college underachievers. *Personnel Guid. J.*, 1966, 44, 243–247.

Dilley, N. E. Group counseling for student teachers. *Educ. Administ. Supervis.*, 1953, 39 (4), 193–200.

Dreese, M., Group guidance and group therapy. *Rev. educ. Res.*, 1957, 27 (2), 219–228.

Dreikurs, R., & Corsini, R. J. Twenty years of group psychotherapy. *Amer. J. Psychiat.*, 1954, 110, 567–575.

Driver, Helen. *Counseling and learning through small group discussions.* Madison, Wis.: Monona Publ., 1958.

Durkin, Helen. *The group in depth.* New York: Int. Univ. Press, 1964.

Eiserer, P. E. Group psychotherapy. *J. Nat Assoc. Deans Women*, 1956, 19, (3), 113–122.

Ford, D. H. Group and individual counseling in modifying behavior. *Personnel Guid. J.*, 1962, 40, 770–773.

Foulkes, S. H., & Anthony, E. J. *Group psychotherapy.* London: Penguin Books, 1957.

Freud, S. *Group psychology and the analysis of the ego.* London: Hogarth Press, 1948.

Fromm-Reichmann, Frieda. *Principles of intensive psychotherapy.* Chicago: Univ. of Chicago Press, 1950.

Glanz, E. C. *Groups in guidance; the dynamics of groups and the application of groups in guidance.* Boston: Allyn & Bacon, 1962.

Gorlow, L., Hoch, E. L., & Telschow, E. F. *The nature of non-directive group psychotherapy.* New York: Columbia Univ. Press, 1952.

Grier, D. J. *Orienting students through group counseling.* New York: Teachers Coll., Columbia Univ., 1950.

Hare, A. P. *Handbook of small group research.* New York: Free Press, 1962.

Hewer, Vivian H. Group counseling, individual counseling, and a college class in vocations. *Personnel Guid. J.*, 1959, 37, 660–665.

Hoch, E. L., Ross, A. O., & Winder, C. L. (Eds.) *Professional preparation of clinical psychologists.* Washington: Amer. Psychol. Assoc., 1966.

Hoppock, R. *Group guidance: principles, techniques, and evaluation.* New York: McGraw-Hill, 1949.

Iffert, R. E. *Retention and withdrawal of college students.* Washington: U.S. Govt. Print. Off., 1958.

Kadis, Asya L. Applications of group therapy to educational processes. In Asya

L. Kadis & C. Winick (Eds.), *Group psychotherapy today*. New York: S. Karger, 1965. Pp. 243–249.

Kadis, Asya L., & Winick, C. (Eds). *Group psychotherapy today*. New York: S. Karger, 1965.

Kelsey, C. E., Jr. Group counseling: an annotated bibliography. *J. psychol. Stud.*, 1960, 11, 84–92.

Kemp, C. G. *Perspective on the group process: a foundation for counseling with groups*. Boston: Houghton-Mifflin, 1964.

Klapman, J. W. *Group psychotherapy, theory and practice*. New York: Grune & Stratton, 1946.

Lawrence, Ray M., & Kiell, N. Group guidance with college students. *Int. J. group Psychother.*, 1961, 11, 78–87.

Leopold, H. Selection of patients for group psychotherapy. *Amer. J. Psychother.*, 1957, 11, 134–637.

Lifton, W. M. *Working with groups: group processes and individual growth*. New York: Wiley, 1961.

Lubin, B., & Lubin, Alice W. *Group psychotherapy: a bibliography of the literature from 1956 through 1964*. Michigan: Michigan State Univ. Press, 1966.

McKinney, F. *Counseling for personal adjustment in schools and colleges*. Boston: Houghton Mifflin, 1958.

Moreno, J. L. *The first book on group psychotherapy*. New York: Beacon, 1957.

Moreno, J. L. (Ed.) *The international handbook of group psychotherapy*. New York: Philosophical Library, 1966.

Mullan, H., & Rosenbaum, M. *Group psychotherapy*. New York: Free Press, 1962.

Murphy, G. Group psychotherapy in our society. In M. Rosenbaum & M. Berger (Eds.), *Group psychotherapy and group function*. New York: Basic Books, 1963.

Poser, E. G. Group therapy in Canada: a national survey. *Canad. psychiat. Assoc. J.*, 1966, 11, (1), 20–25.

Powdermaker, F., & Frank, J. D. *Group psychotherapy*. Cambridge, Mass.: Harvard Univ. Press, 1953.

Pratt, J. H. The class method of treating consumption in the homes of the poor. *J. Amer. Med. Assoc.*, 1907, 49, 755–759.

Pratt, J. H. The group method in the treatment of psychosomatic disorders. *Psychodrama Monogr.*, 1946, No. 19.

Raines, M. R. Helping college freshmen identify problems through a case conference. *Personnel Guid. J.*, 1956, 34, 417–419.

Redl, F. Psychoanalysis and group therapy: a developmental point of view. *Amer. J. Orthopsychiat.*, 1963, 33, 135–148.

Rinn, J. L. Group guidance: two processes. *Personnel Guid. J.*, 1961, 39, 591–594.

Rosenbaum, M. Group psychotherapy and psychodrama. In B. B. Wolman (Ed.), *Handbook of Clinical Psychology*. New York: McGraw-Hill, 1965. Pp. 1254–1274.

Rosenbaum, M., & Berger, M. M. (Eds.) *Group psychotherapy and group function: selected readings.* New York: Basic Books, 1963.

Satir, Virginia. *Conjoint family therapy.* Palo Alto, Calif.: Science and Behavior Books, 1964.

Siegel, M. The personality structure of children with reading disabilities as compared with children presenting other clinical problems. *Nerv. Child,* 1954, 10, 409–414.

Siegel, M. Compulsory education and adolescent personality. In M. Krugman (Ed.), *Orthopsychiatry and the school.* New York: Amer. Orthopsychiat. Assoc., 1958. Pp. 235–244.

Siegel, M. Group orientation and placement counseling. *Personnel Guid. J.,* 1960, 38, 659–660.

Siegel, M. Group psychotherapy with gifted underachieving college students. *Commun. ment. Hlth. J.,* 1965, 1, (2), 188–194.

Slavson, S. R. *The fields of group psychotherapy.* New York: Int. Univ. Press, 1956.

Szasz, T. S. *The myth of mental illness.* New York: Hoeber-Harper, 1964.

Spotnitz, H. *The couch and the circle.* New York: Knopf, 1961.

Thompson, A. S., & Super, D. E. (Eds.) *The professional preparation of counseling psychologists.* New York: Bureau of Publ., Teachers Coll., Columbia Univ., 1964.

Warters, Jane. *Group guidance principles and practices.* New York: McGraw-Hill, 1960.

Willey, R. DeV., & Strong, W. M. *Group procedures in guidance.* New York: Harper, 1957.

Wolf, A. The psychoanalysis of groups. In M. Rosenbaum & M. Berger (Eds.), *Group psychotherapy and group function.* New York: Basic Books, 1963.

Wolf, A., & Schwartz, E. K. The psychoanalysis of groups: implications for education. *Int. J. Social Psychiat.,* 1955, 1, 17–24.

Wolf, A., & Schwartz, E. K. *Psychoanalysis in groups.* New York: Grune & Stratton, 1962.

Worcester, E., McComb, S., & Coriat, I. H. *Religion and medicine.* London: Methuen, 1908.

Part III

Function and Practice

GENERAL

Chapter 6

The College Admissions Process

IRVING KRONGELB

Historical Background

The years since World War II have seen in the United States a dramatic increase in the numbers of young men and women graduating from high school and going on to college. Sparked by the unprecedented opportunities provided through various forms of governmental assistance, on the one hand, and by the mounting pressures in our society for higher levels of education and training, on the other, this development has brought new and more challenging problems to the field of education at all levels.

In the 57th report of the president of the College Entrance Examination Board, Frank H. Bowles (1960, p. 100), referring to increasing admission pressures, notes, "By the end of the 1960's it will be generally accepted that all high school graduates with an IQ of 100 or higher (in other words, half of the age cohort and more than half of the high school graduates) may be expected to continue formal academic work for at least one and in many cases two more years." More recently, in considering the implications of expanded educational opportunity on a national scale, the Educational Policies Commission (1964) reported,

> High school graduation has been increasing at an average rate of about 1.5 percent per year, and it lies now at about 65 percent of the eligible age group. The percentage of high school graduates going on for degrees in higher education has also been rising at a rate of about one

Irving Krongelb is Assistant Professor, Department of Student Services; and Assistant Director of Admissions, Brooklyn College of the City University of New York.

percent per year. The number of new admissions for degree credit in the fall of 1963 was about 58 percent of the number of high school graduates of the preceding spring. If these trends are extended for a decade it will mean that 80 percent of a whole age group will graduate from high school, and nearly 70 percent of them will seek further education. The numbers involved in such extrapolations are impressive. With approximately 4 million young Americans in each one-year age group, this would indicate 3.2 million high school graduates annually, of whom upward of 2 million would seek admission to college. (pp. 31–32)

At the same time, there has been a concerted effort to identify those among our high school students and graduates who have the capacity for advanced work beyond high school but who, for various reasons, have not been able to think in such terms or have not achieved the kind of academic record which would normally place them in competition for places in college or both. Much of the impetus for this effort has come from governmental and private activity in programs for the disadvantaged, in general, and in the determination to broaden the base of educational and economic opportunity, in particular. The approach which has gained strong support in recent years among educators and others is expressed in the following statement by the Educational Policies Commission (1964):

> Unless opportunity for education beyond the high school can be made available to all, while at the same time increasing the effectiveness of the elementary and secondary schools, then the American promise of individual dignity and freedom cannot be extended to all . . . In the future, the important question needs to be not "Who deserves to be admitted?" but "Whom can the society, in conscience and self-interest, exclude?"
>
> A person cannot justly be excluded from further education unless his deficiencies are so severe that even the most flexible and dedicated institution could contribute little to his mental development. There is reason to expect that most persons capable of completing the studies of an American high school are also capable of further growth toward a free mind . . . the nation seems increasingly determined to raise the level of real opportunity for all. As measures are taken to this end and as research and experience improve the quality of education, the percentage of the population completing high school and capable of significant further intellectual development should continue to rise. (pp. 5–6.)

The implications of these developments are many, and their effects have been felt in the high school and college setting with increasing intensity over the past several years. For persons engaged in guidance and counseling, in particular, and in all phases of the educational enterprise, in general, these developments have an undeniable day-to-day, bread-and-butter quality.

For one thing, colleagues in the high schools have found themselves devoting more and more attention to the guidance of their students, particularly in the area of precollege guidance, and to the myriad tasks they are called upon to perform in the more mechanical, but nonetheless required, aspects of the movement of their students from high school to college. At the same time, of course, college personnel, particularly those concerned with the guidance and admission of students, have been pressed to devote more time and energy to closer, more active liaison with their high school colleagues in a concerted attempt to make more effective the entire process of selection of students for admission to college and to make as smooth as possible the transition of the successful candidates from the high school to the college setting.

Another aspect of this development has been the accompanying growth in the numbers and types of institutions of higher education. Of particular significance has been the expansion of junior or community colleges, which offer (1) two-year terminal programs for the student whose needs or abilities make a career-oriented two-year program (in business or technology, for example) the preferred type of higher education for him, and (2) two-year transfer programs for the student who plans to go on to a baccalaureate degree but who either prefers a junior college nearer his home or who falls short of meeting the requirements for admission to a four-year college and for whom the junior college represents an opportunity to prove himself in a less demanding, often less competitive setting. A second area of rapid growth in American higher education in recent years has been the evening college, which makes available a wide selection of college programs to increasing numbers of students of all ages who, for a variety of reasons, find it more expedient to continue their studies during evening hours.

The High School and College Planning

The marked increases in the numbers of young men and women planning for college, as well as the large numbers of those whose immediate goals lie outside the sphere of college planning, have posed significant challenges for colleagues engaged in guidance activities in the high schools. In fact, insofar as planning for college is concerned, it has become increasingly apparent in recent years that the pressures on and in the schools—from students, parents, and others—begin in the junior high school (the seventh and eighth grades) and often even before. Much of the militancy of parents' groups, for example, can be attributed to anxiety over the extent to which the school systems in which their children are being educated will or will not provide the academic support for easy movement into college. For those parents whose children are not planning to go on to college, the problem becomes one of trying to ensure that the schools will provide the training and the skills which will fit the youngsters for jobs, for the assumption of domestic responsibilities, and so on.

One of the more difficult tasks confronting guidance counselors is that of working with parents whose assessment of their child's potentialities and consequent setting of their child's goals are more emotional than rational. The following examples may be cited:

1. The parents who overestimate their child's capacities and set goals which the child may find it difficult, if not impossible, to realize.
2. The parents who underestimate their child's capacities and, in so doing, fail to provide the encouragement and support which the child needs in considering his goals.
3. The parents who make choices and decisions for their children without considering the attitudes and opinions of the youngsters themselves.
4. The parents who allow themselves to be influenced more by status considerations—their own as well as those of relatives and friends—than by realistic appraisals of their children, and who therefore resist attempts by their youngsters or by others to make them aware of such reality.
5. The parents who cling to old fashioned, often culture-bound views of education and who attempt to manipulate their children accordingly; e.g., parents who subscribe to the view that a college education is unnecessary—"especially for girls"—or those who place major emphasis on "getting out and making a living." Such views, to be sure, are often combined with a sense—itself often quite realistic—of economic and financial inability to support a youngster in college.

Very often, the counselor is placed in the rather difficult position of attempting to resolve conflicts between pupils and their parents when their respective attitudes about planning for the future are in disagreement. Situations of this sort represent a real challenge to the skill and resourcefulness of the counselor since he must, with maximum objectivity, provide parents and pupils with the kind of factual support which will help them to resolve their differences, while at the same time helping them to see the shortcomings in the emotionally toned attitudes to which they feel committed—all of this, of course, without actually making their decisions for them!

These aspects of the high school guidance program are commonly approached in a group setting, through lectures, panel discussions, and question-and-answer sessions of one kind or another arranged by the guidance staff and the parents (or parent-teachers) association. Such programs ("After high school—what?," "Careers after high school," and so on) are variously planned as school assembly programs involving only the students and school personnel; or as special programs, during the school day, to which parents are also invited; or more commonly as evening programs intended primarily for parents, but with students often included as well. Such programs may be scheduled at any time during the high school years, but they occur most frequently during the junior year or the first part of the senior year. Depending on the size and location of the high school, and with appropriate allowances for variation to meet the needs of a particular area and a particular student body, invited authorities at such meetings may include any or all of the following:

1. High school personnel (principal, guidance staff, district superintendent or coordinator, chairmen of departments, and the like).
2. College representatives.
3. Employment service representatives.
4. Representatives of business and industry.
5. Representatives of the armed forces.
6. Alumni.

Very often, of course, such group functions are supplemented by individual conferences arranged to meet particular needs as they arise.

High school counseling specifically geared to the needs of college-bound students has, without question, become a major specialized area of service in recent years, and one of the key elements in the high school administrative structure is now the college office. Here, typically, one will find a college coordinator, supported by a staff of college advisers and clerical aides (the latter very often student aides serving as volunteers for service credit), ministering to the needs of those students who are planning to go on to college after completing their high school studies.

Fundamentally, the task of identifying and guiding college-bound youngsters needs to be viewed as yet another element in a continuing process of guidance throughout the school years. For the youngster who is moving toward college, the process comes to a feverish culmination in the last year or year and a half in high school, and it is then that the services and talents of the college adviser take on critical importance. (Science Research Associates, 1959)

The services of the college coordinator in the typical high school will include the following:

1. Gathering, collating, and maintaining various kinds of information concerning colleges (college bulletins, booklets of information, application materials, directories, etc.).

2. Publicizing (through classrooms, assemblies, bulletin boards, the school newspaper, periodic bulletins or announcements, or by personal contact) the latest information concerning the various phases of precollege guidance.

3. Arranging assemblies and conferences for pupils, parents, and school personnel with college representatives. A pattern frequently employed is the College Night program, which brings to the high school a number of representatives from different colleges; each college representative is assigned to a specific room to which parents and their youngsters may then report for discussion and a question-and-answer period. College Night programs are generally scheduled in such a way as to permit visits by each family to two or three college representatives in the course of the evening.

4. Coordinating the administration of the various tests which have by now become so much a part of the precollege guidance program in American high schools. The two major testing agencies serving college-bound students in the United States at the present time are: (a) Educational Testing Service (Princeton, New Jersey, and Berkeley, California) and (b) American College Testing Program (Iowa City, Iowa). Both these agencies have published numerous booklets and bulletins of information (q.v.) for use by guidance counselors and applicants.

5. Interpreting the results of precollege tests as an aid in counseling—along with school records, teachers' reports, and so forth. Test results can be extremely useful, especially in doubtful cases, as an aid in encouraging some students in their choices and providing alternate choices to others.

6. Advising students of college application procedures, deadlines, and other pertinent information and coordinating the maintenance and gathering of school materials (records, recommendations, and the like) required for the proper preparation and forwarding of application materials. This is especially important in some areas (New York City, for example) where large numbers of applicants from many high schools make application to the same institution or complex of institutions. For example, the City

University of New York, which at this writing offers undergraduate training in six four-year colleges, one upper division college, and six two-year community colleges, with day and evening programs, has established a University Application Processing Center which receives and processes most of the applications from high school students applying to the units of the City University (applications to John Jay College of Criminal Justice and to the upper division college, Richmond College, are not processed through the Center). Each applicant indicates six choices, in order of preference, from among the eleven available choices among the colleges in the City University and, since admission standards vary from one unit to another, the applicant is considered, in turn, for any or all of the six units listed as his choices. Thus, a single application becomes operationally a multiple application for many applicants. This obviously requires very close coordination between the high schools and the City University as a whole, over and above the working liaison between the high schools and each of the colleges individually. For the City University of New York, this coordination is accomplished through a high school-college articulation committee—consisting of representatives of the high schools, the Board of Education, the colleges, and the City University—which meets regularly to discuss policy and procedures governing admission to the City University.

7. Maintaining liaison with colleges and universities. This is, to be sure, a reciprocal operation since the colleges, for their part, are vitally interested in maintaining effective working relationships with the high schools from which they draw their students. The college coordinator in the high school may employ a number of techniques in this connection, including visits to the colleges, invitations to college admissions representatives to visit the high school (often in conjunction with the scheduling of interviews for applicants), reading of newsletters and other announcements published by colleges, as well as mail and telephone communication.

8. Compiling records of the accomplishments of graduates during their college years and beyond. Such information is obtained either on the initiative of the college coordinator, who solicits reports from the colleges and from the students themselves, or from reports rendered by the colleges in periodic feed-back communications to the high schools. These records are very helpful to the college guidance staff in the high school, since they provide information which counselors can use in steering applicants toward one college or another, as well as in boosting school morale in general and the morale of college-bound youngsters in particular.

9. Keeping colleagues (particularly the principal, the chairmen of the

departments, and personnel in guidance assignments) informed of changes in college admission requirements and of successes and failures of students in their attempts to gain admission to college, and advising appropriate action to be taken by the school in particular situations. Thus, for example, recent changes in college admission requirements in the direction of requiring additional units of high school mathematics or foreign language necessitated immediate consideration of modifications in the patterns of subject offerings in the high schools. The college coordinator in the high school is usually the first to know of such matters and must therefore carry the responsibility for initiating appropriate action.

10. Performing such other duties as may, from time to time, be assigned by the principal or guidance coordinator or be necessitated by changing conditions.

It should be clear from the foregoing that the task of the college coordinator, particularly in a large high school which sends most of its graduates on to college, is a difficult, taxing, and challenging one. It is not always easy to juxtapose the pressures which are brought to bear by parents, youngsters, community representatives, and the school administration, but the college coordinator is often called upon to do just this. This calls for a high degree of skill, knowledge, and diplomacy, tempered by a keen insight into what is likely to be the best choice for each youngster. The college coordinator must attempt to be realistic to an extreme, particularly in dealing with students and their parents, while at the same time trying to project the best possible image of the high school in contacts with college representatives and the community as a whole. The proper organization of the college office in the high school, with adequate facilities and with a staff large enough, skilled enough, and wholly dedicated to its mission, becomes a major administrative responsibility in the high school of today.

One other aspect of the role of the high school merits our attention at this point. The increases in numbers of applicants for admission to college have understandably led to a general raising of standards for admission. This in turn has led to a heightened sensitivity at the high school level to the task of providing the extent and quality of preparation which will enable students most effectively to meet the competition. In practical terms, this development has manifested itself in two ways:

1. The process of identifying and encouraging youngsters with demonstrated or potential ability begins long before they enter high school. In many school systems in which pupils are offered the option of an ac-

celerated (two-year) or an enriched (three-year) junior high school program, the assignments are based, at least in part, on teachers' reports, previous marks, and performance on required tests. Thus, there is a tendency to earmark the more capable youngsters for continuing attention.

2. The curricular patterns in high schools have undergone considerable change. More and more, high schools are offering more extensive options in advanced high school courses (for example, mathematics through the calculus, the fourth year of foreign language, and advanced courses in the sciences) and college-bound students are being urged to take these. In addition, the proliferation of college-level courses in the high schools—using college course syllabi and texts—has been very extensive, and more and more high school students each year are earning exemptions in college courses, with or without college credit, on the basis of their performance on Advanced Placement Examinations or on examinations given by individual colleges at the time of admission.

College Admissions

The relentless pressures on colleges in recent years to provide places for more and more students have underscored rather sharply the central goal of every college admissions program, namely, to select for admission those students who show the greatest promise of benefiting from what the college has to offer them. To this end, admission requirements have been subjected to continued re-examination and refinement, with changes pointed rather consistently in the direction of greater selectivity. This has progressed to the extent that promising athletes, for example, must also show academic promise in order to gain admission in many colleges, and even the children of alumni now find themselves subjected to the same careful screening as any other applicants.

Standards for admission may vary considerably from one institution to another within an overall framework of institutional policy and, in the case of municipal and state colleges and universities, law. It is interesting to note that even in state colleges, where graduation from high school in the upper half or upper three-fourths of the class may be sufficient to satisfy scholastic requirements for admission, there is now increasing agitation for more selective admission requirements. Typically, criteria for selection will be built around any or all of the following considerations:

1. Academic achievement as measured by school grades, rank in class, achievement tests, and reports from teachers.

2. Academic potential as estimated from tests (for example, the Scholastic Aptitude Test or the American College Testing Program examination) or from teachers' appraisals.

3. Special indicators of academic capacity, such as completion of honors subjects or participation in science fairs.

4. Personal maturity as gauged primarily from teachers' recommendations and from personal interviews with an admissions officer.

5. Evidences of leadership and school citizenship as measured by the record of participation in extracurricular activities, service squads, and the like.

6. Relationship between the applicant's record and his stated goals; for example, a consistently weak mathematics student who applies for admission to a pre-engineering program would obviously be subject to exceptionally careful scrutiny.

7. Special considerations which may pertain to a particular college at a particular time. Thus, a college which is anxious to attract students with special talents (in art or music, for example) may give heavier weight to such talents than to other elements in the applicant's background. Another factor which may often influence decisions is the much-discussed geographical quota; admittedly, colleges will reject qualified applicants if too many apply from the same high school or the same locality.

A major task which falls to the lot of the admissions officer is that of getting to know as much as possible about the high schools from which his freshmen are drawn. The admissions officer will want to know, for example, how strongly he can rely on high school grades and recommendations; how well different high schools prepare their students for college; and, in general, the kind of educational and community experience provided for students by a given setting. Nor is it at all unusual for administrators and other colleagues outside the admissions area to turn to the admissions officer for this kind of information.

The admissions officer has several resources open to him for securing such information. One way, of course, is to visit the schools to confer with the principal, the college advisers, and department chairmen and teachers; to talk with applicants and potential applicants; and, in general, to assess what the school is doing for and with its students. Another way is to study —or to have department chairmen study—actual syllabi and course materials being used in the high schools. A third technique often employed is to maintain detailed follow-up records of students from the time they commence their college studies. Just as such data have value for the high school college adviser at his level, so is it useful to the college admissions officer in evaluating the credentials of applicants to have on hand comparative data relating their high school backgrounds to their subsequent performance in college.

Closely related to the foregoing is the notion of the image which the college wishes to project to the world outside—to colleagues in the high schools and in other institutions of higher education, to potential applicants, to the community at large—and it is often through the admissions process that this is accomplished. One of the guides which is usually prepared by the admissions officer of the college and which is widely used in this respect, particularly by college advisers in the high schools, is the freshman class profile. The profile typically summarizes the essential characteristics of the freshman class and includes data on such items as age, high school averages, college board examination scores, high school preparation in specified subject areas (particularly language, mathematics, and science), major choices, parents' occupations and education, high school honors and activities, and so on. A useful reference in this area is the *Manual of Freshman Class Profiles,* published biennially by the College Entrance Examination Board. The 1965–67 edition of this manual includes profiles for 419 member colleges of the College Entrance Examination Board.

The counseling and public relations aspects of the admissions officer's work clearly begin long before the more mechanical selection process itself, and admissions officers are typically quite busy with visits to schools, lectures and discussions before parent and community groups, visits to their own campuses by interested individuals and groups, and planned programs for selected audiences which are designed to impart information, familiarize outsiders with campus facilities, and clarify points of doubt concerning the particular college or university. It is interesting to note that such activities are considered important and worthwhile even in public institutions which do not have to engage in active recruiting for students.

At Brooklyn College of the City University of New York, for example, the Director of Admissions each semester schedules a "College Day for High School Juniors and Their Parents." The feeder high schools are invited, on a rotation basis from one semester to the next, to send junior year students and their parents to the college for a program, usually scheduled on a Sunday afternoon, which includes (a) a talk by the Director of Admissions on offerings and admission requirements, (b) a talk by the Dean of Students on aspects of student life on the campus, (c) guided tours of campus facilities in small groups conducted by student members of the Student Orientation Committee, and finally (d) panel discussions with members of the faculty on offerings and opportunities in the various fields of study. This program has been eminently successful in relations between Brooklyn College and its feeder high schools, attendance on a given Sunday afternoon running to 1200–1500 students and parents.

In addition to these personal contacts, the admissions officer is often involved in the preparation and distribution of printed materials of various kinds. College bulletins are typically quite uninspiring and incomplete insofar as information on matters other than curriculum is concerned; furthermore, since official bulletins or catalogues are usually considered valid for extended periods of time (usually two years), they tend to become outdated rather quickly in many respects. It thus becomes important for a college to publish supplemental materials which will help to impart a feeling for the more dynamic, more comprehensive aspects of campus life and will transmit, as required, information about changes and new developments to the off-campus community. Very often such materials, especially those directed specifically to the high schools, are prepared by the admissions officer; at other times they become the responsibility of a public relations officer who receives and coordinates for publication information from many colleagues (including, of course, the admissions officer).

Another area—much more directed to the individual—in which the admissions officer performs a vital public service is that of precollege counseling per se. The typical college admissions office can expect to be on the receiving end of an endless stream of requests for information, assistance, and advice—on a twelve month basis! Such requests may come from applicants and potential applicants; from fathers and mothers, wives and husbands; from public figures and community representatives; from colleagues at various levels; and even from students already enrolled in the college who are convinced that the admissions office must surely have all the answers. For, to most people, the admissions officer *is* the college, and this can often place him in the unenviable position of having to explain and even justify policies and procedures which fall, strictly speaking, outside his area of responsibility.

Most inquiries which come to the admissions office are, of course, pertinent to the admissions function. It is unfortunate that many colleges do not provide the facilities and the staff for performing this function with full comprehensiveness. Fundamentally, persons who bring their problems to the admissions office are seeking some sort of pre-admission counseling. Ideally, therefore, the admissions office should be a place where such persons can sit down with a skilled and knowledgeable counselor who has access to all available pertinent records, has the training to analyze and interpret them, and has the time and patience to give the visitor the information and assistance he needs. Such arrangements are unfortunately not always possible, and it has become customary to deal with most inquiries on a mass basis—a form letter, a mimeographed notice, a reference to printed matter, and a proliferation of all kinds of information booklets, guides to applicants, and the like. The situation is further complicated by the fact that admissions functions in some colleges are decentralized, two or more offices sharing responsibility for various parts of the admissions program; thus, an inquiry may be directed to one office, while the required records and other materials are being processed in another.

The duties of the admissions officer in the area of precollege counseling and public relations tend to be essentially similar, with due allowances for variation to meet local needs, from one institution to another. At the very least, every college assumes an obligation to keep the public, as well as the academic community, informed of its purposes and objectives, its facilities and offerings, its accomplishments, its plans for new developments, its need for continuing support, and of course its policies governing admission and the procedures related thereto. It has already been suggested that the admissions officer characteristically contributes a major share of the effort in this direction.

When we move to the more specialized area of college admissions per se, however, we find interesting differences in the role of the admissions officer, reflecting obviously the variations in admission requirements from one institution to another. The following major patterns are already discernible:

1. If admission is based on the applicant's having or not having completed specified units of high school work and his having achieved a minimum high school average or college entrance test score, the admissions officer's role in determining eligibility for admission will be minimal for the greater part of the entering class. Once he has, in conjunction with designated colleagues (the President, the Registrar, and the Dean of Faculty or Instruction, perhaps), established the minimum average or score to be accepted, he can turn his attention to the special cases and to the other aspects of the admissions program.

2. If, on the other hand, admission is based on a comprehensive evaluation of every element in each applicant's background, the work of the admissions officer is clearly much more involved. In the typical situation, he will sit as a member of a committee on admissions where he and his

colleagues, individually or in committee, will evaluate all materials submitted by or on behalf of every applicant. In this type of admission procedure, obviously, there is full opportunity for considering each applicant's strengths and weaknesses in comparison with other applicants and for applying whatever yardsticks are considered important by and for the institution at a given time.

In every admissions operation there are always special categories which demand, and receive, more particular attention. It is here that some of the heaviest demands are made on the resources of the admissions office. Although colleges and universities are not all equally concerned with these, the following special categories may be identified:

1. *Foreign students*—those whose previous schooling, in whole or in part, has been completed in foreign countries. A major responsibility in assessing the qualifications of such applicants is that of determining their ability to handle the English language. This generally requires a special examination, arranged by the admissions officer; or, if the applicant is still in a foreign country, arrangements must be made for him to be tested there and for the certified results to be sent to the admissions officer.

2. *Transfer students*—those who have completed or are in the process of completing work at another college or university. For these students, the admission requirements are obviously different from those which apply to students entering as freshmen, and the admissions officer must therefore concern himself with the evaluation of the applicant's college record in addition to all other credentials. Furthermore, many colleges regularly request from the college or colleges previously attended information concerning the applicant's character, campus citizenship, health, and so forth; such information can be extremely useful not only in considering the application for admission but, even more importantly, in providing any special assistance (e.g., psychological counseling) indicated in individual cases.

3. *Unqualified applicants*—those who fail to meet the standards for admission, usually on qualitative grounds. This may include high school graduates who, by law, are entitled to consideration for admission to their state college or university but who do not fall within the stipulated upper half or upper three-fourths of their graduating class. Applicants may also be included who wish to transfer from another college but whose record there is below the level of acceptability at the institution to which they are applying. Many colleges make provision for individual consideration of such applicants and, where the admissions officer—usually working with a

committee on admissions—deems it advisable, such students may be admitted in some provisional or probationary status and given an opportunity to redeem themselves.

4. *Disadvantaged students*—those whose family, cultural, and educational backgrounds have failed to provide them with the essentials for college admission, but who are felt to have the potential for higher education. Through new programs specifically designed to meet the needs of such students or through flexible interpretation of standards for admission to existing programs, admissions officers in recent years have given increasing attention to this group.

The Admissions Officer

We have dealt at length with the work of the admissions officer. Who is this person in actual practice? Actually, admissions officers may function under a variety of titles, varying in many instances with the size and nature of the institution. There are deans of admissions, directors of admissions, and other deans doing admissions work; there are registrars (including in some instances associate and assistant registrars) who include the admissions function in their duties; and there are persons in administrative or clerical positions who carry a significant share of the responsibility for admissions operations. In every case, however, the successful practitioners in this area are persons with a genuine regard for the institution they represent and a deep understanding of the human element in the admissions process; for even in this day and age, when many aspects of admissions work are being reduced to computerized operations, the human factor must still be in the forefront of the admissions officer's thought and action.

More and more the admissions officer of today is a specialist. In the vast majority of cases he has had advanced educational experience, at least through the master's level and often through the doctorate, in such fields as psychology, guidance, education, educational administration, or other areas. Most of his training as an admissions officer has been gained in the field, through actual experience and on-the-job training. He is a member of a college community, often with regular faculty rank; and in many cases he will teach classes, counsel students, and perform other duties normally identified with a college position. He understands his responsibilities to his institution, to his colleagues, to the applicants, and to himself. He enjoys the challenge of one of the most nonroutine positions in the academic hierarchy, and he thrives on hard work. (Hauser & Lazarsfeld, 1964)

Orientation of New Students

With the admission of new students into a college both the college and the students assume a major responsibility: the student, in a sense, agrees to dedicate himself to the task of making the most of the opportunity offered him; the college obligates itself to the task of helping the student to accomplish this. The implementation of this point of view requires careful planning and deliberate effort on the part of the college, for the following reasons:

1. Studies have shown that altogether too many entering freshmen lack real insight into what a college education really is.
2. The range of student motivation for entering college is very wide, and student goals are not always compatible with college expectations.
3. There is much that the entering student needs to know about the various phases of college study and college life if his attendance is to be productive.
4. Increasing numbers of entering students make all the more imperative some planned attention to the individual.

Essentially, these considerations become part of the more general task of helping the incoming student to accomplish, as smoothly as possible, an effective transition from high school to college or from one college to another. The device generally employed in this effort is the program of orientation which precedes the student's first registration in the college.

Approaches to freshman orientation vary considerably from college to college. The objectives, however, may include any or all of the following:

1. To clarify for the student his academic standing and, if he is not matriculated for a degree, to explain how he can achieve matriculation.
2. To acquaint the student with pertinent aspects of the curriculum and to consider course choices for the first semester.
3. To introduce the student to the program of student services, through information and through actual contact with the student services staff (Dean of Students, faculty counselors, student counselors, and others).
4. To orient the student with respect to registration procedures, program planning, and details of scheduling.
5. To initiate certain forms required by the college (e.g., student record folder, registrar's data sheet, health record, and the like).
6. To acquaint the student with established rules of campus behavior, dress regulations, dormitory ground-rules, and so on.

7. To introduce the student to the college's program of cocurricular activities.

8. To provide an opportunity for the student to meet, albeit often through the medium of a large assembly, the college president, deans, directors, and student leaders.

9. To acquire additional information about each student—through tests or interviews—for use by guidance counselors.

10. To check the student's health record and health status.

11. To begin the student's contact with the intellectual life of the college (e.g., through seminars, panel discussions, and lectures) and to consider the essential meaning of the kind of education the college offers.

12. To discuss with the student principles and practices in such areas as effective study habits, test-taking, course and instructor expectations, grading practices, opportunities for honors works, and so on.

13. To provide an opportunity for parents of entering freshmen to gain a better understanding of and a deeper insight into the experience upon which their sons and daughters are embarking and their own relationship to it as parents.

There are many different approaches to the task of orienting new students, as seen in the varieties of programs existing on different campuses. Most programs will employ a number of techniques and combinations of approaches, and there is much experimentation still going on in this area of college service. Most orientation programs begin as soon as the applicant has been notified of his acceptance; his acknowledgment of the acceptance, payment of a deposit, contracting for dormitory accommodations, and so forth are in a sense a beginning of his orientation to the college. Some orientation programs include summer activities (for example, visits by students and parents to the campus, orientation camps or week-ends); some are concentrated in a week in the spring followed by a Freshman Week or similar arrangement before registration in the fall; some are spread over the first semester or the entire freshman year, as orientation courses, variously with and without college credit.

The following specific elements in orientation programs may be identified:

1. Assemblies, meetings, and discussions, in larger or smaller groups including students and their parents, designed to realize some of the objectives enumerated.

2. Conferences, individually or in groups, with faculty counselors for

the purpose of discussing curricular plans and choices, career choices, scheduling of classes and other activities, and for the purpose of informing the student of the various forms of counseling and other assistance available to him in the college's program of student services.

3. Meetings, usually in small groups, with student counselors, dormitory advisers, and the like. The use of carefully selected, interested students is a vital element in most effective orientation programs. Upperclassmen who have been over the hurdles are in a position to provide practical insights which will aid the entering freshman in his adjustment in the midst of confusion, and they are also able to provide a basis for identification which can not always as easily be achieved by members of the faculty.

4. Presentations by student clubs and organizations designed to acquaint the incoming student with the various activities open to him. Colleges and universities are generally agreed that cocurricular involvement of some kind is a vital part of a college education, and students are encouraged to participate in such activities to the extent that their interests incline and time commitments allow. To be sure, it often becomes necessary for the college itself to impose some limits on such involvement, since some overambitious youngsters may have a tendency to become involved in too many activities, to the detriment of their studies.

At Brooklyn College of the City University of New York, for example, the Freshman Week program includes a Club Fair held in a large gymnasium; all entering freshmen attend this function in small groups led by student counselors. At the Club Fair student groups of all kinds present displays and materials which illustrate the scope of their interests and activities, and freshmen are invited to register with the groups which interest them to obtain further information. In addition, the college has produced a half-hour television program, shown to entering freshmen via the college's closed-circuit facilities in conjunction with the Club Fair, which presents a comprehensive introduction to the program of student activities at the college.

5. Administration of various tests designed to implement the program of counseling services. These may include achievement and placement tests (particularly in English, foreign languages, and mathematics), personality tests, interest schedules, study habits, inventories, and so on.

6. Health examinations conducted by the college health service, or screening of student health records prepared by their own family physicians. Very often, of course, the student's placement in physical education classes or his exemption from them will depend on the outcome of such examinations.

7. Discussions, lectures, or seminars based on reading done by the freshmen during the summer preceding their entrance into college. Strong feelings have been expressed in recent years that orientation programs concentrate too heavily on administrative routine and thereby fail to introduce the new student to the intellectual side of college life. It is felt that, since college is intended to be a far-reaching intellectual experience, this experience should begin as part of freshman orientation. To this end in late spring many colleges send their new freshmen lists of materials—usually a few selected books—to be read during the summer. Then, as part of the orientation program, these materials form the basis for discussions usually conducted by selected members of the faculty and often involving outstanding upper class students as well.

The exact nature and scope of the orientation program will be determined, of course, by the nature of the institution, the composition of the student body, and the availability of staff and facilities. In most institutions the program becomes the responsibility of the Dean of Students, the Dean of Freshmen, or the Director of Admissions. (Brown, 1961) In almost every case, however, it is interesting to note that selected students play a major role in the program, with excellent results. It should be noted, too, that the principles and programs discussed apply, with appropriate modifications, to evening students as well as day students, part-time as well as full-time, nonmatriculated as well as matriculated. In fact, for many entering students who are not enrolled as regular full-time students matriculated for a degree, a sound program of orientation and counseling may help to determine their future progress.

REFERENCES

Arbuckle, D. S. *Student personnel services in higher education.* New York: McGraw-Hill, 1953.

Boroff, D. P. *Campus USA: portraits of American colleges in action.* New York: Harper, 1961.

Bowles, F. H. *Admission to college: a perspective for the 1960s.* Princeton, N.J.: Coll. Entr. Examin. Bd., 1960.

Brock, E. P. *Freshman orientation in a new meaning.* Philadelphia: U. S. Nat. Student Assoc., 1959.

Brown, N. C. (Ed.) *Orientation to college learning: a reappraisal.* Washington: Amer. Council on Educ., 1961.

College Entrance Examination Board. *Counseling in school and college.* New York: Author, 1961.

College Entrance Examination Board. *The college handbook, 1965–67.* New York: Author, 1965.

College Entrance Examination Board. *From high school to college: readings for counselors*. New York: Author, 1965.

College Entrance Examination Board. *Manual of freshman class profiles, 1965–67*. New York: Author, 1965.

Eddy, E. D., Jr. *The college influence on student character*. Washington: Amer. Council on Educ., 1959.

Educational Policies Commission. *Universal opportunity for education beyond the high school*. Washington: Nat. Educ. Assoc., 1964.

Educational Testing Service. *Background factors relating to college plans and college enrollment among public high school students*. Princeton: Author, 1957.

Fishman, J. A. (Ed.) Social psychology of school-to-college transition. *J. educ. Sociol.*, 1960, 33, 249–304.

Hauser, J. Z., & Lazarsfeld, P. F. *The admissions officer in the American college: an occupation under change*. New York: Coll. Entr. Examin. Bd., 1964.

Hobart, C. W. Freshman disorientation. In H A. Estrin & D. M. Goode, *College and university teaching*. Dubuque, Iowa: William C. Brown, 1964.

Lehman, E., Ramsay, S. J., & Jefferson, J. (Eds.) A *handbook for the counselors of college bound students*. Evanston, Ill.: Assoc. of College Admiss. Counselors, 1964.

Li, Pei-Chao. Freshman orientation and the goals of general education. *J. Coll. Stud. Personnel*, 1962, 154, 130–135.

Science Research Associates. *Preparing students for college*. Chicago: Author, 1959.

State University of New York. *The admissions officer and his role*. Admiss. Officers Sympos., September, 1963.

Townsend, Agatha. *College freshman speak out*. New York: Harper, 1956.

Traxler, A. E., and Townsend, Agatha. *Improving transition from school to college*. New York: Harper, 1953.

Chapter 7

General, Academic, and Preprofessional Counseling

MYRON E. BERRICK

Defining College Counseling

"College counseling is what college counselors do," seems as good a definition of this field as any other, when one observes the practice. Counseling activity ranges from providing information via handbooks or brochures to being involved in a significant relationship through which a student will attempt to resolve for himself some of the most important problems and decisions faced by young people today. Most students get help in very direct kinds of ways. They need to know about admission requirements or course sequences and prerequisites or other college requirements. The information and advice given is counseling, under this very general definition; and yet neither it nor any other level of counseling just listed is truly counseling unless one important factor is involved. Therefore, the definition might better read, "counseling is what counselors do to help students resolve questions and problems for themselves."

The Job of the Counselor

The major job of the counselor is that of listening, attempting to evaluate the student's problem, and, then, of trying to aid the student in coping most effectively with that problem. It would seem that a principle emerges

Myron E. Berrick is Assistant Professor, Department of Education; and Coordinator, Teacher Counseling and Placement Center, Brooklyn College of the City University of New York.

at this point, which is that the student should be made aware, perhaps through overt discussion of the fact, that he is a partner in the counseling situation. If possible, there should be some expression from the student that he is aware that he is a partner in this effort. The statement may lead to some discussion of how he feels his problem has been dealt with, whether he has developed any greater understanding of its ramifications, and, most essentially, whether he has developed from his interaction with the counselor the understanding that nothing will be done for him that is at all possible for him to do for himself. The advocacy of an informative interchange between counselor and student does not necessarily imply an advocacy of that emotive-inspirational method of counseling which so many people decry. Rather, in a very matter-of-fact, informative approach, both the counselor and the counselee should be aware of some of the underlying implications of their meetings. This does not mean that there is no place for the emotive-inspirational method of counseling; hopefully, something between the two would be the usual practice, and observations made in many institutions with effective counseling programs have demonstrated that this is the case.

General Training of College Counselors

In most college counseling services there are usually both trained counselors and others with no formal training in counseling practices and techniques. There is, of course, a diversity of effort, compatible with the levels of training, and there is a further diversity of techniques used by the professionally trained counselors. This is not so much in terms of a dogmatic adherence to one style or school of counseling, but rather of variations in methodology and technique according to a counselor's understanding of a student's problem. A good counselor will utilize various techniques, none of which may be perfect. He will vary any techniques in which he is comfortable to fit the situation in which he finds himself.

In the training of faculty members for counseling, techniques of counseling must be included; however, exposure to too much concentration on technique may rob the counseling office of a counselor's good potential. Counselors, being human, are anxious and may tend to fall back on structure and techniques rather than remain aware of the individual with whom they are in a counseling relationship. As a result, the counselor may interact with a student counselee in a technically adequate manner yet leave the student feeling that he is in contact with nothing more than a good technician. Since many counseling contacts are for the purpose of obtaining information, there need not be any adverse effects. On the other hand, when a student needs a warm, sympathetic human being and finds a competent technician, there is perhaps a greater level of disappointment than when a student coming to get a program change has to listen to a counselor reminisce about his own college days for five or ten minutes. A guiding principle for counseling practice is that the counselor, as the most responsible person in the counseling situation, should be aware, informed, and human enough to evaluate the situation presented by the student entering his office. The counselor must deal effectively with the situation as it is presented and be free to develop it further, according to his best judgment.

Student Development and the Liberal Arts College

There seems to be a great need in the liberal arts colleges today for a reaffirmation of the student's role in his own development as an educated person. Due in large part to the development of psychological testing and its efficacy in prediction, and due also to the growth and development of counseling and guidance as a profession, the youngster today very often sees himself as a mass of good potential which will be shaped up in the guidance program in the high school and college and led into those courses of study which will then place him in the world to be the most productive of individuals. Very often this view is shared by his counselors, especially those in schools offering preprofessional training. It is unfortunately a truism that success in developing good practitioners does a great deal toward producing stagnation in a professional or preprofessional training program. Success in training permits the development and definition of criteria for success in the chosen field. These criteria can then be used anywhere in the selective processes to furnish evidence of good potential for this, that, or the other profession. The result is that college students or, more particularly, high school students begin to feel that there will be some magical measure of their potential and capabilities which will allow them, when it is revealed, to know what they are good at and what course they should pursue. If this were really true, it would be true in those areas of professional work where there are finite rules and regulations, boundaries of knowledge, and well-established techniques and methodologies.

One of the greatest bastions of hope for the preservation of the spirit of constant change should be the liberal arts college, where every student and faculty member should feel that he is part of a continuous movement which has a beginning and a middle, but never, hopefully, any end. A counseling program, therefore, geared to help a student orient himself, acclimate himself, and adjust and conform to the rules and regulations of the institution might by some definition be regarded as untenable in a true liberal arts program. There need not necessarily be any dilemma involved, however, if the important words, *adjust* and *conform*, are correctly understood. If *adjustment* carries with it the connotation of perceiving a situation clearly and then modifying one's behavior in terms of one's best judgment, *adjustment* and *conformity* are not necessarily horrendous terms. Rather, they are very much a part of the development of the individual's awareness of himself in his environment, which is precisely the job of the liberal arts college. This awareness may be accomplished, in part, by orientation lectures early in the student's career, possibly beginning even before he is in attendance on campus. It may be done through brochures or handbooks given to the student by student advisors or guides, or it may be fostered by a combination of both the written and spoken word.

Counseling for the liberal arts student is effective, then, *only* if the student is involved as a participant and is made to feel his involvement. The paradigm for such a state is this: The college exists and as it exists it has something to offer students; counseling is a process designed to aid students to get as much as possible out of the college as it exists; the student is part of the college. The major role of a counseling service is to help each student recognize his responsibility for dealing with the college, explore his goals and needs, find his own ways of satisfying these goals and needs, and, hopefully, examine the other possibilities that lie before him.

The Academic Process in Action

With respect for the student's needs, among which is a need not to reveal himself too quickly to strangers, the counselor may be able to bring about in the student an awareness of things about himself, the college, and his interaction with the college that were not part of his awareness before. The counselor's function may be one of information giving as well as one of developing certain insights. Whatever a counselor does, he is doing in terms of providing a service for the student. It is in this area that the danger lies: Doing too much may prevent the student's growth; doing too little may interfere with the student's adjustment to the college setting. It would seem, therefore, that there needs to be an orderly growth in the counseling services which are provided for students. These should range from helping students to recognize the existence of the college and what it has to offer and providing information through an orientation program of what the institution requires (the ground rules under which it does exist) to developing for a student a relationship with a faculty member who can be there to disseminate information, listen to a problem, and perhaps give advice and counsel.

All of these activities and the methods and techniques of performing them are part and parcel of the counseling program at the large, urban college with which the author is most familiar. An outline of that program is in order at this time as a reference point to clarify the principles of practice already enunciated. An excellent description and detailed examination of the Brooklyn College Student Personnel Program can be found in Goodhartz (1960). The Department of Student Services at this college, through the Office of the Dean of Students has responsibility for all counseling activities. A number of services are offered to students at all levels, including to those students, while still in their high school years, who are prospective matriculants. A program of orientation to admissions procedures, the core curriculum for the freshman year, the requirements for matriculation and for graduation given to high school seniors and incoming freshmen, and the programs of orientation for the parents of new students are handled through the Office of Admissions. Once the student is on campus, he is introduced to a freshman faculty advisor, who may remain as his counselor for the rest of his stay at the college. The faculty member aids him in making the many transitions necessary in the first year and in getting the best out of the college. Depending upon his sequences of coursework, the student is assigned in his junior year to a different counselor, usually in the student's major department, for curriculum counseling.

The majority of the general counselors are faculty members, recruited from every department of the college, who counsel on released time from teaching assignments in their departments. They range in background, temperament, and outlook as would any representative cross-section of a large college faculty. What they seem to have in common is the willingness to involve themselves deeply in student-faculty relationships. They relate to students as people, and while there is inevitably some carryover of their backgrounds and training to their approaches to counseling, it is not necessarily very direct. It might be expected that a mathematician or scientist would be very forthright and matter-of-fact in his breaking down of a student's problem, as compared to a member of the Modern Language Department, a poet, or philosopher. Experience indicates that such is not the case. A rigorous, definitive, didactic and direct approach, for example, may mark the counseling work of a member of the Classics Department, while a number of physicists are wont to relax with students and allow things to happen. As previously remarked, we are in this case dealing with counselors who are people first and only secondarily counselors and technicians. They are, as noted, recruited from all departments of the faculty, and their training for participation in the program consists of a rigorous indoctrination into the curriculum and the administrative machinery of the college. The rules, regulations, traditions, and practices of the college which have been set down by faculty committees on curriculum are in the main perceptive doctrines well worked out for the development of a well-rounded, educated person. It is the counselor's job to know as much of this material as possible. In one sense, this is a major activity of counseling in a liberal arts institution: the dissemination of information concerning the student's best adaptation to the environment in which he exists.

It is at this point, as previously noted, that there exists the danger of over-counseling, which can change the interaction of faculty member and student from dissemination of information and aid in the development and growth of the student to dissemination of information without regard for the individual in terms of his own unique problems. The feeding of information to students should be a careful process, one which shows some concern for the fact that people digest different informational foods at different rates. The student will be able to absorb information pertinent to him and will be able to relish it for his own ends, but he will not hear information that is indigestible to him at that time. Simply disseminating information, which is a major job of a counseling program in a liberal arts college, cannot be sufficient in itself without high regard for the person to whom it is given. Therefore, the counselor must know something of his student if he is to do any sort of a valid job.

In a college where contact between faculty and student is casual at best, few records exist which would enable a counselor to sit down and pore over a folder giving him the requisite background information. Furthermore, given a half year's counseling in any large center, counselors begin to recognize that there can be great bias and distortion in the evaluations that faculty members write as part of the student's record concerning their contacts with students. This is not to say that such reports of contacts are not most valuable—they are; however, it is also a fact of life that they cannot in themselves be depended upon to give a true picture of the student and his interaction with the college. Scores from entrance examinations, the required evaluations of the Freshman English and Social

Science instructors, grades, psychological test results can, if available, give the counselor a great deal of information about the student and his potential. But, again, they cannot in entirety be relied upon to give the true picture. We make grievous errors when we assume that people remain constant. This is especially so when we are dealing with adolescents, who by the very nature of their concerns and development are not constant in their endeavors. We should expect variation and appreciate it for what it represents—flexibility and freedom on the part of the student. But what does this do to the counselor who is trying to get a picture of the student with whom he is dealing, so that he may know how to present the information he has to present? There is no answer that makes good sense.

At many colleges there is a file for each student. As noted, there are the scores of an entrance examination, the scores on the SAT that the student took in high school, grades from courses completed, and the reports of the English instructor or instructors of other required basic courses who cooperate with the counselors in the freshman year. There may or may not be other information. There is also a data sheet filled out by the student, which gives his family history and some indication of his socioeconomic status. This is a great quantity of information, and yet it tells very little. The student has the ability to tell much more, and the counselor should have the ability to help the student to express and perhaps reveal himself. But the student is not required to provide information, and this must be respected. Therefore, the counselor must have in his armamentarium not only the techniques of ice breaking and eliciting activity in the counseling session, but also the sensitivity and humanness to keep quiet and to be respectful when it is obvious that the student does not wish to participate in a counseling endeavor. There is still information to be gained by both the student and the counselor from each other. There can be mutual respect and pleasantness, and should be, in this interaction; the counselor and student can always fall back on the dissemination of information.

In a liberal arts college there is much the student can learn from the counselor in terms of curriculum planning and procedures. At many colleges this is done via a plan of study, a form filled out by the student in his sophomore year which anticipates the courses he will take to fulfill the requirements for the degree he wishes to obtain. It is the job of the counselor to review the plan of study and to offer suggestions or corrections where necessary. The plan of study by whatever label it is known is the responsibility of the student. It is his job to sample the courses offered by the college in his freshman and sophomore years to determine as best he can what his major interest is and therefore what his major will be in his elective coursework. In contact with a faculty member of that department, usually one who is designated as the departmental counselor, he then ascertains what courses are required by that department in order to graduate as a major. He next fills out his plan of study and brings it to his counselor for review. The counselor, who has hopefully had contact with the student previously, should have some idea of what the student is like as a person and whether in any way the plan may be infeasible in terms of the student's background and potentials. Knowing something about the requirements for entrance into medical school, for example, would undoubtedly make a counselor take certain steps with a student with a very low index in mathematics and the sciences who plans to major in biology in hopes of getting into medical school. The counselor would most probably send such a student to the office of the preprofessional counselor for medical education (if such an office exists). This, it seems, would be one point where a counselor might intervene for the sake of helping a student become more realistic in clarifying his aims. It may be that a student who really desires a medical degree can pull himself up and through the required course work in mathematics and the sciences despite low interest scores on the entrance exams. There are rules and regulations, however, and there are some areas in which there can be very little variation on the part of the student. It is the job of the counselor to inform him of this. Aside from that, the role of the counselor should be one of encouraging the student to develop for him, not only an appropriate major, but to explore as well other avenues in the college, other possibilities for rounding out his interests and abilities. Curriculum counseling is a vital and essential counseling function. The manner in which it is handled determines to a great extent the development of future counseling contacts and may determine whether the student is put on his own early in his college career.

Training New Counselors and Faculty-Student Relations

In the counseling services of most colleges there is usually an indoctrination and training period for new counselors in which they are grounded in the curriculum, the college bulletin, and rules and regulations. There is a system of guidance by more experienced counselors available to them and, in most instances, a constant program of in-service training. Furthermore, with the increasing inclusion of specialists in mental health, there is contact and interaction between the general and the specialized counseling programs. The specialists, clinical psychologists, psychiatrists, and social workers, usually deal with students who have problems of an emotional nature requiring more contact and deeper levels of communication. (See Chapter 11.)

In an increasingly larger number of liberal arts colleges many of the overall activities of the college are combined with what we are here calling the general counseling program. For example, orientation lectures are provided by many departments and preprofessional groups in order to attract students to their programs, and these lectures and other activities are coordinated through the general counseling program. The contact between the general counseling program and the teaching departments is usually made with departmental counselors. Their rapport with the members of the general counseling panel is usually very good, since in many instances a departmental counselor is also a general counselor or has had some experience as a general counselor. (See also, Chapter 17) Faculty members who have had experience as members of the general counseling panel seem to have an advantage over members of their department who have not had such experience when taking over the functions of departmental counselors. Members of the faculty of any one department can usually understand fully the ramifications of the course requirements for their particular department. Given some time as members of the general counseling panel, where they are responsible for knowing overall college requirements (i.e., curriculum requirements for matriculation and graduation), faculty members gain greater breadth and depth applicable in their departmental counseling. The training of the faculty in the requirements for obtaining the liberal arts degree is invaluable, not only in helping them to function as counselors, but in enabling them to understand their functions in the larger context of the liberal arts college. Just as we require that students be made aware of their own involvement in their own growth and development as members of the college, so too, it seems that faculty members need some help in clarifying and defining their roles as members of the college community. It is a very educational experience to sit with a student whose potentials on paper are good, whose potentials as they appear in his contact with you are high, and who is hampered in his attempts to get into some specialized program because he has a poor grade in one required course. When one can see the effects of various grading systems and practices, for example, one develops a greater awareness of the need to deal individually with the individuals who present themselves. Counseling aids the college instructor in many, many ways. For one thing, there is a kind of feedback the counselor gets if student and counselor relate to each other and can really discuss the student and his progress in the institution.

The counselor can learn much from the student's view of instructors and their place in the scheme of things. There is too little evaluation of the faculty by the student on any basis that really helps the faculty to grow and develop. In this sense a general counseling program works both ways: The training of the instructor in counseling is highly beneficial to him individually and as a member of the faculty. Such experience can produce a greater awareness of the aims and intentions of the college and of the college administration as a whole. In these days of reported dissension between faculty and administration, students and administration, and students and faculty, communication and understanding seem clearly to be fostered by an inclusion of the student in the counseling process, and by an awareness of student-faculty interaction in counseling.

Student Counselors

In the attempt to make the student as much a partner as possible in the affairs of the faculty for the benefit of both students and faculty, counseling programs are taking many steps, including the recent development of programs utilizing student counselors. (Siegel, 1967) These are advanced, superior students who act as dormitory advisers or students preparing for personnel work who take over some of the functions of the general staff counselors (with appropriate safeguards for the confidentiality of information). These programs seem to have been developed in part in an attempt to enable students to feel that there is an easier transition between being a student, or rather a member of the student body, and a member of the faculty. This is most certainly felt by those participating as counselors. The effects on those students who are counseled in these programs is still very much in the process of being evaluated, as are most of the procedures.

The General and the Preprofessional Concepts of Counseling

Departments of Student Services (or whatever title the counseling programs use) constantly evaluate their various counseling programs in the attempt to improve them and coordinate their functioning and to resolve what in some instances are the seemingly incompatible philosophies involved. The general counseling program, for example, with an educative and exploratory outlook towards the college curriculum, and the various preprofessional counseling programs, which are designed to channel the student's coursework into prescribed paths to meet the entrance criteria for certain graduate programs or vocational areas, are theoretically in conflict. That there is usually no conflict is a result of the tendency of the old liberal arts college to disappear in these days of specialization. For the student who sees the liberal arts program as a stepping stone into professional training, the general counseling program is a stepping stone into the preprofessional counseling program. The student for whom college is an education in itself, with the Bachelor of Arts a terminal degree, experiences no conflict with preprofessional programs, since he tends to have little or no contact with them. For the counselors and administrators of the various counseling programs, however, the question of the incompatibility definitely exists, and the direction, scope, and intensity of counseling activity is always under discussion. One of the constant factors in these departments is that when new methodology is devised to make counseling transactions easier the question of where it fits in the resolution of the student's dependency-independency conflict is always a corollary. As this conflict affects the use of the counseling service, it is apparent that for those students who focus on graduate training there is a greater willingness to accept the dependent position and seek out all resources the college can offer in their search for the greater independence in graduate work. Conversely, the terminal B.A. student is more in conflict about expressing his dependency and seeks out the counselor only as required by regulations or when other avenues of information have not proven fruitful. Thus, no matter how defined, college counseling is for those who seek its services.

One group, however, for whom the counseling service should make efforts to insure more than just availability of counseling services is comprised of those students for whom adaptation to college, especially an American college, presents unusual difficulties. Such students would include those educated in other countries, where English may not be a native tongue, and those students presently being pushed into higher education by programs to help the disadvantaged.

Counseling Foreign Students[1]

A bona fide foreign student is one who is studying in the United States on a student or diplomatic visa and who intends to return to his native country after completing his education. However, many colleges extend

1. This statement on counseling foreign students has been prepared by Assistant Dean of Students Shirley Ullman Wedeen, of the Brooklyn College Department of Education. At the time of writing, Dean Wedeen was serving as Coordinator of the General Counseling Program at Brooklyn College.

their definition of a foreign student to include the student who submits for his entrance into college foreign credentials for the major part of his secondary school work. These two categories of foreign students present some similar, but to a great extent, different problems.

Admission questions for all are essentially the same:

a. Does the applicant have the necessary qualifications?

b. Is his command of the English language adequate to his academic objectives?

c. Does the applicant seem to have the personality and desire to meet the demands of a new environment?

d. Have financial needs been assessed and plans made to meet these needs?

On the other hand, when the college has to face the specific problems of different students it finds that there is no prototype of a foreign student. Students from the same country differ, as do those from different cultures. Therefore, when a foreign student is admitted into a college he needs the information and counseling all students at the college receive and in addition that necessitated by his specific needs. Usually he requires more initial counseling assistance in order to find his way around. It is advisable to centralize the counseling of foreign students because they have certain similar problems which lend themselves to group counseling techniques. Then too, a specially designated counselor is in a better position to acquire the information and sensitivities pertinent to these students.

The counselor of foreign students should know who the foreign students on campus are. He should organize an orientation program for these students and should involve other faculty members, to the extent possible, in projects and discussions in order better to orient both groups. He should, moreover, be freely available to his students. It would be advisable to have a newsletter type of publication (numbers of foreign students permitting) through which to circulate pertinent information. A social group might be established in which these students can get together and discuss their problem or other interest areas. Local groups, particularly those groups who may have vested interests in the college, should be involved for the dual purpose of getting to know these students and assisting these students to become accepted members of the community. The foreign student is, in the first place, a student on campus and only secondly a student with certain different and additional needs.

Preprofessional Counseling Services

While the foreign student counseling program just outlined is highly consistent with a general counseling program, for prevocational and preprofessional counseling, additional information and rather specialized services need to be provided. Visa restrictions on working, for example, may interfere with a foreign student's obtaining necessary field experience via paid work. For foreign and native students alike, however, vocational counseling does require more specialization.

In contrast to the lack of definition as to what constitutes a general counseling service, preprofessional or prevocational counseling may be readily defined as that activity which aids in the directed growth of a student from a high school senior to a college graduate qualified for admission into a graduate training program, or a good job. At many large urban colleges the general counseling program is in contact through its admissions programs with students in their high school senior and college freshman years, and supplies those students who have definite vocational or professional aims with information of preprofessional or prevocational programs. Students, for example, who wish to enter the pre-engineering program are required by many colleges to take a special examination as entering freshmen. Students who plan to enter medicine or dentistry may or may not take special examinations, but usually they are advised to contact in their upper freshman term a preprofessional counselor from whom specialized preprofessional counseling services are available. Once the student is out of the admissions program and into the general counseling program per se, he may be advised by his general counselor (on the basis of aptitude and interest scores, where such testing programs exist, or his grades in his freshman year, or the like) to consider entering one of the professions, in which case he will be referred to the appropriate preprofessional counselor.

Where there are such preprofessional counseling programs, they are usually charged with the responsibility of securing information concerning admission into such professional schools or training programs as accounting, engineering, medicine, law, library science, social work, psychology, and teaching. Furthermore, they are often in contact with industrial and commercial corporations, who search out talented college graduates. The preprofessional program may thus aid in job placement or act as an informational resource. Preprofessional programs, however, go much further than simply providing information. They are much more structured and organized than are the general counseling programs, since they have criteria established for them by the professions themselves. The more or less strict adherence to these criteria involves a considerable amount of the student's coursework in the college, but within these restrictions counselors attempt to get the student to broaden as much as he can his scope of interest and sensitivity as an educated person. Contact is maintained with the student throughout the various stages of his college career, and a rather constant evaluation is made of his growth, especially as reflected in his grades. Grade consciousness is one unfortunate result; and, whereas in the general counseling program the student might discuss many factors involved in fallen grades, the preprofessional student attempts to justify it and promises to do better next term. Whereas a general counselor may be seen as an ally in the student's attempt to grow, the preprofessional counselor is often seen as a roadblock and sometimes as an enemy whose opposition must be overcome if the student is to progress as he should.

Contact with parents is one of the functions of college counselors, and preprofessional counselors (or those counselors or administrators delegated to implement retention or dismissal where grades are low) come into contact very often with irate or excited parents. Since the recommendation of the preprofessional counselor is frequently very important for admission into graduate schools or industrial programs, the preprofessional counselor must exercise extreme care in the decisions he makes. It is for these reasons that counselors very often stick to the requirements and the rules and regulations. In this sense, the demands of their job force them into being technicians, since there very often can be no room for a warm, sympathetic approach in the role they play. People, being people, tend to persist in their demands with warm sympathetic human beings and try to be the exception to the rule; therefore, pre-professional counselors cannot function in the same fashion as the general counselors, unless there is no great difficulty in entering the desired profession.

A Case in Point

One such example is in teaching, where, because of the teacher shortage of the past twenty years (which seems to be over to a great extent), it was not necessary for a student who desired to teach to feel as pressured as the student who desired entrance into a medical or other professional school. The demands of the college, of the Department or School of Education, and, in a sense, of the profession of teaching itself, could be overlooked by a student who wanted a job as a teacher. Boards of Education, especially those in urban areas, out of their desperate need for teachers were filling classroom vacancies with college graduates possessing the barest minimum of the requirements of the Departments of Education of the various states. Therefore, the professional counseling program for teaching was not subjected to the pressures experienced by the more competitive professions. Now, however, as the desperate teacher shortage seems to have come to an end and jobs have become more difficult for unqualified people to find, pressure will begin to mount, and teacher counseling will need to work out for itself a role which will hopefully combine specialized and general aspects of counseling.

Such programs will have to cope with the increasing demand for liberal arts training for specialists in teaching and with the demands of the many states who are codifying the preparations which are or are not acceptable for certification as a teacher. In the teacher counseling program with which the author is identified, for example, a program of counseling procedures has been worked out which includes dissemination of information via brochures and orientation meetings prior to college entrance, required contact in the sophomore year for a formalized plan of study, and availability of counselors beyond the required contacts. This program is a testing ground for many of the principles of practice enumerated and the source of observation basic to the many arbitrary statements made. The program attempts to combine the best aspects of general, preprofessional, and vocational counseling services and to benefit the students and faculty members who participate in it.

REFERENCES

Arbuckle, D. *Student personnel services in higher education.* New York: McGraw-Hill, 1953.

Arbuckle, D. Client perception of counselor personality. *J. counsel. Psychol.*, 1956, 3, 93–96.

Brodbeck, J. L. Need for more specialized counseling services. *Counsel.*, 1956, 14, 1–4.

Froehlich, C. P. A criterion for counseling. *Psychol. Monogr.*, 1957, 71, No. 15.

Gordon, I. J. Guidance training for college faculty. *Nat. Assoc., Deans Women J.*, 1953, 16, 69–76.

Goodhartz, A. S. (Ed.) *A commitment to youth.* New York: Bookman Assoc., 1960.

Hardee, M. *The faculty in college counseling.* New York: McGraw-Hill, 1959.

Hilton, T. Alleged acceptance of the occupational role of teaching. *J. appl. Psychol.*, 1960, 44, 210–215.

Horst, P. How much information on test results should be given to students: views of a research psychologist. *J. counsel. Psychol.*, 1959, 6, 218–222.

McGowan, J., & Schmidt, L. *Counseling: readings in theory and practice*, New York: Holt, 1962.

Rogers, C. *Counseling and psychotherapy*. Boston: Houghton Mifflin, 1942.

Samler, J. An examination of client strength and counselor responsibility. *J. counsel. Psychol.*, 1962, 9, 5–11.

Siegel, M. Training of students as assistants in counseling. *J. Nat. Assoc. Stud. Personnel Admin.*, 1967, 3, 139–142.

Tyler, Leona E. *The work of the counselor*. (Rev. ed.) New York: Appleton-Century-Crofts, 1961.

Vance, F., Grams, A., & Berdlie, R. *Parents and the counselor*. St. Paul: State of Minn., Dept. of Educ., 1960.

Williamson, E. Some issues underlying counseling theory and practice. In W. E. Dugan (Ed.), *Counseling points of view*, 1–13. Minnesota: Univ. of Minn. Press, 1959.

Chapter 8

Student Activities Programs

ARCHIE MAC GREGOR

A Rationale For Student Activities

The college cocurricular program is a substantial contributor to the undergraduate learning process. While learning in all of its aspects may be broadly defined, each student program must stand the test of meeting this requirement in some way. At a time when pressures for funds, space, personnel, and other university resources have never been greater, programs owing their support primarily to tradition, sentiment, or pleasure purely for pleasure's sake cannot be sustained. Historically, the claims most frequently made for student activities have been that through these experiences colleges were developing leadership and citizenship, social poise, and other desirable personal qualities, such as sportsmanship. Today, considerable evidence is available supporting these claims to some extent and with certain qualifications. But additional educational values not previously considered now also indicate the necessity for a strong program of student life.

Student activities personalize for countless students a college existence that could otherwise be routinized, automated, and devoid of warmth. The opportunity for counseling individuals which grows out of the relationship between the student or student leader and the faculty adviser can sometimes offset the sense of rootlessness that might otherwise become over-

Archie Mac Gregor is Assistant Professor, Department of Student Services; and Assistant Dean of Students (Student Activities Program), Brooklyn College of the City University of New York.

powering on a large campus. This is particularly true in the nonresidential urban campuses in which an increasingly large proportion of college students are enrolled. The holding power of student activities can offer a meaningful interlude, during which personal developmental problems or problems of career choice or motivation are resolved, thereby saving students who might otherwise be lost. Moreover, student activities may directly supplement the classroom. The increasing growth of academic clubs and substantial intellectual programs in every field offers practical application of or extension of formalized instruction. Information about career fields and graduate schools, opportunities for student-sponsored trips, individual research projects, and preliminary tutoring or other service experiences in the community can all relate helpfully to the academic program.

Student activities can also contribute to the sense of community. This should not be in the older sense of citizenship training via shallow rules of procedure and the emphasis upon forms of students' rights. Rather, it should be in terms of awareness of the campus as a community and the students' obligations to it and in terms of service to the larger community beyond the campus. It should be the objective of the college to see that the student culture reflects through effective faculty guidance and rules of procedure the best of the larger culture rather than the mode. Student politics for example should not be accepted at a less than statesmanlike level simply because this level is sometimes prevalent in the larger world.

While the contributions of a good student activities program to an undergraduate education are significant ones, an inspection of all of the college catalogues in America would probably not reveal a single college offering a bachelor's degree program with a major concentration in student activities. The insistence of some few students upon devoting an unreasonably large proportion of their time to student activities, to the point that participation becomes a flight from the classroom if not from life itself, is a disservice to all concerned. College regulations limiting the extent of participation and requiring the attainment of minimum academic standards should be explicit and carefully enforced within the framework of a good counseling situation designed to assist those who are failing in this way. Procedures designed to contain those students who grossly abuse their right to join in student activities, either by over participation or in other ways, should be appropriately placed by each campus on the spectrum at opposite ends of which are rules which would be excessively permissive and rules which would establish virtually a police state. Neither polar situation is adequate preparation for living in a truly free society: An excessively permissive situation with an absence of organization does not really support learning or activity any more than an authoritarian situation. The meaning of *appropriateness* for each campus can best be developed gradually through experience and consultation of students and faculty, interim errors being made in favor of giving students freedom and having confidence in their integrity and good faith.

Since student activities contribute to the development of the self and to an awareness and appreciation of the concept of the community, and since these activities are an extension of the educational process fundamentally grounded in the classroom, two additional premises logically follow. First, student activities must be as adequately supported as are other college programs. In general this should mean direct financial contributions by the college to the maintenance of college-wide activities such as the student council and student newspaper and indirect support, primarily in the form of counseling assistance and overhead costs (space and the like), for individual groups which are not college-wide in nature. It also follows from the educational purpose of the student activities program that the responsibility for its development and well being should be that of the faculty.

One final aspect of this rationale is the need for an attitude of creativity and innovation. The student activities program should be based upon a contemporary philosophy of life and learning. This would include an awareness of the endemic nature of change in our culture and a desire to base such change, not upon an unreasonable desire for endless change for its own sake, but rather upon research and research-based planning. Among the many areas in student activities which currently require systematic study are the potential role of students in college policy making, a definitive analysis of the relationship between academic success and student activities participation, the impact of the growing numbers of graduate students on student activities, and the entire field of late adolescent student values in personal living. An endless number of other topics could be listed. On many campuses such research is taking place, sometimes with foundation support, as a joint venture of faculty and students.

Administering the Student Activities Program

The Faculty Adviser and Student Participation in Leadership

Every group which is formally recognized or has any other kind of official standing on the campus should have an adviser. Two schools of thought exist concerning his role. Some authorities suggest that the adviser is a resource, an encourager, and in effect that "he who advises least, advises best." The majority, however, subscribe to the view that, although the primary task of the adviser is to offer expert guidance, there will inevitably arise occasional situations in which the faculty adviser will be forced to try to tactfully exercise overt controls. These situations will arise most frequently in the use of funds, in membership procedures and elections, and in the relationship of the group to the campus and the community, especially through publications carrying the college name. The mandate for minimal faculty controls of this nature stems from the legal involvement of the college in the activities of its groups, the moral obligation which the college undertakes by having encouraged the group to form using its facilities and drawing its members from the college's students, and the educational desirability of relating the work of the group to instructional goals. Efforts to relieve the college of this at times rather burdensome responsibility are continually made by those who find the idea of faculty supervision of student activities inconvenient or unpleasant. These efforts include measures such as placing student publications in a separate corporation and other tactics which might at least lessen legal responsibility.

To be of greatest assistance, faculty advisers should be drawn from the permanent career staff. Exceptions will have to be made to this policy, but the practice of assigning as group advisers new staff members who are unfamiliar with the campus and its policies is particularly unfortunate. Wherever possible the group should have the privilege of electing or inviting an adviser of its own choice. This will not be possible for groups whose activities involve college credit (bands, orchestras, and the rest) or in those cases in which the adviser will receive assigned teaching time or a new full-time adviser is being hired. Some colleges do invite students in these cases to list qualities that they seek in a good adviser or do sometimes involve students in some way, perhaps indirectly or informally, in the actual selection process. Whatever the situation, no group should be permitted to function for any length of time without an adviser.

The adviser's primary tasks are to serve as an educational leader and a source of strength and continuity for the group. This role may be performed in many ways; the adviser, however, should certainly be present at meetings at which the group holds elections, has guests from off-campus, or holds large functions at which a question of negligence might arise as a result of his absence. Depending on the amount of money involved, the adviser should be involved in handling group funds. He should assure that there are written records of the work of the group, and should file written counseling appraisals of the work of its leaders. The group should consult with the adviser, but having consulted him, need not be bound by his advice except in matters such as the handling of funds and other limited areas which may be developed on each campus. Counselors on assigned time should file written schedules indicating when they will be involved in the work of advising their groups.

While considering the role of faculty advisers, it seems appropriate to give thought to the matter of *students' rights* or *student academic freedom.* Associated with this is the time-honored or time-worn concept of *in loco parentis* to which organizations such as the United States National Student Association (Johnston, 1962) have expressed strong opposition. Other national organizations have made suggestions which would limit substantially the degree of supervision over the activities of student groups currently being exercised on many campuses. The concept of students' rights is a changing one; however, in general it appears that the courts have been consistent in upholding the right of the university, using reasonable procedures, to supervise individual students acting in a way which might reflect upon the university. Events in the history of American and European university life indicate that violence or near violence have frequently been the order of the day and that student deaths and injuries and attacks upon professors have been not at all uncommon. Recent student excesses have happily been increasingly verbal. The tide of current student activism, however, includes participation in demonstrations and other activities on and off campus in ways that are sometimes not considered legal and are occasionally misdirected. Among these are attacks upon individuals with whom students disagree, not the least of which are censures in gross terms of college administrators.

From the standpoint of education and learning, college should insist upon at least minimum standards of behavior. A recent issue of *Antioch Notes* describes undergraduates as "novices in freedom" and states the need for some forms of control by suggesting that students, with little to lose, are not "sensible" in adult terms; that they have not been accustomed to being held responsible and are not aware of possible consequences; that they have no sense of timing and expect things to happen right away; and that they harbor much "mythology and demonology" concerning values and other matters. (Keeton, 1965)

From a practical standpoint, many of the suggestions made to secure greater student group privileges would prove unworkable in a well-administered student activities program. However, a great margin for student freedom and expression does exist. Faculty-student committees, for example, comprise one of the widely used procedures for student participation in the leadership of student activities. These may be standing committees on a variety of subjects not limited to student activities and may have a very considerable budget of power. A second procedure, which has been pioneered for a quarter of a century at Brooklyn College, is a student adviser leadership program. In this program students serve as faculty advisers to social groups, exercising all of the responsibilities of senior advisers. Participation is on a selective basis; the students chosen enroll in a sequential series of five seminars in which they are given instruction about college policy, trained to work with groups, given the opportunity to explore in depth the area of student values, and otherwise carefully instructed while they serve as advisers. Experimentation is proceeding in the use of these students as counselors in the general counseling program.

The leaders' conference is another widely used method of developing independent and responsible student leadership. Presemester conferences for freshmen, early fall and late spring weekend meetings for elected student leaders, and leadership institutes of up to two weeks in length run by regional and national organizations are all common occurrences. Ideally such meetings should be held away from campus so that the participants will be inaccessible for routine interruptions; however, the facilities offered by the modern student center may serve as the meeting site if desired. Such conferences have proven their effectiveness in raising morale and encouraging creative leadership, provided that they are carefully planned with a substantial agenda and adequate financing, the student guests paying at least a part of the cost.

Through these and other measures, efforts are being made to develop leadership affirmatively and to cope as well with the problem, receiving increased attention, of the destructive leader. A few students see in student-group leadership opportunities, not for service or personal growth and learning, but rather for the expression of generalized anger or resentment. Others are motivated by careerist goals or by the need to reassure themselves in an unhealthy way that they are keeping up with their peers or surpassing them. Unfortunately, the inexperienced undergraduate sometimes selects the vocal, aggressive leader without regard to his other qualifications. Undergraduates also subscribe to the myth that certain leaders are indispensable and must not be replaced no matter what tactics these leaders use to achieve their purposes. Counseling assistance for destructive leaders is complicated by the fact that they are often unaware of the true nature of their difficulties. In working with these students, the faculty adviser should maintain careful written records as a basis for future counseling and a calm attitude of firmness and fairness.

Whenever possible in advising student activities, it is desirable to work with groups of students rather than with individuals. Apart from the economy of skilled time represented, experience increasingly indicates that many tasks can be accomplished more effectively in a group than in an individual situation. Many campuses might save staff time also by reviewing the number of student group activities currently on a semester basis (student elections, group room assignments, and the like) that might profitably be switched to an annual basis. Continued study of all procedures used in advising groups is recommended.

General Student Activities Administrative Policies

funds

The use of the student activities funds in many colleges centers about a college-operated bank in which are kept all student-group funds, including those from college sources and from individual student members. The advantage of this policy lies in assuring that sound business procedures are followed and in counseling students about wise expenditures. A situation fraught with potential heartache is transformed by the well-run activities funds depository into a learning situation for future business and professional people and homemakers.

In our culture, youth is given the privilege of spending a tremendous amount of easily acquired money. Simple activities have been replaced by more sophisticated and proportionately more expensive ones. The total student activities program, including expenditures by groups, easily represents several hundred thousand dollars annually and on some campuses this figure may exceed one million. Students typically approach group spending from two premises: that all of the members of the group are honest, and that there is no need for the red tape represented by formal business procedures. Faculty members at times also subscribe to the shoe box approach to financial management in the absence of other routinized facilities. In addition to avoiding the possibility of loss and offering an instructional opportunity for group treasurers and other members in collecting, safeguarding, and disbursing funds, a systematic account affords a permanent record of the group's activities and receipts for its expenditures. Accounts are audited so that each successive treasurer is relieved of his obligation in an orderly way. The funds of smaller groups thus receive professional attention that would not be available through a commercial bank. Convenient facilities on the campus, moreover, discourage procrastination in depositing funds.

If a bank is to be maintained on campus, every group should be required to participate. This will make it possible to centralize counseling in budget making and in drawing contracts, in addition to assuring uniform practices in the handling of money. Faculty advisers may be required to countersign withdrawals above a certain amount. Students should be advised to consult a specialized financial counselor before arranging events at which admission is to be charged, before running charity drives, and before involving themselves in the sale of any items. They should also have professional assistance before signing contracts or committing themselves to large purchases and should be required to file copies of all contracts. Certainly any contract carrying the signature of a college employee should receive careful scrutiny. Other services generally offered include selling tickets for group events, taking orders for yearbooks and other items, handling student insurance, and sometimes even cashing small checks. Standard deposit slips and payment order forms must be designed by each campus. All employees of student activities banks must be bonded, and the entire bank is subject to regular professional audit. The increasing amount of money being handled in student activities banks amid the heavy traffic of college offices, moreover, poses a substantial security problem that merits the attention of professional firms in this field. Many professional educators are presently unaware of the size of the funds expended.

SCHEDULING

A second general student activities administrative procedure, particularly useful for nonresidential colleges is the scheduling of reserved time for the cocurricular program. During this weekly or twice weekly period classes and other regularly scheduled college activities that would prevent student participation in the cocurricular program are not held, so that students will be free to meet with groups that they have chosen to join. The reserved time is equally helpful to faculty members, who use it as the occasion for departmental meetings, individual student conferences, and other work. Brooklyn College, for example, schedules these hours on Monday and Wednesday from noon until two P.M. throughout the academic year. (Sober and Mac Gregor, 1963)

Maintenance of central schedules of group activities in the student activities office, combined with publication of a noninstructional calendar will avoid group conflicts. Social rooms and other areas reserved for student activities may be assigned by the individual responsible for producing the central schedule. Groups should be encouraged to inform the office as early as possible of the appearance of prominent guests and other special activities likely to draw students away from regular programs. A student board may be established to resolve disputes and protect groups that have cleared dates and prepared programs from having these programs effectively destroyed by other organizations that plan competing agendas on short notice.

OFF-CAMPUS ACTIVITIES

A topic of controversy is that of student group off-campus activities, and particularly those activities in which the name of the college is used. Social groups usually file housing codes in which they commit themselves to certain standards of behavior. Violators of student-developed standards, individually and as groups, are subject to discipline. Friction between college social organizations and their neighbors in college communities has been a source of difficulty for generations.

Political and social action groups on many campuses, however, have recently become much more active off campus and have sometimes declined to delineate proposed off-campus behavior. The standard advocated is that of legality, it being argued that groups who break the law will be subject to its penalties. It is claimed further that student rights are impinged upon when student groups are required to list in their constitutions forms of off-campus behavior in which the group plans to engage. Double jeopardy is involved, it is said, when individual students are disciplined on campus for illegal activities committed off campus. This departure from traditional prerogatives of American universities has culminated in one case in students insisting that the college intervene in behalf of a student arrested during an off-campus student-group demonstration on the grounds that the student arrested was at the time engaged in a college activity.

Until rather recently some colleges denied students the privilege of forming campus chapters of entirely political organizations. This practice, now rapidly disappearing, may account somewhat for current extreme student views concerning privileges that they should have in using the college name. Some colleges are convincing the students to develop general codes of behavior which serve as standards and guidelines but which are not strictly enforced. Others are establishing uniform regulations covering political activities on and off campus, violation of which subjects the student and his group to disciplinary action. Still others are requiring individual student groups to list in their own constitutions the general categories of activity on and off campus in which the particular group intends to engage. Examples would be participation as a student group in primaries and general elections, fund raising, picketing, housing surveys and other studies, and so on. A small faculty-student committee prepared to meet on short notice may be authorized to permit the group to proceed with activities that had not been foreseen at the time the constitution was prepared until it can be regularly amended. Students who knowingly engage in unauthorized activities are subject to discipline.

The requirements of sound educational policy, possible legal involvement in the activities of student groups using the college name, and responsibility for students injured on school trips preclude granting a student club carte blanche authority to engage in all kinds of on or off campus activities. Common sense precludes an educational institution encouraging in the normal course of events activities that are not legal. Nor should the college compromise its obligation to discipline students who bring discredit to its name.

Within the framework of these rather moderate limitations, however, current practice suggests that student groups should be given the opportunity to combine learning and action in a wide range of off campus activities, the general categories of which have been agreed to in advance through consultation of students, faculty, and administrators. Wherever possible students should be encouraged in these activities to accomplish their objectives through meaningful and substantial service programs, opportunities for which can be found in virtually any community, or through educational programs, using direct agitation only as a very last resort and not as a primary part of the group's program.

GUEST SPEAKERS

Another area of student rights, formerly a center of controversy, is that of guest-speaker privileges of student groups. Some campuses have denied their facilities to communists or have had other provisions requiring the college to limit specific speakers or classes of speakers, frequently at the behest of state legislatures or boards of trustees. As a matter of policy it seems desirable to permit student groups the widest possible latitude in inviting speakers of all shades of opinion, and increasingly this practice is receiving support from educators, as well as judicial experts. In general, having permitted its facilities to be used for guest speakers, the college should permit them to be used by all guests student groups wish to invite. Exceptions would be cases in which the speaker's appearance would disrupt the regular educational process because of noise, the time scheduled, or some other substantial reason. Speakers under judicial consideration or who have been dismissed from the college may be instructed not to use the campus as the place in which to discuss these matters. Other rare, special situations are best handled through negotiation and persuasion in a general situation in which the students are permitted to invite whomever they wish. Should it appear that one or more campus groups are systematically abusing the guest-speaker privilege in some way, modifications of this basic policy can be developed then.

Student groups having guests should file informational cards in the student activities office well in advance, listing the name of the speaker, the organization he represents, the date on which he will appear, and other information that may be desired. These cards should be a prerequisite for the speaker's appearance. The college should not be in the position of being uninformed about guests using its facilities. Over a period of time, cards registering guest speakers often prove to be useful as research data.

STUDENT ELIGIBILITY

Student leaders, including all officers, chairmen of standing committees, representatives to the student council, and holders of major positions on student publications, should be required to meet a minimum standard of academic eligibility based upon performance during the semester or year before the one in which they are to hold office. This standard should be developed to meet the needs of each college, but is usually the equivalent of a *C-plus*. Eligibility should be determined by having the student file a card at the beginning of the semester in which he is to serve, which may be checked against the student's record. Other tests of eligibility sometimes used include the number of semesters of participation in student activities and the number of other offices held. In general students who are not eligible, academically or otherwise, should not serve. But this decision should be made following a counseling interview, and the director of student activities or dean of students should have authority to grant waivers in appropriate cases. A record of waivers granted to individual students should be kept to assist counseling these students in future semesters. In addition to eligibility cards, filing of program cards showing where student officers may be found at various times will expedite the work of the student activities office.

All students, whether or not they are officers, should be encouraged to maintain cumulative record cards in the office of student activities. These can be used after their graduation as an enrichment of their permanent records. The students may list memberships in individual groups, offices held, any honors won, and may also list part-time employment.

The entire matter of student eligibility should be approached within a flexible framework keyed to individual counseling. It may be in the best interests of some students to permit them, for a time, to hold offices for which they are not academically eligible. In other cases, a degree of strictness is indicated. The yardstick should be the contribution which this activity is likely to make to the academic success and personal growth of the individual concerned.

Awards

Although the problem of choosing awards winners is one of the more sensitive ones in student activities personnel work, the granting of such awards is a traditional ingredient in student activities programs. Awards are given as a mark of distinction, particularly for service, and are thought to raise morale. In recent years some colleges have reduced or eliminated the special award, but most do grant a key, a crown, or some other small emblem to student activities leaders. Sometimes these keys are granted simply on the basis of so many years of service or participation. On other campuses they are supposed to represent the attainment of an exceptional level of performance. Where length of service is the consideration it is possible to grant two levels of award (as silver and gold). Where excellence is the primary consideration however, it is best to have only one award.

Colleges granting special awards beyond the key or crown, usually at the request of civic organizations, alumni groups or business firms, find that the number of these awards tends to proliferate. It is difficult to resist agreeing to confer more awards in a situation in which some are already being given, and the prospective donors are frequently determined to be included. Since the winners are normally chosen by a faculty committee, the cost of conferring such awards in staff time can be rather substantial.

The importance of choosing winners appropriately is heightened by the fact that an award is often accompanied by a rather definite list of the winner's qualifications. The students involved, however, sometimes tend to consider certain positions (e.g., president of the student council) as assuring the holder of winning an award regardless of his performance or other attributes. Therefore, it is necessary that a college granting special awards for excellence in student activities periodically remind the students of the need for sportsmanlike acceptance of a decision which is a very subjective one. Some student leaders find not winning such an award a threatening experience and show almost a necessity to react in an immature way when they are not among the list of the winners.

Students should be discouraged at the outset from participating in leadership activities in order to win awards. While high standards must be maintained, the number of key awards should be sufficiently great so that winning one does not become a matter of excessive importance. The matter of accepting special awards with large monetary prizes not based on financial need is one that many colleges should restudy. Certainly a college not currently granting such special awards should think twice before beginning to do so. Student activities awards are commonly given out at a special dean's tea or other social event. This can be a most pleasant late spring occasion if the work of the faculty awards committee has gone well.

The Student Center

The student center (or union) movement in the United States has enjoyed tremendous growth since the Second World War, but actually began to develop around the turn of the century. The Association of College Unions was founded in 1914 at Cornell University, and many college unions were built during the 1920's. The role of the student union varies from campus to campus. In general it began as a social organization. Today the union usually serves as a recreational and social center but also concentrates on the development of at least one additional area of student life, frequently that of the fine arts and other cultural activities. Particular interest has been seen in programs related to student values. On larger campuses the student union may be a complex of several buildings rather than just one. Or there may be separate union buildings at various points on the campus. The designs for such buildings have become increasingly creative, and are of tremendous variety. Courses in the administration of union buildings are currently offered in several graduate schools of education.

Student participation in the management of the student center is frequently provided through separate policy and program boards. If a group of volunteers willing to contribute to some of the more mundane work can be developed, the possibility of future promotion to these boards can be offered to this group. Financing is usually arranged through a student fee, and a separate corporation with its own board of trustees or other governing board may be established. The problem of financial soundness is one of the most difficult ones facing the union. Other problems involve prevention of student management from slipping into the hands of a small clique and assurance that the program will be educationally sound but not so overly structured and professionalized that it lacks spontaneity and freedom.

Developing the Individual Group

Recognition of new groups should follow standard procedures agreed upon in advance and consistently followed. Many colleges grant to the student council the privilege of chartering new groups, sometimes subject to review by a faculty-student committee. In chartering new groups it is desirable to avoid duplicating the purposes of existing groups, and for this and other reasons an explicit written statement of the purposes of the new group should be required. In general it appears wise to permit the formation of any group that does not discriminate in its membership or advocate discrimination or illegal or violent actions. A group which is denied recognition because of its political or other attitudes will probably operate covertly in a way which can be more destructive of good order and more attractive to the immature mind than the group could possibly be in the light of day.

The group requesting recognition should submit to the student council or student activities office a form containing its name and purpose, a specified minimum number of prospective members, and the names of its officers and faculty advisers. Once this has been received, the group may be given campus space and other privileges for a limited time in order to prepare a constitution, secure additional members, and plan its activities. A model constitution available to all groups can assist the new group and assure the college that standard procedures will be followed in sensitive areas such as elections, handling of funds, amendments to the group's list of purposes, and so on. The model should be prepared by the student council in consultation with an appropriate faculty member or members. In the event that the new group's constitution is not forthcoming within a reasonable period of time, the group should be denied the use of campus rooms, publicity facilities, and other resources until this is accomplished.

Provision should be made for the establishment of various types of organizations. In addition to the long-term club or other organization, there should be a less structured but nevertheless well-organized research or study group and a special project group. A study group would be limited in the size of its membership, would not usually have meetings open to the general student body, and would function for a limited period of time to accomplish its research purposes. A special project group would organize on a short-term basis to accomplish some special purpose, such as a memorial program or support of a political candidate outside of regular party channels. Study groups and special project groups would have the advantage of requiring fewer members and a much more rudimentary constitution than other groups (a simple statement of purpose should suffice) but should be required as other groups to have a faculty adviser.

Simple but definite provisions should also be developed on each campus for the revision of student group constitutions. Such revisions should also be approved by the student council before they take effect. A permanent folder which will be a record of the life of the group should be maintained in the office of the coordinator of student activities or the dean of students. The folder should contain annual reports by the officers of the organization, perhaps countersigned by the adviser. Preparation of these reports should be the occasion for student evaluation of the group's work and for planning for the year ahead. The folder should also contain the group's constitution with any revisions, its membership list, lists of its officers, and programs or other items of special interest.

In working with individual groups a series of standardized forms will be of inestimable value in speeding group programs at a minimum cost in group time and college money. A form for recognition of new groups, a model constitution, and a membership list have already been mentioned. Other forms will be needed for registration of groups (names, addresses, and phone numbers of officers; meeting rooms and times; and signature cards for group treasurers and faculty advisers, if they are to countersign expenditures) and for publicity announcements. Larger colleges will reproduce for distribution lists of recognized organizations. Forms may also be desired for group cosponsorship of college events and to bring some order into the process of individual or group representation at off-campus conferences. Forms of the housekeeping or nuisance type may also contribute to tension free and economical procedures. These forms may be requisitions for audio-visual equipment, smoking permits, maps showing the campus and the location of its buildings, or other items for which a need is felt. A good form should be patterned to meet the particular program of one campus. It should be as simple as possible, easy to fill out, and should require only the minimum information needed. It should be attractively designed of standard size with consideration for permanence and ease of reference. A student activities form should be developed with student involvement and cooperation and should be continually reviewed to assure that it is still needed.

Larger student activities offices may wish to issue publications describing their programs. Priority should be given to the development of an annual brochure containing a calendar of noninstructional programs. Such a calendar will avoid scheduling of events during holidays or conflicting programs by two groups designed to appeal to the same audience. A bulletin of information listing college policies related to student activities is an important second aide. Beyond this, the college may wish to assist individual groups or associations of groups in the preparation of informational brochures about their programs for use with freshmen, new faculty members, alumni, and others.

Local associations of similar groups will logically form on each campus and on some campuses it may be desired to use these as the basis for the organization of the student council. Such organizations will include a college interfraternity council, a panhellenic association, and a house plan association. There may also be an association of academic clubs, religious groups, and political and social action groups. Of these, perhaps the academic club association is a currently emerging type that is most promising in terms of its potential for campus scholarly service. Associations sponsor leadership institutes, pool resources for common projects, standardize rushing and other procedures, and act as spokesmen for the individual groups. These associations should have constitutions, officers, and in other ways meet the same requirements as their member groups.

A truly surprising number of national student organizations also exist (apart from the individual national fraternities and sororities) for social organizations, student publications, student government, political activity, and for other purposes. Tremendous numbers of students are represented in these organizations. Members gain the advantages of a relationship with other college students; support for minimum standards and assistance with programs are usually also offered. The groups sometimes act nationally as spokesmen for their members. Membership in such organizations involves costs, such as attendance at national conferences, where failure to attend can mean that the college's participation is only nominal. Other hazards include the possibility that the organization may not be permanent, that it may become politically or otherwise oriented in a way which will not reflect the thinking of the students of the college, and that it may attempt to interfere in internal matters on its member campuses.

It is suggested that membership in such national organizations be at the discretion of the students, who must pay the costs, but that tangible evidence of value received be obtained annually in written form as a basis for consideration of continued membership. There should also be provision for periodic referenda among successive generations of students so that renewal of membership will not become automatic. Faculty and administrative involvement in the decision to join such an organization is also indicated by the fact that membership gives the national organization the privilege of using the name of the college, which is not the exclusive possession of its students. A typical campus might belong to the National Interfraternity and Panhellenic Conferences, the Association of College Unions, and one of the politically oriented groups.

Problems of Special Groups

PUBLICATIONS

Student publications have been a mainstay of the college cocurricular program for many years. With the passage of time, increasing stress has been placed upon quality and intellectual content, and in the modern program productions such as the humor magazine have decidedly declined. To the newspaper, the yearbook, and the literary magazine have been added journals devoted exclusively to the humanities and to the pure or social sciences. A good college publication should meet the same standards in terms of responsibility (though obviously not in terms of production) as any other publication. It must be accurate, first of all: The students given this vehicle for self-expression must perceive their traditional ethical obligation to check facts. Beyond mere accuracy in the selection and publication of material that is factually correct, the publication must have honesty: Its intentions must be constructive. Finally, the college newspaper should be fresh in its use of language and in what it says.

Perhaps, the most difficult of the problems faced in accomplishing these objectives is the perennial shortage of students who can write well and are able or willing to give the necessary time. A formalized annual search for such students by student editors and faculty advisers, possibly centered on English classes, should be given consideration as a method of meeting this need. A broad base of participation, rather than control of the publication by any clique, should be the objective. A second problem area is the content of the publication. Land mines in the road include ill-considered humor aimed at individuals and the printing of social gossip. Student newspapers have a tendency to lose balance in that influential students secure the printing of too much sports news or too detailed a summary of a favorite lecture or an intensive summary of every detail of the weekly meeting of the student council. Quarterlies devoted to the fine arts or other subjects can get similarly out of proportion. Other problems include the use of space and the layout of the publication in a way that is both pleasing and economical, and the matter of student reporters having access to and being mature enough to be able to handle privileged information which will provide the background information necessary to be fair.

Part of the answer to these problems lies in the selection of the leadership. Admission of many candidates to lower positions is the best assurance that there will be adequate choice as the organization promotes from within to the top positions. The editorship of a student publication has always been a sought-after, prestige position. Consideration has been given to the possibility of compensation for such positions, and many campuses do assist students at least by covering a part of their expenses. Systematic training of junior members is probably the best assurance of having fully prepared leadership.

The faculty adviser of a publication should work on the premise that the students given the authority to produce it will act responsibly. While the structure should permit prereading of manuscripts when the adviser feels that this is necessary, as a matter of policy in a well-established student publication, the adviser may feel that he should consult and suggest but not necessarily monitor. From time to time the quality of previous issues may require closer inspection of immediate future ones. Pressures upon the students of a special nature from off campus or substantial evidence that the editorial staff over the longer term has not been in support of the best interests of the college, might also suggest that prereading is required or some other measures needed. In general it is the college that is really the publisher of student journals, and it is the college that must assume final legal responsibility.

On many campuses, as has been indicated, policy for student publications is made by a faculty-student committee. Advertising is an area of frequent concern. Most campuses do not permit certain classes of advertisements. However, once the overall classification has been agreed upon (e.g., student travel) it is impractical except in occasional cases to check the reliability or other attributes of individual advertisers. The general policy of the publication, therefore, should be to accept all ads from within the approved category. All new publications should obtain approval from a student or other board so that there will not be a splintering or duplication of periodicals and a corresponding reduction of quality.

Religious Groups[1]

A second important area of college life has been that provided by the religious organizations. A notable series of revivals swept many campuses in the nineteenth century. Today, guidance for their members is provided

1. See also Chapter 14, Religious Counseling.

by the Newman Apostolate, the B'nai B'rith Hillel Foundations, and various Protestant organizations. Larger campuses or campuses on which there are large numbers of students from one faith have separate buildings serving as centers for members of these groups. Their services include religious observances, teaching of courses, counseling individual students, and service and social programs. Their work is sometimes coordinated by a council composed of members of all groups.

Academic Clubs

The academic club is a growth area in student activities in which many new individual programs are being combined with greater student participation. A large campus may have dozens of such groups, each supported in some way by the appropriate college department; they serve as a gathering place for students majoring in each field, as distributors of career information, as a supplement to the classroom program, and as spokesmen for students on matters of their department's curriculum. Many of these clubs in recent years have conducted outstanding individual and group research projects, sometimes with foundation grants. They also offer a social alternative and a sense of belonging to the student who may not have joined a fraternity or other group. Some academic clubs are linked to national professional or preprofessional bodies that offer prizes and in other ways encourage the work of campus chapters. Alumni working in various fields can also contribute to the efforts of campus undergraduate clubs in their profession.

One other recent development is the academic club association. This organization may act as the spokesman for the combined academic clubs; it may produce a newsletter or other publication designed to highlight club programs; it may sponsor subject matter conferences cutting across the narrow lines of individual club interests; it may offer workshops concerned with membership and other problems of individual groups; and in other ways it may generally serve to strengthen the total academic club program. It is wise to state in its constitution that this association will not be drawn into the national political and social questions which often occupy much of the time of campus-wide student councils or in other ways compete with that larger organization in matters not directly related to academic clubs.

Social Groups

Organized social groups date their origins on American college campuses from the eighteenth century. Frequently serving as literary societies, their earliest contributions were intellectual as well as social; they achieved growing prominence following the Civil War but encountered opposition because of accusations of secrecy and snobbishness. Further criticism stemmed from the tremendous personal consequences sometimes involved for the individual who was rejected by the Greek letter group of his choice. Gradually other types of college groups arose and began to fulfill some of the needs which once had been met only by the social groups. Amidst continuing doubts about the fairness and meaningfulness of some of these organizations, admission to the fraternity or sorority has continued to be a matter of great significance for many late adolescents.

What is the role of the modern fraternity, sorority, or house plan? Its social and recreational aspects, run at a high level, continue to be a worthy use of student time. But too often the social group's total program is limited to these areas. A common addition among men's groups is an elaborate intramural program. Encouragement for scholarship is another facet of social group life claimed for both men's and women's groups. While the claim may sometimes be more ritual than substance, it is true that academic achievement among members of social groups is often higher than achievement among the total student population. While this may be because the groups tend to admit the more attractive, alert students, an effective social group program can stimulate friendly academic rivalry among groups, sponsor tutoring programs, offer incentives for excellence in scholarship, enhance pride in the college, and otherwise contribute to an environment conducive to scholastic success. Service programs on the campus and in the community are also among the contributions of social groups. In counseling social groups, the author sometimes uses the existence of some service or other citizenship activity as a rough test of the health of the group. There are, of course, national men's and women's organizations devoted primarily to these activities. Perhaps the greatest raison d'etre of contemporary college social groups, however, is their contribution to human relations—learning to live with one's fellows—and to personal growth.

In recent years, some of the newer and better college dormitories have combined attractive lounge and study facilities for small groups with a better-supported, more orderly life than that of the hectic, disordered, and overcrowded fraternity house. Prompted to some extent by this, and also by other important factors, many social groups are carefully reconsidering some of the practices which have made them most vulnerable to criticism in the past. Rushing and pledging practices are chief among these. The concept of deferred rushing under which lower freshman at least would not be eligible to join social groups has received serious consideration on some campuses and has been tried with various results. The advantages of deferred rushing, if any, are uncertain; and the financial and other impact upon the groups can be a serious one, at least temporarily. Much wider success has met efforts to shorten other rushing and pledging practices, to simplify them and render them more constructive and fair. A coordinated rush committee of student members usually establishes uniform and sensible procedures in this area. The embarrassing juvenile pledging practices of another day have been substantially replaced with service activities, although continual faculty attention is needed to assure that good intentions are equalled in practice.

The tendency of many social groups to become excessively the domain of students whose aptitudes, interests, appearance, or other characteristics are always just the same should be resisted. Overt discrimination based on race or religion seems to have been largely removed from the charters of social organizations. But much remains to be done in an educational way to build groups that really offer the diversity that would logically emerge from fair play and good judgment, groups in which greatest happiness and personal growth can occur.

In addition to the Greek letter groups many colleges encourage the development of house plans. These are smaller, more easily started organizations with less formal trappings of tradition and ritual. Sometimes these groups do not perpetuate themselves but exist only through the college careers of a specific group. Nonresidential, they often do occupy smaller quarters for social and recreational purposes. They usually omit the pledging period entirely, admitting new students directly to full membership. A ceiling on total membership maintains the closeness of the group. It is not at all unusual for these organizations to be more vital and influential, and to have more prestige, than their older Greek counterparts.

Every campus having such social groups maintains an interfraternity council and a panhellenic and house plan association. These groups set standards, act as spokesmen for their constituents, and sponsor ambitious and expensive programs that would otherwise not be possible. At Brooklyn College, for example, preliminary thought is being given to the development of an intersocial-group federation or cabinet that would minimize competition and otherwise support the work of all three social group associations.

Apart from their programs, particularly important questions of college direction of social groups arise in the areas of membership (already discussed), business management, and housing. Social federations sponsor concerts involving thousands of dollars. Individual groups are employers, and purchase and occupy real estate. They may collect large amounts annually in dues. They should have the support and guidance of a trained faculty adviser in all of these endeavors. Particular attention of the adviser should be given to assure that the students receive fair value in making purchases and that they are not taken advantage of by more sophisticated business people. Another area of financial guidance is that of good taste and restraint in the tendency, especially of fraternities, to make purchases which are ill-conceived attention getters. One such small area of common extravagance is in the purchase of quantities of loving cups, statues, and other awards. Many other, more extreme wastes of funds by social groups could be listed on every campus.

The relationship between the college and the off-campus housing facility that will certainly be considered by the community to represent the college should be spelled out in a written housing code. Each facility should be required to develop and submit its own set of house rules for approval. The college should know the location of each of the groups using its name. These facilities should be visited periodically by the faculty adviser and should be open to him at all times. The individual house guide should answer questions about safety procedures and should include statements about what is to happen in the facility, when it is to happen (days and hours), how noise is to be controlled, where the students are to park, and how the facility is to appear and be taken care of. Every group should be required to meet minimum standards contained in the housing code it has filed, and the college should be able to suspend the group if this is not done.

The Social Affairs Board

On a large campus it is desirable to have a student board coordinate dates and programs for social events to avoid conflicts in scheduling. The work of this board should be supplemented where possible with the services of a trained counselor, experienced in planning social affairs, who can assist with budget and procedures. Together the board and the counselor can encourage a program of social events for all students, in addition to maintaining standards at dances only for members of organized social groups. A successful college social event is well planned. Key items are the budget, the date, the names of the students in charge, the general theme or purpose of the event, the place in which it is to be held, decorations, entertainment and refreshments. All of these items should be in writing. In general the large, impersonal dance has been replaced by smaller affairs, perhaps more elaborate than formerly, but with an emphasis on intimacy.

Each campus will need to develop its own measures safeguarding its students and assuring that excesses will not occur. The question of vandalism is a nation-wide one of deep significance; however, insistence upon faculty attendance, strict compliance with the law related to the consumption of alcohol, careful identification of those who attend, and a preference for events attended by couples rather than single students will improve the prospects for success. The practice of selling tickets at the door is decidedly less desirable than selling them in advance.

THE STUDENT COUNCIL

One of the great needs in college student activities at this time is for a new nomenclature that will clarify the misunderstandings and communications breakdowns resulting from the use of the term *student government*. Only slightly better is *student council,* which carries a more advisory tone but is closely linked to the secondary school. There are many areas of college life in which students can play an important role sharing in decision making; however, the idea that students should be encouraged to think of themselves as "governing" the college is fundamentally unfair to the undergraduate who has a right to expect honesty and frankness from professional personnel. The college has tremendous interests in its name and property and is responsible for administering its funds. The students have presented themselves to be educated and seek the credential the college offers. The cocurricular program is simply one of several teaching devices directed toward this end. The students frequently are minors, and will be at the college for only a short time.

What then are the tasks of the student council? A questionnaire distributed to members of the class of 1963 at Brooklyn College (Mac Gregor, 1963) asked the students, then seniors, to list two or three important functions that an effective student government might fulfill. The most frequent response was to convey student views to the college administration. Second most frequent was the suggestion that the student government should coordinate and develop student activities, particularly cultural exchange programs and other programs of an artistic nature. A third frequently mentioned purpose was the improvement of communication among students. Next, students suggested that an effective student government might be the voice of the students beyond the campus in community affairs. Betterment of faculty-student relationships was mentioned by some students, and sponsorship of social functions was indicated by others. In addition, twenty other possible purposes of student government were mentioned at least once. These included student welfare activities (e.g., insurance and group travel), building college spirit, raising funds for worthy purposes, a free tutoring service for college students, improvement of student dress, "control of the beatniks," assistance in orienting freshmen, and "protection of student rights." In all, twenty-seven distinct purposes or activities appropriate for student government were suggested.

In spite of the potential area of service for student government, on many campuses it is not an effective, legitimate expression of student wishes. Columbia College students, for example, voted in 1962 not to have formal student government at all, and since that time it has been replaced with an informal cabinet of student leaders who meet periodically with the Dean. The inadequacy of student government is a favorite subject for editorials in undergraduate newspapers on many campuses. One weakness of student government is lack of communication. The contribution actually being made is often not known or appreciated by the students at large. A second weakness is the dilemma of structure. Direct elections from the student body deteriorate almost universally into a situation in which a handful participate and the student government becomes the property of a fraternity or other group. So much energy and expense are frequently devoted to the election campaign that the winners are unwilling to contribute serious effort to service after they have won. The need to generate enthusiasm during the campaign prompts the creation and debate of meaningless issues on which nothing worthwhile can later be based.

A better alternative is election to the student government from interest groups, such as the clubs or other organizations. The students are acquainted with the candidates for whom they are voting. The winners have a constituency to whom they must report. There is no need for an expensive, disruptive, and sophomoric campaign. The attention of the student government is directed to the student group program, which probably should be its area of greatest influence anyway. The difficulty with election of student governments from student groups is that at first glance the structure appears less democratic than the direct election system and it is difficult to maintain campus support for it. Students seeking student government memberships, moreover, join groups primarily in order to acquire their seats, so that, unless care is exercised, the student government can still become the province of a special group.

A third weakness of student governments is in their members. It is natural that this activity should attract future lawyers and political science majors and that these students would be more effective in winning campaigns. To the extent that students from any one major area are overly represented, however, the student government is less equitable than it otherwise might be and its advice will be less well received by students and faculty. Students with aspirations for careers in government or public life also tend to involve the council in excessive debate over national questions. Unfortunately, these questions are not always of serious concern to all students, and the answers to them are generally beyond the capabilities of student government. The result is one of frustration and disillusionment.

It appears, therefore, that a new concept of student government is needed which would start with a new vocabulary, stress service, work and responsibility, develop statesmanship among students from many major areas, and communicate well with the students and faculty and enjoy their support. Such a student government should have a clear and reasonable budget of power, understood and agreed upon. The selection of members for this new student government would be the most important factor. Training for leadership in a democracy should not be superficial. Possibly underclassmen seeking to be student government members should take a required course about the organization of the college, the nature and perception of good leaders, discrimination between trivia and matters of lasting importance, and the other pitfalls which commonly hamper the student in the attainment of happiness and growth as a student government member. If only it were possible to obtain well-trained and favorably motivated candidates so that American college student government would not be in the embarrassing position of producing annually thousands of future political bosses of low repute, then the debate over the structure of student government could assume the secondary importance it deserves.

Citizenship and Service Activities

The many volunteer activities offered to college students are an alternative way of strengthening citizenship attitudes and developing worthwhile personal qualities. Virtually every campus has a blood drive and a campus drive fund; in recent years students have been increasingly aware of service opportunities off campus and determined to relate to community movements to assist the disadvantaged. Colleges should provide meaningful programs building upon this determination so that the experience will be a useful and satisfying one. Some colleges have had off-campus volunteer programs for many years. One of the older examples is Phillips Brooks House at Harvard University which has been providing volunteers for various areas of social work since 1900. A model today perhaps is the Columbia

College Citizenship Council. (Lee, 1965) Under the guidance of a student committee of fifty, Columbia men contribute their time to hospitals, schools, community centers, and government offices. Oberlin college students and faculty members travelled to Mississippi during a recent winter recess to rebuild a burned church there. Students at the University of Miami maintain a service organization on call twenty four hours a day for campus and other emergencies. Many other examples could be cited.

In conducting such programs, the college should lend support to assure the educational quality of the effort and to protect itself from possible legal entanglement in the event of injury or other difficulty. Students should be well oriented and trained in advance. There should be continuing meetings conducted by campus specialists to strengthen the program as it takes place. Prudence also indicates that off campus the students should be working under the auspices of a recognized private or public agency. This agency should be committed to supply on-site professional personnel to answer students' questions and offer supervision and other help. The activities must be meaningful so that the student is satisfied and is learning, but not so difficult that he is placed beyond his depth in a situation for which he has no solution.

Student Travel

Student group trips and charter flights are an expanding area of student activities counseling for the present affluent and idealistic college population. Student attendance at conventions and participation in work projects in other parts of this country and in other countries is common. Student travel for pleasure and learning is a burgeoning field. Under the favorable arrangements permitted by the United States Civil Aeronautics Board, campus charter flights may be organized of faculty members, students, and their immediate families. Various private national and international organizations also sponsor student travel. Each college should develop its own set of standard procedures governing student and faculty participation in trips. Questions to be resolved include who may organize such trips, under what limitations may students participate, how are the trips to be financed, and what is the legal and educational relationship of the college to them.

Student Activities for Graduate Students

An expanded program of service to graduate students may be needed in the field of organized student activities. This possibility has received greater attention because current disturbances on many campuses are led in large part by graduate students who apparently are dissatisfied with the culture and also with their own continuing student careers. Such activities should be quite different from those offered undergraduates in the degree of graduate student self-direction, in intellectual content, and in objectives. They should be less formalized, paying greatly diminished attention to the status of student leadership positions. A university with large numbers of graduate students is missing a potential area of educational achievement and may be playing an expensive and reckless game if it ignores the social and intellectual cocurricular needs of these students.

Dormitory Counseling

Counseling programs in college dormitories include aspects of personal and academic guidance and student activities work. In recent years, managers of student residence programs have given renewed attention to this phase of the student personnel program. One reason for this increased attention to dormitory counseling is the severe price of student vandalism. Prompted in part by the impersonal and austere dormitory living conditions resulting from the overcrowding which has been becoming more aggravated since World War II, student destruction has been a serious problem in an era of rising costs. In addition, personnel workers have become more aware of the educational opportunities inherent in dormitory living. These two factors have encouraged inclusion of seminar rooms, small lounges on each floor, libraries and study areas, music practice rooms, and many other improvements in new or redesigned buildings. Funds have been provided for student snacks and other informal social occasions designed to build a sense of participation and loyalty among small groups of residents.

These improved dormitory facilities have frequently been accompanied by the development of counseling staffs composed of graduate students. A common pattern is a ratio of counselors to students of about one to fifty, the counselor living on the same floor with the undergraduates. These counselors are instructed not to act as professional people but as slightly older brothers or sisters. It is best if such counselors serve for a maximum of three years. They usually receive a room and a small honorarium or salary, which may include meals. Graduate counselors are supervised by a professional worker who is readily available. The practice of employing married couples as counselors and giving them an apartment within or adjacent to the dormitory is perhaps less common than heretofore.

An almost standard procedure is to require freshmen in residential colleges to live in the college dormitories. Legal support can be found, however, for requiring all students to reside in college facilities. In practice, or because of the relative desirability of certain facilities, some colleges maintain dormitories largely for freshman only. Such dormitories are more difficult to control, and the process of assimilation into college life proceeds better if freshmen are mingled with upperclassmen. Most dormitory counseling programs, in part to combat this problem, seek to obtain expressions of student desires and to involve the students in the work and policy making of the dormitories through an elected student dormitory council.

Special restrictions upon women students residing in college dormitories are called for by parental expectations, the need to provide for the safety of women students, and by the fact that it is doubtful that traditional social attitudes regarding women have perceptibly changed. However, on many campuses, procedures have become more permissive in permitting women and men students alike to have guests of the opposite sex in their rooms during specific hours and under specific conditions agreed upon. Begun as experiments, these freer arrangements rarely are terminated and generally receive favorable reports from college personnel.

A problem of consequence which is frequently not settled satisfactorily is that of obtaining medical and psychological assistance for dormitory residents, especially during evenings and weekends. It is necessary to have counselors well versed in the procedures agreed upon in the event of emergency and to test the channels for obtaining assistance from time to time to be sure that they are still functioning. Will the emergency telephone number really bring help? How quickly?

Other problems which are of continuing or emerging importance are provision of housing for married college students, improvements in the social standards and educational quality of life in fraternity houses, and the relationship if any of the college to the housing of students seeking private rooms or apartments.

Student Loan Programs

General Considerations

As the difficulties of financing college education have increased and as the society in general and particularly the Federal government have faced the growing importance of higher education, student loan programs have proliferated. It has been estimated that the amount of money being borrowed annually by college students has increased twenty fold in the last decade and that loans outstanding have increased from about thirty million dollars to approximately eight hundred million. (Hill, 1965) A great variance exists from institution to institution in terms of procedures for granting such loans, student eligibility for loans, size of loans, amount of interest, and other matters.

Loan programs are established to assist promising but needy students in their quest for education. In the administration of the programs, responsible college officials are continually confronted with questions of the reasonableness of particular requests. Should a student seeking to become independent of parental control be granted a loan if parental income is so high that he would not normally qualify? To what extent should the funds of the college, or government funds being administered by the college, be hazarded through loans to students who, however needy, do not appear to be personally stable? These and countless other individual problems indicate the need for careful screening of written college records concerning applicants and for insistence upon filing of extensive information by the candidate. Such screening should be the work of faculty members, rather than members of the business staff of the college, intricately involved as it is with other aspects of the student's undergraduate and personal life. Conversely, the matter of collection of the loan and the exit interview related to collection are better assigned to members of the financial staff who are trained in business procedures. There also should be agreement between business and faculty staff members about information to be elicited from the student for future collection purposes and about the safeguarding of vital loan records.

The use to which students propose to put loan funds should be determined by having them file detailed budgets. The availability of funds at a reduced interest rate and the forgiveness feature for future teachers encourage some students to borrow for purposes which are not essential. Some students will be encountered who consider the privilege of borrowing Federal money at a low, subsidized rate of interest almost an inalienable right. Others hesitate to borrow under any circumstances, even though need for a loan may be indicated, and must be encouraged to make proper use of the borrowing privilege. In general the case load will be somewhat heavier in the fall semester than in the spring, so some slight shifting of personnel may be required for peak periods. While an interview is recommended, it may be necessary and possible to approve some loans on the basis of inspection of the student's record folder, application, and supporting parental information.

Sources of Loan Funds

Beginning in 1959, the Federal government began providing funds under the National Defense Education Act of 1958 with which participating colleges could make loans to needy students. Preference was intended for students with good records, especially in science, mathematics, engineering, and modern foreign language. Students who enter elementary or secondary school teaching enjoy a forgiveness feature in the amount of ten percent of the principal for each of a maximum of five years taught. By June of 1965, about six hundred million dollars had been made available to students through this program. (Hill, 1965) Interest at three percent starts one year after the student has completed his education. Once payments have started, the principal is usually repaid through a maximum ten year annual payment procedure. Financial need must be shown to qualify; a maximum amount of one thousand dollars a year may be borrowed, and the total may not exceed five thousand dollars.

An increasing number of states offer guaranty loan programs, usually at a somewhat higher rate of interest than the Federal program. Under these programs, the college screens the student and approves the loan which is then made by a bank after further checking and final state approval. Responsibility for collection is generally left with the bank, the state guaranteeing that there will be no loss after reasonable collection efforts have been made. Such programs are far less cumbersome for the colleges to administer but frequently carry a higher rate of interest for the student. In New York State the loans are subsidized so that the student is charged at the same rate as under the Federal plan. In most states time alloted for repayment is less generous than under the Federal plan.

A number of foundations and national religious or fraternal organizations also contribute to student loan funds or make loans to students directly. In addition, most colleges maintain a modest emergency loan fund administered informally and supported by student group activities or gifts from alumni. These loans are often used to tide the student over until a larger, more permanent arrangement can be made through one of the sources above. Such small loans are also helpful for students who would not normally borrow but who face a temporary emergency. Since the procedures are rather flexible and interest is not normally charged, many institutions have found it desirable to insist that these loans be repaid before registration for the semester following that in which the loan is made.

THE EMERGING PROBLEM OF COLLECTING STUDENT LOANS

The increasing volume in number and amount of student loans is a development in higher education of recent date. Some of the earliest loans under the National Defense Education Act have not as yet matured. The responsibility for collecting these loans, however, lies with the colleges that made them, and is proving to be the major proportion of the administrative cost of the loans. It has been suggested that the cost of collection may in some cases greatly exceed the amount of the loan. The concern of the Federal government about the collection of these loans has prompted the publication of a manual of collection procedures (Comm. on Labor . . . 1965) and even led to the consideration of establishing a central collection agency.

Colleges making loans should protect themselves by making very sure that the student does understand that he is making a loan, and that it will have to be repaid. One simple procedure would be to have the student file a written proposed schedule of payment. If the college is going to make loans, moreover, it should be sure to acquire standard collection information including such items as names and addresses of siblings, employers, and friends; bank references; and other financial information not usually found in student records. The student's plans and obligations should then be reviewed in a substantial and well-recorded exit interview. Changes in the Federal legislation have been proposed which would make the annual payments permitted only at the option of the college and that would reduce the grace period to six months following graduation. Such measures would also increase the facility of collecting loans made under the auspices of state or private programs.

Staffing for Student Activities

Questions of staffing a student activities organization have, in general, been subordinate to the practical reality that colleges have not been willing to allocate sufficient numbers of substantially qualified professional people to this area. Student activities staffing has consisted chiefly of either the recent young graduate lingering nostalgically at his alma mater or the low-ranking career individual with credentials deficient in a manner preventing his entrance into the higher circles of academic life. The folly of inadequate student activities staffing in numbers and quality of personnel has manifested itself with increasing urgency in the fields of student rights and the declining standards of behavior in social organizations. Recognition of the need for intelligent and well-trained colleagues on substantial blocks of assigned time and of the need to accord adequate prestige to this work has brought within the past few years a significant trend toward quality.

The ideal Student Activities Counselor would be a scholar, trained in a discipline, or an exceptionally well-trained generalist. His specialty could either be student personnel work or one of the traditional academic fields. As a faculty member he might teach one course and would also contribute to the research, publication, and other scholarly endeavors of the institution. As a matter of vocational interest, he would have a long term commitment to student activities seen as a substantial part of the program of learning of the college. He would enjoy the same opportunities for advancement available to other colleagues. The current shortage of personnel has resulted in the prevalence of the Masters degree as the educational requirement for work in this field. However, those institutions requiring the Ph.D. for tenure and promotion to higher rank should make the same demands of student activities personnel, offering appropriate monetary, status, and intellectual incentives to reduce turnover.

A large organization would seek a variety of backgrounds in its student activities staff. In selection, primary attention should be given to the quality of the training and the skill and experience of the applicant rather than to knowledge of a seemingly appropriate subject area. A psychologist developing a leadership program may make of it a needlessly intensive therapy situation; a social scientist may involve the student government in endless wrangling over the niceties of political structure; what is needed is an individual with judgment and dedication rather than training in any one specific field. And, as in selection of staff for other fields, traditional orientations should be reconsidered and generally discarded in the light of the changing world. The author, for example, was temporarily rather surprised when in a recent year the Interfraternity Council officers readily expressed willingness to accept a woman as Adviser to College Fraternities. In areas such as this, students will frequently be far ahead of their older colleagues.

The ability to persuade students and to win their affection and loyalty is particularly helpful. Student activities counseling proceeds in a difficult situation in which the counselor's options for action and authority are extremely limited on the one hand by the students' conception of their rights and privileges, and on the other hand by the College's expectations of quality. Patience, the ability to work slowly but persistently toward a given goal, and the capacity to work well under continuing stress are essential qualities. While dedicated to service, the student activities counselor must sometimes be a good gambler in his daily work situation.

To what extent should students be involved in the selection of the student activities staff? Here is a field in which they will feel that they have a special province. A reasonable approach appears to be a maximum informal involvement in the procedures of selection without in any way compromising the structure which provides for faculty appointment of their peers. Wherever possible, for example, candidates should by all means be introduced to student leaders. Offering the candidates tours of the campus, inviting them to stay for lunch, and a variety of other semi-social situations presents opportunities in which students may gracefully be given previews of those under consideration. All candidates may be described to students, although candidates' confidential records may not ethically be shared with them. Progress reports about the status of reference checks and other matters should be made available. In general, the students must feel that they are involved in some meaningful way in the selection if it is expected that they will accept the winning candidate. A counselor who is wanted and for whom the students feel some enthusiasm will have a tremendous advantage at the outset. Placing the candidate briefly in some fair relationship with the particular group of students involved may give the selection committee quite a valuable indication of the candidate's appropriateness for a given position.

Some colleges are experimenting with situations in which students interview in a formal way, usually in the presence of faculty members, candidates for student activities positions before their employment. Situations may also be found in which students serve as actual members of committees responsible for the appointment of staff members. Careful consideration of matters of policy, however, should precede such commitments. Can the students function intelligently in this role if they are to be denied access to the confidential information on the basis of which an equitable decision must be made? If they are to participate in selection, should they not be involved in tenure and promotion? If the students are to be substantially involved in the structure for the selection of paid student activities counselors, and if these counselors are to have full status equal to other members of the faculty, should not the students be involved in the hiring of geology, biology, and history professors?

A few miscellaneous thoughts need to be mentioned in conclusion. First, the leader or administrator of the student activities program bears a heavy responsibility for the educational quality, the good order, and the enrichment of campus life. Such a task requires the full-time services of a person of excellence. Second, the student activities office is frequently a depository for a number of routinized tasks which, though potentially intricate, can safely be delegated to a high level clerical person under the supervision of a professional person. As part of the process of upgrading a student activities staff, therefore, it would be important to study the work assignments to be sure that maximum use is made of workers at each level. Third, as increasingly elaborate and expensive programs develop, and in view of the increasingly litigation-prone and civil liberties-conscious society that is emerging, the services of an accountant and of an attorney as part-time consultants directly available in the student activities office would be a tremendous asset. Finally, the problem of inbreeding is especially difficult in student activities where recent graduates are relied upon. Their undergraduate associations will give them an initial advantage but may ultimately hamper their effectiveness. A variety of staff from different geographical, social, and undergraduate backgrounds with different specialties will be the most precious resource of any student activities program.

REFERENCES

Bakken, C. J. Student rights as seen by a lawyer-educator. *Coll. Stud. Personnel*, 1965, 6 (3).

Brubacher, J. S., & Willis, R. *Higher education in transition.* New York: Harper, 1958.

Committee on Labor and Public Welfare, Subcommittee on Education. *National defense education act of 1958, as amended by the 88th Congress.* Washington: U.S. Senate, 1964.

Committee on Labor and Public Welfare, Subcommittee on Education. *Report on collection of national defense student loans.* U.S. Senate. Washington: U.S. Govt. Print. Off., 1965.

Coulton, T. E. A *city college in action.* New York: Harper, 1955.

Goodhartz, A. S. (Ed.) *A commitment to youth.* New York: Bookman Assoc., 1960.

Higher Assistance Corporation. *Manual of purpose and procedure; guaranteed student loans.* New York: Author, 1964.

Hill, W. W. *An analysis of college student loan programs.* New York: United Stud. Aid Funds, 1965.

Johnston, N. (Ed.) *In loco parentis.* Philadelphia: U.S. Nat. Stud. Assoc., 1962.

Keeton, T. Crazy like parents. *Antioch Notes*, 1965, 42, No. 4.

Lee, C. B. The Columbia College citizenship program. *J. higher Educ.*, 1965, 36 (4).

Mac Gregor, A. Our graduates speak out, a report on the class of 1963. Unpublished report, Brooklyn Coll., Dept. of Stud. Serv., 1963.

Mueller, Kate H. *Student personnel work in higher education.* Boston: Houghton Mifflin, 1961.

Sober, Margaret E., & Mac Gregor, A. Club hours at Brooklyn College. *Nat. Ass. Stud. Personnel Admin.*, 1963, 1 (1).

Stroup, H. *Toward a philosophy of organized student activities.* Minneapolis: Univ. of Minn. Press, 1964.

U.S. Department of Health Education and Welfare. *Manual of policies and procedures, National Defense student loan program.* Washington: Govt. Print. Off., 1964.

Williamson, E. G. *Student personnel services in colleges and universities.* New York: McGraw-Hill, 1961.

Chapter 9

Placement Counseling

ROBERTA BAKER

The College Placement Office

Rashdall (n.d., p. 108) complained in his history of medieval student life, "The brilliant pictures which imaginative historians have sometimes drawn of swarms of enthusiastic students eagerly drinking in the wisdom that fell from the lips of famous masters have perhaps somewhat blinded us to the fact that the motives which drove men to the university exhibited much the same mixture and much the same variety as they do now." The universities in the Middle Ages and later served an intensely practical purpose: they opened the doors to the professions, the clergy, the law, and medicine. Colleges and universities still open the door to the professions, and now to the world of finance, merchandising, scientific achievements, and many others as well. A student, however, needs assistance in finding the doors that will open to the particular combination of specific or generalized education and talents he has developed in his progress through a liberal arts or specialized curriculum. In order to look efficiently for the proper doors, he needs placement counseling, a product of many images—usually projections of various people associated with or dependent on a college.

First of all, and most importantly, what does a student expect from placement counseling? Initially, he probably expects the placement counselor to get him a job, one that pays well and is interesting. On the other hand, some students expect little or nothing from placement counseling

Roberta Baker is Assistant Professor, Department of Student Services; and Assistant Dean of Students (Career Counseling and Placement Center), Brooklyn College of the City University of New York.

because they do not know what types of services are available. Some may never have heard of or needed help from the placement office. Still others may have developed an antipathy to counseling of any kind and may prefer not to seek help from placement counseling. This last, the individualist, must be left to his own ingenuity, the assistance of friends, relatives, personal contacts, commercial agencies, and any other sources he can find. The student who uses placement counseling services correctly sees them as an extension of his education, a preparation for his entry into the world outside school, and a counseling arm of the college—not an employment agency. Additionally, there is the consideration of what the students' parents expect from the placement office. Parents have the right to expect solicitude and consideration for their children from the placement function in both public and private institutions. The most obvious reasons for this right are that the school stands in loco parentis and that the parent is a taxpayer or a supporter of the institution through tuition or endowment dollars. This surely gives him the right of expectation, if not that of involvement and interference. (The mother who calls the placement office to find out why her son has not been seen in recruitment interviews is the well-known illustration.)

A variant form of expectation comes from the placement officer's faculty colleagues. This source ranges from the professor who seeks a summer position for his brilliant son attending another institution to the faculty member who is unaware of the purpose, function, or existence of the placement office. On some campuses, faculty members of several departments serve as part-time placement counselors. This is indeed desirable, especially when these faculty members represent different disciplines, varied work backgrounds, and current contacts with the business, industrial, and governmental communities.

Alumni also often make demands of the placement office. Where staff, budget, and space allocations of the placement office permit, alumni are welcome to return or write for assistance in relocation, job seeking, or job changing. On the other hand, alumni can often be of service to the institution by providing entry positions in their firms for recent graduates. Naturally, they expect the placement office to refer attractive and well-educated students for employment—at least as well educated as they had been when they were graduated.

In its turn, what does the college administration expect from the placement office? Ideally, it expects a competent counseling unit which assists students in formulating job campaigns and makes the proper type of job referrals and makes other types of counseling referrals when necessary.

It should expect a smoothly running, efficient administrative unit which serves as liaison between the academic world and the world of business and industry. The placement office should endeavor to promote intra-college relations and public relations off campus. In doing this, it can be expected to prepare reports, statistics, and facts about where students have gone and what they are doing. The wise administration also can look to the placement office for realistic advice in curriculum planning.

Preparation

The references listed at the end of this chapter comprise some of the professional literature which prospective or currently involved placement counselors should read, review, and check for effective counseling. The conscientious placement counselor is also conversant with the daily news reporting of the geographic area that most strongly influences the employment of his students. This means reading the newspapers with financial pages, trade journals of firms employing a large number of graduates from the school, and government publications. Keeping abreast of what is happening on the national and congressional fronts can also mean a great deal to the students the placement office is trying to help. Another important publication for the placement officer to read and display prominently is the alumni magazine of the school, of which some universities may have several for the different colleges of the school.

What the unsophisticated student should be advised to read to become better acquainted with his goals is a related problem. Digging through the multiplicity of *how to* books, pamphlets, and articles can be discouraging to both college students and alumni. The subject of some articles is fairly obvious from reading the title; for example, The National Commission on Safety Education's book *Careers in Highway Safety* would obviously interest students of highways, safety, transportation, or public transport. But the liberal arts student who is investigating a broad number of areas and subjects is faced with a problem of selecting articles and books to read that can seem almost insurmountable. In the first place, many of the books in the field are designed for high school students. Furthermore, there are very few, if any, college placement offices which can afford to purchase and house the many new publications that appear on the publishers' lists daily.

One way to assist the student in solving this problem is to refer him to the list of professional associations in *Placement Services for Personnel in Higher Education*. He can probably also find other sources on his own. A highly recommended book for both counselors and students is Allan Rood's

(1961) *Job Strategy*. At times, a brochure, pamphlet, or booklet specifically tailored to the interests and needs of a particular institution's students can be best. This need not be too elaborate, but it should be interesting, provocative, intriguing, and down-to-earth to capture and stimulate the student's interests. Attending college is a reading occupation, and for most students, unless some immediate reward can be earned from the venture, reading is usually limited to classroom texts, areas of special interest, and supplemental readings in the library. Consequently, attempts to help the student help himself must arouse his interest and show him some promise of reward.

The student, as well as the placement counselor, has homework to do in starting to solve his problem. It is, perhaps, too pretentious to label the student's situation as a problem; although it can mean a step into the unknown for some students, it is for many the logical next step. The student, especially in urban areas, may have attended elementary, junior high, senior high school, and undergraduate college in the same community. While he may not leave one geographic area to assume his role in the outside world, he does enter a different level of maturity. This is true even of the student who has the intermediate step of a prep school and college away from home. The new world may be less competitive than the academic one, but it may well be more thwarting in different ways: It demands decision-making ability and moves a great deal faster; it encourages individual, personal initiative in some instances and in others restraint and forbearance; it may be paternalistic, but it may be cut throat. In addition, it may ask fewer or more hours of work than school did; it may depress the individual or exhilarate him. In any event, it is different from the school world of regimentation and youthful freedom, of authority figures and subordinates, of dispensers and receivers of knowledge.

Perhaps an even greater change is demanded, however, of those who do not leave the school milieu. Standards of maturity and wisdom that can truly be a challenge are expected of those who progress through graduate training and return to teach, lecture, or do research in a college setting. This can be evident in the first teaching positions of young, inexperienced elementary schoolteachers.

Reaching the Public

At what stage does the placement office try to interest and intrigue the college student? A better question might well be: When does the placement office *not* try to interest the students in the college? The stimulating of healthy self-interest in their futures should start during freshman week. A continuous film showing of the College Placement Council's "Where Do I Go From Here?" (see Appendix B) may be used to expose the entering student to the facilities and services available through placement. An invitation to faculty members to attend may result in positive awareness of available services on a different level. The placement counselor or one of his staff can also volunteer to explain the services of placement at a freshman class meeting, although this may not be feasible in some schools because of the size of the class, scheduling difficulties, and other factors. Additionally, some form of attractive registration handout describing the services of the placement office may be effective and helpful.

The primary purpose of publicizing the placement office with the freshman class is to acquaint the student with one of the pedestrian and prosaic services of the placement office, the counseling of students about their responsibilities to themselves, their studies, their college, the community, and the prospective employer when they seek and obtain part-time jobs while in full-time or part-time attendance at college. There are almost as many reasons for wanting or needing to work while attending college as there are students seeking work. Among the most common are the following:

1. Need for money for living expenses or tuition.
2. Need for independence from parents.
3. Need to assist at home.
4. Saving for graduate school.
5. Saving for marriage.
6. Reluctance to accept any more money from parents.

Another reason for many college students' needing to work, a real as well as a good reason, is the need to support a car and its required insurance.

Some colleges discourage the freshman student from attempting the quite difficult task of adjusting to the regimen of higher education at the same time that he undertakes a time-consuming job; there seem to be none that prohibit it absolutely. Some colleges view part-time work orientation as part of the counseling process and part-time jobs are an integral part of the placement office. Other colleges assign this function to the personnel or other office, usually under the dean of students. Where the function is fulfilled by the placement office, in like manner, part-time clerical work, laboratory assisting, dining room or kitchen work, and other student-aide types of work on campus are often handled by the placement office. In some instances the placement office performs a follow-up function in evaluating each student's performance on the job from written comments and observations received, even making this job evaluation a part of the student's permanent record folder. Such evaluations can be particularly helpful to the student and the placement counselor at a later date when the student is looking for a career position.

With the government's increased interest in improving opportunities for disadvantaged and underprivileged college-age youth, many placement offices are welcoming the chance to assist in the sponsored employment on and off campus of students who would without this assistance have little opportunity to attend school. The cooperation of the institution and the federal government, which underwrites the major financing, is opening up opportunities that should result in benefits to the individual student, to the institution, to the community, and to the society as a whole. These supervised programs are administered autonomously by the colleges. It is not unlikely that an institution's participation in the governmental projects will be made a requirement for participation in loan projects and other financial assistance programs of the government. In many cases, the application for, the handling of, and the accounting for these funds are the responsibilities of the placement officer supplemental to his counseling responsibilities.

In addition to the government's increased interest, private foundations have found it worth while to promote the higher education of young people who might otherwise not have the incentive or assets. These projects often require the cooperation of the placement officer and his staff. For example, a foundation decides to support a two-year 100,000 dollar pilot project to attempt to find out the best way to encourage and motivate students who would normally not attend college. In the course of the project, the foundation pays all school and tutoring expenses for the youngsters and gives them a small allowance of eight dollars per week while in attendance. The placement officer may find that he has the responsibility of assisting these youngsters in trying to locate part-time work as well, which can present a particularly delicate counseling job. Because of financial need, the students' parents may object to their being in school at all, while the students may object to the type of menial part-time work which alone is available to them in the outside world because they have no saleable skills. Their attitudes may need bolstering with positions of some status. To meet this need, assistance from the various college departments may be requested in placing the students in student-aide jobs within the college. Communication with firms outside the college may also find employment for those students who require full-time work while in attendance at college. To accomplish satisfactory results, however, expert and skillful counselors must be available in other places besides the placement office.

Tutoring

The placement office in some institutions affords preprofessional training for exceptionally able students in the form of tutoring services to the community. Students who have demonstrated to the placement counselor that they are eager to work with less able students or those with learning difficulties can, in fact, be excellent emissaries to the community and receive in return valuable experience. Their attitude and talents as creditable representatives of the institution to the community must be appraised by the placement counselor first; then their ability and competence in the subject matter must be verified by the various departments of the college. Approval should be restricted to those students who have had at least an advanced elective course in their discipline and an excellent grade point average. Referrals may then be provided through the placement office.

Students with tutorial ability can earn money considerably in excess of the usual paid rate of part-time college workers. The need for this type of tutoring and referrals depends on the size of the community, the accessibility of public transportation or the number of students who own cars, the pressures within the community for academic excellence, and the reputation of the college in the community. An example of the wide range of educational opportunity afforded is met by a placement office in the New York City area for a tutor in remedial reading for a thirty-five-year-old longshoreman who, because of traumatic experiences as a child, had never learned to read. Such preprofessional training is also excellent for student teachers who wish to add individual instruction to their experience.

Legal Implications

Other problems may arise in connection with work and placement of college students. Some states require adolescents under 18 or 16, depending on the state laws, to obtain working papers to assure society that their work is not dangerous or harmful and that employers are treating them fairly. With the admission age of college students decreasing each year, as it seems to, the placement counselor must be conversant with federal and state labor laws and with any special regulations or exceptions of his local area. Knowledge of the cultural mores of the college community is also helpful. One college placement officer received a call from a prospective employer who stated quite politely, but emphatically, that he was interested in employing a student from the college, but he would much prefer it if the applicants for the position would come for the interviews without their mothers.

Knowledge of hazards to part-time student workers is also a responsibility of the placement officer. He must be prepared to provide appropriate counseling if a student somewhat hesitantly tells him that she had worked as a receptionist in an office for three days when her employer made unwelcome advances and invited her to the mountains for a weekend before she fled. The placement officer must be prepared to act if a student reports that, from a placement office job referral, he worked for a firm for a week and a half, was fired with some vague excuse, and has received only promises but no actual pay. In these cases, he should know the applicable laws and agencies and an acceptable method of handling the situation. Similarly, he must be prepared to investigate complaints about students and their actions and to counsel them.

Other Duties

Some placement officers have the responsibility of hiring and testing the skills of applicants for clerical positions within the college. Depending upon the size of the institution, this can place quite an onerous and time-consuming burden upon the placement officer. This also may leave him exposed to the vagaries of office politics, as well as many and conflicting pressures from different administrators of the college. In conjunction with placement in many colleges, the counselors have found it expedient and helpful to include aptitude or other testing within their scope. Some placement counselors are psychological counselors in other areas of the college, and oftentimes these duties are inextricably linked. Some colleges, on the other hand, have separate testing bureaus or offices, the privilege being given to the placement counselors to request the administration of tests to students. The results are returned to the counselor for interpretation with the student. Counselors must be extremely judicious in administering tests to some students, because a student will frequently request a battery of aptitude tests as if he were going to a computer for answers to his career and job problems. This type of student must be made aware that aptitude testing can provide only limited assistance in the process of learning what one wants to do with one's working life. On the other hand, aptitude tests as an adjunct to counseling can, if skillfully used, help in placing the student. (See Chapters 4 and 10 for further discussions.)

Transfer Students

There is another group of students whom it is wise for the placement officer to anticipate, if he can locate them. These are the students who have transferred to his institution from other colleges or universities and who may require a little extra help in their adjustment to the new college. Some of them may not be aware of all the expenses involved in the new school. Some may have underestimated the living costs of the new institution and be forced to seek work to meet these living expenses. In addition to the usual counseling given to transfer students, information about the placement office counseling services should be made available to them immediately.

Cooperation with Clubs

One way of reaching students and helping them establish a relationship with the placement office is to volunteer the services of the placement officer or his assistant to orient academic clubs on campus to the use of the office and its connections with the world outside. In some instances, fortunately, this is not necessary because the club advisor to the academic club is even more knowledgeable about the requirements within his field in the world outside the college campus than the placement officer. It is then that the placement officer has the pleasure of consulting the faculty advisor for information and help in counseling students in that field. On the other hand, an academic department may have been unable to develop rapport and contacts with firms and agencies, sometimes by reason of the very nature of the field or discipline. In this case, the placement officer should be delighted to speak to the academic club involved, to set up a mock interview for a club meeting, or even to bring a comprehensive listing of jobs available for members of that particular club. He may even be able to assist the club in setting up its own specific occupational files for use by its members, or he may help the club make arrangements for speakers at club meetings.

Career Conferences

In addition to setting up occupational files, an academic club or group of clubs may be interested in cosponsoring a career conference. The career or job conference may last any amount of time—an hour or a day. Usually, however, if time is spent in planning a good program it is desirable to allow at least a full hour for presentations of various types with time for questions and answers. When a number of clubs join with the placement office in sponsoring a program, however, it is often wise to plan a full-day affair with displays and experts in attendance to answer questions for the entire time. Examples of such programs would be "Careers with Uncle Sam," with the political science and history clubs, a panhellenic sponsored meeting on "Unusual Careers for Women in 1970," or a modern language clubs conference on "Careers for Language Majors." Cosponsorship with the placement office should mean that the students serve as hosts and hostesses to the visiting speakers, perhaps at a luncheon, serve possibly as chairman of the conference, and assist with the publicity for the program. It seems desirable for conference speakers to be drawn from the business or industrial communities outside the immediate academic one. It is generally true that the expert or authority is from out of town. Since competition for potential audiences is fierce on most campuses, planning as far in advance as possible is advisable. Even so, the unlooked for may happen. One placement director found a long-planned career conference scheduled to compete with a more recently promoted John F. Kennedy Memorial Library Drive. The career conference attendance was predictably cut quite severely.

Dropouts

Many placement counselors find themselves faced with the problem of assisting students who are required for financial, family, or other reasons to withdraw from school either temporarily or permanently. These students are required to seek full-time employment to support themselves or to help at home. Some of them will attempt full-time work and part-time attendance at an evening school. Other students will be school dropouts because they have not been able to make the grade academically, for whatever reasons. How does one help these young people, and for how long should they be permitted to use the services of the placement offices? The answer to the last part of the question depends, of course, on the philosophy of the college placement office and the college administration and the amount of time available for counseling students who are not currently enrolled in school. Certainly, some effort should be expended in their behalf. The answer to the first part of the question depends, too, on the routine and administrative procedures of the placement office. The students should be given supportive counseling, as many actual job referrals as they can qualify for, assistance in preparing for interviews, a chance to peruse occupational literature, and an open door to the placement office, especially in emergency cases. Some of the most rewarding experiences for placement counselors can come from assisting these students. If the placement office has compiled a list of free placement agencies in the vicinity, this too can be helpful. Advice in the use of commercial placement agencies is warranted at this time, and information should be given such students about the applicant's rights and privileges in using these agencies.

Personal and Societal Images

A group of students who will probably require special handling and more than average counseling time includes the older or mature women who have returned to college after interruptions for marriage and family. Each college will have a varying number of these students, depending on how much encouragement they are given when applying for admission or readmission. The student may have no skills or marketable training for part-time work, and this is probably not what she wants. If widowed or divorced, she is likely to be the main support, emotional and financial, of her immediate family and may well be burdened with debts. On the other hand, she may have a husband who earns a comfortable living and wants her to indulge her hobbies. Whatever the reason for her return, and there are many, she is normally serious in her pursuit either of knowledge or a vocational goal, although not realistic about her experiences, capabilities, or marketable assets in the business world. She may not realize that, while she resides in a state that has passed certain antidiscrimination laws, she may face covert discrimination in some businesses because she is a woman and because she is older than the usual graduating senior. These prejudices must be faced honestly, and it is to be hoped, with a sense of humor, and the determination to try just a little harder. Anyone seeking advice about solutions to individual problems should review the material in public and college libraries, as well as occupational files in placement offices and government publications. There is much available. A good place to contact the older female college student is through her social organization. There is usually one on each campus, depending on the number of such students enrolled at the school. The mature woman has extremely valuable qualities to contribute to work, and should be encouraged to develop them.

Prejudice and discrimination enter into placement in various open as well as covert ways. Fortunately, the most obvious prejudice, that against Negroes, seems to be fading. It may even be developing into a reverse type of prejudice, requests coming from firms especially for qualified Negroes. Of course, each placement office has several types of special requests (e.g., in New York City, the requests for Spanish-speaking interviewers for house-to-house surveys). Job orders expressing selectivity of one sort or another range from the conscientious director of a project settlement house who needs a mature, Negro, married mother with typing speed of 50 words per minute and stenography speed of 80 words per minute to work with unwed teenage Negro mothers to the telephone call for a part-time stock boy who cannot be a Negro. (The phone call was recorded by a Negro student aide in the placement office.) This latter type of request is fortunately becoming rarer.

As each college has developed an image among employers and the governmental officers who hire the products of the college, so have some firms and agencies acquired an image among the placement officers who send students to them as applicants. Some businesses are associated with the informal, unvoiced, and unconfirmed idea that they will employ only American-Irish Catholics from the County of Cork, while others are thought to prefer Sicilian-Americans or some other ethnic group. Even government agencies are not untainted with this type of grapevine gossip. Certainly, much of it is an undeserved carryover from obsolete policies. It does, however, affect counseling techniques and may reinforce a desire to protect some students from rejection.

Even though every firm and agency wants to hire the best young men and women produced by each college, what is the best to one company may not be the best for another. This is indeed fortunate. If a recruiter for an accounting firm will spend time only with students in the upper tenth of the class or those who have *B* or better averages, where do the students go whose grades may have suffered because of illness or work (for experience or other reasons) or faulty early career goals? Where does the would-be doctor go whose overall average has been hurt by a lack of language aptitude and an inflexible college language requirement, and who is now unacceptable for a medical school? This student needs counseling, as does the C student.

If a college or university grade index is skewed because of heavy competition among the students, because of college policy about grades, or because of the faculty's insistence on some type of arbitrary standards, the students from this school may not stand up too well in job competition with students from other universities. How then does a recruiter from a business firm or public accounting agency make an evaluation of the graduates of different colleges? How does he choose among them? Study of the performance records of graduates of different schools may be the best answer. The standards of a school may change over a period of five years or so, however, and the calibre of the faculty and the students may improve over that same period. In that case, of course, other criteria will be applicable.

Senior and Graduate Recruitment

Recruiters are the business or government representatives who visit college campuses during the recruitment season to conduct brief interviews, administer tests upon occasion, and do the preliminary screening of baccalaureate graduates, Master's degree graduates, and Ph.D. candidates who are seeking positions. The recruiting season usually extends from mid-October to mid-May, except that in those schools with only one graduation the season is usually limited to the spring. It is important to note here that an increasing number of graduates are continuing their education with graduate or professional work of some kind. Their reasons for this include the reluctance to leave the security of the academic world, reluctance to enter the armed services, genuine desire for further knowledge, recognition that further education is necessary for advancement within a profession, and indecision about what to do with their futures. Some undergraduate schools are now discovering that at least 70 to 80 per cent of their graduates plan to continue their education immediately upon the granting of the undergraduate degree. This does not mean that *all* of the top 70 per cent of the class go on for further work. The students who are in the market for jobs after four years in college occupy a continuum within the grade range of the graduating class: included will be a few of the best students as well as some of the poorest.

Recruiters may be personnel people whose job is to promote college relations or to hire new employees on all levels, as well as to handle union problems and governmental red tape within the company. One top-level company representative, for example, interviews (or rather supervises interviews of) 25,000 applicants per year. Among the recruiters are engineers, mathematicians, accountants, chemists, and other specialists among the sciences and business. All of them are people knowledgeable about their firms. Almost all of them are willing to serve as extensions of the counseling services of the college. In many cases, they may give the student practical advice and help in seeking jobs. Most of them are competent, interesting, and able speakers, and many of them are excellent public relations representatives for their firms. Each reflects the personnel policies of his organization; therefore, it behooves the placement officer to know as much as possible about the policy of the organizations to be represented on his campus. Integrity seems to have been gently promoted among recruiters, as well as placement officers, by the establishment of The Statement of Principles and Practices of College Recruiting. (Teal and Herrick, 1962, pp. 21–26) All students are expected to practice the type of integrity spelled out in this statement.

Let us assume that the recruitment season has been successful. Students and recruiters have been cooperative and helpful. All students have filled out the proper type of résumé forms and have reported their courses and cumulative grade-point averages accurately. All have appeared promptly for their interview schedules and surprised the recruiters by being able to talk knowledgeably about the firm. Students have read company literature and recruiters know something about the college. Faculty members have been most cooperative and have been eager to assist in the entertainment of visiting recruiters at luncheons. Reports from the recruiters at the end of the season point to a successful year. Almost all of the candidates for positions have been offered them. Those students who have not firmly accepted positions have declined offers because they have been offered assistantships or fellowships for graduate study at leading universities and will continue their education. This utopian moment is the time to start (or continue) preparing for the next year's recruiting season, making and confirming invitations and commitments to visit the campus during the next academic year.

Difficult Placements

Unfortunately, there will be students who have carefully prepared résumés, reported grades accurately, appeared promptly for interviews, taken all the federal, state, and city civil service entry examinations, are being graduated honorably, if just barely so, with a C average, but who have little to offer an employer. In addition, there may be a few students who have physical or appearance handicaps: A slight case of obesity, for example, might make placement of a student quite difficult. The handicapped student who has been attending college under a scholarship and assistance from the Vocational Rehabilitation Service probably has counseling assistance from them as well as from a special counselor on the campus (if the school has one for handicapped students), but this same student may come for additional help to placement. The busy placement officer may be able to do little more than refer the handicapped student to the proper agencies for help, or he may possess some contacts and knowledge which can be helpful. In any case, he should be receptive, understanding, supportive, realistic, and hopeful.

What, however, of the misfit and the left-over after the recruiting season is finished? What about the student who may be able to adapt himself to an academic atmosphere for four or more years and achieve graduation, but who is unable to leave the comforting solace of campus and dormitory? With him, indeed, a placement counselor has a special problem. Even though the counselor may be a trained psychologist with a Ph.D. in counseling or clinical psychology, would it be proper and wise for him to undertake therapy with the student? The answer would seem to be an emphatic "No." In the first place, rarely would he have as much time to devote to an individual client as would be required to bring a case to solution. Next, he might be faced with conflicts of interest resulting from the student's private revelations and the college interests. Then, too, he would be faced with the problems of possible involvement with the student and consequent danger to the objectivity of his attempt to place the student in a job. Where, then, does the young person obtain assistance in helping him to function with today's society? The answer can be various. (See also Chapter 11 for elaboration.) He may be referred with his knowledge and consent to the proper counseling agency on campus, or he may be referred to an off-campus resource. Often the nature of the referral depends on the student's ability to pay, the prognosis of length of treatment, and whether or not the student can permit his parents or guardian to know of his situation. Needless to say, the placement counselor still has the responsibility of assisting the student with placement.

The foregoing discussion is based on the assumption that the student is not currently in therapy or receiving psychological assistance in some other form. The individual who states at some stage in his placement counseling that he is in therapy, that he is limited in his pursuit of a position by the fact that he will be required to remain with his therapist for another year or so, and that he is restricted in the amount of stress he should be exposed to in the course of employment presents a different problem. Does the placement counselor present this situation to the recruiter or job contact as a special situation, does he ignore it, or keep his fingers crossed? The manner in which he advises each student depends on the circumstances, the job market, the advice and suggestions of the therapist (if the counselor has, with the consent of the student, consulted the therapist), the willingness and readiness of the student to accept realistic suggestions, and many other factors that come to light within the counseling process.

In the full economy of the 1960s, there is little doubt that the student or graduate who appears to possess no more than the acceptable number of idiosyncrasies, eccentricities, and personality neuroses, who has managed to struggle through four years of college, who can talk intelligibly and coherently, who is clean-shaven, whose grammar is not objectionable, who looks clean and dresses in general conformity to most of society's standards, and whose handicaps are not too visible will eventually be placed in some remunerative activity. This may be accomplished through the activities of his own friends and family, services of the college placement office, registration with a secular or commercial, or social agency service, or by coincidence and good fortune. The initial opportunity may not be exactly what the student has in mind and he may accept the position as a compromise, or he may be the determined young man who achieves a "million-dollar-club" rating in the insurance business in his first two years of employment. Whatever happens ultimately, he will probably find a position following his graduation from college.

Difficult placements may include the young man who seems eminently well equipped to handle a special type of job, who does not wish to continue in graduate school, who is eager to compete with his peers and seniors in business, but who has not yet fulfilled his military obligations. Fortunately, there are firms and agencies which look with tolerance on this young man and are willing to hire him on the supposition that upon completion of military service he will return to them a more mature individual who may have even more to offer than he did originally. This is, of course, not true of all employers.

The young lady who is engaged and plans to marry also may find job hunting a disappointing venture at times. Firms looking primarily for stability among their employees view her with suspicion. The attrition rate among young female employees is very high, especially after marriage. The engaged young woman faced with the task of supporting her husband while he is enrolled in a distant medical or graduate school may find herself relying on a fund of self-confidence when all other indications seem doubtful about her obtaining a position before relocation. The young lady who possesses a teaching license that will be honored or needed where she relocates is indeed fortunate. She possesses preparation that is much more marketable at long distances than are other skills. Some colleges of the same religious order do honor requests for placement assistance from graduates of sister or brother institutions in other parts of the United States. In urban areas, however, many are so thoroughly overwhelmed by the size of their own student bodies that they are able to assist students from other schools only minimally, if at all. Relocated students must then rely on social, state, and commercial agencies in those areas, and correspondence as well as leg work when the young ladies are visiting their fiancés is recommended. One recent advance that has helped students in this type of venture is a move by some large companies to set up their own centralized referral system for employment in their offices throughout the country. It is almost unnecessary to mention the priceless value of the *College Placement Annual* (Kauffman) to students searching for positions out of their immediate geographical area and to all employment candidates generally.

Teacher Placement

As mentioned before, teacher placement is somewhat different from placement for other types of positions. In some institutions, teacher placement is supervised and handled by a centralized college placement office. On other campuses, teacher placement is a separate office and the functions of placement are decentralized. In fact, the teacher placement office may be next door to the placement office, but the two offices may operate quite differently, separately, autonomously, and with different forms, though cooperatively. In the first instance, a science student who is qualified to teach physics as well as perform beginning research work in a laboratory might file his student teaching and academic references with one placement office for the purpose of investigating both teacher positions and opportunities in business and industry. He would reasonably expect to be required to see both the teacher placement counselor and a regular placement counselor, although these functions may be centered in one person. In the second instance, the same student would be required to file his dossier and references with the teacher placement office and see a teacher placement counselor. He would then be required to file proper forms in the placement office and see a placement counselor for the purpose of seeking positions other than teaching. Whether the placement offices on a college campus are centralized or decentralized depends on the college philosophy, the attitude of the education department on campus, the history of the placement office on that particular campus, and the personalities of the placement counselors. Persuasive arguments can be given for the advantages of either way of handling placement.

The amalgamation of the two types of placement offices in one seems to work especially well in assisting graduate students, M.A. graduates, or Ph.D. candidates. This is the more true in that some graduate students are still uncertain about whether they wish to enter teaching or some other area and are equipped to do both. Since many graduate students, however, must work to help pay tuition fees and living expenses, placement counselors have found a ready supply of inexpensive labor for jobs offering tuition remission in schools conferring graduate degrees. In turn, there are many requests for this type of help. On the other hand, some large universities have specialized placement offices serving various schools, such as the school of social work, law, or library science. At this time, it is extremely important to emphasize the invaluable aid which a student's mentor or thesis advisor can give him. He can mention the student's talents at professional meetings, recommend him quite personally and effectively for positions, and verify intellectual attainments. In fact, in some instances where personal effort on the part of the advisor is responsible for a student's obtaining a position, the placement office is the last to know of the appointment.

Summer Placement

An important aspect of placement on every level throughout the college, including faculty members who seek rewarding experiences in or out of the academic world, is placement for summer positions. As Professor George Davenel of Queens College of the City University of New York so aptly phrased it in a personal communication, "there is summer work and work in summer." One type earns money for the student or faculty member; the other gains valuable experience for him as well as remuneration. Though still rare enough to be highly prized, it seems that opportunities to learn and earn in the summer are increasing. If the placement office can publicize opportunities in the form of a summer job guide or similar publication, there will be many eager readers. Other faculty members are a good source of information about opportunities for students during the summer.

For the student to whom money is not the primary purpose in summer work, emphasis should be placed on the value of volunteer work. How much good can be gained by a political science major working in the office of a state assemblyman or other politician, a would-be lawyer in the law office of an alumnus of the school, a prospective researcher in the laboratories of a local hospital, or a social worker in an orphanage or children's home is immeasurable. The placement counselor can play a significant role in helping students to relate their summer plans to their academic or vocational interests.

Foreign Students

Summer work will be especially important to the students who come from foreign lands. It is wise, however, for the foreign student to clear his intentions with the foreign student adviser on campus before he seeks work and referral from the placement office. The foreign student adviser may have knowledge of opportunities which are unknown to the placement office. Foreign students on an F-1 visa in regular attendance at their colleges are also permitted to work during the regular term. At the present time, according to immigration restrictions placed on foreign students, the student must exhibit financial need for such employment (except for summer work) and may not exceed twenty hours of employment per week. In the event that the needs of a foreign student cannot be met through the placement office or the foreign student adviser, the student should be referred to international agencies which have more extensive contacts. Counseling of foreign students necessitates the placement counselor's knowing at least a little about the attitude toward work, the social hierarchy, and the pay scales of the student's home land. The placement counselor must also be prepared to provide encouragement and support in the student's difficulties with language, transportation, and related problems.

Evening Students

Many colleges and universities have evening divisions in their schools. These include graduate, baccalaureate, two-year liberal arts, and two-year terminal vocational studies programs. If the placement office has received recognition from the college administration, it is likely that it can provide additional services for those students who must or wish to attend school in the evening. This includes many who are engaged in full-time employment during the day and attend school only part-time in the evenings. There are major differences between evening and day students in that the evening students are usually more diversified in their ages, their interests, their abilities, and even their personalities. It is among these students that one finds the technician, the legal secretary, the bookkeeper-becoming-accountant, or the latent philosopher. Very often, also, one finds retired people who enter college or come back to college after a long interlude to acquire new skills or training. Some become thoroughly discouraged about the prospect of upgrading themselves. The extension of placement services to evening students to meet the unique needs of this population is clearly necessary.

Alumni

Obviously, all students, part-time or full-time, day or evening, liberal arts or technical, should be eligible for the counseling services of the placement office. The question of permitting alumni access to these services, however, produces variable responses around the country. As mentioned earlier, some placement offices operate under monumental pressures. Ratios of approximately 3000 to 1 are not uncommon when one considers the total number of students at a school and the number of counseling hours or counselors available. Some schools operate under even more disproportionate ratios. In such cases it is extremely difficult for the counseling staff to assist alumni efficiently. Yet as more and more opportunities for experienced people become known to the college placement counselors, it is of value to attempt to assist alumni wherever possible. This type of activity will also enhance the rating of the placement office with the alumni association, the administration of the college, and the business and governmental community. The College Placement Council has developed a unique method for matching college alumni and jobs with participating firms through its computerized GRAD system. A graduate may request service through his college placement director (if participating) or directly from the College Placement Council Data Center in Bethlehem, Pennsylvania. This procedure can make the placement director's job of assisting alumni easier and more productive. For the present, it may be said that placement offices provide personalized attention and services to alumni whenever feasible.

Professional Memberships

The placement officer should become a member of one or more regional placement councils of the College Placement Council (Bethlehem, Pennsylvania) as soon as practicable and permissible. Membership in this organization provides invaluable assistance to both the neophyte and the experienced counselor. Its publications are the sine qua non of placement counseling: the *Journal of College Placement, The College Placement Annual, Salary Surveys,* the *Directory of College Placement Offices,* and the revised *Principles and Practices of College Recruiting.* The eight regional placement associations hold professional conferences, attendance of which is extremely advantageous. The placement officer may also choose to join the local Chamber of Commerce, if it is an effective organization, or some other such group of the business community. If permitted, he may join a professional body consisting of personnel people from all fields. He probably will want to belong to either or both the American Psychological Association and the American Personnel and Guidance Association. Within the latter, there are the National Vocational Guidance Association and the American College Personnel Association, both of which publish valuable information. Whether he chooses to belong to other local, regional, or national organizations depends on his time, energy, interest, and budget.

Personnel and Budget Administration

Budgets are very important considerations in the administration of a placement office. Again, practices vary among different colleges in regard to the allocation of funds for placement. Some placement officers are governed by a predetermined budget established by the Dean of Students, Vice President, or other college officer who supervises the operation of the office. In other cases, the placement officer must plead for every expenditure of the ordinary operating routine, must remain uncertain about whether he will be able to attend professional meetings as the college representative or must go at his own expense, and must remain equally uncertain about how his operation will be supported from year to year. In other schools, the expenses of the placement office are supported by the alumni organization. In still other schools, the placement office is considered an integral part of the business operation of the college and operates on an annual budget. Most placement officers recommend this last method.

The status of placement officers and counselors varies among the different schools, as well. The placement officer is considered by some schools to be one of the academic faculty and is assigned tenure and otherwise accorded all benefits and privileges (including vacations) granted to faculty. In other schools, the placement officer is considered one of the administrative staff and treated accordingly, which may include working a twelve-month year with a two or three week vacation. In still other institutions, the placement officer may be occupied only part-time in placement activities and devote the remainder of his time to such areas as teaching, the alumni office, college personnel management, or related activity.

However the arrangements are made on a particular campus, it would seem advisable, unless the whole college community decamps for the summer vacation, to operate the placement function on a twelve-month basis. The business and governmental communities operate on a fiscal year calendar; so should all placement offices unless cogent reasons suggest otherwise. Summer jobs come to the placement office as late as August for those students who have been engaged in summer school. Plans, moreover, must be made for the coming recruitment season. Information concerning available part-time jobs comes in continuously, and the phone rings constantly.

If the placement office is to be a twelve-month function, then there must surely be sufficient staff to man the office, take phone calls, keep the bulletin boards and occupational library up to date, counsel students who come for help, and maintain continuity by planning adequately for the next academic year. Actual practice points out that some offices function with one full-time (or even half-time) placement counselor and a secretary who provides all clerical assistance. Another placement office operates with a director, two associate directors, seven counselors, and a large clerical staff. Bigness, in this case, means increased service and efficiency. In all cases, counseling, education, and service should be the goals of the office, and staffing should be adequate to these goals.

Space is to be prized almost as much as personnel and budget. Teal and Herrick (1962) in their excellent treatment of this subject, spell out a desirable norm for college placement offices. Although these standards seem like a utopian dream to many placement people, the goal has been reached on some campuses, undoubtedly as a result of excellent public relations on the part of the placement director and the vision of the college administrations. Even in some of the largest universities, the visiting recruiters are apologetically provided with interview cubicles which do not afford privacy and which are crisscrossed with steam pipes. In other institutions, the recruiter is afforded the best of accommodations for interviewing, but is rarely invited to the placement office because of its decrepitude.

Gratuitous though it may seem, it is necessary to point out that adequate space is essential for clerical, secretarial, and placement counseling operations in the interest of the students being served.

Placement directors and counselors may be of all ages and of both sexes, as well as coming from various types of experiential backgrounds. They communicate freely and share ideas willingly as a general rule. It is desirable for them to have had some acquaintance with the business world as an employee at some stage in their careers. Professor Nancy D. Stevens of Hunter College described the ideal staff applicant in these terms: "The composite picture of the preferred applicant for a position on a placement staff was a man or woman who had a master's degree in the general field of guidance and counseling with either three or five years of work experience in the field of business and college counseling, and who was between the ages of 25 and 35." (1965, p. 234) The consensus of people already in placement is that the placement counselor should be chronologically mature, well trained, and experienced. There is some evidence that the trend in seeking new placement directors is to look for someone with a Ph.D. in psychology or guidance who has college experience in counseling and teaching. Most college administrators take the position that a placement counselor should complement the climate, culture, purposes, and policies of his school. In addition to such professional placement personnel, who spend a major portion of their time in placement work, there are faculty members who by volunteering, assignment to the office, or primary interest in their students and the fields in which they teach can be useful adjuncts to the placement office. Motivation is so very important in placement counseling that a willing social scientist is better used for six counseling hours a week than an unwilling counseling psychologist.

Summary

Placement counseling is an educational and service function complementary to the purposes of the college or university: the education and training of its students. The placement program should be an integral part of the institution. Counselors in a placement program look upon their role as catalytic in the transition of students from the academic world to responsible positions in the outside world. The program views itself as a half-way house between school and career, a passageway of exit and entrance.

REFERENCES

American Personnel and Guidance Association. *NVGA bibliography of current occupational literature.* (Rev. ed.) Washington: Author, 1966.

Baer, M. F., & Roeber, E. C. *Occupational information.* Chicago: Sci. Res. Associates, 1964.

Crawford, A. B., Clement, S. H., & Harrower, N., Jr. *The choice of an occupation, part one: general principles of orientation.* New Haven: Yale Univ., Off. of Counsel., Placemt. and Res., 1959.

Forrester, Gertrude. *Occupational literature.* New York: H. W. Wilson, 1964.

Kauffman, W. E. (Ed.) *The college placement annual.* Bethlehem, Pa.: College Placement Council, Annually.

Kauffman, W. E. (Ed.) *The Journal of College Placement.* Bethlehem, Pa.: Coll. Council, Four Times A Year.

McKinney, F. *Counseling for personal adjustment in schools and colleges.* Boston: Houghton-Mifflin, 1958.

Mohs, M. C. *Service through placement in the junior college.* Washington: Amer. Assoc. of Jr. Coll., 1962.

Odiorne, G. S., & Hann, A. S. *Effective college recruiting.* Ann Arbor, Mich.: Univ. of Mich., Bur. of Industr. Relat., 1961.

Pitt, G. *The twenty minute lifetime: a guide to career planning.* Englewood Cliffs, N.J.: Prentice-Hall, 1959.

Rashdall, H. *The Universities of Europe in the middle ages.* Vol. 3. New York: Oxford Univ. Press, no date. Ch. 14.

Read, Julia E. *Career counseling and placement in higher education: an annotated bibliography.* Convent Station, N.J.: Coll. of Saint Elizabeth, 1964.

Roe, Anne. *The psychology of occupations.* New York: Wiley, 1956.

Rogers, C. R. *Counseling and psychotherapy.* Boston: Houghton-Mifflin, 1942.

Rood, A. *Job strategy: preparing for effective placement in business and industry.* New York: McGraw-Hill, 1961.

Siegel, M. Group orientation and placement counseling. *Personnel Guidance J.*, 1960, 38, 659–660.

Stevens, Nancy D. A changing concept of college placement. *J. Coll. stud. Personnel*, 1965, 6, 233–235.

Super, D. *The psychology of careers.* New York: Harper, 1957.

Super, D. E., & Crites, J. O. *Appraising vocational fitness by means of psychological tests.* New York: Harper, 1962.

Teal, E. A., & Herrick, R. F. (Eds.) *The fundamentals of college placement.* Bethlehem, Pa.: The Coll. Placemt. Council, 1962.

U.S. Department of Health, Education, and Welfare. *Placement services for personnel in high education.* Washington: Govt. Print. Off., 1961.

U.S. Department of Labor. *Employment and earnings statistics for states and areas 1939–63.* Washington: Govt. Print. Off., 1964.

U.S. Department of Labor. *Occupational outlook handbook.* Washington: Govt. Print. Off., Annually.

Part IV

Function and Practice

SPECIALIZED

Chapter 10

Vocational and Career Counseling

RICHARD E. GRUEN

Student Career Counseling Needs

College and university students are searching for self-awareness. They are in quest of answers about themselves and the world around them. The questions about themselves are often imposed from without, but there are also deep rumblings from within, in their trial and error attempts to answer the questions, "Who am I?" "Where am I going?" "What kind of life do I want to live?" In their quest for a variety of identities, so much a part of the developmental pattern of late adolescence and early adulthood, the task of career identification takes on major significance during the college years. Because of external institutional, societal, cultural, and familial pressures, the question of career identification becomes crucial for college students in liberal arts colleges, especially in the sophomore year. This is the time in most colleges when students must choose a major.

Other aspects of the developmental process are certainly involved and very much related to the clarification of career goals: the integration and crystallization of the self-concept, the need to explore and to test values and roles, dependence-independence strivings, emancipation from the parental home, ego-integration, and the increased awareness of sexual role and identity. The college student is asking himself in many ways: "What are my needs?" "What really are *my* values?" "Can I find a career in which

Richard E. Gruen is Assistant Professor, Department of Student Services, Brooklyn College of the City University of New York.

I can express myself?" "To what extent will this or that career satisfy my needs?" "Do I have the ability to be successful in this or that course of action?"

College and University Responsibilities

One of the major purposes of higher education is to give the late adolescent or young adult college student as much equipment as possible to help him fashion his own orientation toward the world and to help him live happily and productively in the varied areas of his life. In recent times many colleges and universities have taken on the responsibility of helping young people develop personally as well as intellectually, vocationally as well as academically. It is important to note that whole persons *can* be developed without diluting the intellectual experience that college primarily needs to be. The intellectual life need not be compromised when self-discovery is another and congruent imperative. It is not really possible to compartmentalize the individual. The implementation of ideas, the marriage of cognitive and affective processes, the holistic notion of the total personality, the relationship and cross-fertilization processes—this is higher education at its best.

By looking at the late adolescent and young adult developmentally, and by seeking to understand this transitional phase of growth, one cannot help but see that career development is inseparable from human or personal development. It is incumbent upon a first-rate college or university to have on its staff, in proportion to the student population, a significant number of professionally trained personnel concerned with the personal development of students. Within this realm, there are needed professional persons, principally concerned with the potential careers of the student body. These professionals should have strong backgrounds in the behavioral sciences and theories of vocational development and the developmental process of late adolescence and early adulthood. They should be equipped with the latest information pertaining to careers, which is forever changing, and they should know where to get information that is objective and reliable. They should be motivated to keep up with change and to remain flexible in their own personal orientation toward the world and open to new ideas. The ability to initiate and sustain growth-provoking relationships with students is imperative, if means are to be found to achieve positive ends. The need for counseling specialists in the career field who understand the aims of liberal education and the processes of human development is pressing. One of the goals of colleges and universities should be to provide the student with what he cannot do without in a rapidly changing society.

Let there be no mistake about the fact that a major motivation of college students in pursuit of higher education is the preparation for a career. The press of American society, the prodding of parents, the historical thrust for social and economic mobility in the American value system are important factors to be considered in the context of meanings attached to higher education today in the United States. Next to the choice of a lifetime partner, the choice of career is probably the most important series of decisions an individual is called upon to make. This series of choices among college students often crystallizes significantly and sometimes even culminates during the course of the college experience. These are years of exploration, experimentation, the deepening of interests, and the intensification of purpose. Career development is no longer thought of as an event, but as a continuous process. Higher education should aid this process.

Counseling centers in colleges and universities tend to be moving away from a vocational counseling specialty toward a more holistic perception of student problems. Counseling centers tend to invite the more "interesting" or more "important" problems; vocational planning, unfortunately, is not perceived in most instances as one of these "important" or "interesting" problems. Despite the fact that there is a great need for further theoretical underpinnings in the area of vocational choice and vocational development and the fact that the field is interdisciplinary, it would be a mistake to assume that vocational counseling is ancillary to the work of a university counseling center or to the purposes of the university.

The Nature of Career Counseling

Specialized career counseling in the college or the university is designed to help students who are experiencing some degree of anxiety or ignorance, either through lack of exposure or distortion of perception, in the choice of a major or a graduate or professional school and in the tentative choice of career. It includes assessment of interests, values, aptitudes, and intellectual ability, as well as attitudes and feelings. Implicit in it is an understanding of self-concept development. It is concerned with the dynamics of decision making and the working through of choices as well as the understanding of work-value patterns.

In liberal arts curricula, as elsewhere, there are many students who experience a sense of drifting or ennui, display a lack of goals, and evidence aimlessness. Lacking information about themselves, the outcomes of possible majors, specific careers, and the meaning of a liberal arts education, many of these students have not been able to direct or mobilize themselves as a result of orientation or advisement sessions. In some cases there is considerable resistance to self-appraisal, scrutinization of possible careers, and the realities of the labor market. Particularly common are those students of high intellectual ability who are not utilizing their inherent potential, and who are at odds with or in rebellion against the aims and purposes of the education given them.

Vocational counseling is a process of growth in exploring occupational choices. It involves a greater understanding of self and of value systems on the part of the college student; a greater awareness of the opportunities available to him from specific majors; a realistic assessment of his intellectual capacities, achievements, interests, preferences, and abilities; and an effort to produce a climate for realistic vocational planning at the student's particular stage of development. For the college student especially, the choice of the major is a step in his vocational development.

Super, Crites, Hummel, Moser, Overstreet and Warnath (1957) state,

> The term *vocational development* is used to denote the process of growth and learning which underlies the sequence of vocational behavior. It thus includes the more common concept of occupational choice, but avoids the pitfall of suggesting that choosing an occupation is an event occurring at a point in time. It includes also the concept of vocational adjustment, but by comprehending both of these concepts it avoids the misleading implication that they are separate and distinct. The development nature of vocational orientation, choice, entry, adjustment, and retirement calls for a broad term which puts the emphasis on process over a period of time. (p. vii)

Of great importance to the realistic career counseling of college students is the work of Bradburn and Davis (1962), who remark,

> The vast majority of the nation's college graduates have their sights set on attending a graduate or professional school. In fact, almost 8 of every 10 seniors plan to continue their education sometime in the future, according to findings of a recent survey of college graduates conducted by the National Opinion Research Center.
>
> Data for the report were based on self-administered questionnaires completed in the spring of 1961 by 33,982 June graduates sampled from 135 colleges and universities.
>
> Among the major findings in the survey of the career plans of America's college graduates were:
>
> Seventy-seven per cent of the seniors said they expected to attend a graduate or professional school at some point in their careers.

> Sixty per cent of the graduates planned to go into some sort of professional field.
>
> Fifty-five per cent said they had a definite job lined up after graduation. (p. 30)

The writer has juxtaposed Super's definition of vocational development with the findings of Bradburn and Davis to illustrate the fact that, with more and more of our undergraduates going on to graduate and professional schools, career counseling in the undergraduate college and university is in a process of significant change.

Ginzberg and Herma (1964) state,

> Central to a comprehensive theory of career development is the realization that the individual, especially the talented individual, is constantly confronted with options. . . . During his preparation for a career in professional, technical, or managerial work the individual must make a series of decisions over a period of at least ten years; almost twice as long must elapse before he becomes established in his career. . . . (p. 9)

It has been emphasized here and elsewhere that career development is part of personal development. The major construct here is that a body of theory, however in conflict, must be available to organize formulations that may be applicable, and that may, in themselves, serve as tools for research. Tiedman (1965) states,

> the idea that the career may be personally determined provides a context with which we can consider career development through liberal arts and work . . . the fundamental nature of the personally determined career is that of action guided by thought. The personally determined aspect of career development requires charting the development of a system of thought in action which lends direction to the pursuit of personal advantage through educational and vocational activity. (p. 1)
>
> The person is able to reflect upon himself as an agent of his activity of a vocational nature. When a person does so, he is able in relation to the experience accumulated during the course of goal seeking: (1) to reflect upon past events, (2) to anticipate future events, (3) to form goals; and (4) to create plans both for the attainment of formed goals and for the revision of goals and/or means. I elect to refer to this condition as that of "career" when such behavior exists in relation to vocational activity. . . . (p. 3)

According to Super (1957),

> Vocational guidance is the process of helping a person to develop and accept an integrated and adequate picture of himself and of his role in the world of work, to test this concept against reality, and to convert it into a reality with satisfaction to himself and benefit to society. (p. 197)

Most of the more recent authorities in the field of vocational counseling agree that career development is concerned with behavior. Roe (1956), applying Maslow's theory of needs, believes that a person's behavior is almost always motivated, and is also almost always, biologically, culturally, and situationally determined as well.

The blending of all of the social sciences is necessary for the full understanding of career counseling and career development. This is especially true where college students are concerned because of the multiplicity of variables in their lives and the rapid changes that are taking place in American professional, corporate, managerial and bureaucratic life styles.

Student Reactions

Pearlman (1965), in an effort to ascertain the views of college students regarding their mental health experience, found:

> The extent of their admitted troublesome reactions was about the same for "family interrelationships," "career decisions," and "relationships with the opposite sex." . . . Career decision making appeared to be another plaguing experience for many (over one third) of the graduates, as disturbing to them during their college years as intrafamilial relationships and relationships with the opposite sex. It is of interest that the higher ranking graduates were as much affected by these problem areas as the lower achieving students. . . . (p. 279)

Student reaction to the area of vocational development during the college years was studied by Gruen (1966) as a part of a larger survey of college seniors at Brooklyn College of the City University of New York. The following are some student reactions:

> Vocational growth and development has [sic] been absent in my college experience. I have had none, and I am still not sure of my life's ambition or purpose.
>
> My liberal arts college experience did not stress vocational growth and rightly so.
>
> Vocational growth and development is a personal problem and has little to do with school.
>
> I have had very little time to explore and experience a field of study. I would never have been in my area if a stranger had not suggested that I take a particular course to fill in my program during a summer session. I would never have had the time to take such a course until my senior year, when it would have been too late to select a major. I was just lucky.

> I found a field I had really not known about in high school, and through contact with certain professors became imbued with an enthusiasm for that field.
>
> I became interested in too many fields, unable to specialize and unable to make any decisions about a future career. But at least I know what I *don't* want to do.
>
> Certain individuals were forced into a major field after two years in spite of the fact that they were not ready to make this decision.
>
> There are too many students for a really effective vocational counseling program to be developed or to be useful to the student.
>
> I was very well prepared in my field and can proudly say, I had some of the finest scientific instruction available in the United States.
>
> My vocational growth was not due to my school experience but rather to summer work experience. Again, the students' main purpose for choosing a profession is monetary and social. They do not try to apply themselves to their chosen field or the work itself. They are always looking for ways they can gain prestige.
>
> As my own indecisiveness and lack of preparation in terms of a vocation is a function of my own personality, I would hesitate to attribute it to a failure on the part of college. I suspect that I didn't avail myself of the opportunities provided.

In John Hersey's novel *Too Far to Walk* (1966) the protagonist John Fist, a college student in desperate search for his identity, says to his friend,

> My trouble is, I want to major in everything. I want to be like that Gutwillig character, slice right through all the listings in the lousy catalogue. Boy, what a poly histor that cat is! . . . (p. 33)

At another point in Hersey's novel, John says,

> I want to major in magic, I want to be a magician. A physicist-architect. A physicist-ecologist. A geneticist-politician. I want to be able to use calculating machines from A to Z. You know, devise the dog tag with all your medical and emotional and educational history on it, everything about you, which you wear around your neck at all times, and then, you see, when you have to make a decision you just insert the dog tag into the Fist machine, a thing like a vending machine, along with a data ticket with your question on it and whirr! (p. 34–35)

At still another point in the book John suddenly breaks out, "I don't want to be fenced in! This majoring business. With all the variety that college has to offer, you ought not to be forced to make a choice in your second year . . ." (p. 76) Hersey's novel is so current in terms of this college generation, it includes nothing less than a student protest. Relevant to this discussion, one finds again in Hersey (p. 135),

> Spinter was leading them all; he looked gaunt, with great pools of foul March weather in the hollows under his eyes. He was carrying a crudely hand printed cardboard placard:
>
> ABOLISH THE MAJOR
> INTELLECTUAL IRON MAIDEN

One of John's peers in an earlier part of the novel asks,

> Say, what're you doing about your major? Deadline's Tuesday, you know, that prelim option thing.
>
> I haven't decided. That blank doesn't mean anything, does it?
>
> I figure English. I mean I'm going to do law, and my father says the law schools all complain about their students can't put together a decent sentence. . . . (p. 32)

One of the writer's students states in his term paper a very common theme among college students, "College has come to mean for me the place that society has forced me to come if I want a good job with prestige, security, and high pay. . . ."

The Administrative Place of Career Counseling

There is somewhat of an altercation in the field of college student personnel work in terms of where career counseling belongs organizationally. Some say career counseling should be a function of the counseling center where vocational problems are looked at within the framework of the developing personality. Here, vocational planning, selection of a major, assessment of interests *may* turn out to be secondary in importance to the counselor, and perhaps the student will obtain little information as to requirements, qualifications for particular careers, appropriate labor market information and the like.

Pustell (1965) points out,

> a strong case can be made for a single, unified counseling center. Matters which ordinarily concern the psychiatrist, the vocational counselor, the counseling psychologist, and the clinical psychologist can be handled in the same setting with great advantage. Unnecessary duplication of services, and a nonfunctional segmentation of the student and his problems are thereby avoided. A situation in which the college student must decide whether to classify himself as material for a vocational counseling center, a psychology department clinic, or a medically

> sponsored mental hygiene service tends to perplex and sometimes even frighten the student. He may, for example, want psychological help, but being hesitant to discuss or classify himself as a "real case," he avoids the medical service and settles for an indirect discussion of his emotional difficulties in the course of vocational counseling. If the vocational counselor happens to be a qualified therapist, the student is in luck. Otherwise the real need may go unmet. Even when a referral is attempted, resistance to making a change to an unknown agency is often difficult to overcome. And even in those cases where the counselor is qualified to provide the therapeutic counseling himself, he runs the risk of a jurisdictional dispute with the medical service. The fact that such disputes can be settled constructively in many cases is no reason for creating them in the first place. The single integrated psychological-vocational service recommends itself highly as an ideal solution. (p. 171)

Others say that career counseling is inextricably bound to placement and that career counseling belongs organizationally to the Placement Office. Indeed, in recent years there has been a movement toward Career Counseling and Placement Centers. Hoppock (1966) makes the following point:

> Career counseling is a means to an end. The end is successful placement of the student in a job in which he can be reasonably useful and contented. Helping a student to decide upon a career objective may lead only to frustration if the objective proves to be unattainable.
>
> Too many counselors and counselor educators are content to help the student to establish a career objective and to start movement toward it. Too many counselors do not follow through until the objective is attained. . . . But to be effective, career counseling must be closely related to placement and to the realities of the employment market. It must not become so divorced from placement that the counseling is done almost entirely in terms of the abilities, interests, needs, and problems of the student, with comparatively little attention to the possibility in finding a job in the career that the student selects. This kind of pseudo-career counseling is being done by far too many trained counselors already. And this is the kind of counseling placement offices will get if they are staffed with counselors who wish to separate themselves from the evaluation of their work which they cannot escape at the point of placement. . . . (p. 126)

Stevens (1965) sees career counseling and placement as interrelated:

> The college placement field is in a stage of transition. Older philosophies underlying the principles of placement operation are being challenged. A newer philosophy is developing which is concerned with the psychological dynamics of personality and behavior exhibited by placement clients. (p. 233)

Still others state that career counseling with college students is an entity unto itself and that there should be a Bureau of Vocational Guidance and Counseling separate from the Placement Office and the Counseling Center. This is the most traditional approach. It is interesting to note that Williamson (1965) quotes Yoakum (1919) with the following with regard to this organizational framework:

> The principal functions of the bureau are to obtain accurate data on each student, to codify the requirements of different professions, to supervise the use of tests and to provide means whereby each student may become acquainted with his abilities and the requirements of the occupations in which he is interested . . . all the problems can be investigated . . . in a scientific manner and will initiate and encourage research in this field. (p. 100)

The problem really resides in the professional qualifications of the counseling staff, their specialties, and where *they* are located in the particular organizational model of the college or the university.

It is important to know what is meant by the various levels of career counseling, guidance, or advisement. Max Siegel, Max Weiner, and Austin B. Wood (1965) state,

> With respect to a possible career or careers, an individual investigates and learns about, chooses (or drifts into), prepares for, enters, works at, and remains or withdraws, and possibly moves on to a subsequent choice as a result of an almost infinite number of influences. Different individuals enter college at different stages in this process. A college program of career counseling, then, must operate on different levels, and in many cases may have to start before a student ever sets foot on campus. That is to say that certain aspects of a recruiting-admissions-freshman orientation program will inevitably deal with, or touch upon, the subject of careers. In attempting a long view of this matter, we found ourselves distinguishing between (1) "career orientation" to which category we assigned the more general exploration of the widest possible variety of occupations in the world of work, including introductory information on qualifications for various jobs, preparation of the work itself, rewards both material and non-material, what it may mean to one's family, and similar considerations; (2) "career information" which was the term we began to use to refer to much more specific and detailed information on a single career or family of careers. This involves concrete information on current job opportunities, income statistics, promotion possibilities, etc.; and (3) "placement" which involves the culmination of the preceding functions in helping the individual to seek out and to land a specific job, appointment, or position. . . . (p. 2)

Personality Variables in Career Choice

It is now more widely accepted that many requests for career counseling from late adolescents at the college level often have deeper implications in the search for identity. Erikson (1965, p. 218) has pointed out that it is the inability to settle on an occupational identity which disturbs young people.

Colleges and universities request through questionnaires, direct confrontation, and other information-getting devices that students indicate their vocational choice upon admission. Although this information is sometimes useful (mostly in terms of change, in the opinion of this writer), the student sometimes feels that there is something wrong with him if he does not know the answer. If college is a time, especially in the first two years, for exploration and exposure, are not college personnel asking for something that has not yet crystallized? Are we not saying to the students, "You ought to know!"? As Watson (1966) says,

> He [the student] is in the process of changing from a dependent child to an independent man, and he is also in the process of changing his social status. . . . One of the student's primary goals in going to college may be to move up in the social scale, to become someone quite different from his parents. . . . (p. 71)

As a result of many kinds of stresses, both from within and without, the student may wish to change his major, perhaps several times, much to the chagrin of college administrators, teachers, and some counselors who need to feel that everything is neat and well packaged. The present trend toward an upgrading of specialty education in the undergraduate curriculum puts further pressure on the student. In this regard, Sanford (1965) emphasizes,

> It is risky to construct or to speed up liberalizing education in the interest of hastening a student's ascent of a professional ladder, and it may well be a good idea *not* to discourage the student who wants to change fields at a comparatively late stage in his training. . . . (pp. 643–644)

The fact that many students experience a considerable amount of stress in their inability to choose a major is pointed out very well by Galinsky and Fast (1966):

> In late adolescence the task is to make an integration of the diversity of previous identifications and role experiences . . . it is the problem of establishing and integrating character modes into a unified pattern of functioning. Since this task is a difficult one, an unsatisfactory com-

> pletion is not uncommon. . . . Choosing a vocation involves a kind of self definition that forces one to say to the world, "This is what I am." It is precisely the lack of internal wherewithal to make such a declaration that immobilizes some people when they are faced with having to choose. Although they may wish to avoid declaring themselves, adolescents are always painfully aware of the demand that some decisions be made. The incompatibility between the internal inability and external (as well as internal) demand creates a great deal of additional discomfort. . . . (p. 89)

The importance of personality variables in the choice of a career cannot be underestimated. The clusters of personal characteristics within specific majors and careers have been studied and some theories have been formulated, however much in need of further research they are. Watson (1966, p. 76) states, "Ideally, the choice of a profession is made in response to personality needs, but once chosen, the profession tends to mold the personality of the chooser." Recognition of personal characteristics and psychological needs is given scant attention by some counselors, especially those vocational counselors in colleges and universities whose training predates the more current theories of the developmental processes. College students, themselves under the pressures of an other-directed society which influences them in terms of material well-being, social status, prestige, and glamorous life styles, tend to forget about their inner needs and sense of self.

Watson (1966) points out,

> For a young man in an American college, the choice of a career is a crucial and frightening experience. Rightly or wrongly he feels that the choice he now makes will determine the whole course of his life, that a mistake will be irreparable, and, often, that he has not the maturity and wisdom to make that choice. He has grown up in a society where the primary questions are not, "Who are you?" "Who was your father?" but "What do you do?" and "What does your father do?" He is keenly aware that the work a man does determines not only his social standing but the rewards he will receive in money, prestige, and pride of achievement. Often, he is much more aware of this than he is of his own needs and drives. . . . (p. 76)

Sharp (1962) reports on a National Science Foundation study conducted by the Bureau of Social Research in 1960–1961, a nationwide survey of June 1958 graduates,

> There are many implications in these survey data for the counseling and guidance of students now in college or about to enter college. Whether one likes it or not, it is clear that the choice of a major may well turn out to be a serious career commitment—not only for the pre-

professional student, but for students majoring in the arts, sciences, and humanities as well. Some doors are almost automatically closed and others opened once a decision is made to major in history, business or English. Selecting a given undergraduate institution often predetermines career outcomes—if a student is restricted in his choice of a major because of limitations in the types of programs offered, he is probably permanently ruling out study or work in areas not available to him as an undergraduate. Yet it is common for students to select their school and especially their major field of study without giving much thought to the long-term implications of their choices, perhaps in the mistaken belief that they are not making major career decisions when choosing a field of undergraduate study. (p. 7)

Davis (1965) reports on a very detailed study, conducted by the National Opinion Research Center, of over 33,000 1961 college graduates from 135 colleges and universities,

Viewed abstractly, the changes during the four years of college hardly suggest that college experience is decisive for occupational choice. On the whole, the students come out oriented to the jobs they chose as freshmen, and on the whole, the changes that do occur appear to be the continuation of trends that began before entry into college.

Viewed in more detail, the changes during college are sufficient to justify considerable interest in the process: (1) half the students change or choose a career during college; (2) particular fields such as engineering, medicine, and the social sciences change considerably in popularity; (3) the reversal of direction for the social sciences suggest a strong effect of college on choice for that field. . . . (p. 76)

Gruen (1966) surveyed the senior class at Brooklyn College of the City University of New York. The senior survey, called *Our Graduates Speak Out,* is an intensive annual study of the senior class. One of the open-ended items of the *Graduate Questionnaire,* Class of 1966, reads as follows:

At some time in your college career, was there a change in your motivation for college work? 1–Yes; 2–No.

If "Yes," in what year was this change apparent? 1–Freshman; 2–Sophomore; 3–Junior; 4–Senior.

If "Yes," what was the nature of the change and what precipitated it?

Over 60 per cent of the seniors responding "Yes," indicated a change in the sophomore or junior year. Some of the more typical responses follow:

As a junior, I was able to take the courses *I* wanted. I was doing what I had first come here for and I was totally involved and truly excited. . . .

In my sophomore year I became more serious about my courses and realized I couldn't just coast through. I became aware I was judging majors on the inadequate evidence of introductory courses and that I was making a choice of a life's work. . . .

In my sophomore year I became acclimated to college and began to take elective courses. I believe this precipitated positive change. . . .

Realization that I would soon leave the fantasy and comparatively easy world of the teenager, dependent upon others, and I would soon have to rely on my own initiative. . . .

When I entered college as a freshman, my goal was career training. I wanted to be a teacher. A teacher needs a college education, therefore I was in college. Towards the end of my first year, I realized that college was more than a career training center. A whole new world of ideas and attitudes then opened up to me. . . .

In my freshman year, I attended because my parents demanded it of me. In my sophomore year, I began to appreciate the necessity of a college education. In my junior year, I began to appreciate the value of my studies in broadening my intellect. In my senior year, the degree became a major source of accomplishment and pride. . . .

There was a great increase in motivation when I decided on my major. This was precipitated by a number of things. (1) The advice of a number of my professors; (2) the interest in the courses themselves; (3) contact with another student who graduated from college and met with success in this field. . . .

I both lost interest in one field and found that I both enjoyed myself and benefited more from another. . . .

The all too often "sophomore slump" is precipitated by too long a period of required courses. When I was able to branch off into my major, my work became self-motivating. . . .

Most of the respondents indicated that their major or their change of major precipitated a change in their motivation for college work. Many students indicated that a peer relationship or interpersonal relationship with an adult (often a professor) motivated a change in a more positive direction. Change in major in the junior year precipitated positive direction and increased motivation among many students. College counselors only infrequently influenced the vocational decisions of students.

Career Counseling in Groups

Brooklyn College has offered group career counseling for sophomores and seniors in addition to individual career counseling. Group career counseling was instituted in 1960 and conceived of as more than orientation or information-giving sessions. It was conceived of as a more dynamically oriented group activity but was not considered psychotherapy, although to some extent it utilized psychotherapeutic techniques. Emphasis was placed on greater self-awareness, self-definition and the processes of decision-making. The group career counseling effort organizationally came under the aegis of the Specialized Counseling Program which provides individual and group psychotherapy for matriculated students in the college. The group sessions were centered around the problems of sophomores and seniors from a normative crisis and developmental point of view. Occupational and other kinds of information were dovetailed and combined with this point of view.

The sophomore group was designed to help second-year and some third-year students who were experiencing more than the average stress in making a choice of a major (or changing a major) with a view toward future career choices. During the first few years the groups met for eight weekly one-hour sessions a semester. In later years the number of sessions was increased to twelve weekly one-hour sessions. Students selected for the groups were also invited to attend career conferences sponsored by the Career Information and Placement Program as well as those sponsored by departments, preprofessional programs, or academic societies. Assessment of interests, values, and intellectual capacity were made, *where appropriate*, through the use of tests, the results of which were interpreted only within the context of counseling. Every effort was made to convey the idea that tests were not a magical formula that would solve the problems of the students and that test results had to be synthesized with many other variables. The results of interest, values, and aptitude assessment were discussed within the group setting. Individual or group personality and intelligence tests were interpreted in individual sessions with the students. All students were invited to make individual appointments with the counselor to discuss special problems. The groups initially were composed of as many as fifteen or twenty students. However, in later years the number was limited to no more than ten for each group. All students were screened prior to acceptance. Some of the student problems that emerged from the sophomore groups over the years centered around the following:

1. Why am I in college?
2. The dynamics of choice and decision making.
3. Personal considerations in educational and career planning. Personal characteristics of individuals in given major fields and careers.
4. The meaning of a liberal arts education.

5. Parental pressures involving major choice.
6. Occupational and educational information pertinent to specific careers; offerings of the various academic departments and preprofessional programs of the college.
7. Implementation of the self-concept in choice of major and career.
8. The expression of suppressed feelings about the college experience and the demands and stresses perceived.

The senior groups were designed (1) to help lower and upper seniors who displayed more than the usual stress with regard to their immediate and long-term goals; (2) to provide the needed support for selected students to bridge the transition from campus to career or graduate school. Here also the number of sessions was increased from eight to twelve weekly sessions and students were screened beforehand. Some of the problems that emerged from these senior groups centered around the following:

1. "Senior blues," senior depression and separation anxiety.
2. Dependence, independence, and emancipation strivings.
3. The dynamics of choice, decision making, and career planning.
4. What can I do with my major?
5. Perceptual distortions of specific professions and careers, life styles.
6. Educational, occupational, and labor market information regarding entry jobs.
7. Graduate school programs and their career outcomes.
8. Senior Recruitment Program and Placement Services.
9. The occupational outlook.
10. Planning a job campaign.
11. The employment or personnel interview (including role-playing interviews).
12. Preparation of the résumé and letter of application.
13. Self-assessment.
14. Parental pressures.

Students in the senior groups, on the whole, experienced more than the usual transition problems of decision making at this important choice-point of their lives.

Students who desired or needed information *only*; students desirous of taking tests *only* outside the context of concomitant counseling; students who could resolve their problems by seeing a general counselor, preprofessional counselor, or career-information and placement counselor; and students who needed psychotherapy were not included in either the sophomore or senior groups. Students in most of the groups felt that the group counseling helped to develop their feelings of ego strength. The students very often were able to see themselves in their peers and were able to help each other. The group effort also provided a situation in which more students at the college could be seen for career counseling in a given semester. However, the group effort was not a substitute for individual career counseling.

The primary motivation for attending college of the students found in both sophomore and senior groups was vocational, but they did not know which major or which career. Distortions, stereotypic thinking, fallacious as well as unrealistic thinking appeared to be prevalent in all groups. Perceptions of salaries on entry jobs were particularly unrealistic. The fact that the choice of major was not irrevocable, the notion that career choice was not an event but a process, the fact that one could go on to medical school or law school without a major in science or political science, and the fact that industry and government welcomed the liberal arts graduate often irrespective of college major came as a great surprise to many of the participants in the groups. The characteristic late adolescent absolutes, dogmatic thinking, and polar-opposite processes were equally observable. The fact that students in the groups as well as those in individual career counseling sessions knew about the life styles of various professions, but had little information about precise requirements, qualifications, and specifications for particular careers corroborate the findings of Beardsley and O'Dowd (1962). Seniors were beset by a multitude of anxieties as they realized that they were going to have to implement their plans. Naiveté with regard to employment and personnel interviews, and value systems that were quite willing to accept a crass manipulation of interview responses and deliberate distortion of backgrounds were also in evidence. Worry over reporting draft classifications and engagement and marriage plans to personnel recruiters and interviewers provided much stress and many questions of ethics among the seniors. Some students were so anxious and frightened by the thought of leaving familiar surroundings that they seriously considered going to graduate school as a means of prolonging adolescence or avoiding the draft, rather than because they needed more education for particular fields or desired further learning.

Common to students in both the sophomore and senior groups over the years, as well as those in individual counseling, was their poor understanding of a liberal arts education and what it means. Their impressions of liberal education and its non-negotiable character have caused this writer no small degree of anxiety. The impressions of students, often sounding like those of a feature writer of a large metropolitan newspaper, have been reported by Ginzberg and Herma (1964) in their study of individuals with high intellectual potential:

> The school I attended (an Ivy League College) apparently considered its duties discharged upon the completion of my studies. I was cut adrift to fend for myself in a world which is not particularly kind to those who possess a so-called liberal arts education. As a broad intellectual base this education was fine. But for the pursuance of a definite career, and as an aid in earning my own living, this training was practically useless. . . . (p. 31)

Probably one of the finest studies that has recently been done with implications for our bright and capable undergraduate students in the colleges and universities of this country can be found in Ginzberg and Herma's (1964) book, *Talent and Performance*. According to their earlier study (1951) *Occupational Choice*, a significant number of young people in college appear to crystallize their career choices during their junior year, as they approach the end of their teens. In the later study they point out,

> Until he confronts the reality of work no individual can know whether his plans, indeed his choice, were sound or not. . . .
>
> Just under three quarters of the entire group (72 per cent) reported that their occupational goal was related to their later actual field of work first in college; 22 per cent said that this happened in graduate school; only 6 per cent stated that they completed their formal education without having crystallized an occupational goal that was related to their later work. That college was the period during which most of the respondents reached a choice about their future work is underscored by the additional finding that only about one-third of the group had an occupational goal in college that was unconnected with their later work. . . .
>
> Teachers at every level from high school to graduate school, were most frequently singled out as having played an important role; the only other group of individuals mentioned with any frequency were employers. Only a few referred to relatives. . . .
>
> Young people must make choices in college and in graduate school with respect to a major subject and these choices usually bring them closer to the clarification of their occupational goals. . . . (pp. 51–53)

In one of the most fascinating parts of this book, Ginzberg and Herma explode some myths. With particular reference to individuals with high potential, they did *not* find that (1) a large proportion of young men complete college without knowing what they want to do; (2) teachers have a considerable influence on the occupational choices of their students;

(3) military service is a seriously disruptive influence on the career planning of young people; (4) early marriage is a serious deterrent to a man's acquiring a doctorate. (p. 65) They discuss career patterns in terms of (1) straight pattern, (2) broad pattern, and (3) variant pattern. They are among the few authors and researchers in the field who speak at length of value orientations in the choice of a career. Referring to value orientations they state that *values* are the generalized principles to which the individual has committed himself, which in turn help him to choose and order the alternatives that he encounters in any number of life situations. The subtleties and complexities as well as the interrelationships that are found in the field of career choice are succinctly expressed by these workers in their breakdown of value-orientation types into (1) individualistic types, (2) leadership types, and (3) ideological types. (pp. 114–116)

The Goals of Vocational Guidance

What today, in the late sixties, are the goals of vocational guidance? In a recent effort to meet the demands of an ever-changing society, the National Vocational Guidance Association has taken upon itself a reexamination and reconceptualization of vocational guidance. Addressing himself to this issue, Tennyson (1966) states,

> Work has not lost its purpose, as some believe. Although technological progress inevitably changes the character of work and man's relation to it, there is no reason in the world why change cannot be structured in ways that will provide man with a more meaningful vocational existence. . . . (p. 2)

In this writer's opinion, a holistic approach to work and the meaning of work is inescapable. Bertrand Russell (1961) has noted the profound variability among human beings in their tendency to regard their lives as a whole. Russell encourages the habit of viewing life as a whole as an essential part both of wisdom and of the true morality.

In this framework, educators and vocational guidance workers have tended in most recent years to focus attention upon career planning as a life process, in which the traditional aims of selecting an occupation no longer suffice. Borow (1964, 1965) warns about the dysfunction between conventionally practiced vocational guidance and economic conditions in contemporary society. Patterson (1964) emphasizes the goal of finding a vocation consistent with one's self-concept. Hoppock (1963) describes the choice of an occupation as a means to the end of being reasonably useful and contented in one's life and work. Roe (1956) underscores occupational adjustment as a facet of life adjustment. Super (1963, p. 3) pictures the vocational counselor's task as "helping a person to formulate an adequate idea of himself and to find a role appropriate to the kind of person he conceives himself to be and seeks to become. . . ." Tennyson and Blocker (1962) regard career planning as a process which is developmental in character.

The just-cited points of view are clearly in the mainstream of educational philosophy in the 1960s, but were anticipated almost forty years ago by Alfred North Whitehead (1929), who stressed that education must impart both technique and intellectual vision and should turn out students with both technical and liberal backgrounds. In this spirit, the goals of vocational guidance become the goals of a free society in which students make an effective transition to adult responsibility.

Qualifications for Vocational Counselors

The qualifications for vocational counselors, especially in colleges and universities, are of extreme importance. They must be professionally trained and they must know a good deal about the processes of higher education. Vocational counselors in our colleges and universities are dealing with subtle and complex problems of relationships and interrelationships. We must accept the fact that the training of vocational counselors must be of a high level of interdisciplinary education and performance, to cope with such problems.

Requirements, training, terminology, and personal qualities are summarized by Super (1964), who states,

> In *colleges and universities* those who are professional counselors, rather than professors with individual advisory functions, are generally called *counselors* or *counseling psychologists* in recognition of their concern with educational, personal, and social adjustment as well as with vocational development. The teaching role which they often play in an academic department strengthens bonds with the profession of education or with the discipline of psychology. Tenure, advancement and prestige, as well as the satisfaction of teaching and research, are likely to come to those who have the doctorate and academic as well as counseling appointments. The term "counseling psychologist" therefore gains in popularity in the profession; in everyday usage "counselor" has more appeal because it sounds more "normal." (pp. 557–558)
>
> The recommendation of training at the doctoral level for counseling psychologists, and the clear trend toward expecting more and more psychological sophistication on the part of those who counsel. . . . (p. 559)

> Those who do vocational counseling have a special role to play, but they must be broadly trained and they do need the psychological sophistication so frequently stressed today. . . . (p. 560)
>
> The increasing recognition of the importance of both emotional and reality problems, and of the need to work with both as they manifest themselves in client contacts, justifies some optimism concerning the health, vitality, and future of vocational guidance in our colleges and universities. (p. 573)

The 1964 Greyston Conference, reported by Thompson and Super (1964) reviews in considerable detail the recent history of counseling psychology, as well as employment locations, duties, methods, training, and other characteristics of counseling psychologists.

Some Guides for the Career Counselor and Administrator

The writer makes the following recommendations for those who do career counseling in the college or the university:

1. Learn all you can about what is known and what has been hypothesized about the characteristics of the late adolescent and young adult college population in the nation as well as on your own campus.
2. Learn all you can about what is known and what has been hypothesized about the dynamics of career development and theories of occupational choice.
3. Keep up to date with the contributions of the social and behavioral sciences to vocational development and career counseling.
4. Know the environmental press on the students in your institution and its influence on value patterns.
5. Know the student culture on your campus and its influence on value patterns.
6. Know the relationships of career counseling to other aspects of counseling in the college or the university, especially psychological counseling and the placement service.
7. Be able to change gears as a counselor in terms of the degree of depth necessary in working with a wide range of college students in search of a major and tentative choice of a career.
8. Keep up to date with occupational information, requirement, and qualifications for careers for college graduates. Know the labor market. Know the resources.
9. Keep up to date with graduate and professional school information with regard to requirements and qualifications.

10. Learn how to use group techniques in career counseling.

11. Follow up the graduates of your institution with respect to their career choices and job satisfaction five years after graduation.

12. Remember that it is at the point of placement that you can best evaluate the effectiveness of your counseling.

The writer makes the following recommendations to student personnel administrators with regard to career counseling:

1. Establish a tier system of career counseling services to meet the needs of the wide range of needs on your campus. Spread your nets wide. Remember that different levels of depth are necessary. Initiate career orientation for freshmen, perhaps a required course in careers for sophomores and juniors, career conferences, testing services, depth or specialized career counseling for those who need it, and a strong career counseling and placement program.

2. Get the instructional departments in the college or university involved in your planning and activities. Get the alumni involved.

3. Do not get upset because college students change their majors. This is not a mark of instability. Plan accordingly.

4. Provide well structured liaison and communication between career counseling and psychological counseling.

5. Choose your professional personnel carefully. Make sure that your counselors meet the needs of students rather than their own status needs with regard to the type of counseling they prefer to do. Choose counselors who are flexible and who can move around with facility in the various latitudes of counseling.

6. Determine the career counseling needs and the organizational framework as a result of institutional research and the needs of your particular student body.

Concluding Remarks

To conclude that the student populations of our colleges and universities are all late adolescent and young adult would scarcely be accurate. There are increasing numbers of mature adults in our institutions of higher learning, in regular sessions as well as evening sessions, schools of general studies, and special programs designed along the lines of the *new college* conceptual framework. There are mature men involved in the process of changing their occupations, and an increasing number of women who desire to change their life styles, initiate a change in careers, or who desire to enter the labor market for the first time. Many of these mature adults are in need of career counseling. Their problems are often very subtle and complex. Colleges and universities have a responsibility to help these adults define or redefine their career goals. There are few well-qualified career counselors in our colleges and universities, proportionate to this growing population, who are capable of handling these problems. There is a growing need for college career counselors who will work with this population. More particularized training and experience should be required for these students.

Colleges and universities also have some responsibility for counseling the prospective dropout and students who are dropped for poor scholarship. These students also have subtle and complex problems. It is striking that many college dropouts give as their reason for failure or boredom something in the nature of the following as typical responses: "I was just going to college aimlessly." "I had no goal and didn't know what I could do or couldn't do." Here too is a fertile field for professionally trained specialists in career development and counseling. In conclusion, it should be succinctly restated that both experience and research have suggested that vocational development is a central aspect of human development and vocational guidance a central function of college counselors.

REFERENCES

Barry, Ruth, & Wolf, Beverly. *An epitaph for vocational guidance.* New York: Bur. of Publ., Teachers Coll., Columbia Univ., 1962.

Beardslee, D. C., & O'Dowd, D. D. Students and the occupational world. In N. Sanford (Ed.), *The American college.* New York: Wiley, 1962.

Borow, H. (Ed.), *Man in a world at work.* Boston: Houghton-Mifflin, 1964.

Borow, H. Emerging conceptions of career development: some implications for counseling. Paper read at Virginia Personnel Guid. Assoc., Arlington: April, 1965.

Bradburn, N. M., & Davis, J. A. The career plans of 33,000 college seniors. *J. Coll. Placemt.*, 1962, 23, 30 ff.

Caplow, T. *The sociology of work.* Minneapolis: Univ. of Minn. Press, 1954.

Carter, E. M., & Hoppock, R. College courses in careers. *Personnel Guid. J.*, 1961, 373–375.

Davis, J. A. *Great aspirations: the graduate school plans of America's college seniors.* Chicago: Aldine, 1964.

Davis, J. A. *Undergraduate career decisions.* Chicago: Aldine, 1965.

Dennis, L. E., & Kauffman, J. F. (Eds.) *The college and the student.* Washington: Amer. Council on Educ., 1966.

Eastern College Personnel Officers. *Career counseling and placement in higher education: an annotated bibliography.* (Selected references from periodicals, journals and research sources.) Available from: Miss Julia E. Read, Chairman, 1964 ECPO Project Committee, Career Guidance and Placement Department, College of Saint Elizabeth, Convent Station, New Jersey, 07961.

Erikson, E. H. Growth and crises of the healthy personality. In C. Kluckhohn, H. A. Murray, & D. M. Schneider (Eds.), *Personality in nature, society, and culture*. New York: Knopf, 1956. Pp. 185–225.

Galinsky, D. M., & Fast, Irene. Vocational choice as a focus of the identity search. *J. counsel. Psychol.*, 1966, 13, 89–92.

Ginzberg, E. *Life styles of educated women*. New York: Columbia Univ. Press, 1966.

Ginzberg, E., Ginzberg, S., Axelrod, S., & Herma, J. L. *Occupational choice: an approach to a general theory*. New York: Columbia Univ. Press, 1951.

Ginzberg, E., & Herma, J. L. *Talent and performance*. New York: Columbia Univ. Press, 1964.

Goldman, L. *Using tests in counseling*. New York: Appleton-Century-Crofts, 1961.

Gruen, R. E. Our graduates speak out: a report on the class of 1965. Unpublished manuscript, Brooklyn College, C.U.N.Y., 1965.

Gruen, R. E. Our graduates speak out: a report on the class of 1965. Unpublished manuscript, Brooklyn College, C.U.N.Y., 1966.

Hersey, J. *Too far to walk*. New York: Knopf, 1966.

Hoppock, R., & Gruen, R. E. Professional preparation for college placement? *J. Coll. Placemt.*, 1965–66, 26, 26 ff.

Hoppock, R. *Occupational information*. (2nd Ed.), New York: McGraw-Hill, 1963.

Nosgow, S., & Form, W. H. (Eds.) *Man, work, and society: a reader in the sociology of occupations*. New York: Basic Books, 1962.

Patterson, C. H. Attitudes toward work. *Voc. Guid. quart.*, 1959, 7, 2–4.

Pearlman, S. The college student views his mental health experience. *J. Amer. Coll. Hlth Assoc.*, 1966, 14, 277–283.

Pustell, T. E. A unified college counseling center. *J. Coll. Stud. Personnel*, 1965, 6, 171–174.

Roe, Anne. *The psychology of occupations*. New York: Wiley, 1956.

Russell, B. *The conquest of happiness*. New York: Liveright, 1961.

Samler, J. Where do counseling psychologists work? What do they do? What should they do? In A. S. Thompson, & D. E. Super (Eds.), *The professional preparation of counseling psychologists*. Report of the 1964 Greyston Conference. New York: Bur. of Publ., Teachers Coll., Columbia Univ., 1964.

Sanford, N. (Ed.) *The American college*. New York: Wiley, 1962.

Sanford, N. The human problems institute in general education. *Daedalus*, 1965, 94, 642–662.

Sharp, Laure M. Career patterns of recent college graduates. *Occup. Outlk quart.*, 1962 (February), 3–8.

Siegel, M. Work for all. In A. S. Goodhartz (Ed.), *A commitment to youth*. New York: Bookman Assoc., 1960, pp. 145–168.

Stevens, Nancy D. A changing concept of college placement. *J. Coll. Student Personnel*, 1965, 6, 233–235.

Super, D. E. *The psychology of careers*. New York: Harper, 1957.

Super, D. E. *Appraising vocational fitness*. New York: Harper, 1962.

Super, D. E. The professional status and affiliations of vocational counselors. In H. Borow (Ed.), *Man in a world at work*. Boston: Houghton-Mifflin, 1964.

Super, D. E., Crites, J., Hummel, R., Moser, Helen, Overstreet, Phoebe, & Warnath, C. *Vocational Development*. New York: Bur. of Publ., Teachers Coll., Columbia Univ., 1957.

Super, D. E., Crites, J., Hummel, R., Moser, Helen, Overstreet, Phoebe, & Warnath, C. *Career development: self-concept theory*. New York: Coll. Entr. Examin. Bd, 1963.

Tennyson, W. W. (Ed.) Testing our capacity to change. *Newsltr NVGA*, 166 (5), 1–2.

Tennyson, W. W., & Blocher, D. H. Career development. *Bus. Educ. Forum*, 1962, 16.

Thompson, A. S., & Super, D. E. (Eds.) *The professional preparation of counseling psychologists*. Report of the 1964 Greyston Conference. New York: Bur. of Publ., Teachers Coll., Columbia Univ., 1964.

Tiedeman, D. V. Career development through liberal arts and work. *Voc. Guid. quart.*, 1965, 14, 1–7. (a)

Tiedeman, D. V. (Ed.) Trustees seek enlargement of our goals and programs. *Newsltr NVGA*, 1965 (4), 1–8. (b)

Wannamaker, Mary. A presentation of library research as a basis for the reconceptualization of vocational guidance. Unpublished manuscript, Univ. of Minn., 1966.

Watson, Gladys H. *The Brooklyn College student: a pilgrim's progress*. New York: Twayne Publishers, 1966.

Whitehead, A. N. *The aims of education*. London: Williams & Northgate, 1929.

Williamson, E. G. *Vocational counseling: some historical, philosophical, and theoretical perspectives*. New York: McGraw-Hill, 1965.

Wood, A. B., Weiner, M., & Siegel, M. Report of Committee on Career Counseling to the Dean of Students, Brooklyn Coll. Unpublished report, 1965.

Yoakum, C. S. College personnel research. *Sch. & Soc.*, 1919, 9, p. 559. Cited by E. G. Williamson, *Vocational Counseling: Some historical, philosophical, and theoretical perspectives*. New York: McGraw-Hill, 1965.

Chapter 11

College Mental Health

SAMUEL PEARLMAN

Public Health Concepts

The concern about the mental health of students in colleges and universities has historically paralleled, in broad perspective, the focus on the mental health needs of the general population. Over the past four decades, concepts of public health (Caplan, 1964), normally referable to the epidemiology of disease and the efforts to eradicate or control medical illness on a community basis, have had a measure of impact on higher education. The parallelism has by no means been steady or consciously designed, but at this point in time is able to be analyzed in terms of gross trends. Its discussion here will serve as an introduction to the later materials of this chapter.

One

The arraignment of mental illness as the "most insidious of human afflictions" (Srole, Langner, Michael, Opler, & Rennie, 1962, p. 8) has its counterpart in higher education in the recognition of the high personal losses in efficiency, social relationships, and career mobility among college students as the outcome of affective dysfunction. No successful effort has as yet been made—and the utility of any such effort is open to question—to estimate these losses in fiscal terms, in the manner and with the tech-

Samuel Pearlman is Associate Professor, Department of Student Services; and Coordinator of the Specialized Counseling Program, Brooklyn College of the City University of New York.

niques already applied to the dollar-cost drainage of mental illness in general on the national income. (Malzberg, 1950; Fein, 1958) Typically mentioned in the literature, however, is the unspecified deprivation to the nation of the leadership potentials of disturbed students. (Group, 1957)

Two

Epidemiological surveys in general mental health areas have been reflected in the efforts of college personnel and professional associations to delineate the nature and scope of mental health problems on the campus. For the most part these efforts have brought forth many interesting bits and pieces of information from a variety of institutions, and in a constructive way they have begun to meet the insistent challenge of a past director of the National Institute of Mental Health for "facts—many facts, accurate facts . . ." (Felix & Kramer, 1952, p. 152). Rarely, however, have the data been found to have a common base and meaning; and the logic of their research designs must be accepted with considerable reservations. Several broad-gauged investigations of *what is*, *where*, and *to what extent* have been reported, and the specific pluses and minuses of these will be discussed later. What has yet to be accomplished here in the college mental health field is at the level of the analyses of the Joint Commission on Mental Illness and Health (1961) and of the Midtown Manhattan Study (Srole et al., 1962).

It is clear to this writer that the growth and development of mental health services in colleges and universities have usually anteceded a full awareness of needs, emphases, and directions, and have therefore lacked a built-in base for program evaluation and innovation. The desire to do something in response to emergent stress situations on a campus has, more often than not, brought with it piecemeal solutions and a resulting poor integration of concept and action. Furthermore, the objective of wresting new knowledge through *basic research* in college mental health, without regard to immediate program utility, has only recently begun to take hold within the design of higher education. (Group, 1962; King, 1964)

The increasing research interest in college mental health may be illustrated with a brief comparison of the extent of the published literature in this field over two periods of time. For the period from March, 1919, to January, 1947, a mimeographed report on "Publications on College Mental Hygiene" (Yale, n.d.) listed 239 items, the majority of which were published in the decades of the twenties and thirties. A later bibliography on student mental health, covering the years from 1936 to 1955, contained 1803 listings and abstracts of books, articles, and reports. (Funkenstein &

Wilkie, 1956) With due regard to the overlapping years of coverage, this bibliographic expansion has the flavor of a publication explosion and has been maintained in recent years. Articles and reports on college mental health have continued to be published in a wide variety of journals. Four national periodicals, however, heavily weighted toward this topical area, are presently on the scene: the *Journal of College Student Personnel,* a quarterly issued since 1959 by the American College Personnel Association; the monthly *Journal of the American College Health Association* (formerly *Student Medicine*), first issued in 1952; the quarterly *NASPA,* the journal of the National Association of Student Personnel Administrators, initially published in December, 1963; and the *Journal of the National Association of Women Deans and Counselors,* now completing its third decade of publication. Clearing-house programs, both governmental and private, designed to abstract the literature on college students and student personnel services, have also been appearing to supplement the information available in these four major periodicals. Of particular value in the private domain is the quarterly publication (first issued in 1965) of the College Student Personnel Institute (Claremont, California). In the national capital, the U.S. Office of Education (Department of Health, Education, and Welfare) has established the Clearinghouse for Studies on Higher Education. In recent years as well, a number of academic institutions have established frameworks for research, notably the Center for the Study of Higher Education at the University of California (Berkeley), the Center for Research and Training in Higher Education at the University of Cincinnati, and the Mellon Foundation for the Advancement of Education at Vassar College.

Three

Public health achievements in preventing physical disease have, as a matter of course, spurred the search for methods and programs of preventing mental disturbance. (Gruenberg, 1953; Goldston, 1965) This medically oriented approach, in time conceptualized and framed in social-action terms, had had slow acceptance by college administrations and faculties prior to the period of the Second World War. Much of the resistance was dissipated by a stabilized understanding of institutional responsibility for personnel services to students, by the very gradual inclusion of psychiatric support within the framework of established medical services, and by the impact of the presence on campus of numbers of war veterans with neuropsychiatric disabilities. Farnsworth (1965, p. 21), in a statement that could not easily have been made a quarter of a century ago, has highlighted the change of institutional climate that has worked through to the present: "The question is no longer whether psychiatric services should be provided but which ones are appropriate, considering the nature of student populations, particular institutions, and certain factors fundamental to the educational process." The development of psychiatric services within the medical structure on campus has been corelative with the mental health efforts of specialists in the guidance and counseling field, and since the latter have maintained as much concern as the former in the rendering of mental health services to students and faculties, some problems of overall jurisdiction and management have arisen in troublesome fashion. The counseling specialists in mental health (who may include psychiatrists and social workers in their service arrangements, but typically remain within the framework of the office of the Dean of Students) have raised serious questions as to the wisdom and appropriateness of incorporating without change a purely medical model into the campus service structure for mental health, and then of considering this model as the hub around which all other mental health services of the college will revolve. At present, where the parallelism in structure has developed, effective working arrangements for liaison have also been developed, although with an implicit measure of professional uneasiness. A further comment of Farnsworth (1962, p. 816) is very much to the point here: "Collaboration sometimes becomes difficult because of personality needs or qualities of the individuals concerned, but there is no theoretical bar to working together with mutual satisfaction."

Nevertheless, through whatever institutional channels it has been able to find expression, the preventive public health theme is to be considered multifaceted in both concept and application. Where well-developed college mental health programs are found, at least *three levels of preventive action* may be perceived, each of which is understandably intertwined with the others in the actual rendering of services:

1. An effort to lower the incidence of aberrant expressions among students.
2. The development of arrangements through which morbid processes, already ongoing, will be arrested or shortened in duration or maintained without advanced complications.
3. The establishment of a system of rehabilitation for distressed students or groups of students.

In their application to the mental health demonstration project at the University of Florida (Gainesville), these ideas were explicitly stated by Barger (1964) as follows:

> One of the central concepts of the public health approach is prevention. Now, an event which occurs over time can be "prevented," at any stage of its development, from proceeding to the next stage, if something is done to interrupt its development or progression to a succeeding stage. For conceptual simplicity prevention has been thought of in terms of three stages or levels in the public health literature. That is, primary, secondary, and tertiary prevention.
>
> Primary prevention refers to action programs aimed at preventing disease from developing, or, in the case of a mental health program, preventing the development of emotional disturbances. The infectious agent or its carrier is eradicated, or the host is made invulnerable to infection as with vaccination. Such programs are referred to as primary prevention.
>
> Secondary prevention, on the other hand, refers to any action program designed to identify and treat illness in its early stages, before it becomes a serious illness, or emotional disturbance. Secondary prevention is directed toward the prevention of serious illness, not toward the prevention of illness occurring.
>
> Tertiary prevention refers to the treatment of illness, in the interest of preventing crippling, permanent damage or death. (p. 52)

One cannot fail, however, to recognize the tendency among college mental health workers both to accept and decry, at the same time, the application of this classical preventive design to the college setting. This mixture of attitudes is reminiscent of the argumentative dialogues between concerned individuals or groups—first, between those who are inclined to view all individuals as potential patients and those who prefer to spend their professional energies on the enhancement of healthy personalities (Frank, 1953); and, second, between those who deprecate the value of any service except that directed to the individual distressed student and those who maintain an exclusive focus on the concept that "the college is the patient." It is interesting that neither stance in any of these seemingly artificial debates negates nor diminishes the importance of the preventive approach. Nevertheless, as each point of view remains unintegrated with the other, college environments will perforce reflect sharp differences in their service arrangements for mental health. A zone of comparative clarity and consensus can surely be reached as a base for constructive action in college mental health programs, *if the preventive concept can be removed from its exclusive relatedness to mental illness and become more firmly grounded on the positive growth aspects of the student in his special environment.*

Significant material support for this latter viewpoint may be derived from two sources:

1. The satisfaction of the delegates at the first International Conference on Student Mental Health (September, 1956; Princeton, New Jersey; sponsored by the World Federation for Mental Health and the International Association of Universities) with a definition of *mental health*, which contained nothing directly connotative of mental illness: "The mentally healthy person is one who is developing toward personal maturity. Maturity is reached in the same degree as the individual can independently and in a fruitful way overcome his internal conflicts, realize his own aims in life and responsibly live in fellowship with others." (Funkenstein, 1959, pp. 417–418) In balance, the delegates did emphasize that positive mental health did not mean adjustment under all circumstances, conformity, freedom from anxiety and tension, constant happiness, the absence of personal idiosyncrasies, the undermining of authority, or an opposition to religious values.

2. The general agreement in the literature that the most significant personal gains from psychotherapeutic assistance will accrue to those college students who have not as yet established *rigid and chronic* patterns of neurotic reaction, but rather, in their present maturational progression, have been *acutely* overwhelmed by inner and outer pressures, in response to which they have resorted to deleterious (often archaic) defensive expressions.

This same keynote for college mental health has been well illustrated by Blos (1946. Others include Allport, 1964; Farnsworth, 1962; Nixon, 1960, 1964) as an outcome of his own experience with the mental health of college students:

> Cases which come to the attention of the psychological counselor are as diversified as might be expected. Gross mental disturbances are referred to clinic or psychiatrist with the help of the family. Neurotic conditions are, if possible, also referred for psychotherapy or psychoanalysis. This leaves us with a bulk of disturbances which do not fit into any of the customary classifications of personality disorders. In fact, when I tried to classify 387 cases, I was appalled to find that classification would indeed be fitting them into a procrustean bed, for the sake of typology. I began to realize that I was dealing with case material which was basically different from cases seen in a mental hygiene or child guidance clinic; the difference being that no definite symptom complex had developed in these cases. A dysfunction had made its appearance in a limited field of the student's life, which rendered college an unsatisfying or unsatisfactory experience.
>
> Complaints of this kind rarely come to the attention of psychiatric or mental hygiene services outside the college, because the individual is

> still in the state of seeking solutions by managing the environment or by isolating his conflicts in the process of symptom formation. It is precisely in this state of personality disturbance, when a maturational conflict is acted out rather directly in a displaced form, when the symptom has not yet crystallized into a symptom complex, that psychological counseling is called for. This type or state of personality disturbance is, in fact, the legitimate field of psychological counseling. (p. 572)

This more or less common view has been partially offset in the reported experiences of a number of mental health workers, who have insisted that "students at college mental hygiene clinics are often underdiagnosed," in terms of the formal psychiatric nomenclature (Selzer, 1960); that the symptomatological range among college students is "indistinguishable from that seen in an adult psychiatric clinic" (Swartz, Posin, & Kaye, 1958); and that "there has been a sharp increase in the number of severely disturbed cases seen in the Student Health Service during the six years covered by this research" (Weiss, Segal, & Sokol, 1965).

Four

The area of college mental health has tended to become imbued with the sense of community which has uniquely pervaded public health thought. Over the years it has been made clear that the management of emotional disorders could be more effective and shorter in duration if accomplished at or close to the home base of the individual. Both logic and experience have pointed to the local community as the natural unit of population for the proper development of a coordinated program of prevention and treatment and of the promotion of mental health. The only consideration in the present instance has been as to whether collegiate institutions as such are natural communal entities and might justifiably be expected to incorporate mental health services within their educational structures. The consensus on this point has been dramatically positive; and the kind of definition of the term *communities* deemed appropriate to campus environments has been that of Williams (1961, p. 131): "units of population, the members of which share certain values in common, toward which they feel a significant degree of loyalty and identification, and in which they could—but do not necessarily—find all aspects of living." Still to be brought into this dynamic college design, however, is the active promotion of the open-door concept for students from socioeconomic segments of the general population, to whom collegiate opportunities have not been previously available. A look at both the present and future reveals a significant degree of convergence of the demographic patterns of the nation and the colleges, and a consequential broadening of the population base for higher education.

There are obvious advantages to the perception of the college as a unique community with special opportunities for mental health service, research, and training. Indeed, in at least one aspect, the setting has been described as "an ideal place for research and innovations in psychotherapy." (Comer, 1965) In general, the focus has been on the comparatively high degree of homogeneity characterizing the student body in such factors as age range, intellectual endowment, verbal facility, health status, family background, career and social aspiration, and maturational needs. Realistically, the college is favored with such a remarkable juncture of human circumstances and resources, with diminished variability, as to be able to proffer mental health services with desirable simplicity, greater depth, and clearer target than would be feasible in the community at large. Erikson (1961) has expressed this thought with remarkable facility:

> Colleges, of course, are foremost among the institutions which permit the study of comparable inner problems under demonstrable conditions. Students are men and women of the same age group, who share a certain range of intellectual endowment and a converging set of motivations, and who compete in life tasks dictated by a known tradition which they have (more or less) freely chosen as a trusted style. Colleges, furthermore, offer young people a sanctioned interim between childhood and adulthood. Such a *moratorium* is often characterized by a combination of prolonged immaturity and provoked precocity, which makes colleges not only good study grounds, but—as the surrounding communities always have been most eager to note—breeding grounds for deviant behavior of all kinds, whether such behavior is attributed to the influence of scholastics or humanistics, radicalism, existentialism, or psychoanalysis. (pp. xiii–xiv)

Crucial to this view is the recognition of institutional organization, partly visible and partly assumed through its operations, as providing for an interplay of psychological and sociological factors which, in turn, evolves into what may be termed a mental health climate. The structural dynamisms inherent in this circumstance are important to a comprehensive understanding of collegiate ecology; yet, admittedly, the nature of the organic interdependence of college and student, and the outcomes of their symbiotic relationship, have yet to become the subject of serious investigation. One of the most cogent formulations representative of this social-psychological conceptualization is that of Sanford (1963, pp. 17–22).

Prevalence and Incidence Studies: Epidemiological Data

Explosive is the term currently used to characterize the rapidity of increase of our national population. The demographic projections for the college-age populace have been no less dramatic: within one decade, by 1975, as it is anticipated, the category of 18-to-21-year-old individuals will rise by more than thirty per cent to the level of nearly 16 million. By that date, nearly 9 million of these young people will be enrolled in various institutions of higher learning. Past experience has indicated that forecasts of this type are on the conservative side; but, whether higher or lower limits of estimate are involved, there cannot be any question that higher education is due to be confronted with the pressures of mass education similar to those now apparent in the primary and secondary school systems. No less important than the matter of numbers, however, will be the opening of the registration doors in colleges and universities to a widening spectrum of social classes. What is expected under these correlated circumstances is an expansion of mental health services somewhat similar in scope, although not necessarily in kind, to those already being applied to the general population.

The need to know, in mental health terms, what it is that prevails in higher education has become a matter of urgency. Epidemiological data, validly and reliably brought forth, must be acknowledged as the first-order derivation of efforts to determine the structure and direction of college mental health services. This fact-finding problem was designated by King (1964) as having the number-one priority in present research. In his analysis of this problem for colleges and universities, King concluded that two types of studies were particularly relevant: "The first deals with emotional problems as seen by the professional. Note has been taken of the fact that many people feel the standard psychiatric nomenclature does not do justice to the conditions which occur. Also, the frequency of various symptoms and conflicts in different colleges is unknown. . . . The other study seeks data about emotional problems from the students' own point of view." (p. 329)

The published literature is replete with scattered information on numbers, rates, and types of mental disturbances among college students generally and in particular institutions; some of the studies and reports date back to the third and fourth decades of this century. An examination of these documents is bound, however, to raise issues of considerable complexity. Not only is there a question of the soundness of their investigative designs, but also a matter of difficulty in assessing widely dissimilar bases of data collection and interpretation. Comparative analyses of the presented data, more often than not, tend to become stymied by this mixed range of methodologies. These difficulties have been highlighted in Baker's (1965) critique of reported indices of psychological disorders in college populations:

> Probably the most important factor, one which represents a condition that must be specified in the construction of an estimate, is the definition of disturbance in terms of degree of severity necessary for professional attention to be indicated. Other factors include whether the investigator goes to the student body in a general search for signs of pathology, or waits for students to present themselves (or to be presented) to mental health services; the readiness with which students seek help from college mental health facilities as opposed to others available, or as opposed to none at all; the kind of population selected for study in terms of academic and social accomplishment and apparent health; whether diagnosis is made from clinical-type interview material or from psychological tests; the relative proneness or reluctance of workers to diagnose pathology; how closely the student is studied; whether the measure employed is based on a shorter or longer segment of the college career; and possibly cultural differences in the student body. (p. 539)

Other points of descriptive neglect have been the size of the student population, the nature of the larger community within which the institution functions, sex and age differences within the student groups, and the possible differential patterns of mental health expression from the freshman to the senior years. (Baker, 1963; Baker & Nidorf, 1964; Freedman, 1960; Miller, 1963–1964; Pearlman, 1950, 1958)

With due regard to these methodological considerations and problems of depth and scope of content, it is nonetheless appropriate to review a selection of the incidence and prevalence reports in the field of college mental health, within the following frame: general and multi-institutional surveys, studies of individual colleges and universities, and canvasses of student reactions.

General and Multi-Institutional Surveys

The typically encountered statement is that ten per cent of all college students have emotional problems of an order serious or severe enough to warrant the intervention of professional assistance (Farnsworth, 1965; Group, 1957). In some instances, this figure has been gauged as a conservative one (Blaine, Coon, Farnsworth, Munter, & Walters, 1964). Grounded on the experiences of the larger colleges and universities with clearly structured mental health services, it represents an extrapolation of the numbers of students requesting and using these special facilities. A cautionary approach to this mode of generalization is obviously in order in the light of the range of differences among institutions of higher learning. Most reported data, as will be noted, are derived from medical offices or health services, and rarely concern themselves with the records of other offices and agencies of the college or university which are no less likely to be rendering mental health assistance to students.

In one of the earliest reported surveys (Morrison & Diehl, 1924), a questionnaire sent to 20 universities having well-organized health programs revealed that none employed a mental hygienist. Mental health service programs were known to exist in a few institutions, however, but their common aspects rarely came to public view; in a number of instances, they were semi-formal structures developing out of the concerns and commitments of a few professionals, whose efforts were just beginning to be regularly budgeted by their respective institutions. Two surveys of broader scope were accomplished in the mid-thirties. That of Diehl and Shepard (1939), for the American Youth Commission (American Council on Education), was based on the questionnaire responses during 1935–1936 of 549 colleges and universities. Fewer than one quarter of the schools were found to have provisions for some sort of mental hygiene counseling. In 202 of these institutions, it proved possible to identify a total of 67 psychiatrists, psychologists, and psychiatric social workers, and in only 11 instances were there indications of student counselors with special assignments in the mental health area. No information was provided by the investigators, however, as to the numbers of students seen in these services. The broader canvass of Raphael and his colleagues (Raphael, 1937; Raphael, Gordon, & Dawson, 1938) covered the facilities of 865 colleges and universities, and for the 479 responding institutions, fewer than half (41 per cent) revealed a noticeable type of consultation service for disturbed students. Only 142 schools (about 30 per cent) were considered to have well crystallized services, while the arrangements in the remainder were describable as loosely organized and irregular in operation. Among the well-organized services, 43 were clearly under health-service psychiatric direction, but in the main (in 99 institutions) the services were made available to students through deans' offices and personnel departments. Raphael did make an effort to determine the extent and kind of student contacts, but the replies he received to this facet of his questionnaire were too few and indefinite to make possible meaningful tabulations or comment.

About ten years later, shortly after the end of World War II, a questionnaire distribution by Fry (Group, 1949) to the 4,765 members of the American Psychiatric Association, which produced 2,238 returns, indicated that there were only 30 psychiatrists actively engaged on a full-time basis in established college mental hygiene programs, and an additional 63 affiliated on a part-time arrangement. A further group of 114 were tallied as tangentially related to higher education as visiting psychiatrists or consultants. The 1953 data of Moore and Summerskill (1954) and Moore (1960), based on 938 institutions, were largely focused on general medical services, but did point out that 17 per cent of the colleges and universities had some provisions for mental health diagnosis and treatment. Where the mental health facilities were structurally manifest, 98 institutions were found to be employing one or more psychiatrists on their respective staffs, and 125 were noted as having one or more psychologists within this service area.

None of these surveys was particularly useful, except indirectly, in providing information on the prevalence of emotional disturbances among students. They served essentially to point out that a problem did exist and that a movement to cope with this problem was steadily gaining force. In 1953–1954, in preparation for their report to the Fourth National Conference on Health in Colleges, Gundle and Kraft (1956) delineated a more rounded picture of the mental health resources for college individuals. Their questionnaires went out to all four-year colleges and universities with more than 250 students and all two-year colleges with more than 500 registrants in the United States and Canada. Completed returns were received from 728 institutions out of a canvassed total of 1,141. Only 99 schools (14 per cent of those responding) were found to be maintaining special facilities within their health services to deal with emotional problems. Of these institutions 87 had psychiatrists, 52 had psychologists, and 17 had social workers, either on full-time or part-time assignments; and for the first time noted anywhere in the literature, graduate students in training were being used in a systematic fashion to render service within 13 universities. In the total figures, bringing together both full-time and part-time individuals, there were 166 psychiatrists (inclusive of psychiatric residents), 115 psychologists, 32 social workers, and 49 graduate students. There was no evidence in this report, however, of the existence of any professional workers in collegiate agencies outside of the jurisdiction of the regular health services. It was interesting to note that the typical mental health team, consisting of a psychiatrist, psychologist, and social worker, was a feature of 16 universities. It was also clear that the likelihood of the existence of a formal psychiatric service was in direct proportion to the size of enrollment of the institution. For example, in schools with 10,000 or more students, 13 out of 16 had well-developed mental health services, while 549 out of 601 colleges with fewer than 3,000 in enrollment were reported as having no regular mental health facilities.

Gundle and Kraft's (1956) data included the percentages of students seen in the mental health offices of 99 schools, relative to their respective total registrations. Their overall mean value was 4.7 per cent, with a distribution of individual means from 0.61 to 40 per cent. In their analysis of this result, they had this to say:

> We were surprised that there was such a wide range, but the 40 per cent figure was an exception and for one small institution. From the questionnaire we deduced that these were primarily screening interviews where a large number of individuals were seen one time. Most institutions were reasonably close to the mean. This figure is interesting in view of the assumption that has frequently been made that a well run service will see about 10 per cent of the student population. . . . In the light of our findings this figure may have to be revised; five per cent seems to be more reasonable and accurate. Aside from a few small colleges where as much as 15 to 40 per cent of the student population is seen in one hour screening interviews, our questionnaires reflect that even in well-organized and adequately staffed services, the percentage of enrollment seen may be only as high as 6.5 per cent. Any higher figures reflected primarily screening practices. It appeared that the greater the enrollment, the smaller the percentage of the enollment which was seen, even though the units in larger universities have a larger staff. (p. 68)

This last point deserves special note, in that it revealed a tendency among the well-established university services to devote more diagnostic and therapeutic time and to engage in more comprehensive efforts per student than would be the case in smaller institutions with more limited staffs.

On the basis of his own review, Whittington (1963) vouched for this more reasonable and accurate figure of five per cent for students seen in the psychiatric clinics of university settings. Even this statistic, he asserted, "certainly exceeds prevalences reported in other subcultures." (p. 28) Paulsen (1964) was nonetheless inclined to maintain the reliability of his own general estimate, stating that from 8 to 12 per cent of a student body were severely troubled and enduring complications in their campus living; that another 10 to 15 per cent were mildly to moderately troubled but without serious impairment in social and academic functioning, and that a still further 20 per cent could benefit from professional contact, if only for an hour or two.

During 1962 Robbins (1963) conducted a survey of the 64 institutional members of the Pacific Coast College Health Association; replies were received from 46 of these colleges and universities, all but two of the nonrespondents being privately supported institutions of under 2,000 enrollment. The range of enrollment among the respondents was from 1,161 to 25,000 for the tax-supported group, and from 697 to 13,000 for the private institutions. Among the 46 colleges and universities on which his tabulations were based, 23 used psychiatric or psychological consultants for the mental health screening of entering students, and 34 made psychiatric appointments available to students subsequent to the registration period. While no data were presented here on the numbers and proportions of students using the existent mental health services, it was apparent that most of the reporting institutions limited the number of visits per student and generally restricted the professional contact time to cases easily amenable to treatment.

Seven leading universities (Cornell, Colorado, Kansas, Illinois, Northwestern, Purdue, and Wayne State), known to have psychiatric facilities of moderate scope, were reported by Wilms (1965) as having a yearly average of 4.4 (range: 2.3 to 6.2) patients per 100 students in the campus population. The average span of interviews per student was from 2.6 to 8.0, with a mean of 5.0 contacts for the entire group of institutions. Where there was any variance from this latter overall average, according to Wilms, it was in part the outcome of the custom on some campuses to provide routine screening examinations for education and nursing students and in part due to the relative openness of the psychiatric service to students, faculty, and administration.

Running through most of these larger surveys are concepts pertinent to clinics, student patients, and formal psychiatric medicine. While there is a peripheral awareness in some of the data of the broader aspects of college mental health and the constructive roles of nonpsychiatric college agencies and professional personnel, the central emphasis on the medical model remains strongly in evidence. The regular and now firmly established student health service patterns, all under medical direction, have tended to become absorptive of the campus mental health programs in general and the nonpsychiatric professional personnel attached to them. This is a process which has brought to the fore an old and repeated theme that, since anything related to health falls to the medical profession, anything touching on mental health must, as a matter of course, fall within the province of psychiatrists as prime movers. While due recognition is accorded to the ancillary cooperation of counselors, psychologists, social workers, and others in the college mental health field and to the fact that college mental health problems are only in small part the problems of psychopathology, there is a continued insistence on the part of many psychiatrists, either individually or through their professional associations, on their right to or primary jurisdiction over the management, direction, and supervision of college mental health programs. There has been relatively little flexibility in this attitude, unfortunately, with the result that innovative approaches in college mental health have often been hampered. In terms of the broader concepts of mental health, more commonly accepted now in a preventive public health framework, it is important to recognize that the more extensive contributions are being made in college settings by nonpsychiatric professionals under such functional designations as "psychological counseling," "clinical counseling," and "personal counseling" and that the efforts of these individuals are more closely bound up with the positive mental health-inducing activities of campus life than those of the psychiatric clinics or centers.

There are few general surveys of psychological counseling activities in higher education. In 1961 Congdon and Lothrop (1963) attempted to assess this area of service on a nationwide level, covering 109 colleges and universities of a nonsectarian, coeducational type ranging in enrollments from less than 2,500 to over 10,000. (Two thirds of the responding institutions were either state or municipally supported.) They found that only 76 schools offered psychological counseling or psychotherapy and only about half of these had this service established in an independent status or unit. The larger schools were more likely to have this service and to make it the exclusive function of a specific office on campus. As the institution increased in size, however, the percentage of a student body seen for psychological counseling tended to drop, in this instance from 12 to 2.5 per cent, an outcome which approximately matched that of Gundle and Kraft (1956). Nugent and Pareis (1965) submitted the following query, among others, to the directors of over 1,000 officially recognized college and university centers throughout the United States and Canada: "Does the College have a psychiatric unit for students as a part of its immediate administrative structure?" Sixty per cent of the reporting institutions had registrations ranging from 1,500 to over 15,000. Of the 454 respondents, 80 per cent indicated the absence of such a psychiatric unit, and 176 of them revealed no manifest arrangement for the use of psychiatric consultants. Within those institutions which did have provisions for psychiatric consultation, the data inferred that no more than about twenty counseling centers employed psychiatrists as full-time members of their staffs. It was interesting to note, however, that only slightly over half of the counseling directors believed their respective colleges or universities should have distinct psychiatric units. In a somewhat less inclusive survey of 117 university and college counseling center staffs, Cass (1961) estimated that approximately 70 per cent had some sort of psychiatric consultation service available to counselors and their students.

The fact-finding canvass of Cowen (1960) was concerned with the activities of psychologists in undergraduate personal counseling and psychotherapy within 50 mental health programs. With but two exceptions, his data were derived from all the institutions of higher education which were listed in 1958 as having Ph.D. training programs in clinical psychology approved by the American Psychological Association. The universities varied in size of undergraduate enrollment from approximately 725 to 26,000. All 50 schools answered affirmatively to the question, "Do you provide counseling or psychotherapy for undergraduates with personal, social, and emotional problems?" A follow-up series of queries, eliciting responses from about 70 per cent of the counseling programs, explored the extent of the therapeutic services rendered to the students. Cowen found that the number of students seen during a year for personal counseling and psychotherapy ranged from 15 to 750, the midpoint figure being about 125. The average number of sessions per student was nearly 11, but the median figure of 6 was considered by him to be a more accurate reflection of the central tendency in this instance. An indication of the more intensive psychotherapeutic work done in certain institutions appeared in the wide span of data on the mean numbers of interviews per student—2.5 to 95 sessions. One questionnaire item, intended to define the types of staff members devoting time to personal counseling and psychotherapy, brought forth the following result: 49 per cent of the counselees had been seen by the regular staff psychologists of the center, 45 per cent by graduate students in training, and 6 per cent by other personnel, usually medical. In this regard, Cowen (1960) remarked,

> These overall figures do not however capture the variation among schools; for some, 100 per cent of undergraduate therapy is done by staff while for others it is done by graduate students. Moreover the data are overweighted by exclusively psychological facilities, or by the psychological facility in a university which is also known to have separate psychiatric facilities. Doubtless they would change drastically with inclusion of comparable information from the many student health psychiatric facilities actively in operation." (p. 68)

In summary, certain impressions have been left with this writer following his review of these general and multi-institutional surveys:

1. As yet, the prevalence picture of college mental health remains extremely spotty and without adequate delineation. The sole reliance in the surveys on a questionnaire approach and on a limited number of queries, along with gaps in the sampling procedures, has given a superficial cast to outcomes. This does not diminish the importance of these generalized efforts: they are rightfully to be considered a part of a long-range developmental process of investigation, and are undoubtedly preliminary to the application of more advanced and refined methods of research. The presently existing data, even though of limited utility, are sure to lead to combined extensive and depth studies of prevalences in colleges and universities, in epidemiological patterns similar to those already in effect for urban and other communities. At the moment, what we are left with is an emphatic confirmation of the emergent mental health pressures on all campuses, and a consensus that the resolution of the associated problems must rest with the institutions themselves in balance with their accepted educational missions.

2. Incidence reports derived from multi-institutional surveys have produced variable results. The criteria for data collection, the explicitness of research criteria and definitions, and the consideration of institutional qualities and differences have only too often been conspicuous by their absence. Not unexpectedly, "facts" have tended to be dealt with in procrustean fashion, squeezed into statistical conformity with predesigned frames. The commonly seen figure of 10 per cent of a student body as having emotional disturbances serious enough to warrant professional assistance can only be reckoned as relevant to a few institutions with well-ordered psychiatric arrangements. Incidence investigations for a wider range of colleges and universities, even when based on the same or similar sources of information (e.g., the psychiatric services of student health facilities) have come up with percentages which are significantly higher or lower. Several factors must be adduced for a partial explanation of this mixed circumstance: *first*, much of the data has been pulled solely out of the experiences of psychiatrists in the college health centers and then projected without due caution onto entire student bodies; *second*, the health center data, which have constituted the fundament of most multi-institutional reports, have remained isolated from, and therefore uncombined with, the mental health statistics of other campus agencies (ACHA, 1961); and *third*, little weight has been given to the private efforts of

students, especially in urban settings where off-campus psychotherapeutic help may be more readily available, to deal with their upsetting reactions unbeknownst to their respective institutions (Farnsworth, 1965; Pearlman, 1966).

3. Over the past half century, except for the period of World War II, the college mental health movement has been gathering considerable momentum. Its early progress was slow, at times unsteady, and, more often than not, its impetus was dependent on the leadership of a number of key individuals in psychiatry and psychology. Such advances as it has had have to a degree paralleled, although with some lag, the cultural trends toward the acceptance of community mental health needs and action programs in the nation. There are relatively few reservations now about the role and value of mental health services in educational settings (Farnsworth, 1965); the major uncertainties pertain rather to the locus of these services within institutions, their scope and functioning in varied types of colleges, the qualifications and types of professional personnel to be employed, and administrative relationships.

4. Dual service arrangements exist on many campuses in the mental health area, one of which, for the sake of convenience, may be termed the counseling division, the other of which is an integral part of the medical or health service. In a fully organized mental health program, each may be found to function independently of the other, even with similar personnel patterns, but with an agreed-on degree of collaboration or liaison; or both may overlap each other and share functions and personnel. These styles of coexistence have proven to be workable by and large, but the inherent tensions in this balancing of structures have become noticeable in some instances and have already given rise to considerations of a need for a new model for mental health service in higher education. In the less developed programs, this duality tends not to exist, since most of the mental health activity, as far as it exists, is carried on by counseling or clinical psychologists, at times with the consultative assistance of psychiatrists who may or may not be members of the medical center staff. There is as yet only a figurative handful of social workers in college-level programs assigned either to the counseling division or to the health offices. An expansion in the use of graduate students in clinical psychology under close supervision has been evident in the mental health programs of some universities; and where the latter have affiliated medical schools and hospitals, a few resident psychiatrists will be found to be rendering service to students.

5. An expected conclusion from a review of the surveys is that the

larger the college or university, the more formally structured and regular is its mental health service. More unexpected, however, is the revelation that the more organized the service, the smaller is the percentage of the student body that was seen therein. The most probable interpretation of this datum is that, despite the availability of a larger staff, there is increased diagnostic and therapeutic time accorded to each accepted student; at the same time, there is a greater possibility that the amount of allocated time away from direct service is increased and is devoted both to programs of faculty orientation and consultation and to research endeavors.

Studies of Individual Institutions

The same issues of reliability and validity which have been touched upon with respect to multi-institutional surveys are also relevant to the assessment of the prevalence and incidence studies of individual colleges and universities. The comparability of these published reports, often lacking in explicit definitions, criteria, population delineations, and other research requirements, is necessarily severely curtailed. It is not unusual to discover at times that case-finding and case-reporting have tended, frequently without significant awareness on the part of investigators, to turn into case-making with obviously biased outcomes. The present selection of studies is intended only to develop a limited type of generalization, essentially with the view of clarifying the directions that further research must take.

Reviewing the experience with emotional disorders in the health service of Harvard University during the past decade, Farnsworth (1965) noted that from 8 to 9 per cent of the student body (about 14,000 enrollment) sought psychiatric help each year. In addition, he estimated that an unknown number of students, to the extent of 3 or more per cent of the university registration, arranged for private psychiatric assistance in the nonacademic, urban community. Mental hospitalization occurred in 15 to 25 cases per year for reasons of psychotic reactivity; but, in constructive outcome, about 70 per cent of those leaving the university because of psychoses were able eventually to return to their campus studies, and in three out of five instances were sufficiently capable of maintaining their psychiatric improvement to the point of graduation. In a somewhat different collegiate setting, Nixon (1964) "guessed" that 15 to 20 per cent of the psychologically normal student population at Vassar would, if the opportunity existed, be willing to seek the services of a counselor or psychotherapist; and, in the course of an academic year, he estimated that about half of this group tended to visit him as a psychiatrist.

These two approaches to data collection, as far as they go, reflect the typical difference in epidemiological perception that runs through most other reports. In the one instance, there is a statistical dependence on treated cases of illness in a specific agency of the institution; in the other, there is a trend toward focus on total-health and total-illness calculations. Both approaches have merit, but the former, despite its more limited results, dependent as it is on full-fledged cases coming to a fixed place, is seductively easier to take. Both Farnsworth and Nixon attempt prudently, as do many others, to establish a partial convergence between the two methods of investigation, although with limited success.

A prime illustration of the effort toward partial convergence is available in the morbidity report of Evans and Warren (1962) at the main branch of the University of Wisconsin. They reviewed the medical records for a ten-year period (ending in 1959) of both the Student Clinic and the Student Infirmary, which provided the health services for a student population averaging about 13,500 per year. Over the decade, they found the utilization rate of the clinic outpatient services to vary minimally between 2.5 and 3.0 visits per year per student, and year by year it was noted that between 5 and 10 per cent of the student body were hospitalized in the infirmary. With specific reference to emotional illness, the infirmary admission rate remained quite constant in the course of any one year, while psychiatric consultations in the outpatient Clinic tended to reach high levels in June and September, coincident with the opening of the summer and fall semesters. More significant for our purposes was their effort to group their data into yearly patterns and broad clinical syndromes. The "Big Four" among the illnesses of the young adult in college proved to be, in order of frequency, respiratory infections, gastrointestinal upsets, skin diseases, and psychiatric problems. The appearance of this last category in its relatively high position among all morbid conditions in the university was a new finding, according to these investigators, since emotional and psychiatric problems had not previously been found to be among the first ten common illnesses in morbidity reports based on nonacademic communities with large populations. Apart from the value they gave to their experimental design in producing accurate figures, Evans and Warren adduced the following circumstances as explanations of the higher psychiatric illness figures for college students: "first, the greater likelihood of the emergence of emotional problems in university students as opposed to those in a more stable working environment and secondly, the availability and low cost of counseling and psychiatric services in our student health department." (p. 586)

A variety of designs of considerably smaller scope has been applied in individual institutions to determine local incidence patterns. Using a questionnaire method which categorized respondents in three dimensions (intrapsychic function, interpersonal function, and social role function), each of which encompassed varying degrees of clinical disturbance, and supplementing their tabulations with the interview judgments of psychiatrists, Smith, Hansell, and English (1963) surveyed a 20 per cent sample of the 1965 graduating class of a metropolitan, church-affiliated liberal arts college of moderately small size (less than 1,800 in enrollment). For the 86 subjects of their study, 58 per cent were found to be without significant psychopathology, 30 per cent showed subclinical disturbance, and 12 per cent were rated as "clinically disturbed." No hospitalizable case was discovered in the entire group. Comparing the students in their progression from the first to the second years of college, the group as a whole was described as improved in its mental health status, showing 10 per cent more "well" individuals and 6 per cent fewer "clinically disturbed." Whether this improvement was to be charged to psychiatric intervention or to the unaided process of maturation was not stated in this report. In any case, what is left in the absence of much more knowledge, qualitative and in terms of living experience, about this small group of subjects is an incidence of detectable psychiatric disturbance that is higher than encountered elsewhere; but what this fact means for this particular institution is not indicated.

Weiss, Segal, and Sokol (1965), using a combination of psychiatric data from the health service at Dartmouth College and from Minnesota Multiphasic Personality Inventory protocols of six successive classes of entering freshmen, tried to determine the prevalence trend over the six-year period beginning in 1958. Their data were based on 1,036 subjects out of a student universe of 4,389. According to their criteria and definitions, they found 11.5 per cent of their subjects to be significantly emotionally impaired in a clinical sense, but the outcome impressing them most was the sharp increase in incidence of such impairment over six years, from 6.9 per cent of the entering students in the class of 1962 to 16 per cent of the entering students in the class of 1967. They claimed support for this increase as real, in that over one quarter of the most impaired students and fewer than 6 per cent of the least impaired had seen a college psychiatrist at least once in their academic careers.

The experiences of Selzer (1960) and his coworkers at the Mental Hygiene Clinic of the University of Michigan were brought to bear in argument against the tendency in the literature "to implant the idea that little if anything is wrong with most students who seek help at a college mental hygiene clinic." (p. 131) Reviewing several hundred referred students ($N = 506$) psychiatrically interviewed over one and a half years (1957–58), and applying the formal psychiatric categories, he asserted that over 80 per cent fell into the three major psychodiagnostic classifications, psychoneurosis, personality disorder, and schizophrenia, with the latter reaching the level of 21.7 per cent. With the three major diagnoses accounted for, there remained only a small residue of students defined as having "adjustment reactions" (8.3 per cent), a milder type of disturbance which he claimed was falsely more accepted in the mental health services of other universities and was typically underdiagnosed. The extent of the psychotherapy given to his group was noted by Selzer: the students were seen over eighteen months for a total of 961 interviews, 25 per cent of them meeting with him in session five or more times. The classification of diagnosed psychosis had been less drastically accorded to students at Michigan in the earlier study of Raphael (1937)—1.4 per cent of the total enrollment at the university. Braaten's clinic data (1961) at Cornell revealed a ratio of only three diagnosed psychotics per thousand students, for a total in 1958–59 of 31 in a student population of about 10,000.

The case evaluations of Swartz, Posin, and Kaye (1958) appeared to tally with those of Selzer. In summarizing the diagnostic categories of 322 students seen for psychiatric reasons in the four years from 1952 to 1956 in the division of student health of Boston University (about 10,000 enrollment), Swartz, Posin, and Kaye considered 78 per cent of the students to have problems consistent with long-standing and deep-seated emotional difficulties or neurotic reactions with full-blown obsessive or depressive symptomatology. Psychotic reactivity was noted in as much as 7 per cent of the group. "Emotional problems basically of recent onset, or of a situational nature, are not what we find most commonly." (p. 227), he concluded. At the University of Massachusetts, the student clientele of the mental health service, in full-time operation only since 1961, was described (Allen & Janowitz, 1965) as a mixture of neurotics, psychotics, curiosity seekers, immature characters, somatizers, troublesome dormitory companions, cultists, sexual deviates, and relatively healthy adolescents with minor adjustment problems. The students dealt with at this university during 1961–63 numbered 636; 6.5 per cent were classed as psychotics, about one third were thought to be suffering from neurotic or characterological disorders, and another third showed the transitional adjustment reactions of adolescence. Of the cases 78 per cent were seen for 4 or fewer sessions, the average for the entire group being approximately 4 visits per case.

In each academic year at the Mental Health Clinic of the University of

Kansas, it was reported, about 4 per cent of the student body were seen, mostly on a self-referred basis. During 1957–58 and 1958–59, over 500 students visited the clinic, manifesting the full range of psychiatric illness except for the "diseases of old age" (Whittington, 1960). Whittington (1961) subsequently made an interesting effort to determine the differences between the *clients* of his institution's Guidance Bureau and the *patients* of the Mental Health Clinic. His results, based largely on interview reports and MMPI protocols, seemed to indicate more severe symptom patterns in the patient group, although an issue may be raised as to the nature of the diagnostic set of the clinic staff. At the University of Chicago (Elson, Ichikawa, & Kohut, 1963), the reported data indicated an average student load per year of 400, approximately 15 per cent of whom were carryovers from the preceding year. Comparing the first 200 students seen in 1938 with 349 students seen for the first time in 1962 at the mental hygiene clinic of the University of Missouri, Landfield, Nawas, and O'Donovan (1963) felt that the present students were facing difficulties of a more severe nature: "Academic complaints have more than tripled, and medical complaints and sexual problems have more than doubled. The number of students with suicidal potential has increased sharply." (p. 204) Diagnoses of acute or borderline psychosis rose from 1 per cent to 3 per cent in this quarter century of the clinic's operation.

As has been implied in other data, some university mental health clinics have hospitalization facilities available in affiliated infirmaries or in the hospitals attached to their respective medical schools. An example of this functional relationship is evident in the report of Kuehn (1965) on the Student Health Center of Indiana University. During the period of January through March, 1965, 424 students were seen in the mental health clinic, and of this number 52 were admitted to the inpatient service with psychiatric diagnoses. Only 10 of the students withdrew from the university following hospitalization, the balance developing sufficient personal reintegration to resume their studies. Kuehn's comment on this rate of hospitalization, which was apparently higher than that found in other institutions, was that his clinic used "elective" and "noncritical" admissions on frequent occasions as part of a total treatment program, on the basis of his experience that limited periods of hospitalization encouraged a rapid return to normal college life and reduced the number of dropouts under psychiatric conditions.

One of the largest universities (Yale), with well-developed clinic facilities, reported that in the 1964–1965 school year 970 individuals were seen in its Division of Student Mental Hygiene. A majority of them

($N = 412$) were undergraduate students, the balance ($N = 385$) being derived from the graduate and professional schools. Clinic service was additionally being rendered without special emphasis to a mixed group of employees, faculty, student dependents, and former students. Of the regular students, three fifths were self-referred, and about 7 per cent were afforded contact on the recommendations of off-campus sources (family, friends, and nonuniversity physicians). About one third were brought to the clinic's attention by administrators, faculty, other students, and health service physicians and nurses. During the year, for the entire caseload, there were 6,720 individual therapy hours and 887 visits for group therapy. (Davie, 1966) At a similarly large institution (Stanford), about 15 per cent of a student enrollment of 10,000 had contact with the mental health service during the academic year (Paulsen, 1964). Most (60 per cent) of these individuals experienced a resolution of their problems in the course of one or a few sessions at most; about one fifth required contact of from 10 to 20 hours, and the remaining 20 per cent received long-term therapy, including at times periods of hospitalization lasting from one to three weeks. These professional contacts, it should be noted, were not always continuous, since treatment intervals of several months, or even years, occurred in a number of instances. What is of significance in this institutional report, as well as others, is that students were able with appropriate mental health support to remain on campus and to function within acceptable academic limits.

At Harvard (McArthur, 1961), almost 600 cases were dealt with in the psychiatric service during the academic year 1956–1957. In the effort to classify these students in psychiatric terms, about one quarter were finally diagnosed as neurotic, another quarter were designated with other labels, mostly depressive reactions and schizoid states, and a third quarter were conveniently accorded "problem diagnoses," since there seemed to be no identifiable psychiatric ailment. The remaining quarter included a scattering of administrative problems, "adjustment reactions to adolescence," "adult situational reactions," and requests for information. McArthur was frank enough to state that the use of this diagnostic nomenclature was not very valid, especially (as he charmingly phrased it) "when applied to the adolescent chameleon." In the Harvard Graduate School of Arts and Sciences, which had no medical unit but shared psychiatric facilities with Harvard College and with the other graduate schools, 100 of the 1,500 enrolled were seen by the psychiatric service during one academic year. (Nelson, 1961)

Hall and Barger (1964), at the University of Florida, combined their data on clinic cases from both the University Mental Health Clinic and the University Counseling Center for the two classes admitted in 1961 and 1962. In their total sample of 6,764 students, they found that 464 (6.85 per cent) had been seen for mental health reasons, two thirds of them being male students. In their subsequent report, for the academic year 1963–1964, Barger and Hall (1964) produced somewhat similar figures, but also indicated that 8 out of every 10 patients were either self-referred or physician-referred, and that about three quarters of the students had only from one to four interviews with the professional personnel. A mixed pattern of diagnostic classifications was evolved for this group of students: no diagnosis was listed for 82 individuals, and among the others, 2.2 per cent were noted as psychotic, 25 per cent were labeled as having psychoneurotic reactions, 20 per cent were classified as having "personality disorders," and nearly one third were designated as having "transient situational conditions."

The reader will be alert to the fact that practically all of the data reported above have been derived from the medical or health services of colleges and universities. Relatively little information of a comparable type was available from those centers or agencies in higher education institutions which were not directly affiliated with health services but did render mental health services. These services generally tended to fall to the jurisdiction of the Dean of Students, and were headed by nonphysicians (usually psychologists). Data from several of these units are presented here for purposes of illustration.

At San Fernando State College (California), with a registration of about 9,000 students, 15 per cent of the student body requested individual counseling or group therapy. Sessions with these students averaged 2.5 per student during an academic year, with a range for the total group of from 1 to 54. (Palmer, 1963) The counseling service of Columbia College (New York) during 1962–1963 reached 331 students, or 12.7 per cent of the college enrollment. These students were not necessarily performing poorly in their courses, and many were found to be active in student activities, athletics, and campus social life. About half came to the counseling service completely on their own initiative; the other half sought help at the suggestion of someone else on or off campus. (Miller, 1963–1964)

At the psychological clinic of Clark University (Massachusetts) during 1964–1965, 131 students (including several graduate and former students) were served, in a number of instances by graduate psychology students or interns under supervision of the regular staff. (Baker, 1965) Of these, 60 per cent were seen in short-term psychotherapy up to a maximum of four visits; only 25 per cent were afforded longer-term contacts, averaging 14 hours for each. About one out of six presented such psychological circumstances as to make it advisable to refer him to an agency or private practitioner outside of the university. The majority of the students proved to be self-referred. In an earlier report of this psychological clinic, covering the experience of six academic years, Baker and Nidorf (1964) noted a general decrease in the incidence of appeals for psychological services as the classes moved from freshman to senior years. In part, this result could be accounted for by the attrition of those individuals who were not able to meet the stressful demands of the academic experience; but it could also be the outcome of a process of positive accommodation on the part of many students to these same stresses as they proceeded and matured through their four-year period of education.

At Brooklyn College, the direct mental health service is located within the Office of the Dean of Students and is essentially staffed by clinical psychologists. During the 1956–1957 academic year (Pearlman, 1958), the number of referrals amounted to about 3.5 per cent of the college enrollment of 7,700. As a group, for the most part, the referred individuals were at the age of 18 years or over (90 per cent), at the level of the freshman and sophomore classes (56 per cent), and more heavily balanced toward the male group (58 per cent). Somewhat over 50 per cent of the referrals were evaluated as acceptable for on-campus psychological service, and about one out of every six students in the total group was either referred to community sources of assistance or was found to be already in the process of receiving such help. Two thirds of the referrals were made by the general counseling and administrative offices, and another one fifth by members of the teaching faculty; and since these offices, along with the faculty, constituted the first line of screening for distressed students, the extent of the walk-in or self-referrals was comparatively low (5 per cent). In a follow-up study of this group, comparing the students who had accepted intensive psychological counseling with those who rejected their manifest need for such help, Watson (1961) concluded that the counseled individuals after two years had responded in such fashion as to become distinctly superior in scholastic achievement as measured by the extent of their continued attendance in college and their graduation with honors: "They were more successful in dealing with academic failure, more able to make a valid decision about whether to remain in college or to withdraw. They were more likely to have elicited favorable comment relative to behavior other than academic achievement." (pp. 103–104) Watson did not, however, make any attempt to prove that counseling alone was responsible for these results. As she viewed it, psychological counseling served essentially as a positive catalytic agent for those individuals whose personality structures enabled them to accept help for self-mobilization in periods of emotional crisis.

Several generalizations may be drawn from the above and other reports on the mental health services of individual institutions:

1. The numbers and percentages of the students afforded direct service in college institutions varied according to design and objectives developed for such service, the kinds of staff assigned, and the leadership opportunities permitted to professional workers. A narrow definition of the concept of mental health has tended in many settings to develop structures and procedures which focused on the treatment of mental illness, in which instances the services to students were routinely to be found in the psychiatric sections or divisions of the college medical offices. The formal diagnostic categories, typical of clinics and hospitals, were usually applied in these instances, and the training biases of professional workers were often reflected in what has been called *overdiagnosis*. The reports of mental health counselors not directly affiliated with the medical offices, whether they were psychologists, psychiatrists, or social workers, did not show this same degree of emphasis on pathological nomenclature.

2. The larger universities tended to budget their mental health services in a regularized and well-ordered fashion, and without any reflection that monies expended therefor constituted a loss to classroom and teaching expansion. Where these larger universities were located in developed urban areas, a reliance was shared with the available community mental health resources for service to students; and if these community resources were extensive, students were often to be found using them on their own initiatives and without reference to college facilities and records.

3. The more prevalent treatment method has been that described as "brief psychotherapy," whether group or individual; but the delineation of this therapeutic procedure as it was being effected in the collegiate environment has as yet remained unclear. Furthermore, group and community approaches to mental health enhancement have continued in a state of flux in college or university settings, although there has been fairly common agreement that the usual one-to-one or small-group treatment patterns are no longer able to meet campus mental health needs.

4. The development of mental health service arrangements in some universities has been accompanied by the structural incorporation of a training mission for mental health workers. While none too well organized at present, a movement is already proceeding to open the area of student

services to the training of counseling and clinical psychologists and psychiatric residents in the graduate and professional schools. The training has usually taken the form of field work, practicums, and internships and residencies, always within a framework of supervised practice, and has been a gladly accepted burden upon the available professional staff time and energy. There have been obvious counterbalancing compensations in increased service time to students and in the awareness that such training might eventually expand the numbers of new professional individuals seeking careers in college mental health.

5. The allocation of research time for the investigation of college mental health problems and the specific employment of research-minded individuals on mental health staffs have not as yet been generally recognized as important. Only a few institutions of higher education have such designated titles as "research psychologists" or "coordinator of research" in mental health; most are reluctant at this time to use precious service time for investigations and assessments, despite the long term values accruing from such endeavors. The research gap is partially being filled by the increasing availability of foundation and governmental funds, but in a spotty fashion, and with little attention to the need for cooperative and long-term studies.

Student Reactions to their Mental Health Experiences

As the served individuals, personally experiencing the stresses of growth and social development within the college community, students constitute the most important component in the provision of mental health services. Their needs and reactivity, both on individual and group levels, obviously must be gauged and then reflected in institutional arrangements. Most canvasses of student reactions have focused on the elicitation of problems and problem areas; relatively few have touched upon the students' efforts by and large to resolve their tension states through their inherent ego strengths. It is also well recognized by this time that the reported numbers of students who seek professional assistance in the mental health units of colleges and universities do not encompass those who have arranged for personal help elsewhere. The several reports briefly summarized here will serve illustratively to note what directions the investigations of student reactions have taken and, by implication, the areas which require further research.

Canada's Mental Health (1964), in announcing the formation of an advisory committee at the University of Toronto to study the adequacy of psychiatric aid for students, reported that three students had committed suicide and about a dozen others had made suicidal attempts during the previous year. A survey of a sample of 400 students, early in 1964 had also indicated that 72 per cent of the men and 74 per cent of the women admitted to feelings of despondency and depression. Other common problems revealed by the students were excessive burdens of study, general feelings of inadequacy, difficult relations with the opposite sex, fear of "nervous breakdown," overeating, and conflicts over home and peer moralities.

At Yale University two items included in a large questionnaire sent to a representative sample ($N = 1,280$) of all four male undergraduate classes asked how frequently the students had been bothered by certain specific problems (loneliness, nervousness, insomnia, headaches, and indigestion), and to what extent any personal problem had interfered with their activities (studies, athletic participation, extracurricular participation, recreation, sleep, sex life, and relations with people). (Rust, 1960) His data were based on the responses of 833 subjects. The most frequently checked problem on the scale was "nervousness;" over one in three of these Yale students said he was bothered by nervousness "very often" or "fairly often." The next most frequent problem was "loneliness," checked by almost one quarter of the sample. The other three problems drew fewer responses: "insomnia" (11 per cent), "headaches" (9 per cent), and "indigestion" (8 per cent). On the second question, designed to determine the areas of functioning interfered with, 28 per cent of the sample indicated being bothered by a personal situation which either seriously interfered with or gave them some difficulty with studying. Approximately one fifth of the subjects stated that they currently had some special problem which troubled their "sex life," "relations with people," and "athletic participation." In addition, the students were asked as to whether they had consulted anyone about a personal problem during the current year: 31 per cent answered yes. It was also revealed that, among the respondents, 12 per cent had been patients in the Student Mental Hygiene Clinic of the University; but it was interesting to note that three quarters of those who had checked four or more personal problems on the scale had never been seen at this Clinic. Certain of these data suggest the necessity for experimentation with new service programs for students, as well as new paths for research efforts. A somewhat similar effort to assess the nature, frequency, and severity of students' personal problems was undertaken by Rust and Davie (1951) at Southern Connecticut State College and produced somewhat similar outcomes.

The largest reported canvass of student reactions in a single institution was that undertaken by Pearlman (1966) at Brooklyn College. The entire graduating class of 1964 ($N = 2,632$) was requested to answer a confidential 18-item questionnaire on their self-judgments of their academic efficiency in the light of troubling personal problems and on their thoughts and actions regarding professional assistance. About 1,900 of the seniors submitted completed forms, over 1,200 of them taking the initiative to add or append written statements of their personal viewpoints. Asked directly whether their respective scholastic indices would have been higher if as students they had not been "troubled by personal problems" at some time during their college careers, no fewer than 1,000 (55.2 per cent) of the respondents) answered yes, and these students were to be found strongly represented in each of the tabulated levels of achievement from the lowest to the highest. The trend of the data was quite clear: the lower the scholastic index of the graduate, the more likely it was that he felt his academic efficiency would have been improved by the absence of "personal problems." This conclusion, however, did not serve to diminish the import of the fact that two out of every five of the highest-ranking students claimed to be affected by troublesome concerns; indeed, they were as much shaken by personal circumstances as the lower scholastic groups, except in their concerns about academic skills and study habits. In the over-all figures, it appeared that a substantial majority (estimated at about 65 per cent) of the graduates admitted to the negative impact of one or more specific problem areas on their scholastic performance. The data indicated that the respondents were less affected by "personal and family finances" and "social relationships generally" than by other areas. The extent of their admitted troublesome reactions was about the same for "family interrelationships," "career decisions," and "relationships with the opposite sex." Standing out sharply in the statistics, however, was the emphasis on "academic skills and study habits": 949 of the respondents (53.8 per cent) noted their difficulties here. Career decision making seemed to be another plaguing experience for many (over one third) of the seniors, as disturbing to them during their college years as intrafamilial relationships and relationships with the opposite sex. It was of interest that the high-ranking graduates were as much affected by these problems as the lower-achieving students.

A further inquiry was made of the graduates as to whether, in the light of their expressed problems, they had given consideration in thought or action to the matter of securing professional assistance. Over 95 per cent of the graduates responded to this item, and about one third of them admitted to experiencing such intense personal reactions during their college period as to warrant the *thought* of seeking professional help. Even some of those who did not so acknowledge at this point later indicated that they had sought and received such professional assistance. In any event, thought preceded action in the movement toward mental health support, but did not always lead to action. While 1 out of every 3 seniors did consider the advisability of assistance, only about 1 out of 14 had taken advantage of the available campus facilities, about 1 out of 20 had made contact with a community clinic or agency, and about 1 out of 12 had established a private relationship with a psychologist, social worker, or psychiatrist. What was of further significance here was that the patterns of thought and action on professional help were not statistically different for the high, middle, and low achievers. This was not unexpected, since the experience of college mental hygienists has shown that successful intellectual or academic performance is no safeguard against, and indeed at times may even be a reflection of, emotional disturbance.

The Brooklyn College survey included two items to check the attitudes of the graduates to the existence of psychological services on campus. One of the items inquired of each graduate whether he would be inclined to recommend these services to other students in emotional distress. The response of the entire group was 47 per cent "Yes" and 42 per cent "Maybe," the remainder being in the negative. In their written comments, the "Maybe" respondents generally leaned toward the "Yes" category, but manifested an unwillingness to express a forthright judgment on the personal needs of other students. The second item asked whether the graduates felt the college should provide psychological services (a mental health unit, possibly) to students. The potential benefits of such an arrangement were more positively viewed by the group: 70 per cent answered "Yes" and 21 per cent answered "Maybe." Here, in the remarks of the "Maybe" respondents, the only significant qualification related to the matter of privacy and the confidentiality of contacts and records once psychological help was sought on campus.

Reviewing the responses of the seniors in general, it was quite clear that the attitudes of the students toward mental health support had changed in a positive direction over the past two decades. Their present approach to mental health problems was more open and frank, and often a focus for discussion in their peer groups; and their unwillingness to use the available mental health resources on or off campus was considerably less trammeled with personal and social guilt. A generalized differentiation was apparent among the graduates in their thinking about mental health and mental illness, in the sense that a resort to professional assistance was viewed more as an opportunity to release constricted energies for more effective living than as a means of repairing emotional damage for survival purposes. More research on student opinion and involvement in the campus designs for mental health is manifestly needed in the present era.

Existent Service Models in College Mental Health

Most of the visibly structured mental health programs of colleges and universities have simply grown over the years, and their forms in development have been dependent on knowledgeable and understanding administrations and the efforts of a few leaders in college mental health. It is the intent of the writer to describe three different models of service current at this time, without endeavoring to assess their general and institutional values and effectiveness. For more detailed information on specific programs, the reader is referred to the published literature, sparse as it may be (ACHA, 1961; Blaine & McArthur, 1961; Farnsworth, 1957, 1964; Funkenstein, 1959; Wedge, 1958; Whittington, 1963).

The Medical-Psychiatric Model: Yale University

Health problems at Yale University are dealt with in a service, the Department of University Health, headed by a director who reports administratively to the provost of the university. An advisory Board of University Health is available to the director, who serves as its secretary. The members of this advisory board are, *ex officio*, the dean of the medical school, the university provost, the university treasurer, the director of the athletic association, and the dean of the faculty of arts and sciences; in addition, there are special members appointed for short-term *ad hoc* assignments, depending on the current interests of the board and the department. The board acts in a coordinative capacity for university health activities, and also assists in the determination of health policy and programming. (Davie, 1966)

Within the framework of the Department of University Health, there is a Division of Student Mental Hygiene, responsibility for which is assigned to a psychiatrist-in-chief. In the internal divisonal arrangement, clinical services and training fall to the jurisdiction of a director and research and evaluative activities come under a coordinator who acts for the entire health service (in both the medical and psychiatric divisions). The coordinator of research not only has administrative charge of his own office and of scheduling research meetings for each division (medical—once a month; psychiatric—twice a month), but also serves as a resource person for all staff members with research interests and in a liaison relationship with all other university offices interested or engaged in research on students.

The Division of Student Mental Hygiene, physically a part of the University Health Structure, which is centrally located on the university campus, serves a student population of approximately 8,000 individuals. Its current (1966) professional staff consists of 17 members, 6 of whom are full time and all of whom together are the working equivalent of a full-time staff of 10. Represented on this staff are the disciplines of psychiatry, psychology, social work, and sociology, equivalent to five psychiatrists, two-plus clinical psychologists, two-plus psychiatric social workers, and one half-time sociologist. In addition, there are three part-time trainees in psychology, and three to four full-time third or fourth year residents in psychiatry. Four hours per week of one of the full-time psychologists are devoted to diagnostic clarification; and a third-time psychologist deals with speech disorders.

The division, as a clinic facility, is the only formally designated agency in the university community serving the mental health needs of its population. There is no counseling service center of the general type found on other campuses. As in all institutions, however, there are to be found at Yale many other formal and informal resources to which students and others with mental health problems may turn—chaplains, deans, physicians, nurses, faculty, friends, and so on. The clinic offers brief psychotherapy to students individually and in groups, usually on a once-a-week basis, and is available for consultation and referral services on a limited basis to the faculty and staff. Inpatient facilities are provided, as necessary, by the university infirmary and the psychiatric section of a local hospital. In an average year, approximately 10 per cent of the total student population uses the clinic, and of these about 30 per cent are carryovers from a previous year. To illustrate the service caseload for a group of undergraduates from another point of view, of the 1,066 students admitted to the college in 1958, one fifth were seen at the clinic at some point prior to June 1962, when the class graduated. Of these clinically dealt with, 45 per cent were seen during their freshman year, 23 per cent during the sophomore year, 16 per cent in the junior year, and 16 per cent during the senior year. Of the total number, 30 per cent came to the clinic ostensibly self-referred, 23 per cent were referred by the health service nurses and physicians, 30 percent from the faculty and administration, and 17 per cent from miscellaneous other sources. In terms of diagnosis, about two fifths of the caseload were left without psychiatric labels, reflecting the policy not to categorize students seen in brief contact or for intake only. Of those who were classified diagnostically, 44 per cent received the designation of "adjustment reaction of adolescence," 16 per cent were diagnosed as having psychoneurotic disorders, 28 per cent as having personality disorders, 10 per cent as having psychotic disorders, and 2 per cent as "other." The average number of visits per individual during the four years of the class of 1962 was three.

In addition to helping troubled students, the clinic serves the Yale community in other ways. Individual staff members accept invitations to speak to various student and faculty groups on mental health issues; the clinic is consulted by the college administration in questionable cases of discipline, admission to college, and readmission to college; it is also consulted from time to time with respect to general issues such as adjustment of transfer or foreign students. In addition, meetings are held from time to time with other groups in the college community concerned with student welfare, such as chaplains, nurses, coaches, and freshman counselors, to develop mutual understanding of different viewpoints and to coordinate existing sources of help for the maximum benefit of the individual student. (Davie, 1966, pp. 3–4)

THE SPECIALIZED COUNSELING MODEL: BROOKLYN COLLEGE

By and large, in the process of its historical development, Brooklyn College (with a register of nearly 11,000 full-time students) has included all counseling and health services to students within the jurisdiction of the Dean of Students. Thus, the mental health activities of the college, in their organized framework, have tended naturally on this basis to fall within the supervisory scope of the dean as part of the larger counseling program, rather than as adjuncts of the medical office operations. A system of cooperative relationships, effected through liaison committees, has served to establish the desired degree of functional coordination among the several units. These arrangements are notably different, but in no sense inferior to, those prevailing on other campuses, wherein the existing mental health programs emanate from health or medical departments. (Lawrence, 1962; Pearlman, 1950, 1958, 1960; Siegel, 1956; Watson, 1962, 1963)

The psychological services, presently termed the Specialized Counseling Program, are headed by a coordinator designated by the Dean of Students. None of the staff, who are eight in number, is on a full-time assignment to the program, since their schedules also involve teaching and other duties, but the total service time allocated by them to the program during an academic year is equivalent to the assignment of three full-time individuals, a total of ninety hours per week. All but one (a social worker) of the staff are psychologists; a part-time psychiatrist was available as a staff member until recently, and there is likelihood that this position will be filled within a reasonable time. The coordinator is in a key position to receive all referrals from the faculty, the administrative officers, and the general counselors, to arrange for the screening of these referrals, and to make the appropriate assignments of students to his staff. The referral-intake procedure is clearly organized and, over the years, has become well routinized in operation. Twice during the academic year a memorandum is issued by the program through the Dean of Students to the various academic departments and administrative offices of the college, along with copies of a form (*Referral for Counseling*) which is used for the suggested specialized counseling of specific students. In the use of this form the faculty and staff are encouraged to report without interpretation only what is noted in the reactions and interactions of the referred students; no lengthy personality descriptions or attempts at diagnosis are advised in these reports. As an extension of the intake system, adequate safeguard is made for the confidentiality of all records pertaining to referrals and to specialized-counseling interviews. The procedure calls for all such confidential records to be filed on prescribed forms with the Dean of Students, by whom they are maintained in a closed status, thereafter being made available under special circumstances and then only on the direct authorization of the Dean of Students.

Typically, the receipt of a referral form leads to an intake interview of the student with the specialized counselor, in which interview a determination is made of the special counseling requirements of the student and of the feasibility of dealing with him on or off campus in the light of the recurrence and severity of his presented psychological status or condition. For those students whose affective problems are not considered to be of a chronic, long-standing nature, an assignment is made for specialized counseling on campus for a maximum period of one semester, customarily on the basis of one session per week. In the absence of any available psychodiagnostic test facilities in the intake process, the intake interview has become the sole method of appraisal and judgment. The clinical experience of the intake counselor therefore weighs most heavily in the total procedure. From the overall data it is apparent that only about half of all the referred students are accepted for specialized counseling on campus. The balance of these students are noted as already in an off-campus treatment relationship or are referred on to an appropriate agency following the intake procedures. In a few instances, of course, the referred students prove to be unresponsive to offers of assistance. No further action is customarily taken with this latter group, since the program functions in the main on a voluntary-contact principle, and no compulsion is ordinarily exerted upon students to avail themselves of the service.

An increased use of the staff in consultative capacities has been evident over the years. In this development, the consultative relationships have especially been expressed in four directions:

> 1. In advisement to the classroom instructors with regard to the aberrant behavior, the out-of-line responsiveness, or the low academic efficiency of their students.
> 2. In evaluation of disturbed students for administrative officers who need to make decisions or render judgments in areas related to admissions, dismissals, academic failures, and discipline.
> 3. In direct consultation with faculty members who may be faced with difficult problems or decisions affecting their own professional or personal lives.
> 4. In liaison with off-campus clinical agencies or individuals whose relationships with disturbed students are such as to make cooperative contacts with the program advisable. (Pearlman, 1960, pp. 120–121)

The Parallel Model: The University of Kansas

The descriptions of Whittington (1961, 1963) are here presented as an illustration of a two-pronged service arrangement in campus mental health. A guidance bureau is available to students at the University of Kansas, under the direction of the School of Education, and is designed to provide vocational-academic advisement and personal counseling; it is staffed by counseling psychologists. The Student Health Service, a division unto itself within the structure of the university, contains a Mental Health Clinic staffed by one psychiatrist and two clinical psychologists. In his effort to define the client populations consulting these two agencies, Whittington (1963) has this to say:

> Bright students who complained of academic difficulty and with whom the referring person could empathize were referred to the Guidance Bureau . . . with the clear communication, "I don't think *you're* sick enough to have to see a psychiatrist." On the other hand, seriously depressed persons, those who had committed antisocial, violent, or frightening acts, and those whose illness made empathy difficult for the referring individual were sent to the Mental Health Clinic of the Student Health Service. The Dean of Students usually accepted responsibility for helping those who got in minor scrapes with authority or experienced difficulty in adjusting to group standards of behavior. The

religious counselors saw those who had habitually found in religion a buttress for and extension of their own identity. (p. 52)

Comparing the two client groups (and using a randomly selected control group of freshman students) he found the following differences:

1. The Mental Health Clinic clients were distributed throughout the age range of the university population, while the Bureau counselors dealt with the younger students.
2. The Guidance Bureau clientele almost wholly presented vocational-academic problems, while the clinic group complained commonly about their symptoms of internal discomfort (largely anxiety). However, about one quarter of the interviews at the bureau primarily explored problems of an emotional nature, rather than vocational-academic indecision.
3. The counselors were, or described themselves as being, much more accepting than were the interviewers at the clinic. The latter often questioned the motivations of the students from the start and were more likely to use such descriptive terms as "defensive," "intellectualizing," and "reluctant to elaborate."
4. The usual recommendation for the clinic group was for three or more evaluative interviews, while the Guidance Bureau routinely advised interest and aptitude testing followed up by further counseling.

As Whittington realized, this bit of research raised more questions than it resolved.

The usual pattern of functioning of the Clinic allowed for four evaluative interviews with a student, usually ending with one or more of a number of recommendations: to terminate contacts by mutual agreement; to enter individual or group psychotherapy at the clinic; to effect a referral to an off-campus mental health setting; to prolong and expand the evaluative process; or to effect a rearrangement of the environmental experience of the student. About 1 out of 15 of the clinic students were hospitalized at some time during their evaluation or treatment, most of them for only three or four days as a means of reducing their symptomatic expressions to manageable scope.

REFERENCES

Allen, D. A., & Janowitz, J. F. A study of the outcome of psychotherapy in a university mental health service. *J. Amer. Coll. Hlth Assoc.*, 1965, 13, 361–378.

Allport, G. W. Crises in normal personality development. *Teachers Coll. Rec.*, 1964, 66, 235–241.

American College Health Association (ACHA), Mental Health Section. *Recommended practices.* Unpublished manuscript. Ithaca, N.Y.: Author, 1961.

American College Health Association (ACHA), *Recommended standards and practices for a college health program.* Ithaca, N.Y.: Author, 1964. (Reprinted.)

Baker, R. W. Pattern of initial contacts with a university psychological clinic and its relation to academic stressors. *J. clin. Psychol.,* 1963, 19, 361–363.

Baker, R. W. Incidence of psychological disturbances in college students. *J. Amer. Coll. Hlth Assoc.,* 1965, 13, 532–540.

Baker, R. W. *Report of activities during 1964–1965.* Unpublished report. Worcester, Mass.: Clark University, The psychological clinic.

Baker, R. W., & Nidorf, L. J. Patterns of occurrence of psychological disturbances in college students as a function of year level. *J. clin. Psychol.,* 1964, 20, 530–531.

Barger, B. Change and challenge in college mental health: the University of Florida Mental Health Project. In J. M. Bevan (Ed.), *Impact of changing student culture.* St. Petersburg, Fla.: Fla Presby. Coll., 1964. Pp. 51–68. (a)

Barger, B., & Hall, E. Characteristics and clinical data of mental health clinic patients, July 1, 1963–June 30, 1964. *Ment. Hlth Project Bull.,* 1964, No. 12 (b)

Blaine, G. B., Jr., Coon, G. P., Farnsworth, D. L., Munter, P. K., & Walters, P. A., Jr. The psychiatric service. In D. L. Farnsworth (Ed.), *College health administration.* New York: Appleton-Century-Crofts, 1964. Pp. 69–92.

Blaine, G. B., Jr., & McArthur, C. C. (Eds.) *Emotional problems of the student.* New York: Appleton-Century-Crofts, 1961.

Blos, P. Psychological counseling of college students. *Amer. J. Orthopsychiat.,* 1946, 16, 571–580.

Braaten, L. J. A descriptive study of schizophrenia in a college setting. *J. Amer. Coll. Hlth Assoc.,* 1961, 9, 298–312.

Canada's Mental Health, 1964, 12 (5).

Caplan, G. *Principles of preventive psychiatry.* New York: Basic Books, 1964.

Carnegie Foundation for the Advancement of Teaching. *The flight from teaching: summary of a discussion by the trustee.* New York: Author, 1964.

Cass, W. A. *Personnel policies as applied to universities and college counseling center staff.* Pullman, Wash.: Wash. State Univ., 1961.

Comer, P. E. The college setting as an ideal place for research and innovations in psychotherapy: a case in point. Paper read at Amer. Psychol. Assoc., Chicago, Sept., 1965.

Congdon, R. C., & Lothrop, W. W. *Survey of college counseling practices in the United States.* Durham, N.H.: Univ. of N.H., 1963.

Cowen, E. L. The role of psychologists in university counseling and psychotherapy *J. clin. Psychol.,* 1960, 16, 66–70.

Davie, J. S. Personal communication. February 22, 1966.

Davie, J. S. Research in college: a case approach. Paper read at Invit. Conf. on Ment. Hlth of Coll. and Univ. Stud., Syracuse, N.Y., February, 1966.

Diehl, H. S., & Shepard, C. E. *The health of college students.* Washington: Amer. Council on Educ., 1939.

Eddy, E. D., Jr. *The college influence on student character*. Washington: Amer. Council on Educ., 1959.

Elson, Miriam, Ichikawa, Alice, & Kohut, Betty. The returning patient: an inquiry. *J. Amer. Coll. Hlth Assoc.*, 1963, 12, 235–244.

Erikson, E. H. Introduction. In G. B. Blaine, Jr. & C. C. McArthur (Eds.), *Emotional problems of the student*. New York: Appleton-Century-Crofts, 1961. Pp. xiii–xxv.

Evans, A. S., & Warren, J. Patterns of illness in University of Wisconsin students. *Arch. environ. Hlth.*, 1962, 4, 579–587.

Farnsworth, D. L. *Mental health in college and university*. Cambridge, Mass.: Harvard Univ. Press, 1957.

Farnsworth, D. L. Concepts of educational psychiatry. *J. Amer. Med. Assoc.*, 1962, 181, 815–821.

Farnsworth, D. L. (Ed.) *College health administration*. New York: Appleton-Century-Crofts, 1964.

Farnsworth, D. L. *College health services in the United States*. Washington: Amer. Coll. Personnel Assoc., 1965. No. 4.

Farnsworth, D. L. *Psychiatry, education, and the young adult*. Springfield, Ill.: Charles C Thomas, 1966.

Fein, R. *Economics of mental illness*. New York: Basic Books, 1958.

Felix, R. H., & Kramer, M. Research in epidemiology of mental illness. *Publ. Hlth Rep.* (U.S.), 1952, 67, 152–160.

Frank, L. K. The promotion of mental health. *Ann. Amer. Acad. Pol. Soc. Sci.*, 1953, 286, 167–174.

Freedman, M. B. *Impact of college*. New dimensions in higher education, No. 4. Washington: U.S. Dept. of Hlth, Educ., and Welf., Off. of Educ., 1960.

Freedman, M. B. Some observations on personality development in college women. *Student Med.*, 1960, 8, 228, 245.

Funkenstein, D. H. (Ed.) *The student and mental health: an international view*. Cambridge, Mass.: Riverside Press, 1959.

Funkenstein, D. H., & Wilkie, G. H. *Student mental health: an annotated bibliography*, 1936–1955. London: World Fed. for Ment. Hlth, 1956.

Goldston, S. E. (Ed.) *Concepts of community psychiatry*. U. S. Public Health Service Publ. No. 1319. Washington: Govt. Print. Off., 1965.

Group for the Advancement of Psychiatry. *Statistics pertinent to psychiatry in the United States*. New York: Author, 1949. No. 7.

Group for the Advancement of Psychiatry, Committee on Academic Education. *The role of psychiatrists in colleges and universities*. (Rev. ed.) New York: Author, 1957. No. 17.

Group for the Advancement of Psychiatry, Committee on the College Student. *The college experience: a focus for psychiatric research*. New York: Author, 1962. No. 52.

Gruenberg, E. M. The prevention of mental disease. *Ann. Amer. Acad. Pol. Soc. Sci.*, 1953, 286, 158–166.

Gundle, S., & Kraft, A. Mental health programs in American colleges and universities. *Bull. Menninger Clinic.*, 1956, 20, 57–69.

Hall, E., & Barger, B. A comparison of clinic samples for two years with their original populations of entering students. *Ment. Hlth Project Bull.*, 1964., No. 6.

Joint Commission on Mental Illness and Health. *Action for mental health: final report of the Joint Commission on Mental Illness and Health.* New York: Basic Books, 1961.

King, S. H. Emotional problems of college students: facts and priorities. *AAUP Bull.*, 1964, 50, 327–332.

Kuehn, J. L. College nurses' guide for psychiatric in-patients. *J. Amer. Coll. Hlth Assoc.*, 1965, 14, 100–103.

Landfield, A. W., Nawas, M. M., & O'Donovan, D. A quarter century in the life of a university mental hygiene clinic. *J. Amer. Coll. Hlth Assoc.*, 1963, 12, 202–207.

Lawrence, Ray M. *The personal counseling program at Brooklyn College: a study financed by a grant from the Milbank Memorial Fund.* Brooklyn: Brooklyn Col., 1962.

Malzberg, B. Mental illness and the economic value of a man. *Ment. Hyg., N.Y.*, 1950, 34, 582–591.

McArthur, C. C. Distinguishing patterns of student neuroses. In G. B. Blaine, Jr., & C. C. McArthur (Eds.), *Emotional problems of the student.* New York: Appleton-Century-Crofts, 1961. Pp 54–75.

Miller, S., Jr. Is the college coddling its students? *Columbia Coll. Today*, 1963–64, 11, 13–17.

Moore, N. S. Remarks of . . . In the New York State Association of Community Mental Health Boards, *Mental health and youth* (Fifth Annual Conference). Rochester, N.Y.: Author, 1960. Pp. 82–85.

Moore, N. S., & Summerskill, J. *Health services in American universities.* Ithaca, N.Y.: Cornell Univ. Press, 1954.

Morrison, A. W., & Diehl, H. S. Studies in mental hygiene needs of freshman university students. *J. Amer. Med. Assoc.*, 1924, 83, 1666–1672.

Nelson, R. L. Special problems of graduate students in the school of arts and sciences. In G. B. Blaine, Jr., & C. C. McArthur (Eds.), *Emotional problems of the student.* New York: Appleton-Century-Crofts, 1961. Pp. 186–200.

Nixon, R. E. A challenge for the college mental hygiene service. *Student Med.*, 1960, 8, 340–343.

Nixon, R. E. Psychological normality in the years of youth. *Teachers Coll. Rec.*, 1964, 66, 71–79.

Nugent, F. A., & Pareis, E. N. *Survey—present practices in college counseling centers.* Bellingham, Wash.: West. Wash. State Coll., 1965.

Pace, C. R. Implications of differences in campus atmosphere for evaluation and planning college programs. In R. L. Sutherland, W. H. Holtzman, E. A. Koile, & B. K. Smith (Eds.), *Personality factors on the college campus: review of a symposium.* Austin, Tex.: Hogg Found. for Ment. Hlth, 1962. Pp. 43–61.

Pace, C. R., & Stern, G. G. An approach to the measurement of psychological characteristics of college environments. *J. educ. Psychol.*, 1958, 49, 269–277.

Palmer, J. T. Remarks of . . . In Pacific Coast Health Association, *Proceedings of the 26th Annual Meeting.* San Diego: Author, 1963. Pp. 67–68.

Paulsen, J. A. College students in trouble. *Atlantic Mon.*, 1964, 214, 96–101.

Pearlman, S. *Report on the psychological counseling activities of the department,* 1948–1950. Brooklyn: Brooklyn Coll., 1950.

Pearlman, S. *Progress report on the personal counseling program,* 1956–1957. Brooklyn: Brooklyn Coll., 1958.

Pearlman, S. Mens Sana. In A. S. Goodhartz (Ed.), *A commitment to youth: the Brooklyn College student personnel program.* New York: Bookman Assoc., 1960. Pp. 108–122.

Pearlman, S. The college student views his mental health experience. *J. Amer. Coll. Hlth Assoc.*, 1966, 14, 277–283.

Pearlman, S. Mental health in higher education. In L. E. Abt & B. F. Riess (Eds.), *Progress in clinical psychology, Vol. VII.* New York: Grune & Stratton, 1966. Pp. 191–208.

Raphael, T. Mental-hygiene services for colleges and universities. *Ment. Hyg., N.Y.*, 1937, 21, 559–568.

Raphael, T., Gordon, Mary A., & Dawson, Emma M. Mental hygiene in American colleges and universities. *Ment. Hyg., N.Y.*, 1938, 22, 221–236.

Robbins, W. T. 1962 survey of mental health programs in colleges. In the Pacific Coast Health Association, *Proceedings of the 26th Annual Meeting.* San Diego: Author, 1963.

Rust, R. M. Epidemiology of mental health in college. *J. Psychol.*, 1960, 49, 235–248.

Rust, R. M., & Davie, J. S. The personal problems of college students. *Ment. Hyg., N.Y.*, 1961, 45, 347–257.

Sanford, N. Factors related to the effectiveness of student interaction with the college social system. In B. Barger, & E. E. Hall (Eds.), *Higher education and mental health.* Gainesville: Univ. of Fla., 1963. Pp. 8–26.

Selzer, M. L. The "happy college student" myth: psychiatric implications. *Arch. Gen. Psychiat.*, 1960, 2, 131–136.

Siegel, M. *Progress report on personal counseling, 1955–1956.* Brooklyn: Brooklyn: Brooklyn Coll., 1956.

Smith, W. G., Hansell, N., & English, J. T. Psychiatric disorder in a college population. *Arch. Gen. Psychiat.*, 1963, 9, 351–361.

Srole, L., Langner, T. S., Michael, S. T., Opler, M. K., & Rennie, T. A. C. *Mental health in the metropolis: the midtown Manhattan study.* New York: McGraw-Hill, 1962.

Stern, G. G. Congruence and dissonance in the ecology of college students. *Student Med.*, 1960, 8, 304–339.

Stern, G. G. The measurement of psychological characteristics of students and learning environments. In S. J. Messick, & J. Ross (Eds.), *Measurement in personality and cognition.* New York: Wiley, 1962. Pp. 27–68.

Swartz, J., Posin, H. I., & Kaye, A. Psychiatric problems in an urban university. *Ment. Hyg., N.Y.* 1958, 42, 224–228.

Trow, M. The campus viewed as a culture. In H. T. Sprague (Ed.), *Research on college students.* Berkeley: West. Intstate Commiss. for Higher Educ. and the Ctr for Higher Educ., 1960. Pp. 105–123.

U.S. Department of Health, Education, and Welfare, Public Health Service, National Institute of Mental Health. *Mental health activities and the development of comprehensive health programs in the community: report of the surgeon general's ad hoc committee on mental health activities.* U.S. Publ. Hlth Serv. Publ. No. 995. Washington: Govt Print. Off., 1965.

Watson, Gladys H. An evaluation of counseling with college students. *J. Counsel. Psychol.*, 1961, 8, 99–104.

Watson, Gladys H. *Progress report on the specialized counseling program.* Brooklyn: Brooklyn Coll., 1962.

Watson, Gladys H. *Happy college years: a report on the specialized counseling program.* Brooklyn: Brooklyn Coll., 1963.

Webb, S. C., & Crowder, Dolores G. Analyzing the psychological climate of a single college. *Teachers Coll. Rec.*, 1965, 66, 425–433.

Webster, M., Freedman, M. B., & Heist, P. Personality changes in college students. In N. H. Sanford (Ed.), *The American college: a psychological and social interpretation of the higher learning.* New York: Wiley, 1962. Pp. 811–846.

Wedge, B. M. (Ed.) *Psychosocial problems of college men.* New Haven: Yale Univ. Press, 1958.

Weiss, R. J., Segal, B. E., & Sokol, R. Epidemiology of emotional disturbance in a men's college. *J. nerv. ment. Dis.*, 1965, 141 (2), 240–250.

Whittington, H. G. College campus psychiatry. *J. Kansas Med. Soc.*, 1960, 56, 327–329.

Whittington, H. G. Who helps whom? A comparison of client groups at the university psychiatric clinic and the guidance bureau. *J. Amer. Coll. Hlth Assoc.*, 1961, 9, 345–353.

Whittington, H. G. *Psychiatry on the college campus.* New York: Int. Univ. Press, 1963.

Williams, R. H. Introduction to Part III, community influences and supports on ex-patients' adjustment. In M. Greenblatt, D. J. Levinson, & G. L. Klerman (Eds.), *Mental patients in transition.* Springfield, Ill.: Charles C Thomas, 1961.

Wilms, J. H. How much for mental health? *J. Amer. Coll. Hlth Ass.*, 1965, 13, 422–430.

Yale University, Department of Psychiatry and Mental Hygiene, Division of Student Mental Hygiene. *Publications on college mental hygiene.* (Unpublished manuscript.) New Haven: Yale Univ., undated.

Chapter 12

Counseling the Physically Handicapped

NORMAN KIELL

A Brief Overview

The care of vulnerable groups is one indication of a country's degree of civilization. Barbarians put the old and feeble to the wall; others succour them. It is a justifiable pride of utilitarian social engineering that one especially vulnerable group, handicapped children, has never been so well cared for as now. The story of this achievement is an important one in itself because it highlights the changing attitudes towards all the dependent and vulnerable in society, whether they be children, the sick, the elderly, or the mentally retarded. In the waxing and waning of social provision for the handicapped child is mirrored the fate of all those who depend like him upon organized social provision for their survival.

Russell Criddle (1953) writes, in one of the most sensitive and perceptive autobiographies describing the adolescence of a blind boy,

> The adolescent is continuously torn between his desires and his inhibitions. Before he can recognize that the true source of his distress is sexual, he must break through his inhibitions. Anything which causes displeasure throws the scale toward rejection of the opposite sex. A large nose, a speech impediment, any distressing abnormality, will require the young man or woman to become a little more mature, a little more distressed, before he will seek a positive reaction from the opposite sex. . . . I'm a man in every respect but one, therefore I fall short of being a man by definition. I can't expect to be desired as a man. But I have the desires of a whole man. (pp. 114–115)

Norman Kiell is Associate Professor, Department of Student Services; and Counselor to the Physically Handicapped, Brooklyn College of the City University of New York.

The physically normal adolescent has too many things on his mind to be thinking much about taking care of his health. He cares about his appearance, but that is a very different matter from a concern about his health status. It is only when he suffers from a handicap, real or imagined, that he becomes subject to the condition described by Criddle. Even though he may have learned to accept his disability—strong personalities will be able to adapt themselves even to unfavorable external realities (Fenichel, 1945, p. 577)—the attitude of society may have a compelling effect on him.

Indirect evidence of basic attitudes toward disability is found in the religious practices of the ancient Hebrews, Greeks, and Christians, and direct evidence is found in modern scientific thought. According to Barker, Wright, Meyerson, and Gonick (1953),

> To the ancient Hebrews, as their mores were codified in the Old Testament, illness was considered both a punishment and a sense of atonement. In Greek culture, on the other hand, while disease was odious, it was not an indication of sin but of inferiority. The sick were considered inferior beings and could expect consideration from society only so long as their condition was capable of improvement. The Christian doctrine introduced the view that disease is not a disgrace nor a punishment for sin but, on the contrary, a means of purification and a way of grace. Suffering perfects the sufferer. According to this ideology the sick have a preferential position, and it is a privilege for the healthy to minister to them. According to the scientific view, disabling diseases and accidents are the result of amoral natural conditions many of which can be understood and controlled. (pp. 80–81)

Even though modern man can understand and sometimes control disabling diseases and illnesses, the affective response to the disability can weigh as heavily as the organic difficulty itself. The handicapped young college student has to face not only all of the usual problems of adolescent adjustment but the additional ones presented by his disability. Physical deviations are crucial during adolescence because of the increased importance of the body in the individual's self-concept. In the body ego of cases of morbid ego identity, Erikson (1959) states,

> Those body parts which are supposed to be of strategic importance in the characterization of the race . . . play a role similar to that of the afflicted limb in a cripple and that of the genitals in neurotics in general. The body part in question has a different ego tonus; it is felt to be larger and heavier, or smaller and disembodied . . . It seems dissociated from the whole body, while seeming to loom dominantly in the center of the attention of others. (p. 32)

Literature in the Field

According to one school of thought, the individual's response to his physical disability, while seemingly exaggerated and distorted to the casual observer, is largely a reflection of his peer group's reaction to it. Because the adolescent is so dependent on the group for status, he tends to accept as real the value it places on him.

> More important than the objective handicap inherent in physical defects, especially during the adolescent period, is the social disadvantage at which they place the deviant individual. Deviance from the physical norms elicits a highly negative response from his peers, and almost guarantees that he will be treated differently from his fellows. The lowest common denominators of this differential treatment are devaluation, avoidance, rejection, and accordance of a lower status . . . Disability in adolescence almost inevitably leads to damaged self-esteem. At the very least, it results in hypersensitivity and self-consciousness about the defect. (Ausubel, 1954, pp. 154–155)

Allen and Pearson (1928), on the other hand, concluded from a study, first, that physical disabilities affect the personality not so much through the role of the peer group as through the relationship between the parent and the child; and, second, that a crippling of the personality brought about by the attitude of the parent toward the disability is probably a more serious menace to the future happiness of the individual than a very marked physical disability.

In another study, by Gates (1946), in which autobiographies of crippled adolescents were used, it was suggested that cultural background and personal-social relations in the home may affect adjustment more than crippling does. While one study (Levi & Mickelson, 1952) indicates there is no significantly measurable difference in the social and emotional adjustment between handicapped and normal adolescents, another (Norris & Cruickshank, 1952) reveals marked differences in personality variables and adjustment. Cruickshank's (1952) research showed that handicapped children appeared to have a tendency to withdraw from social contacts and were not as able to evaluate or interpret relationships as nonhandicapped children. For lack of such contacts, fewer normal adolescent interests were revealed while substitute gratification seemed to be sought through fantasy. The data gathered by Broida, Izard, and Cruickshank (1950) suggest that the area of social relationships is one of conflict for the handicapped youngster. Smock and Cruickshank's (1952) study validated this: In Cruickshank's (1951) findings the disabled child seems to have greater need for acceptance than the normal one.

These two contradictory sets of research data, one stating that there are no essential differences between the physically handicapped and the normal adolescent, the other finding significant differences between the two groups, are indicative of the paucity of sound research done in this area. Barker, et al (1953) arrived at the conclusion,

> While there is evidence of weak relationships between physical measure of physique and personality and social behavior . . . methodological shortcomings make it doubtful if this is a true picture of the situation. We are inclined to give more weight to such indirect and nonobjective evidence as the sensitivity of laymen to physical characteristics, and clinical case studies which indicate that normal variation in physique can have tremendous influence upon behavior. (p. 21)

One such sensitive layman was Robert Burton (1927), the 17th century author of the *Anatomy of Melancholy*, who wrote, "Deformities and imperfections of our bodies, as lameness, crookedness, deafness, blindness, be they innate or accidental, torture many men." (p. 251)

The literature on counseling students with special disabilities is fairly comprehensive. Abraham (1956) is concerned with the education problems of college-age persons with seizures. In earlier works, Himler and Raphael (1940, 1945) studied 93 college students with epilepsy and did a follow-up study on them. Lennox, McBride, and Potter (1947), investigating 1,676 colleges and universities, found that 14 per cent of them rejected epileptic applicants and 21 per cent set up admission conditions. Condon (1961) discusses 24 colleges in New York State that admit blind students. McGill and Frish (1960) cover three areas in helping blind students to prepare for college: understanding college procedures, effective study methods, and personal-social relationships. The differential correlates of physical handicap and obesity with grade-point average in college students are discussed by Greenfield and Fellner (1963). Edgington (1963) has surveyed colleges and universities with special provision for wheel-chair students. Fleischer (1953) reviews nine principles for counseling the cerebral palsied college student. Services to the handicapped at particular institutions are discussed by Hardee (1951) at Florida State University, by Fife (1960) at Southern Illinois University, by Berdie (1955) at the University of Minnesota, by Condon and Lerner (1956) at the City College of New York, and by Lerner and Martin (1955) at Hunter College. Condon (1957a) has surveyed 238 colleges and universities to determine the special facilities provided the handicapped. Tucker (1964) has edited an administrative handbook to provide direction to a minimum program for the accommodation of physically handicapped college students. Condon and Lerner

(1955), Grant (1960), Rusalem (1962), and Patterson (1963) all deal generally with counseling the disabled college student.

The literature in the field of the handicapped offers no reliable breakdown of the varieties of disabilities which students attending college have; however, the number of articles and books dealing with the wheel-chair patient, the blind, and the cerebral palsied would indicate that these three conditions are probably the most commonly found on the campus today. Empirical observation supports this inference. Undoubtedly, as the generations of the Salk and Sabine vaccine children mature, postpolio cases will virtually disappear, leaving the blind and palsied students most prominent in the field. Other handicaps, such as rheumatic fever, myasthenia gravis, and epilepsy, present problems of a different level and intensity than are under discussion here.

The Psychology of the Handicapped

In almost every society, physique has a fundamental social significance to the individual in terms of the cultural mores in which he lives, for physique is one of the important criteria upon which social distinctions are based. Barker and his associates (1953, p. 3) have said that a person who lives in a culture where social distinctions are made upon the basis of age, sex, race, stature, beauty, or physical normality will behave, upon observing his own physique, in accordance with his evaluation of these criteria. Similarly, others will react to his physique by accepting or rejecting him in accordance with their evaluation of these physical criteria of social classification. Thus, the adolescent's rate and direction of maturing may have a significant effect on his social acceptance and status, on the efficacy of his participation in a variety of activities, and in all probability, on his emotional adjustment, particularly when a physical impairment makes him conspicuous or prevents him from doing the things his peers do. Two facts seem inescapable: (1) the "right" physique will make personal adjustment easier and life happier, and (2) the "wrong" physique or appearance, ranging from a pimple to a severe physical disablement, will almost inevitably create in varying degrees, sensitivities, frustrations, guilt feelings, anxieties, and so on that would not otherwise necessarily exist and which complicate the adolescent's adjustment processes.

The autobiographies of the handicapped tend to demonstrate this. E. R. Carlson (1941), a spastic paralytic and a physician who founded several institutions to train spastics, says in his memoir, *Born That Way*, that since so many of the handicapped are uncurable, the primary task is an adequate meeting of it at a psychological level. Many accounts of the handicapped reveal an unconscious but very real need to compensate for the impairment. Despite his clubfoot, Byron developed his body through participation in all kinds of sports. But his lameness produced intense inferiority feelings for which he overcompensated by an arrogance in social relationships. In his satirical writings, as in those of the hunchback, Alexander Pope, he inflicted on others some of the pain he felt they had inflicted upon him, thereby reaping a terrible, immortal vengeance. Sir Walter Scott (1914) also overcompensated for his crippled condition:

> My frame gradually became hardened with my constitution, and being both tall and muscular, I was rather disfigured than disabled by my lameness. This personal disadvantage did not prevent me from taking much exercise on horseback and making long journeys on foot, in the course of which I often walked from twenty to thirty miles a day . . . nor do I remember being at all fatigued upon the occasion. (p. 38)

Associate Supreme Court Justice William O. Douglas became an inveterate mountain climber to strengthen his weak and spindly legs, the residual legacy of a bout with infantile paralysis.

> Tactless comments from boys, plus the solicitous comments from his mother, had left him sensitive and determined to prove himself capable. One response was to plunge into study, driving for grades of 100 in all his courses. This he could come near to doing, but it left him dissatisfied with his ability to be like other boys. He stumbled on the story of Sparta in his reading and found that 'they were rugged and hearty people, the kind I aspired to be. So I searched out the literature that described their habits and capacities to see if I could get some clues to their toughness.' Unfortunately, these figures did not serve as models, for in Plato Douglas read the devastating fact that the Spartans did away with their weaklings. Then came the model Douglas was ready for. (Cronbach, 1963, p. 427)

It was another boy, a mountain climber, who inspired Douglas to the sport. Upon the success and satisfaction achieved in it, he built a lifelong interest in mountain climbing and the outdoor life.

The Counselor and the Counseling Process

In a recent survey by Tucker (1964, pp. 58–78) of special facilities for physically handicapped students attending 951 colleges and universities with populations of 1,000 or more in the United States, 121 of them, or 8 per cent, provided counselors for such students. Of the institutions, 340 or about 38 per cent, had Vocational Rehabilitation Service visits made regularly to their campuses. Nearly a third of the colleges had one or more wheel-chair students and more than half had one or more blind students enrolled. The Great Society envisioned by a far-seeing President gives promise of the ever-increasing matriculation of disabled young people into institutions of higher learning.

Before their entrance into college and once there, these students need counselors equipped not only with understanding but also with some special skills to render the services that are requisite. The aim of counseling the physically handicapped is ultimate acceptance and treatment of them by society as equals. Abt's (1954) remark illuminates this, *viz.*, that handicapped people, from a social psychological point of view, are considered to be members of a minority group and to have many of the characteristics, including the special sensitivities and feelings of inadequacy, that minority group members commonly have. A review of the pertinent variables influencing an individual's reaction to physical handicap indicates that uniformity of reaction is not to be expected. (Caldwell, 1952)

In order to be effective, counseling efforts would have to be based upon the unique, idiosyncratic picture presented by each handicapped student's own pattern of attitudes, values, and defensive system. Body image plays a primary role in psychotherapy with the disabled. According to Cath, Glud, and Blane (1957, p. 34), "In every physically handicapped person there are the problems of dealing with the trauma, the need to deny, the repression, the depression. A person must come to terms with the discrepancy between this body image and his body structure. Therapy must cope with severe feelings of depression, guilt, and hostility associated with a distorted body and body image." The specific problems facing a physically disabled individual concern his acceptance of himself and his acceptance by the environment. (Bychowski, 1952, p. 185)

The counselor of the handicapped can be in a position to help in all these facets. The counselor must be sensitive to the needs of the handicapped student (Peckham, 1953), in terms of his acceptance of dependency status (Mussen & Newman, 1958), in creating a setting in which the student can be encouraged to motivate himself (Rogal, 1952), and in helping him to achieve realistic goals. (Garrett, 1952) The counselor of the physically disabled is not a rehabilitation counselor but is concerned primarily with the student's adjustment to the college; thus, he must have special information to counsel these students appropriately. Berdie (1955) singles out some of them:

> The counselor must know how various kinds of physical limitations should be considered in relationship to job opportunities and requirements; what limitations can be attributed to social attitudes, to legal and insurance regulations, and to employer attitudes; and what financial resources are available to assist disabled persons. . . . Special kinds of relationships also must be maintained with . . . medical personnel, with state and federal agencies supporting disabled students, and with families, friends, employers, and teachers. (pp. 476–477)

Inherent in the counseling process is a deep belief in the integrity of the individual and in his capacity and right to determine the way of life that is best for him. Coupled with the belief in self-determination is the conviction that the handicapped student, to attain full self-realization, must know the choices of action possible for him and should be able to look to the counselor to assist him in obtaining those basic health and welfare services he is unable to obtain through his own efforts. (Abrams & Dana, 1957) Thus the goal of counseling is to help the handicapped student achieve the maximum functioning of which he is capable.

The Preadmission Interview

Some institutions consider it advisable to schedule an interview prior to admission between the counselor and the handicapped applicant. This preadmission interview has several goals: to help determine if the applicant has (1) the physical, (2) the emotional, (3) the social ability to survive the rigors of academic life; and (4) to explore his vocational motivation, however tentative it might be. With his findings, the counselor is then able to discuss the advisability of matriculation for the student with the officer in charge of admissions and the college physician. On the basis of their joint evaluation, the applicant is either admitted, rejected, or advised to apply to another institution (possibly a junior college or special training school) better suited to his particular needs.

During the course of the interview, the applicant is asked to describe his handicap, its onset, duration, nature, extent, treatment, and prognosis. In the detailing of the medical history, the counselor is often able to assess the applicant's acceptance of the handicap or its denial, which is, of course, of great significance to his emotional and social life and which therefore will affect his academic progress. It is vital to secure information concerning the present status of the handicap, the frequency of medical attention, and the identity and address of the attending physician. This last will be required should a more informed medical opinion be needed and, once the student is admitted, should the occasion arise when it would be necessary to contact the doctor.

A determination must be made as to whether or not the applicant is physically able to cope with the college environment. Does the blind boy need a seeing-eye dog to get around, and can the college permit an animal in its buildings? If confined to a wheel-chair, is the student able to get from class to class or building to building in the allotted time? Are there ramps leading from the outside of the college buildings for use by the paraplegic or polio victim? Are elevators accessible to the student so that stairs can be avoided? Is parking space available within sufficiently close proximity for those who are able to drive? Each applicable question should be answered in the affirmative to ensure the physical well-being that is paramount to the student's success in college.

Further special consideration for their physical condition may have to be given to certain categories of the handicapped. For instance, a cerebral palsied applicant may not have facility with his fingers, making it impossible for him to take class notes, focus a microscope, hold a test tube, prepare a slide, or perform many other activities which most of us take for granted. How will he—or the blind student—function in the examination situation or the required science laboratory courses? In the counseling interview, the inventiveness of the applicant can be ascertained by the manner in which he responds to these questions.

The last task of the counselor in the preadmission interview is to gauge the social and emotional roles of the applicant. What has been the effect of the handicap on the individual in these two respects? Has the psychic damage been so great that distortions warp his perceptions? Has it interfered neurotically with social relationships? Has he accepted or denied his handicap, and to what extent? How dependent is he on others for support, help, and sympathy? Has there been a resolution of the recapitulated Oedipal conflict or are the parent-child relations of such a nature as to inhibit the learning process? All these questions must be asked.

The preadmission interview is crucial for the youngster's success at college. The counselor must be painstaking in securing the medical data and in determining the nature of the applicant's reaction to his disability, the intellectual and emotional bases of his personality, and his inner resources, limitations, and creativity. This material, combined with the data from the College Boards, achievement tests, high school average, and recommendations, are basic indices for making a judgment to admit or reject the handicapped applicant.

Early Contacts and General Counseling

The difficulties the handicapped student faces, and the kinds of efforts he makes to meet the disability, often serve to build in him an awareness, a resilience, and a strength many normal students lack. These qualities are frequently revealed in initial counseling interviews, which tend to focus on the mechanics of survival. The blind student wants to know where he can obtain a reader; the wheel-chair case asks if there will be some one to help him to get around. When it is called for, an early registration permit should be issued, to enable the student to secure a schedule of classes and room locations which can best serve him physically.

Almost inevitably in these early contacts with the counselor, certain of the handicapped will inquire about test taking. They learn quickly that arrangements must be made by the student himself with each instructor. If it is impossible for him to take the examination at the usual time with his classmates, he may arrange to take it orally, or in the instructor's office, or at home. (Condon & Lerner, 1955) In such circumstances, some students show an unwillingness to be treated distinctively from their fellows, but their acquiescence to reality is a measure of their acceptance of the handicap.

Other mechanical problems may involve granting special automobile parking permits and elevator passes and adjusting the course schedule to the work tolerance approved by the college physician. In some institutions, where the disability (as in the convulsive disorders) may affect the entire class situation, all of the student's instructors are contacted. In other schools this practice is not followed as it is considered an invasion of privacy.

Program planning, program load, and major field are pivotal in every student's academic career. It is no less true for the handicapped. When a student with a disability is admitted to a college or university he is expected to pursue the same courses and meet, with minimal adjustments, the same requirements for his degree as do all other students. (Condon & Lerner, 1956) Adjustment to these demands will depend on the student's physical competence and the nature of the required work. Prior to registering for a laboratory course, it is generally advisable for the student to consult with the chairman of the department and the instructor to determine whether or not to take the course. Delicate instrumentation in the chemistry laboratory may preclude the blind or spastic from participation. Grosser manual manipulative tasks, however, such as may be found in certain geology courses, provide substitute opportunity and gratification for the student wishing or required to engage in a scientific discipline.

The purpose of the early contact, then, is primarily information giving. So far as the counselor is concerned, his paramount function is to establish a working relationship with the student which will provide the warm, trusting climate basic to the counseling situation.

Emotional Problems

By the time the physically handicapped student arrives at college, his ego defense system, like those of the general population, has become well established. If he has been able to develop satisfying object relationships prior to his matriculation, he will generally maintain a good level at college. He will have adjustment problems similar to those of the normal student but possibly of a more intensive nature. Where a neurosis manifests itself, the counselor's task becomes more complex. If the neurosis is severe, a need for therapy may be indicated. If therapy is too threatening, then a supportive counseling relationship may be called for. Of primacy is the awareness on the part of the student that there is a place for him to turn for help should he feel the need for it, a place where he will be accepted for himself, not out of pity or sympathy, but because he is a human being in need of support. Since the emotional concomitants of a physically handicapping condition are of such importance, counseling has great potential value. (Tracht, 1957)

The counselor working with the handicapped views him in terms of the psychosocial forces that have helped to shape him, in terms of the potential that he possesses, based on his past and present resources, for a meaningful life. This view of the handicapped student places emphasis not only upon knowing the individual but upon full knowledge of the resources of the family, friends, and overall community as they have affected and will continue to affect the student's college progress.

Although physically disabled persons exhibit maladjustive behavior patterns more frequently than is observed in the normal population, the kinds of emotional disturbance manifested are not peculiar to them alone. The psychological aspects involved include (1) the unique significance of the physical defect; (2) the effect on social status; (3) the self-concept; (4) acceptance of the handicap; (5) prior personal adjustment; and (6) aids in setting goals for the disabled student. (Garrett, 1955) Jacobson (1959, pp. 135–154) has presented a clinical case in order to enlarge insight into the unconscious motivations of people who have had physical defects since birth or early life. The case demonstrates the narcissistic, aggressive nature of their Oedipal strivings, their rebellions and ambitious aims and claims, their resistance to the Oedipal laws, the spiteful denial of their own conscience, the victory of their unconscious self-destructive trends, and underneath it all, their desperate cry for a love they never receive. While the sources of friction may differ to a degree from the normal student's, their emotional problems are cast in our own vulnerable clay.

The handicapped student's emotional problems arise out of a complexity of reasons: overdeveloped defensive reactions; a distorted body image; social devaluation; a weak self-concept; denial by parents of the reality of the handicap and their feelings of helplessness, guilt, and projection; hypochondriacal tendencies; hostile withdrawal; and extreme timidity, bitterness, or pessimism. While hardly inclusive, these symptoms are characteristic of the somatopsychological aspects of human disability. (Wright, 1960) The efforts of the counselor would have to be mobilized towards strengthening the student's ego so that a sense of adequacy and ability to derive satisfaction from achievement can be developed, and to set realistic goals in personal and vocational areas.

Vocational Counseling

In all cultures, the primary status of the individual is achieved through his occupational role. Whenever socioeconomic roles are differentiated by a functional division of labor or a hierarchy of social prestige values, the typical occupation of the individual defines and symbolizes his relative position in the stratified social organization that almost inevitably results. (Ausubel, 1954, pp. 437–438) The frustrations of the handicapped student when eyeing this world of work come close to being intolerable. The universal need of all men, satisfying work, is frequently denied him, whether because of the unrealistic goals the handicapped student sets for himself or the unyielding prejudice of an uneducated and misinformed public.

The counselor can do much about the former, for he is in a position to exercise the correct amount of leverage to assist the disabled youngster to prepare for and choose an occupation in keeping with his physical limitations, emotional powers, and intellectual abilities. Guiding these students vocationally does not differ esentially from guiding the able bodied: the focus of counseling is the capacities the individual possesses. (Garrett,

1952) Historically, assistance to the physically handicapped has been chiefly the provision of physical repair and mechanical aid. (Menninger, 1950). But the college counselor's responsibility goes far beyond this rudimentary assistance.

A number of recent surveys indicate the great variety of vocational fields chosen by handicapped college students. By far the largest have gone into service fields (Lerner & Martin, 1955), electing education and science. In general, the level of vocational aspirations is towards higher prestige than that of their parents, a phenomenon common to the general population. In a 10-year survey of physically handicapped graduates of the City College of New York to determine their employment success as evaluated by monthly salary, Condon (1957b) found they were nearly on a par with their more fortunate peers. In another study, Condon (1957a, p. 582) concluded that the cerebral palsied, in comparison with the blind and the deaf, had the most difficulty in finding satisfactory employment. Mase and Williams (1964) evaluated the occupational success of 243 severely handicapped college graduates as compared with 224 severely handicapped high school graduates. In a survey of vocational objectives of blind college students in the United States, Asenjo and Axelrod (1957) indicated that the plurality of responses was for a career in teaching.

When a human being is happy, he is motivated by the desire to make the fullest use of his capacities. The universal need of feeling useful in the world of work, of having a gainful occupation on a level of interest commensurate with ability, is as great a need for the handicapped as for any other individual. The successful counseling of the handicapped college student includes the recognition of the need for vocational planning that is realistic and acceptable to him, his family, his employer, and his co-workers.

Administration

Where is the counseling of the handicapped done best? Under whose aegis should responsibility for its functions be maintained? A department of student services? The health office? The medical office? Telling arguments pro or con can be presented for each of these departments but in the final analysis the decision must be based on service to the handicapped student. The latter prefers, generally, to be treated like every other student, so that if the counseling services are quartered in a department of student personnel, the handicapped student would prefer seeing his counselor there. Other factors might seem more paramount to individual institutions, but the overriding variable, to this observer at least, is the psychic comfort of the student.

Another criterion that must be established is the amount of time allotted per semester to the counselor for each of his handicapped charges. A rule of thumb might be two such students for each clock hour. The counselor to the disabled can expect to see his students an hour and a half, on the average, during each term. Peak loads occur at almost predictable times: (1) preadmission interviews in March and April, prior to the applicant's entry into the college; (2) midterm academic standing for those on low scholarship lists; and (3) near the end of the term program planning for the succeeding semester.

Summary

In the Great Society, provision for counseling the physically handicapped is something we all assume. However, the field is a relatively new one, leaving much to be desired in the way of research, physical facilities on the campus, and trained personnel. Millions of dollars have been poured into medical research but comparatively little has been provided for systematic study of the emotional and social effects of physical disability on the individual. The data collected so far have been inconclusive and indeterminate.

While there has always been great awareness of the suffering of the handicapped, and while much is known about the psychology of the handicapped, the most difficult barrier is reaching the individual. Trained counselors and therapists, on all levels, are scarce, and the handicapped student is so much in the minority that administrators do not always want to make the investment of personnel and time to provide special counseling for such few numbers. The general public's conscious and unconscious rejection of the disabled, moreover, limits their acceptance by the community.

Not all of the picture is black, fortunately. From the available data, more colleges are seen to be providing services of one kind or another to the handicapped than ever before. Employment opportunities for the blind and wheel-chair college graduate are increasing, although the same is not true for the cerebral palsied. As discussion of all topics—sexual matters, race, and mental retardation, for example—becomes more frank, the way is open to a greater willingness to deal with the handicapped rather than avoid the problem.

REFERENCES

Abraham, W. Educational problems of college age persons with seizures. *Except. Child.*, 1956, 22, 147–151, 174.

Abrams, Ruth D., & Dana, Bess S. Social work in the process of rehabilitation. *Social Work*, 1957, 2, 10.

Abt, L. E. The psychology of physical handicap: a statement of some principles. *Orthoped. prosthet. Appl. J.*, 1954, 8, 19–22.

Allen, F. H., & Pearson, G. H. J. The emotional problems of the physically handicapped child. *Brit. J. med. Psychol.*, 1928, 8, 235.

Asenjo, J. A., & Axelrod, S. A survey of vocational objectives of blind college students in the U.S. *New Outlook for the Blind*, 1957, 51, 9–16.

Ausubel, D. P. *Theory and problems of adolescent development.* New York: Grune & Stratton, 1954.

Barker, R. G., Wright, Beatrice A., Meyerson, L., & Gonick, Mollie R. *Adjustment to physical handicap and illness; A survey of the social psychology of physique and disability.* New York: Soc. Sci. Res. Council, 1953.

Berdi, R. F. Counseling for physically disabled students. *J. higher Educ.*, 1955, 26, 475–478.

Broida, D. C., Izard, C. E., & Cruickshank, W. M. Thematic apperception reaction of crippled children. *J. clin. Psychol.*, 1950, 3, 243–248.

Burton, R. *Anatomy of melancholy.* New York: Farrar, 1927.

Bychowski, G. Therapy with crippled and disabled. In G. Bychowski & Louise J. Despert (Eds.), *Specialized techniques in psychotherapy.* New York: Grove Press, 1952.

Caldwell, B. M. Factors influencing reaction to crippling disorders. *J. Missouri med. Assoc.*, 1952, 49, 219–222.

Carlson, E. R. *Born that way.* New York: John Day, 1941.

Cath, S. H., Glud, E., & Blane, H. T. The role of the body-image in psychotherapy with the physically handicapped. *Psychoanal. Rev.*, 1957, 44, 34–40.

Condon, Margaret E. A survey of special facilities for the physically handicapped in the colleges. *Personnel guid. J.*, 1957, 35, 579–582. (a)

Condon, Margaret E. 10-year survey of physically handicapped students of the City College of New York. *Personnel guid. J.*, 1957, 36, 268–271. (b)

Condon, Margaret E. Blind college students in New York State. *New Outlook for the Blind*, 1961, 55, 211–215.

Condon, Margaret E., & Lerner, Ruth S. The rehabilitation counselor in higher education. *J. higher Educ.*, 1955, 26, 208–210.

Condon, Margaret E., & Lerner, Ruth S. Program adjustments for the physically handicapped at the college level. *Personnel guid. J.*, 1956, 35, 41–42.

Criddle, R. *Love is not blind.* New York: W. W. Norton, 1953.

Cronbach, L. J. *Educational psychology.* New York: Harcourt, 1963.

Cruickshank, W. M. The effect of physical disability on personal aspiration. *Quart. J. child Behav.*, 1951, 3, 323–333.

Cruickshank, W. M. A study of the relation of physical disability to social disability. *Amer. J. occup. Ther.*, 1952, 6, 100–109.

Edgington, E. S. Colleges and universities with special programs for wheel chair students. *J. Rehabilit.*, 1963, 29, 14–15.

Erikson, E. H. Ego development and historical change. *Psychol. Issues*, 1959, 1, 32.

Fenichel, O. *The psychoanalytic theory of neurosis*. New York: W. W. Norton, 1945.

Fife, W. E. Services to handicapped students at Southern Illinois University. *Rehabilit. Lit.*, 1960, 21, 222–223.

Fleischer, E. Higher education for the cerebral palsied. *Amer. J. occup. Ther.*, 1953, 7, 254, 267.

Garret, J. F. Counsel the man—not the disability. *Crippled Child*, 1952, 29, 14–15.

Garrett, J. F. Psychological aspects of physical disability. *Educ.*, 1955, 76, 119–122.

Gates, Mary F. A comparative study of some problems of social and emotional adjustment of crippled and non-crippled girls and boys. *J. genet. Psychol.*, 1946, 68, 219–244.

Grant, G. The handicapped university student. *Proc. Royal soc. Med.*, 1960, 53, 1054–1055.

Greenfield, N. S., & Fellner, C. H. Differential correlates of physical handicapped obesity with grade point average in college males and females. *J. clin. Psychol.*, 1963, 19, 263.

Hardee, Melvene D. When your client goes to college. *J. Rehabilit.*, 1951, 17, 10–13, 23.

Himler, L. E., & Raphael, T. Epilepsy among college students. *Ment. Hyg.*, 1940, 24, 459–468.

Himler, L. E., & Raphael, T. A follow-up study of 93 college students with epilepsy. *Amer. J. Psychiat.*, 1945, 101, 760–763.

Jacobson, E. The "exceptions": An elaboration of Freud's character study. In Ruth S. Eissler et al. (Eds.), *The Psychoanalytic Study of the Child*. Vol. 14. New York: Int. Univ. Press, 1959. Pp. 135–154.

Lennox, W. G., McBride, M., & Potter, Gertrude. The higher education of epileptics. *Epilepsia*, 1947, 3, 182–197.

Lerner, Ruth S., & Martin, Marion. What happens to the college student with a physical handicap? *Personnel guid. J.*, 1955, 34, 80–85.

Levi, J., & Mickelson, Barbara. Emotional problems of physically handicapped adolescents—a study of ten adolescent boys. *J. except. Child.*, 1952, 18, 200–206.

McGill, W. O., & Frish, Edith. Helping blind students to prepare for college. *New Outlook for the Blind*, 1960, 54, 219–221.

Mase, D. J., & Williams, C. F. *The assessment of college experience of severely handicapped individuals*. Gainesville, Fla.: Univ. of Fla. Press, 1964.

Menninger, W. C. Emotional adjustments for the handicapped. *Menninger quart.*, 1950, 4, 1–7.

Mussen, P. H., & Newman, D. K. Acceptance of handicap, motivation, and adjustment in physically disabled children. *J. except. Child.*, 1958, 24, 255–260, 277–279.

Norris, H. J., & Cruickshank, W. M. Adjustment of physically handicapped adolescent youth. *J. int. Coun. except. Child.*, 1955, 21, 282–288.

Patterson, C. H. Counseling the severely handicapped college student. *Rehabilit. counsel. Bull.*, 1963, 6, 58–69.

Peckham, R. A. Misdirective counseling. *J. Rehabilit.*, 1953, 19, 3–6.

Potter, E. G., & Fiedler, F. W. Physical disability and inter-personal perception. *Percept. & motor Skills*, 1958, 8, 241–242.

Rogal, Ann. Motivation . . . one role of the therapist. *Crippled Child*, 1952, 30, 13–15.

Rusalem, H. *Guiding the physically handicapped college student.* New York: Columbia Univ. Press, 1962.

Scott, W. *Memoirs of the early life of Sir Walter Scott, written by himself.* Vol. 1. London: Macmillan, 1914.

Smock, C., & Cruickshank, W. M. Responses of handicapped and normal children to the Rosenzweig P-F study. *Quart. J. child Behav.*, 1952, 2, 156–164.

Tracht, V. S. Development of emotional and social maturity through counseling and therapy. *Cerebral Palsy Rev.*, 1957, 18, 12–13.

Tucker, W. V. (Ed.). *Higher education and handicapped students.* Emporia, Kans.: Kans. State Teach. Coll., 1964.

Wright, Beatrice A. *Physical disability: A psychological approach.* New York: Harper, 1960.

Chapter 13

Health Services Counseling[1]

RUTH R. FRANKEL

Purpose of Health Counseling

The interest human beings have in their health varies considerably in intensity. Some may have minor problems which are unreasonably magnified, and others may have major problems which are regrettably ignored. The purpose of health counseling is to help an individual recognize his own health problems, appraise them realistically, obtain professional help when necessary, and strive towards better health.

Although Americans in general and young people of college age in particular are comparatively healthy (Hathaway, Milone, & White, 1961), concealed or evident health problems which require detection and treatment are prevalent. Data collected in the National Health Survey (Department of Health, Education, and Welfare, 1963) indicate that an estimated 37 per cent in the 17–24 age group are afflicted by one or more chronic illnesses. The statistics also show that there were 215 acute illnesses per hundred persons in this age group during the course of a year, or approximately 2 acute illnesses per person a year. In the college population, acute upper respiratory infections and other common contagious diseases, skin conditions, digestive disturbances and emotional problems rank high in frequency. (Levin, 1964, p. 18)

Ruth R. Frankel is Associate Professor, Department of Health and Physical Education (Women), Brooklyn College of the City University of New York.

1. This Chapter does not deal with the physically handicapped (see Chapter 12), but rather with the broad spectrum of health services to *all* college students.

Many college students lack the inner sense of well being and enthusiasm for living popularly associated with good health. College students are at times concerned with symptoms of illness, sometimes serious and more often not, but worrisome in either case. Some may keep their troubled thoughts to themselves; and others may take every opportunity, however inappropriate, to discuss them. Health counseling can help students to detect, express, evaluate, and cope with health problems.

Solicited and unsolicited recommendations for improving health are frequently and freely made. Anyone who tries to assist another person with a health problem is unofficially engaged in health counseling. Not all who are so involved are qualified intellectually, emotionally, or educationally for the role which they assume. Parents, clergymen, teachers, physicians, and others in the health or health-related professions are likely to come in contact with problems directly or indirectly related to health; but sometimes even those who are interested and relatively well informed may overlook the health and counseling needs of others. Because the field is so broad and the boundaries so vague, the discussion of health counseling will be limited here to the services available to students through college health services programs.

Development

Counseling of college students through the health service has evolved at an unsteady pace along a tortuous route. The first deliberate step toward improving the health of students was taken in the first half of the nineteenth century when gymnastics, as a body builder, became a campus activity at Harvard, Dartmouth, Williams, Yale, and Amherst. By 1860, physical education was generally accepted as part of the required college curriculum. (Boynton, 1962) At about that time, the first college medical director of a physical education and hygiene department was appointed at Amherst, indicating an increasing awareness of a college's responsibility for the health of its students. By the end of the nineteenth century, first-aid rooms and infirmaries were to be found on college campuses, the former primarily for emergency treatment of athletic injuries and the latter primarily for isolation of contagious disease. In 1901 the University of California became the first to establish a health service. A faculty investigation to improve attendance, in which illness was found to be an important cause of absence, served as the impetus.

The incidence of communicable disease was a positive factor in the growth of the college medical office. Typhoid epidemics at Cornell University in 1903, at the University of California at Berkeley in 1906, and at the University of Wisconsin in 1907 resulted in the expansion of health services. In 1918, a federal effort to control venereal disease created the United States Interdepartmental Social Hygiene Board and also a Division of Venereal Diseases in the United States Public Health Service. A portion of the federal funds, state matched, was granted to colleges, universities, and other institutions for research on education for the prevention of venereal disease. The legislation on this matter, the Chamberlain-Kahn Act of 1918, stipulated that the colleges working with the United States Interdepartmental Social Hygiene Board must agree to establish a department of hygiene and make every reasonable effort to maintain it. During the three years that funds were available (1919–22), 40 participating educational institutions were helped by grants to expand their student health services. Thomas A. Storey, Director of Hygiene at the College of the City of New York, was the first Executive Secretary of the Interdepartmental Social Hygiene Board. Under his leadership, funds for venereal disease control boosted health courses and health services in higher education.

In the nineteen twenties, conferences were held and organizations were formed to stimulate interest in college health. The American Student Health Association was founded in 1920 following a meeting of a few concerned college representatives. The organization was described as an official and authorized organization through which educational institutions might work for promotion of health, prevention of disease, and care of illness among college and university students. In 1922, the President's Committee of Fifty on College Hygiene met to stimulate interest in health teaching. Their report, "The Status of Hygiene Programs in Institutions of Higher Education in the United States" (Moore & Summerskill, 1953, p. 1), was a survey of the health programs in 396 institutions of higher education, pointing to the need for evaluation, standards, and expansion. Other surveys were similar in purpose. They included a questionnaire reported in the Proceedings of the Ninth Annual Meeting of the American Student Health Association in 1928 on 93 institutions; a "Survey of Land-Grant Colleges and Universities—Student Relations and Welfare"; "University Student Health Services" (Griswald & Spicer, 1932); and the comprehensive "Health Services in American Colleges and Universities" (Moore & Summerskill, 1953), which was based on completed questionnaires from 1,157 institutions, 61 per cent of which were recognized colleges in the United States listed in the Directory of Higher Education. These surveys have supplied representative data from which many practical concepts have emerged.

The First National Conference on College Hygiene was held in 1931 "to focus attention upon . . . the basic problems of college hygiene; secure expert analysis . . . and then formulate a consequent statement of their conclusions." (National Tuberculosis Assoc., 1931) Conference reports of this group and of others in the field, scanned over a period of years, direct attention first to the importance of teaching for health, then to the need for environmental hygiene and the expansion of medical services. Modern college health services emerged from a combination of physical education, first aid, instruction in hygiene, control of communicable disease, and medical advice. Programs differed and have continued to differ considerably as the responsibilities of the medical office increased. Advances in medical care have given the health service more to offer the expanding and expectant campus population.

The Scope of Health Services

A fundamental objective of the college health service is the education of students in both personal and community health. The word education does not here imply merely the transmitting of knowledge; its meaning includes a way of life which sets an example for personal practices and community leadership in the future. Activities to carry out this educational function may be classified into two loose categories which overlap: (1) health education, and (2) medical services.

Much has been written on the college students' lack of knowledge and need for a formal course in health. The President's Commission on Higher Education (1947) stated,

> Our colleges and universities are doing far less than they might to dispel the ignorance that lies at the root of the ill health of many of our people. Almost all our colleges, it is true, offer many courses that touch in some degree on the principles and practices of healthful living. But these courses are scattered through a number of departments, and the information contained in them is never brought directly to bear on the practical problems of personal and community health.
>
> What is needed is a course that deals specifically and explicitly with the information, attitudes, and habits the student needs to maintain and improve his own health and that of his community. An important phase of instruction to this end will be emphasis on the fact that health is more than a personal problem, that it has social implications, and that the individual owes it to society no less than to himself to keep his health and energy at their peak. (p. 54)

This concept was restated and supported by the Third and Fourth National Conferences on Health in Colleges in 1948 and 1954 and by the American Medical Association House of Delegates in 1960.

Many colleges have a health course in the required curriculum; but many do not, perhaps because the academic program is crowded with other courses considered more essential in educating the student. If such a course is offered, it may be considered a group counseling experience in which the student explores problems affecting his own age group and the community. As summarized by the American College Health Association (1963, p. 70), the objectives of health instruction should be to develop understanding about the functions of the human organism and its interrelationship with the environment, to encourage behavior promoting optimal health, to develop attitudes leading the individual to cooperate with community and group programs for health protection, and to aid the individual in becoming an intelligent user of health information and services.

Health education courses may or may not be in the same department as the health service. Regardless of administrative ties, health educators who teach the course may be able to reach student groups informally and promote campuswide activities related to health. The informal approach is as important as the formal course, even on campuses where there is required health education. Where there is no curriculum requirement, however, the medical staff has an even greater responsibility for health education. If working effectively, the medical staff is in a position to exert an important influence on health attitudes and subsequent behavior, in addition to the medical services performed.

There are educational and practical reasons for a close relationship between physical activities and the health service, whether in the same or in different departments. Physical education is a part of the total health program, and there is a practical need for providing coverage for emergency treatment of athletic injuries. College administrators, coaches, health and physical educators, and medical personnel should be familiar with the references to health and safety in the "Bill of Rights for the College Athlete"[2]

> Participation in college athletics is a privilege involving both responsibilities and rights. The athlete has the responsibility to play fair, to give his best, to keep in training, to conduct himself with credit to his sport

2. From "The Bill of Rights for the College Athlete," Committee on the Medical Aspects of Sports; reprinted with the permission of the American Medical Association, 535 North Dearborn Street, Chicago, Illinois.

and his school. In turn he has the right to optimal protection against injury as this may be assured through good technical instruction, proper regulation and conditions of play, and adequate health supervision.

Included are:

Good Coaching: The importance of good coaching in protecting the health and safety of athletes cannot be minimized. Technical instruction leading to skillful performance is a significant factor in lowering the incidence and decreasing the severity of injuries. Also, good coaching includes the discouragement of tactics, outside either the rules or the spirit of the rules, which may increase the hazard and thus the incidence of injuries.

Good Officiating: The rules and regulations governing athletic competition are made to protect players as well as to promote enjoyment of the game. To serve these ends effectively the rules of the game must be thoroughly understood by players as well as coaches and be properly interpreted and enforced by impartial and technically qualified officials.

Good Equipment and Facilities: There can be no question about the protection afforded by proper equipment and right facilities . . . the problem lies in the false economy of using cheap, worn out, outmoded, or ill-fitting gear. Provision of proper areas for play and their careful maintenance are equally important.

Good Health Supervision. . . . Including:

First . . . a thorough preseason history and medical examination. Many of the sports tragedies which occur each year are due to unrecognized health problems. Medical contraindications to participate in contact sports must be respected.

Second . . . a physician present at all contests and readily available during practice season. It is unfair to leave to a trainer or coach decisions as to whether an athlete should return to play or be removed from the game following injury. In serious injuries the availability of a physician may make the difference in preventing disability or even death.

Third . . . medical control of the health aspect of athletics. In medical matters, the physician's authority should be absolute and unquestioned. Today's coaches and trainers are happy to leave medical decisions to the medical profession. They also assist in interpreting this principle to students and the public.

Although the primarily medical and the primarily educational programs are dependent upon each other, formal and informal health and physical education have been briefly discussed above, so that health services may be presented separately in some detail. In the "Proceedings of the National Conference on College Hygiene" (National Tuberculosis Assoc., 1931), the following excerpts refer to recommended health services:

> Every college, regardless of size or resources, is under basic obligation itself, or through the parents of the student, or through the available, appropriate community agencies, to make arrangements for the protection, maintenance and promotion of the health of its students and for the detection, treatment and care of those of its students who are physically or mentally sick or socially maladjusted. Arrangements should be made for:
>
> 1. Medical examination, advice, and treatment of physical, mental, and social problems.
> 2. Maintenance of a favorable physical, biological, and social environment.
> 3. Instruction concerning individual, family and community health.
> 4. Student participation in activities to encourage sound physical, mental, and social health habits, attitudes, and standards.
> 5. Creation of a faculty, presidential, trustee, and institutional consciousness of health needs and of educational opportunities related to those needs. (p. 65).

The health and physical education courses recommended have already been discussed; it is the medical care and environmental hygiene that are the basic medical services with which this chapter is now concerned.

Medical Services

Colleges and universities vary greatly in programs offered and responsibilities assumed. The services available depend upon what is considered necessary and practical. The characteristics of the campus population, where the students are living, and the proximity and availability of medical services in the community are factors which influence the structure of the college health program. "Recommended Standards and Practices for a College Health Program," Part I and Part II, and "Ethical and Professional Relationships—A Supplement to Recommended Standards and Practices for a College Health Program," adopted and published by the American College Health Association (1961, 1963, 1964), are required reading in this field. These reports outline a comprehensive college program and establish standards for the services provided. Although the suggested services are not necessarily suitable for implementation in every institution, they can serve as a guide for organizing or expanding a program and for clarifying responsibility.

For convenience in summarizing, the recommended activities of the medical service are here grouped under the following overlapping headings:

1. Health Appraisal and Counseling
2. Records and Confidentiality
3. Emergency and Infirmary Care
4. Preventive Medicine and Environmental Hygiene

Health Appraisal and Counseling

The school physician is primarily a counselor. The evaluation of health status is an approach to the student following the medical examination. The examination of well persons may be given for different reasons during the college years: at entrance and periodically thereafter; at the suggestion of interested teachers and dormitory counselors who have observed atypical appearance and behavior; as a follow-up for correction; as a requirement for participation in athletics, physical education classes, or military training on campus; and as a pre-employment examination in fields such as teaching, nursing, physical education, and civil service.

The medical examination for admission, as well as subsequent examinations, should screen those students who need immediate attention and further observation. In addition to detecting health problems, defects, and disease, the initial contact should introduce students to the medical office and acquaint them with its facilities for advice and treatment. The introduction should help overcome the negative tendency, prevalent among college students, to avoid contact with the medical office. Actual experiences related to health and disease influence future attitudes toward personal and public health problems.

The medical record should provide information on the following:

1. identification of the individual—name, sex, marital status, address, university status.

2. notification in an emergency—relative, family physician.

3. family medical history—diseases which tend to have a high familial occurrence.

4. personal medical history—past illnesses, physical handicaps, artificial immunization (usually for smallpox, diphtheria, tetanus, and poliomyelitis), hospitalizations, symptoms (such as headaches, insomnia, nervousness, chest pains, palpitations, chronic cough, and fatigue), menstrual history for women, birthplace and residence outside the United States.

5. results of the medical examination.

6. results of special tests—urine analysis for albumin and sugar, tuberculin test and follow up of positive reactors with chest X-ray.

7. comments and summary.

8. recommendation to student, home, and school regarding personal hygiene, medical treatment, sports, employment.

9. follow-up procedures—referral for treatment, recall.

The medical examination may be performed by the college physician or, more commonly, by the family physician.

As an example of these procedures in action, Brooklyn College of the City University of New York admits over 2,000 freshman annually. After acceptance a prospective student receives a communication enclosing two letters and a health record folder. The letters, one addressed to the student from the director of admissions and the other to the private physician from the college physician, stress the importance of the pre-entrance medical examination. The completed records are mailed back promptly. The hidden persuader probably is the requirement of this examination for admission. The staff screens the records, checks omissions, and makes recommendations on program limitations. When necessary, the school physician phones the private physician or invites the student for a conference. In the check of the returned forms, many records are found to be incomplete and the students concerned are scheduled for appointments with the college physician during the first semester. At that meeting, the significance of a thorough physical examination is explained. All students are examined in the sophomore year by the college physician. Physicals are required for participation in athletics (semi-annually) and for readmission; students with special health problems are recalled periodically; pre-employment examinations are given to prospective teachers; and as many seniors as possible are scheduled for checkups, especially where the record indicates the need for further counseling.

Because of increased enrollment, Brooklyn College found it advisable in 1964 to replace the college-performed freshman medical examination with preadmission examinations by private physicians. A comparison was made (Axelrod, 1967) between 763 health record charts of all women students in the class of 1968 and 699 charts of the women in the class of 1966. Omission of items on the charts, detected at the routine sophomore examination by the college physicians, were higher in the 1968 group examined by the private physicians. The number of significant omissions was small, however, and some information was perhaps deliberately omitted because of fear that the student might not be admitted, that his program might be limited, or that the record might in some way jeopardize the student. A larger number of less serious conditions was omitted which, if recorded by the private physician, might have been better handled through health counseling in the Health Services office. Axelrod (1967) concluded that the entrance medical examination performed by the college personnel yielded more information than the examination by the private physician, but that the private physicians' examinations were satisfactory. She suggested that the letter to the private physician which accompanies the medical chart give assurance of accepting and accommodating students with disabilities, that the history section of the health chart be more detailed, and that the space for vision bear this warning: "NOT TO BE FILLED IN UNLESS TESTED AT THIS TIME."

A study of 100 randomly selected college freshmen at the University of Rochester (Flinn, 1963) submitting medical records forms from family physicians revealed that 44 had merely cursory inspection, 12 had not been examined, and 95 forms had urine analysis recorded but only 54 students remembered supplying specimens. At the University of Minnesota, however, after 45 years of entrance physical examinations by the Health Service, a change was made to the private physician; and a survey of over 1,100 students admitted under the new system of physicals (Dvorak and Cowan, 1966) indicated that a high percentage of entering students had a good examination by the private physician.

Among institutions requiring a medical examination by college physicians, some have assembly line medicals and others have individual examinations. At Harvard (Levin, 1964) an entering student prepares his medical history form and makes an appointment for a half hour conference and examination. The personal student-college physician relationship at the entrance examination is considered well worth the time and effort because ". . . it constitutes the student's initial contact with the health service and can have a profound influence on his attitudes toward both the institution and his own health. Thus as an educational experience it can serve as an adjunct to the academic process." As a medical advantage, there is ". . . less chance of significant pathology being overlooked." (p. 43)

Following the admission health evaluation, performed either by the private or the college physician, the health service should provide periodic follow-up for those requiring it, should determine if recommended steps toward correction have been taken, and should assume responsibility for the care or referral of those in need of medical, psychiatric, or other supervision. A channel of communication should be maintained between the family physician and the health service. (Levin, 1964, p. 43–45)

Chronic health problems found most frequently among college freshmen are: eye, ear, nose, and throat conditions (including corrected defective vision); bone and joint injuries; skin disorders; allergies; and problems involving psychological adjustment. Prevalence of organic disease is relatively low and adjustment problems are relatively high among college students. (Hathaway, Malone & White, 1961)

In the role of counselor, the college physician or nurse will come in contact with many different problems related to health. Some occur rarely, some frequently, and some are much more serious than others; but all require understanding and skill in handling. A student may be found to suffer from a malignancy, leukemia, or other possibly fatal diseases. Chronic conditions which may require considerable modification of activities are found on campus; for example, blindness, cerebral palsy, heart disease, or severe orthopedic handicaps. Diabetes mellitus, epilepsy, or hypertension may call for some less radical changes in the typical schedule. Tuberculin positive students who are considered high risk for reactivation of tuberculosis should be counseled on the importance of good health habits and medical care. There are other conditions in which the psychological difficulty is more significant than the physical, as in acne. Not to be overlooked by the health counselor are the health hazards, common on college campuses, such as malnutrition, smoking, alcoholism, and drug addiction.

The increased number of married students on campus has resulted in the need for marriage counseling and for establishing policy on referrals for contraceptive advice to married couples. Pregnancy in an unmarried student, sexual promiscuity, venereal disease, and homosexuality are sometimes revealed to the college physician by the anxious student desperately seeking help. The relationship between physician and patient is confidential. Students must be made aware of this if they are to use the health service, especially if they are involved in socially disapproved situations.

The college physician is often in a vulnerable position when controversial or socially unacceptable issues related to health are involved. Premarital sex relations may be brought to the attention of the college physician in a counseling situation and the physician will discuss related problems with the concerned student. Prescribing contraceptives is not generally considered a college health service, but students may be referred for further information. Homosexuality is treated and accepted as a personal emotional problem and is strictly confidential unless it infringes on others. Venereal disease is handled as an infection; and where required by law, it is reported to the health department. Where drug habituation and addiction are criminal offenses, they must be reported. Dean Monro's widely publicized (New York Times, April 15, 1967) declaration on drugs to freshman at Harvard is an attempt to approach the student on the basis of the educational and legal responsibility that the student has to himself, and that Harvard has to the student. The "Monro Doctrine" states that if a student is stupid enough to misuse his time with illegal and dangerous drugs, he should leave college and make room for a student prepared to make better use of the opportunities at Harvard College.

Although medical and psychological counseling are interrelated, these services are not necessarily in the same department; and, if required, contact between the medical and psychological counselors should be made, preferably with the knowledge and consent of the counselee. Records of psychiatric problems and treatment should in any case be separated from the general medical records.

That the college health service program caters to students in general has already been stressed; but there are particular groups on campus which should be singled out for consideration because of special health problems. Among them are handicapped students, married students, foreign students, faculty, and staff. Among the married students, problems involving personal relationships, finances, and child care are common. Among the foreign students, cultural differences in diet and attitudes toward health may indicate a need for special attention. Health problems often require the collaboration of several administrative offices on campus as well as the use of community resources.

The health service has a responsibility to the employees of the college and university. It is desirable to have pre-employment and periodic physicals for all personnel. Medical examinations, every three years for those under 40 years of age and every year for those over 40, have been encouraged at M.I.T. since 1951 and at Harvard since 1956. At institutions where this is not feasible at present, perhaps a start can be made by requiring physical examinations for employees covered by Workmen's Compensation or liability insurance and by promoting campaigns for voluntary physicals. Studies at Harvard (Levin, 1964, p. 49) and the University of Michigan (Tupper, 1962, p. 414) revealed previously undiscovered ailments among faculty and other employees. At Harvard, during 1959–60, about 1,000 faculty and staff members were examined, resulting in the detection of four carcinomas, one case of leukemia, and six other serious diseases. At the University of Michigan, among 1,221 faculty members responding to invitations for voluntary physicals, 900 had previously undetected conditions, including 81 cases of diabetes mellitus, 51 persons with hypertension, 9 cardiacs, 21 malignancies, 4 cases of glaucoma, and 1 instance of active tuberculosis. The value of periodic examinations for early detection of treatable diseases in this group is striking.

Records and Confidentiality

In "A Plea for Uniformity in College Records" (Bowie, 1964), the following record forms are suggested:

1. a detailed history and physical examination form, recommended by the American Medical Association. (American College Health Association forms available)
2. a health inventory form, submitted by the student before enrolling, of educational value to the student filling it out and also of significance to the college physician in counseling the student.
3. a form from the parents on the family's and the student's health, to be sent to the parents before the student's enrollment.
4. a permission form, required for participation in various activities.

Standard-size forms, nomenclature, space left for check-ups and progress notations, ease in filing, microfilming, coding, summary reports, and use of the data for research and computer analysis are practical matters which must be worked out by the staff. Procedures should be reviewed periodically and modified to fit the changing needs of the service. Requests for information are often made by prospective employers, for insurance and disability claims, and by students' private physicians. Records are generally kept at least five to ten years and preferably indefinitely, if not otherwise designated by law. Records are confidential, and the physician may not disclose information without consent of the student, unless required by law.

There may be reason for communication between the college physician and other college offices, parents, private physicians, lawyers, insurance companies, potential employers, and governmental agencies for law, health, and security enforcement. The health service may wish to communicate with members of the university community concerning the welfare of the individual student or of the campus community. The following information may be given to responsible individuals without specific permission of the student concerned:

1. Occurrence, onset, or duration of an illness; but no diagnosis should be mentioned.
2. Estimated degree of incapacity.
3. Severity and prognosis.

4. Specific recommendations relating to academic activities, physical education, athletics, changing residence, withdrawing from school.

5. Recommendation of exclusion if the presence of a student would endanger the student body.

The American College Health Association (1964) indicates specifically the limitations on information disclosed:

> Any information about individual students other than that listed above must be considered a privileged communication between student and the health service and, therefore, subject to the established ethical codes of the medical profession. All personnel involved in the conduct of the health service, including physicians, nurses, aides, clerks, and secretaries, are considered a party to these principles. They represent the physician and are subject to his code of ethics. Specific written or verbal communication beyond the information listed above should be provided only upon the written permission or endorsement of the individual student. (pp. 51–52)

The responsibility of the medical service to parents or legal guardians is stated by the American College Health Association (1964):[3]

> In all cases of serious illness or accident to a student, the parent or legal guardian should be notified immediately. Such notifications may be by telephone and may be followed by written communication in the form of letter or telegram. The student's health service record should record this communication. When such communication to parents or legal guardian is necessary, the Dean of Students may be informed that such notification has been made. In the case of a married student, the spouse should be informed on a similar basis. In the case of the married student under the age of twenty-one, the parents should be informed in such instances even though such an individual is legally considered an adult.
>
> In the case of a minor student, in addition to the above, notification of parents or legal guardian should be made when any condition is discovered likely to be of long term significance, such as diabetes or other chronic disease requiring prolonged care or necessitating adjustment in the student's way of life.
>
> Pregnancy in the unmarried minor student usually requires cooperative effort on the part of the parents, the health service, and sometimes other college agencies. The student should be urged and helped to communicate with her parents or legal guardian and it should be made plain that it is the duty of any physician caring for her to do so in the event of her refusal or inability. It is important that the health service maintain a reputation for confidentiality in this particular area so that women students with this problem will feel free to seek help without fear of widespread dissemination of the information. There should be no in-

3. Reprinted by permission of the American College Health Association.

timation at any time that seeking such help from the health service will result in any action by the health service that may lead to disciplinary action on the part of the academic institution. This does not mean that the health service in any way guarantees that the institution will not take disciplinary action, only that if such action does occur, it will be because of information from other sources and not from the health service. It should be clearly understood that no report will be made to any administrative officer or any other department in the university. As long as parents are informed as outlined above and take responsibility, the health service can advise with them as to the possible course of action for the student. Nothing more need be reported.

When the student has reached the age of twenty-one years, the disclosure of medical information by the physician to the parents is not done without specific written permission of the individual patient. In such cases, it is strictly a matter between the doctor and the patient. Here, again, no report should be made to any administrative office or other department of the university. (pp. 52–53)

The relationship between the college physician and the private physician should be close. When the student is at a distance from home, the college physician may be requested to continue treatment begun by the private physician. If the student is treated by his private physician or referred to the private physician by the medical service, information from the medical records may be forwarded to the family physician. If there is a difference of opinion in an academic situation, the college physician has the responsibility for the final decision and for its interpretation to the private physician.

Care is necessary in releasing information to the press. Details should never be given on an injury or disease. Inquiries about health by a prospective employer may be answered with the knowledge and written consent of the student. However, approving a student for particular employment is a responsibility best assumed by the prospective employer. Information requested by a lawyer or by an insurance company is released only with the written permission of the student or parent of the student if he is a minor. As stated by the American College Health Association (1964), this applies even to government security agencies: "It should be noted that no governmental agency, including the F.B.I., can request confidential information without the written permission of the individual involved." (p. 55) However, local and state regulations require the reporting of certain information to Health and Police Departments. Routine notification of venereal and communicable disease must be made to local public health authorities and evidence of criminal action, such as assault, gunshot wounds, knife wounds, poisoning, and criminal abortion, is required to be reported to the police. These laws apply to all physicians including those in a college health service.

Policy on releasing medical records must be established and firmly kept. The content of such policy is suggested by the American College Health Association (1964) in the following statement:

> Medical records, including X-rays are deemed the property of the health service or hospital. As owner, the health service may restrict removal of the record; however, a court order that authorizes or requires removal of the record must be complied with. The attending physician does not own such records and cannot limit their availability. Only the confidentiality of the records belong to the patient.
>
> Courts have uniformly held that the patient or his designated representative may examine all medical records pertaining to the patient; however, the health service or hospital may supervise the inspection to insure that material is not removed or inserted. Such permission should, of course, be granted only upon written request of the patient. (p. 60)

When a college physician becomes aware of a condition which is of danger to the patient or to others, he may decide it necessary to inform a parent or school administrator. If a student refuses permission, he should be told that this contact must be made anyway. The nonmedical personnel in the medical office should be alerted to the importance of confidentiality as just defined and delimited and the danger of inadvertently disclosing information.

Emergency and Infirmary Care

Services to college students and employees vary considerably from campus to campus. This applies not only to the physical examination and counseling already described, but also to medical care. On some campuses, the health service program is primarily one of first aid in emergency. Where a large number of students are living away from home, it is necessary to provide infirmary care. Upper respiratory infections and gastrointestinal upsets are the common ailments treated in the infirmary, providing the homelike attention not possible in the dormitory or residence away from the family. Hospitalization is required in the advent of serious illness or the necessity for major surgery. At some universities a medical school and hospital may provide specialized treatment.

The medical office must be open during the hours the college buildings are used by students. In residence colleges, 24-hour coverage by physicians is necessary. The college or university may be dependent upon medical facilities available in the area, or it may be equipped for X-ray, physiotherapy, and other specialized services. The medical office must be centrally located and quickly reached by phone. It must meet modern standards of safety and sanitation, provide temporary accommodations for the sick, and be prepared to handle mass casualties. Library facilities and attractive quarters are assumed to be part of the minimal requirements.

A member of the medical staff is expected to be well qualified for his work by virtue of his education, interest and temperament. The director and staff physicians must have a recognized medical degree, experience in general practice, and interest in education. An excellent description (Hurtado, 1963, p. 298) of qualifications for college physicians includes formal training, intellectual alertness, devotion to the specific challenges of student health practice, ability to deal with the student's psychological problems, and also, if possible, a sense of humor, to take in stride the erratic behavior of immaturity.

The medical staff should include a consultant psychiatrist. The nurse on the team should be professionally registered (R.N.), with training in first aid and experience in public health. Assistance from a clerical staff is necessary to handle the office routine efficiently. It is preferable that the personnel be full-time rather than part-time.

The American College Health Association (1963, p. 41), recognizing the dangers of setting arbitrary standards for personnel because of variations in local circumstances, nevertheless makes the following suggestions on staff requirements for outpatient services offered by the Health Service directly:

1. One full time physician per 1,000 students, and 1/10 position for each additional 100 regular students.
2. An administrative assistant when the student enrollment reaches 5,000.
3. One nurse position per full time physician.
4. A pharmacist for student bodies over 4,000 where the clinic dispenses medication.
5. One technician for every 2,000 regular students.
6. One clerk for the first 1,500 students, one for the second 1,500 students, and one for every additional 2,000 students.
7. Environmental health personnel depending on campus needs.
8. Adequate custodial help.

The high incidence of dental defects in young adults and the possibilities of chairside education are arguments for dental services through the health program. In a survey (Dunning, Giddon, & Greene, 1963) of 361 member institutions of the American College Health Association, 292 replied to a questionnaire on dental services. Only 31 indicated that their medical services included dental clinics, and seven of these offered only emergency care or consultation. Dental services, when offered, should encompass preventive dentistry, emergency dental care, and dental health education. The bulk of the treatment should be referred to the private dentist.

The variety and extent of services available through the medical service usually depend upon what is considered necessary, practical, and financially possible. The cost is borne in different ways:

1. by a required health service fee.
2. by a percentage deduction from tuition.
3. by additional fees for special services.
4. by a budgetary allocation.
5. by supplementary health insurance.
6. by combinations of the above.

The American College Health Association (1963) recommends that:

> Direct services to students be paid for out of student fees, preferably fees openly designated in order to counter the rather prevalent idea that the student is receiving "free" services. Under this philosophy, either the student's fee or general college funds may pay for physical examinations. Certain portions of the cost of the environmental health program and certainly the total cost of health education of the formal variety should be a charge against the general college funds. The details of what services the college will provide, and of what charges may be made for special services, will vary from institution to institution, but each college has the responsibility to ensure its students of the best possible medical care. Insurance coverage should be available for those large expenses resulting from medical care which the college cannot provide. (pp. 40–41)

Insurance policies should be written to fit the need of a particular university and should supplement, not duplicate, what the medical service offers. It is uneconomical to insure for what the medical service can provide. When arranged and sponsored by the school for a large group, cost is reduced. Coverage should extend over the full year, including vacations.

The insurance company, the underwriter, receives the premium, assumes the risk, and is responsible for the claims payments. The company should be licensed and approved in the state. In college health insurance, an agency usually represents an insurance company and a broker or agent represents the agency, placing the insurance with the insurance company.

It is important that the college administrator deal with reliable firms and keep track of financial details on premium, claims, and commissions. Common coverage includes services not available through the health service: emergency care (off campus), specialist consultation, hospital expenses, surgery, and medical care in hospitals. Usually not covered are medication (except in hospitals), private nursing, office visits, and house calls.

In the care of patients, institutions and individuals are subject to legal liability for injuries caused through negligence. State laws differ, and each member of the medical staff should be familiar with his responsibilities and liability. Adequate coverage by insurance must be carefully worked out to protect the institution and its employees for specific risks and claims. It is advisable to formulate and distribute to the staff a written statement, signed by the medical director, on policies and procedures related to treatment and medication in anticipated conditions and situations. Precautions include

1. obtaining consent from a student, or parent if the student is a minor, for all optional medical treatment;
2. maintaining accurate and complete medical records;
3. informing parents of injuries and illness;
4. offering top quality medical service.

Preventive Medicine and Environmental Hygiene

Preventive medicine is concerned with the prevention of the occurrence and progression of disease and disability. The prevention of occurrence includes control of environmental factors, artificial immunization, and overcoming predisposing conditions in the individual. The prevention of progression includes periodic health examinations to detect disease at an early stage and encourage treatment. Environmental hygiene implies control of the physical environment which may unfavorably affect physical, mental, and social well being. This area of medical service has been covered to some extent under health appraisal and health counseling, but specific efforts toward control of infectious disease and accident prevention warrant further mention.

An immunization program is required to protect the student and the college community against contagion. Vaccinations against smallpox (within three years prior to matriculation), tetanus (immunization or a booster within three years prior to matriculation), diphtheria, and poliomyelitis are recommended as a requirement for admission. Typhoid and influenza immunization may be advised by public health authorities under certain circumstances, as well as immunization against measles and possibly mumps. Although vaccines are usually given before the student arrives on campus, routine immunization should be offered free of charge by the medical service. Gamma globulin is used for those intimately exposed in outbreaks of measles or infectious hepatitis.

Students, faculty, and staff should be tuberculin tested and X-rayed, the latter to screen tubercular and nontubercular pathology. Chest X-rays should be repeated in the junior or senior year for those who are tuberculin positive; those who are tuberculin negative should be tuberculin retested every few years. Rheumatic heart disease or a history of rheumatic fever calls for follow-up and consideration of antibiotic prophylaxis. If anyone objects to preventive measures on religious grounds, every effort should be made to respect individual rights; however, if the procedure serves the welfare of the group, the individual who objects must comply with the regulations of the college or leave. A chest X-ray, for example, in a tuberculosis case-finding campaign must be taken if it is required for admission.

At times the health service must deal with epidemics of influenza, measles, or chicken-pox which temporarily stretch the infirmary beyond its capacity. The threat of food-transmitted infection must be met by inspecting eating facilities on and around the campus.

Recent tragedies on college campuses involving deaths caused by fires have directed attention to the need for responsibility in student housing. In 1962, a joint committee of the American College Health Association, the Association of College and University Housing Officers, and the Campus Safety Association of the National Safety Council published "Student Housing Standards (1962) Recommended Minimum Health and Safety Standards for noninstitutionally owned Student Housing," which includes the basic requirements of good housing and lists available references. The college administration and the health service have a moral obligation to assume responsibility for safe housing. The Health Service at the University of Minnesota (Daley, 1965) has had a housing inspection program since 1961, and recommends that a trained sanitarian be employed in a housing inspection program as well as in other environmental health services on the college campus.

The college physician is involved in maintaining a safe college environment. To do so effectively, he must be an epidemiologist, a biostatistician, and a social psychologist. He must be aware of the hazards in the college community; he must analyze records and make surveys to identify potentially dangerous areas or activities; and he must have the support of students, administration, faculty, and other employees in order to provide a safe environment. If the college physician is not directly responsible for the danger spots on campus, he is in a position to stimulate interest in improvement. It is suggested that every campus have a committee on health and safety with representation from the medical office, the health and physical education department, the science departments, the administration, the maintenance staff, and the student body. Areas for special attention of such a committee should include housing, lighting, ventilation, fire hazards, disrepair of physical plant, equipment and practices in physical education and the science laboratories, testing of the water supply and swimming pool, supervision of food preparation, education of food handlers, and safety measures for the maintenance staff.

A relatively recent environmental problem is related to the use in research of ionizing radiation and radioactive isotopes. Protective shields and careful monitoring procedures for radiation hazards are safeguards for students, faculty, and maintenance workers in contact with toxic emissions.

In an analysis of accident reports (Scheffler, 1961) on college campuses, the following danger spots were listed in order of frequency of accidents: the athletic field and gymnasium, the physical science laboratories (involving particularly research personnel), outdoors in winter weather, interior floors and stairs, repair shops, and areas where large groups assemble. In 55 per cent of the accidents, the injuries occurred in athletics. Football helmets, mouth guards, safety hats, and contact lenses have been recommended for protection. The number of fractured incisors in competitive sports influenced the National Alliance Football Rules Committee to require that mouth guards be worn in this game. In a survey on mouth protectors in college athletics (Dunning, Gideon, & Greene, 1963), 129 of 292 colleges replying (78 per cent) stated that they were used, in 125 colleges for football only. Hockey, boxing, lacrosse, and wrestling, however, are competitive sports in which teeth can easily be injured, and only 13 schools mentioned any of these sports in their mouth-protector program. "The Bill of Rights for the College Athlete" previously cited is a guide for safety in athletics; its suggestions for protection against injury through good coaching, officiating, equipment, facilities, and medical care should be more widely read and followed. If an accident does occur, a detailed accident report is necessary for the records.

Each contact of the medical staff with the college community through personal counseling, medical care, and environmental hygiene is an educational opportunity to set a memorable example in healthful living and good medical practice.

Research and Evaluation

Research in the medical office is an accepted activity related to better understanding of problems and to improvement of services. Approval for research must be obtained from designated college administrators. Medical research is generally basic, clinical, and statistical. In studies requiring use of records, confidentiality must be respected. In experimentation involving students, faculty, or staff subjects, written consent must be obtained. Policies and forms for research on human beings formulated by the Harvard University Health Service have been published by the American College Health Association (1964). Guidelines are also available from the Public Health Service, Department of Health, Education, and Welfare.

Evaluating policy, services, and results is essential, yet difficult. Kilander and Brown (1964) have prepared a self-evaluation guide which is available for appraising a college health service. The purpose of self-evaluation is to call attention to inadequacies of services judged in comparison with generally accepted standards. Complacency is an obstacle to progress, and self-evaluation of the health services by the medical staff may disturb self-satisfaction but will stimulate improvement.

The student comes to college already molded by home and community. The health program includes a counseling service which must overcome ignorance, misinformation, inertia, and inability or unwillingness to pay for medical care. The evaluative question which must constantly be confronted is whether the health counseling offered will be sufficiently impressive to make some contribution toward the student's healthier living at college and in the future.

REFERENCES

American College Health Association. Recommended standards and practices for a college health program, part I. *Stud. Med.*, 1961, 10, 33–44.

American College Health Association. Recommended standards and practices for a college health program, part II. *J. Amer. Coll. Hlth. Assoc.*, 1963, 12, 35–76.

American College Health Association. Ethical and professional relationships—a supplement to recommended standards and practices for a college health program. *J. Amer. Coll. Hlth. Assoc.*, 1964, 13, 45–89.

American Medical Association, Committee on the Medical Aspects of Sports. *The bill of rights for the college athlete.* Chicago: Author, undated.

Axelrod, Sylvia. Freshman medical examinations: the changeover from college-performed to private physician examinations. Unpublished manuscript, Brooklyn: Brooklyn Coll., 1967.

Bosch, H. M. Some aspects of an effective environmental health program. *Student Med.*, 1960, 9, 150–159.

Bowie, M. A. A plea for uniformity in college health records. *J. Amer. Coll. Hlth. Assoc.*, 1964, 12, 337–342.

Boynton, Ruth E. Historical development of college health services. *Stud. Med.*, 1962, 10, 294–305.

Daley, W. W. Off-campus housing at universities and colleges with 2,500 or more student enrollment. *J. Amer. Coll. Hlth. Assoc.*, 1965, 14, 502–510.

Department of Health, Education and Welfare, United States Public Health Service. *Current estimates from the health interview survey.* Washington: Govt. Print. Off., 1963.

Dunning, J. M., Gideon, D., & Greene, F. B. Prevalence and characteristics of college dental health services. *J. Amer. Coll. Hlth. Assoc.*, 1963, 11, 189–196.

Dvorak, E. J., & Cowan, D. W. Evaluation of the private physician entrance examination: a questionnaire study. *J. Amer. Coll. Hlth. Assoc.*, 1966, 14, 267–269.

Farnsworth, D. L. (Ed.) *College health administration.* New York: Appleton-Century-Crofts, 1964.

Flinn, J. H. The pre-entrance physical examination—fact or fiction. *J. Amer. Coll. Hlth. Assoc.*, 1963, 12, 231–234.

Griswold, D. M., & Spicer, Hazel I. *University student health services.* Publication of the committee on the costs of medical care, No. 19. Chicago: Univ. of Chicago Press, 1932.

Group for the Advancement of Psychiatry, Committee on the College Student. *Sex and the college student.* New York: Author, 1966.

Hathaway, J. S., Milone, H. S., & White, C. Health problems and health surveys of college students. *Stud. Med.*, 1961, 9, 211–217.

Hurtado, E. Contemporary evolution of college health service. *J. Amer. Coll. Hlth. Assoc.*, 1963, 11, 292–299.

Joint Committees on Student Housing Standards. Student housing standards—recommended minimum health and safety standards for noninstitutionally owned student housing. *Stu. Med.*, 1962, 10, 363–393.

Joy, W. W. Health and safety in student housing—a new look. *J. Amer. Coll. Health Assoc.*, 1965, 14, 435–441.

Kilander, H. F., & Brown, W. C. A college health services self-evaluation guide. *J. Amer. Coll. Hlth. Assoc.*, 1964, 13, 218–226.

Levin, O. The medical service. In D. L. Farnsworth (Ed.), *College health administration.* New York: Appleton-Century-Crofts, 1964. Pp. 16–59.

Medical Care on Campus, from *Medical World News*, 1966, 7, 57–69.

Miller, E. A. Student medical insurance and the health service. *J. Amer. Coll. Hlth. Assoc.*, 1963, 11, 247–252.

Moore, N. S., & Summerskill, J. *Health services in American colleges and universities, 1953.* Ithaca, N.Y.: Cornell Univ., 1954.

National Tuberculosis Association. Every college regardless of size. *Proc. nat. Conf. Coll. Hyg.* New York: Author, 1931.
National Tuberculosis Association. Health in colleges. *Proc. 2nd nat. Conf. Coll. Hyg.* New York: Author, 1936.
President's Commission on Higher Education. *Higher education for American democracy.* Vol. 1. *Establishing the goals.* Washington: Govt. Print. Off., 1947. Pp. 50–54.
Scheffler, G. L. Danger spots on campus. *Stud. Med.,* 1961, 9, 336–344.
Tupper, C. F. College professor—his health and health care habits. *Stud. Med.,* 1962, 10, 414–421.

Chapter 14

Religious Counseling

JOHN J. O'SULLIVAN

Historical Background

Any treatment of religious counseling in higher education must be seen against the background of the founding of American higher education by religious bodies. The first colleges were religiously oriented and dominated, from the founding of Harvard College to that of William and Mary. The influence of the churches upon education, however, was too often obviated by a sectarianism which scarred its progress. To this day the fear of favoring a sect continues to prevent a serious confrontation with religion in many state and municipal colleges. Following the Civil War, the state universities began to grow rapidly in number and influence. The legislation which appropriated money for their support nearly always demanded non-support for sectarian instruction and in some cases excluded it altogether. A possible consequence of such legislation may be the present system: public colleges, including state and municipal institutions; private colleges, including many originally organized by the church but later autonomous; and finally, denominational or church-related institutions.

Leaders in state universities were usually eager to avoid the accusation that they were antireligious, but it was not always clear how this could be done without violating the constitutional principle of separation of church and state. Consequently, these same leaders encouraged the campus work of religious groups such as the Y.M.C.A. and, later on, Hillel Foundations and Newman Clubs. As the states vary from one another so do the

John J. O'Sullivan is Newman Chaplain, Brooklyn College of the City University of New York.

colleges and universities. The diverse pattern of American life is reflected in the diverse approach to the relation of the church and higher education. The religious pluralism of the urbanized areas includes Protestants, Catholics, and Jews, whereas the still rural campuses are largely Protestant with some Catholics but without significant numbers of Jewish students.

Religion and Religious Counseling

Since religious pluralism is such a factor in American college life, any counseling program of significance must come to grips with it. Although university life has become more and more secularized, the phenomenon of religion and religious experience is always present. University administrators are hard put to ignore religion when one of the stated purposes of higher education involves the moral and spiritual values of the student. As personnel and counseling programs come to occupy an increasingly larger portion of the university's concern, the problem of religion and religious counseling will mount accordingly. As Arbuckle (1953) has written: "Regardless of the type of institution, religion is an important factor in the lives of many students and it cannot be ignored as if it did not exist." (p. 157) If the university declares that it is seriously interested in religion because of its concern for the student, then it must make room for it in the academic area and in the area of personnel guidance and counseling. Mere lip service to this principle must give way to a serious confrontation with the fact of religion as it affects the lives of so many students. In this regard, the American Council On Education has firmly stated, ". . . institutions of higher education of all types have an inescapable obligation to provide religious guidance as an integral part of their work." (Merriam, 1943, p. 5)

Religious counseling has been going on for a long time in the field of higher education. As Cunninggim (1947, p. 150) has suggested, "Both before and after personnel programs became organized, the religious guidance of undergraduates was furnished informally by faculty members and other interested individuals." When educational institutions were smaller and had not yet begun to assume the roles formerly left to other social institutions such as family or church, informal counseling was a fact. As society grows ever more complex and delegates more responsibility to the educational institution, counseling programs will be forced into being structured to assume these responsibilities. The religious foundations at secular universities will be called into greater cooperation with the university counseling program and the university itself will need to have religious counselors (not campus ministers) on its personnel staff. Many universities already have an office of religious affairs. Such is the situation at the University of Michigan (1958) in which the staff provides counseling for:

> *a.* the student whose personal problems take the form of religious questions, or the student who sees his problem as religious;
> *b.* the student whose relationship with a religious tradition permits him to talk more easily with a trained religious leader;
> *c.* the student who desires religious counseling but does not feel free to discuss a particular problem with the religious counselor of his own faith. (p. 29)

In addition, at Michigan there is a Board of Religious Counselors representing seventeen religious bodies. Referrals are made by the Office of Religious Affairs and can also be made by religious counselors in the various religious bodies. U.C.L.A. and Columbia have buildings for non-worship activities. Earl Hall at Columbia provides offices for religious counselors. At Harvard there is a Bureau of Study Counsel and a Psychiatric Department, in which information and referrals are shared with the respective religious foundations.

Faculty Relations

At universities which do not have officially recognized religious counselors, the campus ministers assume the greatest responsibility for religious counseling. One of the more unfortunate features of such a lack occurs on large impersonal campuses. Thousands of students are unaware of the opportunities offered by the religious foundations. Although faculty and religious foundations have good relations, they are not constant enough to be measurably successful. The process is too sporadic, and mutual referrals take place only on a situational basis. A Catholic student, for example, who seeks help from a counselor on a religious question, is not helped if the counselor does not know that there is a Catholic priest available. A full counseling opportunity can be lost. It is possible that the student would prefer not to seek help from the priest chaplain, but all possible aids should be suggested as part of good counseling practice. To incorporate the facilities of the religious foundations in the staff handbook as well as the student handbook would be a momentous forward stride toward achieving a more inclusive program of counseling. Moreover, providing office space for the campus ministers in the counseling division and disseminating knowledge of this throughout the college community would create a more practical avenue for better relations and better counseling.

Inviting the campus ministers to staff counseling meetings is another valid suggestion for creating greater consistency in the counseling program.

In those private schools which are still sectarian or church related, religious counselors who are not of that particular religious affiliation should be included in the university's counseling program. Although Catholic priests have worked as campus ministers at other than Catholic schools, there does not seem to be reciprocity at Roman Catholic institutions. It seems that such schools should meet this need for the benefit of those students who are not coreligionists with the established sect operating the school. Perhaps the day will soon come when there will be a small Protestant foundation at Notre Dame or Fordham or a Hillel Foundation at St. John's. If the numbers of students do not warrant a foundation, at least a religious counselor or campus minister should be made officially available.

Religious Counseling and Psychological Problems

The boundaries of religious counseling cannot be set off in a neatly circumscribed package. Many of the students who seek the guidance of the campus minister do not have problems which stem from religion at all. This writer cannot agree wholeheartedly with Arbuckle's (1953, p. 170) statement that "what makes counseling in the field of religion somewhat unique . . . is that seldom are religious difficulties ones that can be solved rationally and intellectually." It may be said, however, that sometimes the articulation of the problem by the student is a symptom of emotional disturbance which the experienced campus minister or religious counselor will recognize. He is all too aware that emotionally disturbed students are hardly capable of mature and responsible commitment until the underlying problem is treated. The Christian minister is committed to the Incarnation and knows that emotional health is inextricably bound up with developing as a human person. Before a true commitment is possible, a reasonable measure of emotional health must be attained. The proposition that grace builds on nature must be understood in this context. As Hagmaier & Gleason (1959, p. 6) have noted, "Grace can only do all these things if 'nature' is a whole and healthy and capable of ennoblement." In such cases the campus minister would, of course, refer the student to the appropriate therapeutic office or agency. If the university provides such psychological service, the religious counselor will make a referral. It has been the experience of the present writer that the emotionally disturbed Catholic student seeking psychological help prefers a therapist of his own religious faith. This may not be the experience or preference of other faiths, and systematic research would be most valuable here. When this does occur, however, this usually indicates that the university will be by-passed and the student will be referred to a church-related social agency. According to Msgr. John F. Bradley (Newman Chaplain, University of Michigan; personal communication), the student prefers this type of referral for another reason. He fears having a record of his emotional difficulties placed in his file in the school. Apparently emotional disturbance is still taboo to many. The student is assured in his interview with the campus minister of the confidentiality of his problem. The happy medium is achieved when the counselor and the therapist can cooperate with each other and the student on a continuing basis. The religious counselor must not be too eager to make a referral which will end this particular counseling problem for him. Every door should be left open for a continuing counseling relationship. In order to overcome the fears of the student that the confidentiality of his problem will be violated, a strong public relations program is needed. Confidence must be instilled by the college counseling division and the campus ministers. The benefits will be mutually realized and the results will be felt by the students in whose interest the counseling program operates.

Religious Counseling and Problems of Maturation

The religious literacy of the average college student, whatever his religious preference, is at an elementary school level. His religious knowledge has not matured along with his intellectual growth in other disciplines. As Merriam (1943, p. 40) has pointed out, "without a substantial foundation of knowledge the values in a religious faith are likely to be transitory and undependable." When he comes to the college campus, the student's religious faith is challenged by his civilization, science, and philosophy courses. Perhaps for the first time he is forced to think about his religious faith. Some students build a hard shell around themselves against this challenge. They compartmentalize their faith and refuse to meet the challenge. Others accept the secular discipline as more competent and relevant and quietly put religion aside. Some will seek help from the religious counselor.

A few years ago a young lady came to the writer seeking help in the resolution of just such a crisis. Her religious education had not prepared her for the challenge of the secular disciplines. Her studies in civilization and anthropology had shaken her immature beliefs. She was fast becoming a convinced syncretist. She had consulted her parish priest only to be brushed off as impertinent. Her parents had never undergone a crisis like this and were helpless. She showed a remarkable ignorance of the trends that were current in the Roman Catholic church as part of the renewal process of the Second Vatican Council. Her bitterness was expressed against "dogmatism and authoritarianism and the lack of freedom of inquiry enjoined by the Church." After several counseling sessions, she was introduced to the concepts of freedom and authority as they were hotly debated in the Council and written about without the conciliar sessions. She began to read the contemporary literature on these subjects and finally she discovered the great strides which scientific biblical scholarship has attained. With the closing of the illiteracy gap she was able to weather this crisis successfully.

This example is typical of the religious maturation process and is not limited to one denomination. Jewish and Protestant students have similar problems which are cast in their separate denominational contexts. When the student is made aware of theological disciplines, which are easily the equal in scholarship to the secular disciplines, and when the level of his religious knowledge can be brought up to a parity, the problem is well on its way to resolution. The counseling process can then be shifted from a one-to-one basis, and the counselor can direct the student into religious foundation courses and discussion and study groups. If the university offers courses in religion, the student can be directed to them. The student's religious faith should be challenged, and this challenge can be best effected in the academically competent course arrangements of the university. Although this chapter is not directly concerned with departments of religion, all campus ministers agree that where courses are offered the challenges are even greater than any which the secular disciplines can present.

Religious Counseling and Adolescent Problems

The adolescent years are crucial for shaping the adult religious personality. The religious counselor cannot ignore this factor which has been characterized as the time when the student attempts to define "his place in [that] universe, its acceptance of him, his ability to control and predict it and his life style within it, discovering the rules and standards for charting his way . . . all these processes [making] up the constantly churning turbulence of the adolescent mind." (Walsh, 1964, p. 36) Whether the college student goes off to a residential campus or attends a local commuter college, he will more than likely experience an increase in the adolescent tensions that characterize his relations with his parents. On the campus, he meets with students of such a varied background that his own problems may well crystallize into rebellion against all authority, but it will be mostly directed against his parents. At Brooklyn College, for example, which draws students from the local community, these tensions are verbalized in many ways. The college experience is new to the family grouping. The student is very often the first in his family to attend college. On the one hand, the parents are delighted that their child is in college; but, on the other hand, they cannot comprehend the amount of work the student must do in order to maintain his standing. The available study space at home may be limited. There may be an intrusive, severely limiting lack of privacy. Add to this the factors of pluralism and gradual awareness of current social problems, the overcoming of social and religious prejudices, and the student may be ready to explode against his "ignorant" parents or their college surrogates.

If the campus minister has the reputation of "liking kids," he will be contacted by the student with these problems. The problem is not necessarily a religious problem, but it moves into this area quickly if the student is also gradually coming to a deep religious commitment. He worries about his parents and their "uninformed" religious practice, or worse still, the lack of it. One student was seriously worried about his mother's eternal salvation because she was currently living with a man and already had had five husbands. His own commitment forced him to be concerned about his mother. At best, the religious counselor can deal with such issues by having a sympathetic ear. He can also point out that the attitudes of the parents are perfectly consonant with their social and educational status. He communicates to the student a nonjudgmental attitude toward the parents, by which the student can be brought to see that the chances of changing their attitudes are minimal, and that he will simply have to live with this incongruity until such time as he is free to make his own way. The counselor can suggest alternate study places on the campus or at the religious foundation. He can assure the student that he is always willing to listen to these problems which are so relevant to the student at this time in his life.

Religious Problems

There is no problem that enters into religious counseling as simply religion. The attitude toward religion as a curious and nebulous something removed from life is coming to a long overdue demise. Religion is concerned with the existential person living in and coping with this world. The problem of how to apply one's religious values to the totality of life creates tensions in the college student and gives birth to the counseling situation. This situation occurs when the college student tries to apply his own set of moral values to the diversity of religious backgrounds he encounters in college life. He is exposed to the relative ease of interreligious dating which leads inevitably for some to the serious question of interreligious marriage. Kemp (1964, p. 62) has pointed out the radical importance of this problem: "You cannot deal with the marriage situation without considering whether or not one gives up his church relationship. They are all interrelated."

The campus ministry has achieved an enviable record for mutual cooperation in this matter. Butler (1963, p. 125) underscores this when he writes, "the scandal of God divided has been at least lessened, if not overcome, by the obvious good will and fraternal rapport of chaplains and directors of campus religious organizations." Effective cooperation among religious leaders seems clearly to have been established throughout the country. At the beginning of the writer's association with Rabbi Norman Frimer of the Hillel Foundation at Brooklyn College, for example, it was agreed that any counseling of students on interreligious marriage would be referred to one another. There is awareness that the student couple must inevitably make a personal and responsible choice about such a marriage. Whenever a couple seeks guidance in this matter (e.g., a Jewish girl and a Catholic boy considering marriage), each is counseled in turn. It is true that the obstacles for them in such a union are honestly pointed out. In all cases, however, the free response of the individuals is emphasized, and there is no measure of force or proselytizing exercised. The same degree of mutual cooperation exists when a student begins to consider changing his religion. Mutual referrals are made and the student is counseled about as many potential problems as possible before any kind of formal instruction is initiated. In such situations it will usually be the campus minister with whom the student will consult. The college counseling program can assist by making the proper referrals when such counseling opportunities come to its attention.

Premarital sex experience is another important area of religious counseling. The developing adolescent person is often confused about his relations with members of the opposite sex. He has not yet arrived at a mature personal outlook. He does not function consistently or authentically as yet. Louis Monden, S.J., (1965) describes the ethical conduct of men as occurring on three fundamental levels: the level of instinct, the moral level, and the Christian religious level. However, he writes, "ethical conduct does not find its norms directly in self-donation but in the degree of authenticity of human self-realization as expressed in that self-donation." (p. 8) The college student seeking maturity is constantly pressured to conform to current ethical standards minus the authenticity of human self-realization. His sex education has too often been ignored altogether or has at best been given very little ethical or religious thrust. He is trying to come through these levels of conduct to reach the authentic self-awareness that is personhood. He is reaching out for a maturity which will enable him to be fulfilled in the community of men. The diversity of attitudes toward sexual expression compound his confusion. The religious counselor can assist in the dissipation of some of the confusion by opening the student to opportunities for authentic self-realization. Sex and religion are not opposed at all. A mature religious counselor can exemplify this basic axiom to those students who seek his aid. As Josef Goldbrunner (1958, p. 65) has indicated, "Eros and religion are dependent on one another. Whoever separates them and sows enmity between them creates a division between love for man and love for God." The task of counseling about sex and religion is one of the most important and time consuming concerns of the religious counselor.

Religious Counseling: Whose Responsibility?

Obviously there can be no rigid rules set down concerning the respective roles of the campus minister or religious counselor and the psychological counselor or therapist. Responsibilities will cross back and forth constantly. Some guidelines may be suggested, however, regarding those areas in which the respective counselors will have the most competence. Mutual referrals should be used in addition to the general attitude of continuous cooperation. Those problems that are emotional rather than religious should be referred to the psychological or counseling therapist by the counseling person first contacted, provision being made wherever possible or necessary, for continuous consultative procedures. Questions involving identity or student-parent relationships or crises of synthesizing religious beliefs with secular disciplines can be dealt with by the college staff counselor without necessarily making a referral to the campus minister, but the door should be left open for both. In some instances, the religious counselor (noncleric) can relate better to students because he does not wear any distinct religious or authoritarian garb which could retard the counselor-student relationship. Those problems which have been described as religious per se should be referred to the campus minister. In addition to interreligious marriages and conversion to another religion, vocational guidance when it involves religious decisions (whether to enter the ministry, priesthood, religious life, or rabbinate, for example) should be left within the province of the campus minister. It is to be assumed that a great deal of exchange of information and referrals must take place in mutual cooperation for the significant development of a meaningful religious counseling program.

Professional Qualifications

The religious counselor should have three qualifications: (1) a religious commitment, (2) professional counseling training, and (3) some theological training in his own tradition. If he is an ordained campus minister, he has already acquired from his pastoral experience "the counselor's ear." It would be impracticable to suggest that he now begin to specialize in counseling: As campus minister he is involved in many other projects which prevent this specialization. There are numerous institutes and workshops throughout the summer which may aid in improving his competence. Such workshops would also prove invaluable for the religious counselor of the university staff.

The ideal religious counseling program will be reached in proportion to the recognition that is given to the campus ministry and the university staff of religious counselors. To implement this recognition, the counseling division should provide office space within its own office precincts, especially on campuses which have no permanent religious foundation facilities. Some will doubtless object that the principle of separation of church and state would be violated by such an arrangement. There are no clear cut guidelines for facing this question. It is possible to suggest a parallel, however, with the teaching of religion in public higher education. In his 1964 presidential address to the Conference of the Association for the Coordination of University Religious Affairs, Dr. William C. Tremmel (Personal Communication) documented very well the issue of teaching religion in public higher education. He suggests that the opinions of the Supreme Court since 1947 support pluralistic religion and are not antagonistic to it. He buttresses his arguments with numerous quotations from the opinions of the several justices and concludes that the teaching of religion can be done in a public, tax-supported institution and seems no longer a matter for debate. Leo Pfeffer (1933), the outspoken champion of civil liberties, finds no legal objection to courses in religion in public higher education.

He has written, ". . . tax-supported colleges may constitutionally provide for the objective study of religious institutions, practices, and principles." (p. 432) In a symposium under the general title "Religion and the State University," Dr. Paul G. Kauper (1958, p. 84) concludes, "as long as courses in religion are optional with the student, preference is not given to any single religious faith, the instruction is aimed at understanding and not indoctrination and commitment . . . a persuasive case may be made that this program does not fall within the 'sectarian education' category."

The religious counselor has for his first concern the personal dignity and freedom of the individual. All counseling rests on this attitude as its first premise. Since no force or indoctrination takes place in a good counseling program, it would seem that there could be no objection to a full religious counseling program in the counseling division of *any* college or university.

REFERENCES

Arbuckle, D. S. *Student personnel services in higher education.* New York: McGraw-Hill, 1953.

Bletzer, R. R. The minister as counselor. *Pastoral Psychol.*, 1957, 8, 28–34.

Butler, R. *God on the secular campus.* New York: Doubleday, 1963.

Cunninggim, M. *The college seeks religion.* New Haven: Yale Univ. Press, 1947.

Goldbrunner, J. *Cure of mind and cure of soul.* S. Goodman (Tr.) New York: Pantheon, 1958.

Goldman, A. Psychiatry and Religion. *Relig. Educ.*, 1957, 52, 355–360.

Hagmaier, G., & Gleason, R. W. *Counseling the Catholic.* New York: Sheed & Ward, 1959.

Kauper, P. G. Law and public opinion. In E. A. Walter (Ed.), *Religion and the state university*, a symposium. Ann Arbor: Univ. of Mich. Press, 1958.

Kemp, C. F. *Counseling with college students.* Englewood Cliffs, N.J.: Prentice-Hall, 1964.

Merriam, T. W. *Religious counseling of college students.* American Council on Education Studies, Series 6, Vol. 7, No. 4. Washington: Amer. Council on Educ., 1943.

Monden, L. *Sin, liberty and law.* J. Donceel (Tr.) New York: Sheed & Ward, 1965.

Pfeffer, L. *Church, state and freedom.* Boston: Beacon Press, 1933.

Reissner, A. Religion and psychotherapy. *J. Indiv. Psychol.*, 1957, 13, 165–170.

University of Michigan. *A guide to the resources for student counseling and advising at the University of Michigan.* Ann Arbor: Author, 1958.

Walsh, J. L. The restless generation. (Newman Foundation of Detroit) *Newman Rev.*, 1964 (Winter).

Walter, E. A. (Ed.) *Religion and the state university.* Ann Arbor: Univ. of Mich. Press, 1958.

Chapter 15

Disciplinary Counseling

ERNST KOCH

Dealing with Infractions

Disciplinary infractions in American colleges are generally handled in four major ways:

1. By a student court that hears cases and applies sanctions.
2. By a committee composed of students and faculty members that functions in much the same way as the student court.
3. By individual faculty members on an informal basis.
4. By a representative of the administration. (Bureau, 1964)

The first two methods are educationally unsound, in the opinion of this writer, based as they are on the analogy to a court of law, whose dominant concern is to try cases and to prescribe punishment. By virtue of their composition and procedures these collegiate "courts" can have only a punitive function. Furthermore, aside from the fact that not all types of infraction need to or can be handled effectively in this way, the court or committee system affords reduced safeguards to the student against possible lasting stigma that might be the result of mere public accusation and trial.

The third method is also unsatisfactory. In the first place, when professors act individually there is a marked inconsistency in the action taken

Ernst Koch is Professor, Department of Student Services; Associate Dean of Students; and formerly, Disciplinary Counselor and Professor of German, Brooklyn College of the City University of New York.

as a result of the varying personalities and their conception of their roles. Secondly, there is generally no effective reminder to the student that the institution as a whole has a concern in the matter. In the third place, there is no formal record of misconduct, so that an individual can be guilty of repeated violations without being in danger of institutional detection.

Delegating the treatment of these cases to a single administrator has the advantage that, presumably, there will be more consistency of response and, hopefully, a set of pertinent records. It has the disadvantage that anyone with a major administrative office is too likely to be regarded as an oppressive authoritarian figure and essentially a threat to those students who are already considerably insecure. Furthermore, since administrators are usually overburdened with a myriad of responsibilities, ranging from the trivial to the impossible, they rarely have the time to devote more than casual or peremptory attention to these cases. The general result, therefore, is that the action taken can be little more than either a sentencing or a warning, but in either case an action that is essentially disturbing rather than supportive.

Principles and Practices

Since all institutions and individuals are unique and discrete, it is obviously unrealistic to recommend uniform codification of institutional policy with regard to disciplinary procedures. The following principles and practices are products of the writer's experience, and are recommended to colleagues with appropriate modification consistent with local college conditions.

All infractions are reported to a Disciplinary Counselor (whatever title may be used) who is a faculty representative of the Dean of Students. This concept of the Disciplinary Counselor is predicated on the conviction that colleges and universities are neither correctional institutions nor vocational training grounds, primarily, but educational complexes. Although aberrant student behavior can neither be overlooked or condoned, so that sanctions of one sort or another are inevitable in the disciplinary process, due regard must be paid to the fact that the student is not a criminal but an erring member of the academic community. By judicious treatment, the college hopes to condition the student so that his values and behavior are not only consonant with the aims of the institution but generally socially responsible. Thus, the institution's reactions to the transgressor must be primarily educational, and they can best be translated by an individual dedicated to this proposition who, by temperament and background, is specially qualified to assume such responsibility.

The Disciplinary Counselor, then, should first of all be a member of the faculty. Since this is an extremely important assignment, it should not be turned over to a junior colleague but to a mature member of the staff who is respected by both students and faculty for his character and competence, and who will, in consequence, not be subject to that favorite campus cliché, "stooge of the administration." The Disciplinary Counselor, however, for all his idealism and understanding, should not be so easy-going as to be ineffectual in his actions and thus make his colleagues feel that it is futile to make any referrals. He should be a person who has a good concept of psychological dynamics, who can be flexible, who will be consistent in his judgments and practices, who has the courage to maintain his decisions in the face of any and all pressures, and who, despite any type of provocation, remains consistently conscious of his role as being primarily rehabilitative rather than punitive. Last, but not least, he should be an individual whose manner and appearance can easily inspire confidence and genuine response.

In passing, it might be said that since the number of student infractions is generally relatively small, even on a large campus, it has been found that the time remission or reassignment of one three hour class should be sufficient for the Disciplinary Counselor to carry on his work effectively. This is an important consideration to bear in mind when approaching a senior staff member who would be ideal for such an assignment but who might fear that this responsibility would detract too much from his primary academic interests.

The Disciplinary Process

Disciplinary counseling involves the following process: All complaints of misconduct other than academic dishonesty (cheating, plagiarism, using of crib notes, turning in another student's term paper or lab report) are immediately reported to the Disciplinary Counselor, who investigates the charges, using such supplementary aids as previous records and faculty comments. He interviews the student, takes such action as he deems educationally constructive, informs the student, both orally and in writing, of the action taken, and writes a report for the personnel folder, indicating the nature of the infraction, the student's attitude during the interview, the decision made, and any other factors that may be germane either to a present or future evaluation of the student as an individual. In this connection it might be pointed out that the existence of a general file of personnel folders containing cumulative information of a meaningful sort is not only helpful but imperative if disciplinary counseling is to attain its optimum effectiveness.

The Disciplinary Interview

The best routine to follow in the disciplinary interview is one that puts the student at ease as soon as possible without conveying the impression that the interview is merely *pro forma*. This is best done by asking the student to be seated with a kindly but sober mien. The charges should then be reviewed briefly, after which the student should be invited to give his version of the situation, adding such comments as he may choose. There is now not only a basis for discussion, but also a mechanism for the release of tensions.

Most students appearing for disciplinary interviews are tense, expressing their tensions in a range of behavior from sullenness or open defiance to obvious fright. When, as a result of the just-mentioned techniques, they do not encounter the anticipated arbitrary censoriousness, they usually relax, and profitable exploration is possible. Thus, in years of disciplinary counseling along these lines, the writer has found the great majority of counselees leaving the interview with a feeling of gratitude for a newly discovered awareness. As a matter of fact, even in cases where severe sanction has had to be imposed, students have frequently wished to shake hands at the end of the interview, expressing awareness of the justice of the decision and gratitude for the considerate manner of the counselor.

If decisions are reasoned and rational and not based on a dominantly punitive motive, in all cases except those where serious maladjustment prevents a student from functioning normally, students find a new enlightenment and regard the disciplinary contact as a constructive experience. In cases of serious infractions or obvious pathology, several interviews may be required, including consultation with psychological specialists. All cases, however, should be handled as expeditiously as possible. Nothing can so undermine confidence in the seriousness and competence of the Disciplinary Counselor as inefficient, sloppy, or indecisive procedures.

The Disciplinary Counselor should not interview students in the presence of parents or anyone whose obvious interest is solely to mitigate the anticipated severity of the disciplinary judgment. The misconduct in question is, as far as the institution is concerned, strictly a matter between the student and its representative. Parents have every right to consultation, of course, but this should be reserved for a separate interview or discussion. In this connection the following procedure has been found to be most effective: When a parent calls to arrange for an interview with the Disciplinary Counselor, the secretary asks why the interview is desired, adding that if the aim is to try to effect a change in the counselor's ruling the parent will be wasting his time. If, however, the purpose is to discuss the student in order to find out what the parent might do to assist or support him, the interview might be profitable. In most cases, parents whose motive has been to get a change of decision then drop their request for an interview, whereas parents who are truly concerned with the development rather than with the status of their children always come. The resultant discussions not only afford the Disciplinary Counselor further insight into the problems of the student but also sometimes give him the opportunity of developing a greater awareness in the parent, thereby further helping the student.

Since the institution is, among other things, attempting to help the student in his maturational struggles, the official letter reminding him of the disciplinary action taken should be addressed to him, not to the parent. The latter practice can only lead to resentment and greater personal insecurity.

Academic Dishonesty

In cases of academic dishonesty a departmental committee should be set up for a closed hearing. The committee should consist of the chairman of the department of the subject involved, the accusing individual, and one other member of the department. The student should be informed of the charges before the meeting and should have the opportunity of stating his case in the presence of the whole committee.

After due deliberation, the committee may take such departmental action as it deems appropriate (e.g., give the student a warning or an *F* for the examination or paper, or an *F* for the course). The committee should inform the student of its decision in writing, and then send a review of the case to the Disciplinary Counselor for such other action as may be desirable but beyond departmental jurisdiction. The Disciplinary Counselor then discusses the case with the student or students and takes the further steps that may seem warranted.

The category of academic dishonesty is one of the most disturbing and problematical in the whole area of campus misconduct. If extreme care is not taken by the accusing parties, and if the accusation is not based on convincing proof or an admission of guilt before witnesses, injury to innocent people may result, and it is even possible that the institution may be sued for defamation of character. For this reason it is not only sound practice but imperative that all cases of academic dishonesty be first heard before the aforementioned departmental committee. The Disciplinary Counselor does not have the facts at first hand and is, furthermore, in no way to be considered a judge and jury. The Disciplinary Counselor's role in these cases, therefore, does not properly begin until *after* departmental action has been taken. It is important that departments be clear on this point.

The student should again be apprised in writing of the final institutional judgment and the steps that led to it. He should also be informed that he has a right to appeal to the Dean of Students, who may sustain, nullify, or modify the decision. If the student is unwilling to accept the ruling on this appeal, he should have an avenue of review before a standing faculty-student committee, one of whose functions should be the review of such appeals. In order to safeguard the student from the possible harmful effects of publicity, these hearings should be closed and a record of their deliberations kept in a confidential file. If the student is dissatisfied with this verdict, he should have the right to appeal to the president of the institution, who may wish to discuss the case with a faculty body. The judgment of the president should represent the final formal decision of the staff of the university.

For the protection of the institution and in the interest of fairly assessing the student's personality profile, records of all misconduct should be kept. However, all accusations, deliberations, and verdicts pertaining to other than minor misdemeanors should, for the protection of the student, be kept in a confidential file and be available only to certain key personnel such as major administrative officers, the Disciplinary Counselor, and psychological counselors. These colleagues should use such data with discretion, the primary consideration being the interest of the student where such interest does not jeopardize legitimate rights, privileges, and responsibilities. The material should never be available to outsiders for direct scrutiny.

Discussion

In summation we may say that disciplinary counseling is based on the philosophy that the primary function of the college or university is not only to sharpen the minds of students and deepen their intellectual curiosity, but also to help them with their personal problems. These problems may be a result of maturational stresses or the strains of trying to adjust to a complex world in which the dichotomy between professed values and everyday behavior is so starkly evident in almost every sphere of human involvement. Thus, the aims of the disciplinary counseling process must be compatible with the avowed functions of the institution.

Focal responsibility for this process should be centered in a specialist in this area who utilizes all the resources of the institution—faculty, individual students and student groups, the student newspaper, the administration—to help him achieve these major goals: to develop an increased awareness on the part of the erring student of the aims of the institution; to stimulate an increased tendency in him to accept these aims; to furnish some of the support that will better enable him to act consistently in ways that are consonant with these aims. To these ends, the Disciplinary Counselor should interview every student reported, no matter how minor the infraction. In some cases one interview may be sufficient; in other cases suggested or required referral to psychological counselors may be needed. It is important to remember, however, that a school is not a hospital, and that no degree of disturbance should be considered justifiable cause for ignoring deviant behavior.

Thus, in cases of serious infractions, where there is almost always a history of personal disturbance, reinstatement after suspension should never be permitted without the evaluation of a psychological counselor. As a matter of fact, the Disciplinary Counselor should maintain constant and close contact with the psychological specialist or specialists available, for even in cases of distinctly minor violations the Disciplinary Counselor may become aware of deep anxieties that frustrate a better functioning on the part of the student. It is then his responsibility and contribution to refer the student to an appropriate resource for personal help.

Experience has shown that when the principles and practices just outlined are followed, both student and faculty acceptance of the disciplinary procedures is virtually unanimous. The awakening and nurturing of a sense of responsibility is, of course, too complex an assignment for one person alone. It requires not only the sensitivity of the Disciplinary Counselor, but the positive example of the entire campus community as well. Thus, it is imperative that the Disciplinary Counselor establish and maintain the greatest possible contact with all elements of the campus, so that no one will ever be in doubt about the aims and processes of disciplinary counseling.

Furthermore, and perhaps most important of all, it must be pointed out that success in the area of disciplinary counseling requires, above all, an accompanying moral focus in all our educational activities. We cannot expect a climate of responsibility among our students if our teaching and general counseling programs carried on are in a moral vacuum or if we have teachers who prattle about morality and responsibility but who are themselves guilty of a flagrant breach of these by their unfair or slipshod class and examination procedures or by their obvious disregard of general campus regulations. Irresponsibility does not breed responsibility, and unless the Disciplinary Counselor can point to a pervading climate of responsibility, at least on his own campus, he is engaging in what is fundamentally a futile activity. Thus, it is imperative for him from time to time, through whatever sources are available, to remind his colleagues of their role in providing for emerging personalities the all important example of the mature and responsible human being in a consistently constructive human interaction.

Case Examples

The following cases give examples of actual problems encountered in disciplinary counseling and the manifold ways in which they can be treated.

Case A

Miss X, a brilliant mathematics student enrolled in a special "Scholars Program," was reported by the chief hostess in the student cafeteria late in April for having caused a near riot there. The student had been dancing barefoot in an aisle, thus not only violating the regulation for proper attire on campus, but also obstructing the function of food distribution. When asked to leave she refused and became arrogant. When a member of the staff of the Dean of Students was called she became abusive and hysterically screamed invectives, accusing him as well as the cafeteria staff of fascistic tyranny.

The student was sent for, but before the interview the counselor checked her personnel folder and found comments from several instructors indicating the student to be considerably self-centered. When the student appeared she was sullen and resentful. After briefly and dispassionately reviewing the complaint against her, the counselor invited her comments. In a voice controlled but charged with fury she asked what was wrong with going barefoot when it was warm. It was pointed out that there was nothing wrong with going barefoot in appropriate places, but that the college was not an appropriate place, that she had caused a scene, had obstructed the normal activity of the cafeteria by dancing in the aisles, and had violated a pledge signed upon admission to the school that she would obey the regulations of the institution and give courteous attention to the legitimate directives of its representatives. At that statement she screamed, "You can't talk to me like that!"

Aware that rational discussion was not possible, the counselor quietly informed her that she was suspended from the college as of that moment, that she would not be permitted to re-enter before September, and that even then readmission would be subject to the approval of a personal (psychological) counselor. It was also suggested she see a personal counselor before she left in order to get some suggestions as to how best to prepare herself for readmission. The student said nothing and flounced out of the office. She did not contact the psychological counselor.

In September the student applied for readmission and was referred to the Coordinator of the Specialized (psychological) Counseling Panel, to whom both an oral and written report had been given at the time of the suspension in April. After interviewing the student, that counselor found her not yet emotionally ready to resume her place in the academic community and recommended therapy. The student entered therapy and was readmitted in February after another evaluation.

Although no actual disciplinary counseling could be done at the time of the infraction because the student's rational judgment could not be reached, her subsequent school and personal record shows that the prompt and drastic action was justified, and that only such shock treatment could have motivated her to take the steps necessary to an improved personal adjustment.

Case B

Students of outstanding mental ability seem to be particularly prone to the illusion—frequently fostered by parents and even by teachers—that they should not be subject to normal, routine requirements. Thus, another member of an elite study group, a talented creative-writing student, attempted to purloin a reserved book from the library. Questioned, he said that he had not intended to steal the book, but merely to borrow it for his wife who could not come to the library.

Since severe penalties are imposed for the stealing or defacing of library materials (penalties, it might be added, that are well publicized) and since this student showed not the slightest awareness of personal and community responsibility, and since by his continued insistence on his innocence of any really devious motive he revealed attitudes that made all discussion impossible, he was suspended, with readmission again depending on the evaluation of a personal counselor. He was readmitted after a semester.

A year later he was reported for having made false statements on his admissions application about his academic experience prior to his admission to the College. Since the student could not defend this obvious attempt at fraud, and since he was withdrawn to the point of refusing to discuss the matter, he was suspended from the College, denied college credit for the courses taken prior to his admission to our institution and which he had denied having taken; and since comments were found in his folder by various responsible colleagues suggesting that this was quite a troubled person, the case was referred to the Specialized Counseling Panel for final disposition, where it is now being reviewed.

Case C

Every case requires individualized treatment, as the following clearly shows. Two students were reported for plagiarism on a term paper in a psychology elective. Examination of the folders showed that one had a considerable record of academic dishonesty, even having been once before suspended for cheating. The other folder showed no such history and, as a matter of fact, contained a number of laudatory comments from instructors.

In the long interview with the first student, an extensive history of personal and academic problems was revealed. In view of this history and the condition of the student, she was suspended for at least a year. At the same time she was immediately referred to a personal counselor for guidance with regard to referral for appropriate therapeutic assistance in the community. The student was most grateful for the treatment accorded and said that now, for the first time in years, she felt some hope.

The second student, a young man with a good record, said that he knew he was doing wrong but that pressures had just piled up so at the end of the term that plagiarism seemed the only way out. The matter of expediency was discussed, and what would happen, particularly in professional areas, if expediency became the accepted principle.

Since the student intended to go on to graduate work, he saw the point, and furthermore remarked that, through this incident, and particularly as a result of the detailed discussion of ethics, issues, and responsibilities, he had learned perhaps one of the most valuable lessons in his academic career. In view of the fact that the student had already been given an *F* for the paper and thus suffered a serious grade reduction, and in view of his general personal and academic record, he was merely given a warning and placed on disciplinary probation.

Case D

The names of six students were reported by the chemistry department. In each case the grade of a major test had been raised in the instructor's roll book during his absence from the lab. The students were interviewed individually and all denied knowledge or complicity. Since there were no witnesses, and since investigation showed that the lab instructor in question had obviously invited irregularity by his consistent and gross laxity in the conduct of his class, the students were assigned their original grades but warned to behave in such a way as to be above suspicion. It was made clear that if they were again reported for suspicious conduct, severe disciplinary action could legitimately be taken against them. Since all six were lower sophomores and quite immature, the demonstration of efficient institutional action had an obviously sobering effect on each of them.

Case D

A neighborhood bookstore reported that a student had bought some books and had given a worthless check in payment. The store had honored the check because of the student's college identification card. Subsequently the student ignored all efforts by the bookstore to collect its money. The student had taken a leave of absence by the time the complaint reached the College and was thus not on campus. A letter was therefore sent to her indicating that one of the primary requisites for continued matriculation at the College was a demonstration of good character, and that unless notice was received from the bookstore within a reasonable period of time that she had met her obligations, she would be dismissed from the College. Although the student has not yet petitioned to resume her studies, a week after the dispatch of the warning letter the bookstore indicated that the debt had been paid.

Case F

Although institutions can not and should not serve as collection agencies *per se*, they are obligated to the majority of their students to present an image to the community that will be enhancing to the student. Thus, as in the previous case, where ethics are involved the institution not only has the right but the obligation to take action.

When the office manager of a large bank complained that one of our students had gotten employment with him in June as a result of her assurance that she was going to work there permanently, and then had left in September to go back to school, the student was sent for. The Disciplinary Counselor pointed out to her the manager's justified anger, not only because of the betrayed trust, but also because of the considerable sum the bank had spent for the employment agency fee to hire her. After a considerable discussion of the personal and ethical factors involved, the student asked what she could do. It was suggested that she might reimburse the bank for the agency fee and also send a letter of apology. She agreed to do this. If she had not taken this position voluntarily she would have been informed that unless she made good the loss the bank had incurred through her dishonesty it would be necessary to suspend her.

The student sent a check and in a few days a most valuable letter of appreciation was received from the office manager, valuable because it showed that this man's image of Brooklyn College students as crafty and dishonest had been corrected and also that he had gotten a new insight into the dimensions of the students' responsibility.

Case G

Not all cases are major. As a matter of fact, the great majority are relatively minor: smoking in prohibited areas, violation of dress regulations, lying on the grass, repeated talking in class, and the like. But it is in the interview in these minor cases that one often finds revealing things which can be most helpful. In this connection it should be pointed out that the amount of time spent in the interview need not be, and frequently is not, in proportion to the gravity of the offence. Thus, one may spend no more than five minutes with a sullen, rebellious, withdrawn student, doing no more than reviewing the complaint, explaining that we expect observation of our regulations and the norms of acceptable behavior in an academic setting, giving him a warning and, if it seems warranted, requiring him to see a personal counselor for a professional evaluation for possible subsequent referral.

On the other hand, one may spend considerable time with a minor offender. On interviewing a student who had been reported for smoking in the hall, for example, it was discovered that he had been on his way to an examination and had been very nervous. Further discussion revealed not only an unhappy home situation but considerable pressure on him from his parents to do well academically. Since he was only an average student, he felt frightened most of the time, except when he had a course that was easy or a teacher who seemed kindly.

When the student came into the office he was tense, and in his responses almost stuttered. When he did not encounter the martinet he had expected but a person to whom he could freely talk, he relaxed progressively. After considerable discussion and after he had been given a demonstration of the fact that the primary aim of the institution was to help him in his development, the student perceived the College in a new light. The student was given an official warning for his infraction but was also offered the opportunity of seeing a personal counselor, which he gratefully accepted. Not always can the Disciplinary Counselor achieve such gratifying results, but that should not deter him from making improved human adjustment his primary aim.

Addendum

The assumption that academic disciplining is fundamentally a punitive process is still widespread among both students and faculty members. The adoption of the principles and procedures suggested in the foregoing chapter will change both focus and method from a basic accent on the narrowly legalistic to what has come to be known as "situation ethics" (Fletcher, 1966), i.e., to a greater consideration of the humane. Disciplinary counseling seeks to avoid the type of punitive—and often arbitrary—disciplinary action that has often produced resentment and protest and that—as the appended statement of the American Association of University Professors (AAUP) indicates—still causes concern on the part of some faculty members. Furthermore, when the disciplinary process is carried out according to the principles of disciplinary counseling, the proceedings will not "play a role substantially secondary to counseling, guidance, admonition, and example" (see AAUP statement which follows) but will represent a constructive synthesis of these, and may rightfully be classed as a basic contribution to the total education of the student.

The AAUP, through its Committee on Faculty Responsibility for the Academic Freedom of Students, has published the following draft statement of policy, approved by the AAUP Council (Committee S, 1965):[1]

Procedural Standards in Disciplinary Proceedings

The disciplinary powers of educational institutions are inherent in their responsibility to protect their educational purpose through the regulation of the use of their facilities and through the setting of stand-

1. Reprinted by permission of the American Association of University Professors.

ards of conduct and scholarship for the students who attend them. In developing responsible student conduct, disciplinary proceedings play a role substantially secondary to counseling, guidance, admonition, and example. In the exceptional circumstances when these preferred means fail to resolve problems of student conduct, proper procedural safeguards should be observed to protect the student from the unfair imposition of serious penalties. The following are recommended as proper safeguards in such proceedings.*

A. *Notice of Standards of Conduct Expected of Students.* Disciplinary proceedings should be instituted only for violation of standards of conduct defined in advance and published through such means as a student handbook or a generally available body of university regulations. Offenses should be as clearly defined as possible, and such vague phrases as "undesirable conduct" or "conduct injurious to the best interests of the institution" should be avoided. Conceptions of misconduct particular to the institution need clear and explicit definition.

B. *Investigation of Student Conduct.*

1. Except under emergency circumstances, premises occupied by students and the personal possessions of students should not be searched unless appropriate authorization has been obtained. For premises such as dormitories controlled by the institution, an appropriate and responsible authority should be designated to whom application should be made before a search is conducted. The application should specify the reasons for the search and the objects or information sought. The student should be present, if possible, during the search. For premises not controlled by the institution, the ordinary requirements for lawful search should be followed.

2. Students detected or arrested in the course of serious violations of institutional regulations, or infractions of ordinary law, should be informed of their rights. No form of harassment should be used by institutional representatives to coerce admissions of guilt or information about conduct of other suspected persons.

C. *Status of Student Pending Final Action.* Pending action on the charges, the status of a student should not be altered, or his right to be present on the campus and to attend classes suspended, except for reasons relating to his physical or emotional safety and well-being, or for reasons relating to the safety of students, faculty, or university property.

D. *Hearing Committee Procedures.* The formality of the procedure to which a student is entitled in disciplinary cases should be proportionate to the gravity of the offense and the sanctions which may be imposed. Minor penalties may be assessed informally under prescribed procedures. When misconduct may result in serious penalties, the student should have the right to a hearing before a regularly constituted hearing committee.

* Honor codes offering comparable guarantees, may be an acceptable substitute for the procedural standards set forth in this section.

1. The hearing committee should include faculty members or, if regularly included or requested by the accused, both faculty and student members. No member of the hearing committee who is otherwise interested in the particular case should sit in judgment during the proceeding.

2. The student should be informed in writing, of the reasons for the proposed disciplinary action with sufficient particularity, and in sufficient time, to ensure opportunity to prepare for the hearing.

3. The student appearing before the hearing committee should have the right to be assisted in his defense by an adviser of his choice.

4. The burden of proof should rest upon the officials bringing the charge.

5. The student should be given an opportunity to testify and to present evidence and witnesses. He should have an opportunity to hear and question adverse witnesses. In no case should the committee consider statements against him unless he has been advised of their content and of the name of those who made them, and unless he has been given an opportunity to rebut unfavorable inferences which might otherwise be drawn.

6. All matters upon which the decision may be based must be introduced into evidence at the proceeding before the hearing committee. The decision should be based solely upon such matter. Improperly acquired evidence should not be admitted.

7. In the absence of a transcript, there should be both a digest and a verbatim record, such as a tape recording, of the hearing.

8. The decision of the hearing committee should be final, subject to the student's right of appeal to the governing board of the institution. (p. 449)

REFERENCES[1]

Bacciardi, G. R. Suspension: the approach positive. *J. Sec. Educ.*, 1963, 38, 64–66.

Baron, S. Guidance and discipline. *H. Points*, 1947, 29, 23–25.

Blackwell, T. E. Before expulsion—does a student have the right of due process of the law? *Coll. Univ. Bus.*, 1957, 38–39.

Bonjean, C. M., & McGee, R. Scholastic dishonesty among undergraduates in differing systems of social control. *Sociol. Educ.*, 1965, 38, 127–137.

Bowman, H. J. Review of discipline. *Nat. Ass. Sec. Sch. Prin. Bull.*, 1959, 43, 147–156.

Bureau of Applied Social Research. *Student dishonesty and its control in college.* New York: Columbia Univ., 1964.

1. The Editor acknowledges with deep appreciation the assistance of Dean Murray M. Horowitz, Associate Dean of the College, and Mrs. Thelma Abelew, then Fellow in the Department of Student Services, of Brooklyn College, in the compilation of this bibliography.

Clark, S. G. Let's make the campus disciplinary program effective. *Personnel Guid. J.*, 1955, 33, 393–396.

Cohler, M. J. School discipline by plan. *Amer. Sch. Bd. J.*, 1960, 141, 15–18.

Committee S on Faculty Responsibility for the Academic Freedom of Students. Statement on the academic freedom of students. *AAUP Bull.*, 1965, 52, 447–449.

Conway, M. I. Role of disciplinary action in higher education. *North Cen. Assoc. Quart.*, 1955, 29, 351–359.

Counselor's role in discipline. *Personnel Guid. J.*, 1957, 35, 292.

Evans, M. C. Relations of counseling to discipline. In R. F. Berdie (Ed.), *Counseling and the college program.* Minneapolis: Univ. of Minn. Press, 1954. Pp. 44–52.

Farley, R. *Secondary modern discipline.* London: A. & C. Block, 1960.

Finley, J. W. Student personnel system recommended. *Calif. J. Sec Educ.*, 1946, 21, 21–23.

Fletcher, J. *Situation ethics.* Philadelphia: Westminster Press, 1966.

Fley, J. A. Changing approaches to discipline in student personnel work. *Nat. Assoc. Women Deans Counsel.*, 1964, 27, 105–113.

Foley, J. D. Discipline: a student counseling approach. *Educ. psychol. Measmt.*, 1947, 7, 569–582.

Foley, J. D. Role of counseling in discipline. In E. G. Williamson (Ed.), *Trends in student personnel work.* Minneapolis: Univ. of Minn. Press, 1949. Pp. 201–212.

French, A. O. Dean of men as a counselor and as a disciplinary official. *Coll. & Univ.*, 1950, 26, 54–66.

Froe, O. D. Negative concept in discipline and its relation to rapport in counseling. *Educ. Admin. Supervis.*, 1953, 39, 470–477.

Fromm, F. A. New approaches to counseling and discipline. *Nat. Assoc. Women Deans Counselors J.*, 1956, 20, 31–32.

Gilbert, N. S. When the counselor is a disciplinarian. *Personnel Guid. J.*, 1965, 43, 485–491.

Glicksberg, C. D. Student ethics and the honor system. *Sch. & Soc.*, 1957, 85, 181–183.

Goodhartz, A. S. (Ed.), *A commitment to youth.* New York: Bookman Assoc., 1960.

Goodsell, F. S. Counseling and discipline; excerpts from a panel discussion. *Nat. Assoc. Women Deans Counselors J.*, 1956, 20, 33.

Guide to good practice in the recording and reporting of student disciplinary records. *Nat. Assoc. Deans Women J.*, 1953, 16, 173–175.

Hahn, M. E., & Atkinson, B. H. Sexually deviate student. *Sch. & Soc.*, 1955, 82, 85–87.

Hawkes, Anna L. R. Learning more about purpose formation and self-control. In L. Jones & Margaret Ruth (Eds.), *Student personnel work as deeper teaching.* New York: Harper, 1954. Ch. 16.

Hawkes, H. E., & Hawkes, Anna L. R. *Through a dean's open door.* New York: McGraw-Hill, 1945.

Hewitt, A. K. Counselor's role in discipline. *H. Points*, 1947, 29, 31–35.

Holmes, J. E. Discipline and guidance. *Educ.*, 1963, 84, 151–152.
Horowitz, M. M. Margin for error. In A. S. Goodhartz (Ed.), *A commitment to youth*. New York: Bookman Assoc., 1960. Pp. 169–193.
Hubbell, R. N. Varying perceptions of alleged misbehavior and resultant disciplinary action. *J. Coll. Stud. Pers.*, 1966, 7, 260–265.
Hunt, E. L. Dean and the psychiatrist. *Amer. Assoc. Univ. Prof. Bull.*, 1953, 39, 16–35.
Hymes, J. L. *Discipline*. New York: Bureau of Publications, Teachers Coll., 1949.
Hymes, J. L. *Behavior and misbehavior; a teacher's guide to action*. New York: Prentice-Hall, 1955.
King, A. R. Drinking and college discipline. *Christian Cent.*, 1951, 68, 864–866.
Krause, E. Matter of discipline; Story. *Coll. Engl.*, 1964, 25, 289–293.
Larson, K. G. *Effective secondary school discipline*. New Jersey: Prentice-Hall, 1963. (a)
Larson, K. G. Secondary school discipline; with comments by F. D. Bartlett & M. Luney. *Nat. educ. Assoc. J.*, 1963, 53, 12–17. (b)
McKinney, R. I. Disciplinary philosophy and procedures in a small college. *Assoc. Amer. Coll. Bull.*, 1956, 42, 548–552.
Matika, F. W. Discipline: a long look and a firm stand. *Nat. Assoc. Sec. Sch. Prin. Bull.*, 1962, 46, 193–195.
Miner, R. J. The therapeutic handling of discipline. *Educ. psychol. Measmt.*, 1948, 8, 550–561.
Mueller, K. H. Problems in the discipline program. *Personnel Guid. J.*, 1956, 34, 413–416.
Mueller, K. H. Theory for campus discipline. *Personnel Guid. J.*, 1958, 36, 302–309.
Nugent, F. A. Effective use of high school counselors in disciplinary situations. *Nat. Assoc. Sec. Sch. Prin. Bull.*, 1962, 46, 48–51.
O'Donnell, R. J. Guidance and discipline: never the twain . . . ? *Nat. Assoc. Sec. Sch. Prin. Bull.*, 1962, 46, 51–53.
Ohlsen, M. M. Guidance and school discipline. *Nat. Assoc. Sec. Sch. Prin. Bull.*, 1947, 31, 108–112.
Peiffer, H. C., & Walker, D. E. Disciplinary interview. *Personnel Guid. J.*, 1957, 35, 347–350.
Prusak, R. E. Student, student personnel worker and parent attitudes toward student discipline. *Personnel Guid. J.*, 1961, 40, 247–253.
Rodil, C. F. *Fusion of discipline and counseling functions at the college level*. Washington: *Catholic Univ. of Amer. Press*, 1960.
Scott, J. Disciplinarian or counselor? *Personnel Guid. J.*, 1963, 41, 464.
Seward, D. M. Educational discipline. *Nat. Assoc. Women Deans Counselors J.*, 1961, 24, 192–197.
Sheviakov, G. V. *Discipline for today's children and youth*. Washington: Nat. Educ. Assoc., Dept. Supervis. and Curric. Developm., 1956.
Sheviakov, G. V., & Redl, F. *Discipline for today's children and youth*. Wash-

ington: Nat. Educ. Assoc., Dept. of Supervis. and Curric. Developm., 1944.

Shrewsbury, T. H. What's your verdict? *Personnel Guid. J.*, 1956, 34, 448.

Stern, B. H. What should be done about cheating in college? *Educ. Forum*, 1962, 27, 79–83.

Van Houten, P. S. Positive approach to better student conduct. *Nat. Assoc. Women Deans Counselors J.*, 1965, 28, 88–91.

Whitaker, B. E. Helping students achieve high moral values by combining discipline and guidance. *J. Coll. J.*, 1961, 32, 35–36.

Williamson, E. G. Discipline and counseling. *Educ.*, 1954, 74, 512–518.

Williamson, E. G. Preventive aspects of disciplinary counseling. *Educ. psychol. Measmt.*, 1956, 16, 68–81.

Williamson, E. G., & Foley, J. D. *Counseling and discipline.* New York: McGraw-Hill, 1949.

Williamson, E. G., & others. What kinds of college students become disciplinary cases? *Educ. psychol. Measmt.*, 1952, 12, 608–619.

Wrenn, G. C. Student discipline in a college. *Educ. psychol. Measmt.*, 1949, 9, 625–633.

Wrenn, C. G. *Student personnel work in college.* New York: Ronald Press, 1951.

Chapter 16

Reading and Other Academic Improvement Services

PHILLIP B. SHAW

Growth and Development

Academic improvement services developed during the 1940s to afford remedial aid to deficient students; they flourished experimentally during the 1950s as developmental services available to all students, particularly incoming freshmen; and during the 1960s they have attained educational status as professional, cocurricular services.

The 1940s witnessed a revolution in the composition of the American college student body. Democratic changes transformed the American college from an institution reserved for a select and relatively homogeneous few, to an experience attainable by students of vastly different socioeconomic and educational backgrounds. Along with the traditional college-type, incoming freshmen were students who could afford college only as beneficiaries of the economic revolutions of the 1930s and of the free educational opportunities afforded to veterans of World War II. Coming from homes of noncollege parents and from noncollege-minded high schools, some of these students required remedial instruction in skills or subject matter or both. Accordingly, college administrations instituted reading clinics to enable inefficient students to acquire educational skills that they had failed to develop at high school, and tutorial workshops to repair subject-matter deficiencies in their high school backgrounds.

The professional literature dealing with college reading improvement

Phillip B. Shaw is Professor, Department of English; and formerly, Coordinator, Reading and Study Program, Brooklyn College of the City University of New York.

services of the 1940s reflects the emphasis of these programs upon remedial guidance. The structure of the common program was clinical, the intake concentrated upon deficient students, the materials were mainly of the high school level, and the instruction emphasized drill work. These remedial procedures were centralized about instrument techniques such as tachistoscopes, mechanical rate-pacers ("reading machines"), and films combining the characteristics of the tachistoscope and pacer.

Although the increase of special services at college during the 1940s caused research concerning these services to lag behind them, later researchers took a hard look at college reading clinics. Some attacked the validity of published reports of these programs, in particular (Robinson, 1950) their preoccupation with standardized testing, their subjective evaluations, and their inadequately controlled matching of groups. Some reading research specialists, moreover, seriously doubted the efficacy of the common college reading clinic. They stigmatized the instructional techniques as "mechanical" and the structure as "machine-centered." (Spache, 1955) Furthermore, college reading specialists in general were disturbed that the general faculty tended to dismiss academic improvement courses as "bonehead" services for students who presumably had been lazy at high school or who were simply mentally impoverished. Especially distressing was the common question, "Why aren't the high schools doing their job?"—the assumption being that high school is not a discrete educational experience but only a preparation for the higher experience of college.

That the doubting Thomases did not prevail is evident from the significant proliferation of college reading and other academic improvement services during the 1950s. A visual sign of growth is the increasing length of the annual bibliographies of the Yearbooks of the National Reading Conference for Colleges and Adults during 1954–1960. Statistical evidences of this multiplication are given by two particular surveys. A survey of 1956 (Causey) reported a total enrollment of 57,052 students in reading programs of about 300 colleges, as compared with 33,341 students noted in a survey of the previous year. A later survey (Miller, 1959) indicated that of 170 colleges maintaining reading programs during the latter 1950s, 116 had increased enrollments, 49 of these being doubled. Accompanying these increases was a multiplication of textbooks published for students in college reading improvement courses. According to one study (Fulker, 1958), the number of these books more than tripled during 1946–1955, and in 1956 alone, as noted in another study (Miller, 1957), at least ten such textbooks were published.

Although a relatively few articles about academic improvement services other than reading appear in the professional literature of the 1950s, it is likely that the development of these services during this period paralleled that of reading programs. Subject-matter workshops and other tutorial programs were expanded to provide greater opportunities alike for deficient students and for advanced students who helped the latter. An ever-increasing number of foreign language laboratories arose to serve developmental as well as remedial ends. For example, the report of the 1955 Northeast Conference on the Teaching of Foreign Languages (1956) recommends that language laboratories should include tapes both of *explications de textes* and of lectures that remove the student's concern lest he fail to grasp the content of the lectures in a foreign language. In addition to this remedial service, the report continues, institutions specializing in area-studies, civilization, political science, international affairs, social sciences, etc., should have a library of tapes, discs, and films just as they have libraries of books. A pioneer who supported the language laboratory affording a broad scope of instruction has written (Gaudin, 1962): "Most recent laboratories have been designed primarily for first and second year language learning. The language laboratory can and should, however, play an important role in the study of languages and literature on the intermediate and advanced level." (p. 79)

The vigorous growth of college academic improvement services of the 1950s was due to the continuation of the democratization of college enrollments that had marked the 1940s. Many children of the ever-increasing number of families participating in the higher levels of the national income, and many Korean veterans sent to college by the U.S. government, were the first to represent their families at college. Having the drive to prove themselves there, they sought to become totally engaged in the stimulating experience and they were highly sensitive to their educational needs and opportunities. The expression "the achievement of academic excellence according to one's particular abilities," became a common description of the role of the college. This was countered by another expression, "mediocrity of student performance," which came to be a *mal d'école* against which the college should innoculate its entering freshmen immediately. Thus awareness of the "freshman problem" arose.

The Entering Freshman

The "freshman problem" derives from the fact that high school is a discrete educational experience and not merely a preparation for college, and that college in turn is a discrete educational experience with its unique intellectual climate. College affords the high school graduate taking the giant step from secondary to higher education a new opportunity for self-learning and a new freedom. The student entering college discovers immediately that, compared to high school, the proportion of his learning from books and his learning from teachers has increased significantly in favor of books. Moreover, unlike the high school textbooks to which he is accustomed, his college readings are not extensively edited for appropriate readability. His reading comprehension and attention span are less supported by headings, subheadings, glosses, italicized words, pictures, and other visual illustrations.

When the new college student receives assignments, he is not told what to look for, and his homework is not checked regularly. Course syllabi offer choices of reading. Whether he reads and studies efficiently or takes effective reading and classroom notes is his own concern. Most dramatic of his new freedoms is that he can cut a certain number of classes at will, and that his instructors treat him with respect as a serious *student,* rather than a high school *pupil.* Never before in his educational career has the entering college freshman been so much on his own and hence so responsible for self-development, self-discipline, and self-direction as to his academic skills, attitudes, and goals.

One may ask: Do *successful* high school graduates find college so different from high school that they would benefit from guidance on achieving excellence at college? Statistically speaking, can *many* incoming freshmen benefit from special guidance? As to the first question, probably all college personnel concerned with students' attainment of excellence according to their potentialities will agree with the following statement by a reading-evaluation specialist (Townsend, 1956, p. 112): "Many of the reading skills, habits, and attitudes which are effective in producing good high school achievement are inadequate tools for college reading, even though they are still necessary and still constantly in use." Statistical reports in the professional literature reveal a high incidence of freshmen needs. A director of a reading program of a large university, for example, wrote concerning 1029 students who had completed the freshman year at college (Carter, 1959, p. 156): "68 per cent reported that they had never been taught how to read a chapter effectively, 70 per cent indicated that they had not been taught to concentrate upon a reading activity, 64 per cent had not been shown how to develop an awareness of problems and 70 per cent had not been taught how to critically evaluate a writer's bias and use of preconceived ideas." According to a report from another campus (Halfter & Douglass, 1958), eight years of carefully controlled testing of entering college freshmen revealed that about two thirds of them lacked the reading skills requisite for academic success. A report from still another campus (Hadley, 1957, p. 353) estimates that "95 per cent of college entrants lack adequate study skills." Furthermore, the report continues, a relatively small percentage have reading speeds and comprehension skills adequate for handling all college assignments and a great proportion are weak in notetaking. Thus the academic needs of entering college students are not characteristic only of deficient students nor are they exclusively remedial needs. New college students in general benefit from developmental guidance provided so that they "may become all that they can be."

The Brooklyn College Model

As illustrative of colleges which during the 1950s sought to meet the development needs of its entering freshmen, it is fitting briefly to note the special services of Brooklyn College in this area. Along with individualized freshman orientation and subsequent individual counseling of all incoming students, Brooklyn College maintained a broad program of special academic development services available to good and poor students alike. It provided a Reading and Study Program to afford guidance on developing reading and learning ability. About one third of the entering class enrolled, including students of varying success at high school. Brooklyn College also provided workshops in writing skills, mathematics, physics, romance languages, and chemistry. In these workshops both remedial and advanced students participated, the advanced students being volunteers in a program for deficient students and under the direction of a regular teacher. Furthermore, special honors programs were developed for advanced students in a college subject. Finally, Brooklyn College established a thirty-position Language Laboratory that was a pioneer in affording materials for advanced as well as elementary language students.

Appraisal of the 1950s

The foregoing history of educational services during the 1950s describes the positive aspects. The professional literature of the period is not, however, without negative views about these services. Several reading specialists charged (e.g., Spache, 1955) that college reading improvement services had swung from the trend toward "mechanized" clinics in the 1940s to the tendency toward mechanical "skills-drill" courses during the 1950s. The background of this problem is the explosive growth of college reading services: the recruitment of teachers on released time from regular teaching; the impromptu adoption of aims, techniques and procedures; and finally the great unrestricted demand for these services. Often the characteristics of a program were determined not by educational principles but necessarily by the particular subject-matter orientation of the recruited teachers, the available facilities and materials, and the size of the enrollment. The reliability of evaluations of college reading services also was challenged by researchers. For example, eight years after Robinson's (1950) attack upon supposed validations of college reading services during 1930–1950, an article (McDonald, Zolik, & Byrne, 1959) noted that current reports were still being made on the basis of evaluation procedures that Robinson and other researchers had condemned. In defense of these challenged evaluations, it should be noted that the reliability of the very instruments of evaluation available to reading improvement teachers was seriously questioned in the professional literature. A subsequent survey of reports of college reading services noted (Bleismer, 1959) that the use of standardized reading tests and statistical analyses of gains were indicated in only about half of the reports and that control groups were utilized in a mere two cases. Actually, the other half of these reports, and in fact many published reports of the 1950s, were what came to be called "action research"—descriptions of reading programs and accounts of experimental teaching procedures, both usually presenting subjective premises and conclusions. Some writers expressed skepticism about the prevailing optimism of reports on reading programs, most of which were self-evaluations; one writer (Barbe, 1957) observed ironically that he did not find a single report in the literature on a plan which failed.

In all events, criticisms of college reading programs of the 1950s do not repudiate the obvious effort, enthusiasm, and dedication of the writers of these reports and the apparent gains in motivation of the students. What this criticism did succeed in bringing about was an objective spirit of evaluation of aims, procedures, and results of academic improvement courses in general. These courses had passed through the period of impromptu experimentation. They entered a new period of professionalism during the 1960s.

Professionalism in the 1960s

Three main tendencies have marked the developing professionalism of academic improvement services at the nation's colleges during the 1960s. One is the vigorous growth and achievements of three reading associations.

The second is the elevation of academic improvement services to the status of cocurricular offerings in the new college setting of self-learning. The third is the greater use of counseling techniques to meet the divergent individual needs of students seeking guidance from these services.

The rise of three educational organizations concerned with reading improvement at the college level has marked the developing professionalism of this field. When the International Reading Association was established during the early 1950s, a small but articulate college section was represented on the program of its First Annual Meeting. As only a cursory look at the printed annual programs will show, this college section has flourished increasingly on subsequent programs. In 1964, the Association, which from its beginnings had concentrated upon teaching reading at the elementary level, officially recognized the status of reading improvement at the higher levels by establishing the *Journal of Reading* for articles only on these levels.

The second reading association to rise during the 1950s concentrated upon reading improvement at the higher levels: the National Reading Conference for Colleges and Adults. Its Annual Conferences and *Yearbooks* have given great impetus to the professional status of the field. Thirdly, the latter 1950s witnessed the inauguration of the College Reading Association. This organization's Annual Meetings, published *Proceedings,* and official organ, *Journal of the Reading Specialist,* have afforded to the profession a momentum that is exhibited by the Association's steadily mounting membership and attendance at Annual Meetings.

A significant achievement of the above organizations has been their professionalizing influence upon college reading teachers in general. Annual meetings and subscriptions to published proceedings have brought the teachers into direct contact with the ideas of specialists in their field. Articles scattered among various professional journals available ordinarily only on library shelves have come into the homes of the teachers in the official publications mailed to them as a privilege of membership. Even highly specialized research reports have been a regular aspect of the professionalizing influence of the associations. The National Reading Conference has been issuing annual annotated bibliographies on the teaching of reading improvement to college students and adults. Each of the other two organizations has maintained an active research committee. That of the College Reading Association has circulated questionnaires among the entire membership to solicit and coordinate research projects. The *Journal of Reading* of the International Reading Association contains a regular section on "Research in the Classroom."

Research studies published by the reading organizations have professionalized reading teachers by affording them information both of practical use and of background knowledge concerning reading research. In illustration, two recent surveys (McDonald, 1964a, 1964b) alert reading teachers to the following practical problems concerning tests in a reading improvement program: disagreement about the nature of reading and thus as to the significance of variables that tests on reading purport to measure; indiscriminate use of time-limit and "power" (no time-limit) tests on reading rate; overemphasis upon scores on rate tests that students take without a fixed purpose for reading and that contain comprehension checks affected by students' pretest knowledge and by guessing; the confusion of *identification* (screening out students needing reading instruction) and *diagnosis* (determining the specific kind of instruction each student needs); and, finally, misuse of intelligence test profiles to determine reading potential, as in labelling students "under-achievers" and "over-achievers." These research surveys conclude with two practical recommendations to reading teachers. Owing to the complex nature of reading and the multiple facets of intellect reflected by intelligence test profiles, (1) teachers need to leave the safe, familiar level of objective tests, and instead should make tentative assessments involving the total background of the individual students; and (2) teachers must choose the reading tests which best suit their training, subject-matter area, and educational objectives.

Besides useful information regarding one's own procedures, college reading teachers receive from research studies of their professional associations information about reading research itself, which many do not themselves pursue, but which professionalizes their own mètier. For example, a recent survey (Braam, 1963) in a publication sent to all members of a reading association but addressed to researchers in the field, warns against four research practices:

1. Restricted sampling of populations with the result that either insignificant or untenuous general conclusions are drawn.
2. Acceptance of a "taboo against replication" so that inadequate "verifying research" is conducted.
3. Failure of reading specialists to come out of their isolation and to cooperate with other reading specialists.
4. The absence of needed follow-up investigations.

Another contribution to the trend toward professionalism in college reading courses during the 1960s has been the attention given both by the

International Reading Association and the College Reading Association to professional standards. The former association has adopted two sets of principles: "Minimum Standards for Professional Training of Reading Specialists" and a "Code of Ethics" pertaining to teaching of reading improvement. This concern with standards reflects the recent significant increase of graduate students and facilities in the field of the teaching of reading generally. During the past decade, reading centers have grown all over the nation—at, for example, the Universities of Delaware, Chicago, Miami of Florida, Pittsburgh, Rhode Island, Stanford, Syracuse, Temple, and Teachers College of Columbia.

Reading Improvement as Cocurriculum

The vigorous development and active role of three reading associations described above not only in themselves mark the increased professionalism of the field of college reading improvement; they are evidence of a second aspect of this increase. This is the elevation of these services and of other academic improvement services during the 1960s to the status of cocurricular offerings. The greater recent emphasis upon the learner's role in the pursuit of a college education has enhanced the need for these services. The learner's role is becoming increasingly individual in a setting of greater opportunities for self-learning.

The modern function of academic development services as cocurricular offerings is evident from the widened gap between high school and college procedures owing to the new stress on self-learning at college. The widening is illustrated by the following comparison between the college student of today and yesterday. The modern student, compared to his predecessor, spends more time in the library and reads more from source materials and *books* rather than from *textbooks*. He does more reading, is allowed a wider choice of reading, relies more on his own resources for *explications de textes* and consequent notetaking, and takes tests that pay greater attention to his scholarship, concepts, and values. Furthermore, when the modern student learns formally, he usually does so in large lecture halls where he is expected to learn like one scholar being addressed by another scholar. In this climate of self-education, students need highly developed listening, reading, and associated skills, and also mature attitudes concerning personal development. Students need, furthermore, sophisticated attitudes toward the special characteristics of the new self-education, such as automated learning (e.g., programmed lessons and closed-circuit television) and study abroad.

As cocurricular offerings advancing their students' pursuit of a self-education, academic development services have had to adjust their objectives to their students' immediate experiences in their regular courses. For example, a college reading program that teaches students the following techniques can be behind the times: training students to use a reading-attack formula calling for a preview of headings and the like when the students are reading source materials and regular books rather than specially edited textbooks; requiring students to work out a study schedule to the hour although they are required to spend unpredictable periods in the library; drilling the students on efficient reading of standardized selections without regard to their readings outside of the reading improvement course; and, generally, concentrating on so-called "common" needs of students by uniform procedures not sufficiently flexible to meet their individual needs in their current regular courses. Instruction in an academic improvement service must be geared closely to the students' immediate experiences in their regular courses. As expressed by a specialist on foreign language workshops (Pleasants, 1961, p. 27): "In our workshops, language laboratory programs . . . are considered as 'supervised homework,' i.e., work to be done on subject matter *previously* discussed in class. It is obvious then, that the laboratory . . . is to supplement and implement work done in the classroom." This emphasis upon dovetailing instruction in an academic improvement course to the students' regular college work has received considerable recognition in the professional writings of the 1960s concerning foreign language workshops (e.g., Hocking, 1964), and places this field in the vanguard. Past research studies show that college reading-improvement specialists have not been discovering methods or materials for teaching students to read or study more effectively in mathematics, in physics, in economics, in history, and any of the half-dozen other fields. (Spache, 1958) Recently, a specialist on reading improvement in different subject areas commented that this field is still "in the midst of a period of discovery." (Smith, 1964a, p. 31) This specialist has advanced the field by two major contributions providing information to teachers concerned with reading techniques in different subjects. (Smith, 1964a, 1964b)

In the experience of the present writer, when Brooklyn College adopted a new curriculum in which required area studies displaced required separate courses, students thereafter enrolling in the college reading-study program exhibited quite different needs from those of their predecessors. In social science they were extended by primary materials for homework, by considerable library readings, and, in general, by seeking to evaluate "Our

Contemporary World" (the title of the course). In the integrated science course, "Science in the Modern World," they could not satisfy the course standards by emphasizing memorization of stock problems and of pat laws, equations, and formulas. The students experienced a common need to grasp concepts and values. A familiar request was for guidance on how to answer questions on matter not in the book—to make inferences by critical reading and thinking. The syllabus of the reading-study course accordingly underwent considerable revision, and for some of the standardized reading selections previously used in the course, it was felt necessary to substitute several of the regular books from which the students were learning at the time.

Academic Improvement and the Classroom Teacher

Concerning the immediate educational needs of students in their regular courses, a certain question has frequently arisen in the professional literature. Why cannot the classroom teacher be a teacher of academic skills? The present writer has recommended elsewhere that all prospective college teachers be trained especially to afford appropriate skills guidance as well as subject-matter instruction in their particular freshmen courses. (Shaw, 1961) If such training were given, not only the teachers but also academic improvement courses would become still more professional. In the climate of self-education, as described above, students learn in large classes and from books. When a student feels blocked or unfulfilled in his self-learning, he must consult a special agency: the reference librarian, the personal or departmental counselor, the language laboratory, the reading improvement service, the appropriate workshop. The more guidance he has already received from his regular teachers, the more the special service can afford him advanced impetus toward his pursuit of a self-education.

Counseling and Academic Improvement

As noted above, academic improvement services already are providing instruction to advanced as well as elementary and deficient students. Such diversity of aims has led to the third tendency of these services during the 1960s: an increased use of counseling techniques to meet the divergent individual needs of students seeking guidance from these services.

Counseling techniques are utilized by academic improvement services of the 1960s in two different forms. One relies upon the principles of group therapy, which, applied to academic improvement, has been called the workshop way of learning. Five to fifteen persons meet in groups, often relatively homogeneous, for supervised discussions where individual needs are the basis for choosing the problems to be solved. The significance of this method is that the individual student solves his own problems with the help of the group and the instructor, and leaves the workshop with a plan of action that he believes will fit his given situation (Adult Education Association, 1956). The role of the instructor is illustrated by the following excerpt from a report (Siegel, 1962) of an adult reading improvement program conducted jointly by the Brooklyn Public Library and Brooklyn College:

> In general, the program was characterized by an orderly and systematic introduction of materials, according to knowledge of the group members on the part of the teachers. Students first expressed their interests, exchanged ideas, and revealed their reading problems. The importance of the clinician in helping the group to interact, to establish rapport and become comfortable in this new and even threatening situation cannot be exaggerated. (p. 250)

At Cornell University, students receive group tutoring from student tutors, who, as described in a report (Goodman, 1964, p. 49), have been equipped by the director of the program "with principles used in counseling." In support of group tutoring in preference to individual tutoring, the report states: "The smallness of these groups [five students] permits private instruction but also allows students to realize that others have similar problems. It is felt that everyone benefits from the questions asked by others." (p. 48)

It is evident from the professional literature that use of the workshop way of learning is characterized on the nation's campuses by diversity rather than standardization. Almost all subjects are represented in the literature of the 1960s, including reading improvement, foreign languages, English composition, chemistry, physics, calculus, economics, and even such a specialized area as food chemistry. Diversity also is evident in the duration of workshops, some lasting for a full semester, some for half a semester, and a few for comparatively short periods. Regarding the latter, a recent report (Maxwell, 1965, p. 40), on a Writing Skills Workshop consisting only of four one-hour sessions declares: "Four hours may seem a minimal amount of time to effect any change in writing skills; however, we found that 70 per cent of a group of 45 low achieving students who attended the Writing Skills workshop improved their grades on English themes and 90 per cent of this group passed the Freshman English course."

Flexibility of workshop practices also occur in the combinations of small-group guidance with instruction given in large classes and in individual conferences. At Queens College, New York City, the statement under "Conferences" in the syllabus for a remedial course, English E01 (1965), reflects the adaptability of even an entire semester course to individualization. There are no regularly scheduled conferences for the course outside of class hours. Whenever necessary, conference time is arranged within the class hour, e.g., by excusing a student from doing an in-class exercise not germane to his weakness. A recent report of the Writing Division of the Basic Skills Center of Brooklyn College (McNeil, 1965) illustrates how group and individual instruction can be dovetailed. A program of three fifty-minute periods for six weeks begins with a pretest and a group lecture, followed by individual training sessions, and culminating with a post-test and an individual conference for evaluation. In the course, programs of class and home assignments are designed according to each student's needs; group instruction is based on the individual needs of the students in each group, and every meeting includes an individual discussion with each student of his most recent theme or revision.

The dovetailing of workshop practices with full-group lectures, private supervised study, and individual conferences weds principles of sound education and economy. An experimental advance in this direction is a self-screening technique for students applying for admission to the Reading and Study Skills Laboratory of the University of Maryland. As a substitute for a 15–20 minute screening interview with a counselor, the student applying for the program listens to a five-minute tape recording "covering the same topics that the interviewer typically presented." (Maxwell, 1965, p. 39)

The second form in which counseling techniques are being utilized in academic improvement services of the 1960s is the counseling-oriented reading improvement program. This affords personality and reading guidance jointly. It is based upon the belief that because of the mutual interlocking of a student's reading habits and personality characteristics, instruction on reading skills should be supported by guidance on personality needs. Anticipating the increase of counseling-oriented programs in the 1960s, a reading specialist has described procedures as follows (Spache, 1959, p. 129): "Some students will be assigned to directive textbook-oriented courses, others to supportive machine training courses, others will be offered a laboratory course with a minimum of direction and still others will be given an individualized but closely supervised program. In these various groupings, emphasis upon particular reading skills will also vary according to the personality needs of the students." That this anticipation is based upon actual though modest advances in the latter 1950s is evident from the professional literature. For example, a report on reading programs at Pennsylvania colleges of 1957–1958 (Colvin, 1963) notes only six "psychological-oriented" services, as contrasted to twenty-seven "skills-drill" services and five "mechanistic" services. The writer deplores the paucity of the psychological type.

Some college reading specialists (e.g., McDonald et al., 1959) recommend extensive group psychotherapy as an integral part of reading-improvement services. Others endorse even a broader responsibility for the reading specialist. A report concerning a University of Vermont graduate course entitled "The Analysis of Reading Difficulties" (Mour, 1964, p. 139) notes the following series of instruction: "Presenting the topics within their respective fields were an educational psychologist, an optometrist, a specialist in speech and hearing rehabilitation, a psychiatrist, a pediatrician who specializes in adolescent medicine, the chief of the division of neurology of the medical college, and the instructor of the course." Of course it must be remembered that programs not offering remediation of personal problems along with instruction on reading skills do nevertheless usually provide for the former by referral. For example, the report on the Brooklyn Public Library–Brooklyn College course noted above suggests (Siegel, 1962, p. 252): "In all programs, eye examinations should be recommended to students at the earliest opportunity. When a library is functioning independently, all psychological testing should be avoided and referrals should be made to appropriate agencies."

Judging from the professional writings concerning academic reading improvement during the 1960s, the utilization of counseling techniques in programs employing the workshop way of learning and in counseling-oriented courses will keep step with the increasing emphasis upon the learner's role in the pursuit of a self-education. This inference is based upon the marked increase of counseling divisions as sponsors of reading services. Statistical surveys of college reading courses of the early 1950s fail even to list "counseling" as a sponsor. A study by the present writer (Shaw, 1961) of these courses in 1960, on the other hand, revealed that counseling agencies were significantly represented as auspices (53 colleges), along with education (68 colleges), English (60 colleges), and psychology (33 colleges).

The Future

What of the future of the academic-improvement profession in general? As the library and a student's private study place continue to become, along with the lecture hall and recitation classroom, a major arena for his learning, and as the awareness of the learning uniqueness of each and every human being increasingly underlies educational practices, the profession should go on serving advanced as well as elementary and deficient students. Furthermore, as students' college programs gain individuality from the new practices of advanced credit, exemption examinations, and concentrated honors work, and from the circumstances that—as predicted by a leading educator (Davis, 1962)—one third of the nation's college students will participate in summer study abroad, and colleges will adopt new calendars to grant in four years the Master's degree rather than the Bachelor's, academic improvement services will be centers of individualized training in self-learning.

REFERENCES

Audio-visual aids and techniques in the teaching of foreign languages. Presented at the 1955 N.E. Conf. teaching foreign lang., 1956.

Barbe, W. B. A reading program that did not work. *J. develpm. Read.*, 1957, 1, 17.

Bleismer, E. The status of research in college reading. In O. S. Causey (Ed.), *Fourth yearbook of the national reading conference for colleges and adults.* Ft. Worth, Tex.: Tex. Christian Univ., 1955. Pp. 28–35.

Braam, L. S. Problems in reading research. In C. A. Ketcham (Ed.), *Proc. Coll. Read. Assoc.*, 1963. Pp. 35–38.

Carter, H. L. J. Effective use of textbooks in the reading program. In O. S. Causey (Ed.), *Eight yearbook of the national reading conference for colleges and adults.* Ft. Worth, Tex.: Tex Christian Univ., 1959.

Causey, O. S. College reading programs in the nation. In O. S. Causey (Ed.), *Fifth yearbook of the national reading conference for colleges and adults.* Ft. Worth, Tex.: Tex. Christian Univ., 1956. Pp. 135–137.

Colvin, C. R. Objectives and emphases in college programs. In C. A. Ketcham (Ed.), *Proc. Coll. Read. Assoc.*, 1963. Pp. 22–26.

Conducting workshops and institutes. *Adult Educ. Assoc., U.S.A.*, 1956, No. 3.

Davis, P. H. Changes are coming in the colleges. *J. higher Educ.*, 1962, 33, 142–144.

Fulker, E. L. A decade of progress in college and adult reading improvement. In O. S. Causey (Ed.), *Seventh yearbook of the national reading conference for colleges and adults*. Ft. Worth, Tex.: Tex. Christian Univ., 1958.

Gaudin, Lois. The language laboratory and advanced work. *Mod. Lang. J.*, 1962, 46 (2), 79.

Goodman, Diann S. The student tutorial program at Cornell University. *J. read. Specialist*, 1964, 3 (3), 48–49.

Hadley, S. L. New college students lack study techniques. *Sch. & Soc.*, 1957, 85, 353.

Halfter, Irma T., & Douglass, Frances M. 'Inadequate' college readers. *J. develpm. Read.*, 1958, 1, 42.

Hocking, E. Language laboratory and language learning. *NEA Monogr.*, 1964, No. 2.

Maxwell, Martha J. Innovations in a college reading laboratory. *J. read. Specialist*, 1965, 4 (3), 39–40.

McDonald, A. S., Zolik, E. S., & Byrne, J. A. Reading deficiencies and personality factors. In O. S. Causey (Ed.), *Eighth yearbook of the national reading conference for colleges and adults*. Ft. Worth, Tex.: Tex. Christian Univ., 1959.

McDonald, A. S. Research for the classroom. *J. Read.*, 1964, 8 (1), 58–61. (a)

McDonald, A. S. Research for the classroom. *J. Read.*, 1964, 8 (2), 115–119. (b)

McNeil, Marguerite. Unpublished report. Brooklyn Coll. Basic Skills Ctr.: Writing Div., Day, 1964–65.

Miller, L. L. Evaluation of workbooks for college reading programs. In O. S. Causey (Ed.), *Sixth yearbook of the national reading conference for colleges and adults*. Ft. Worth, Tex.: Tex. Christian Univ., 1957. Pp. 75–85.

Miller, L. L. Current use of workbooks and mechanical aids. In O. S. Causey (Ed.), *Eighth yearbook of the national reading conference for colleges and adults*. Ft. Worth, Tex.: Tex. Christian Univ., 1959.

Mour, S. I. A new approach to an old course. *J. Read.*, 1964, 8 (2), 139.

Pleasants, Jeanne V. *Mod. Lang. Assoc. Conf. Newsltr.*, 1961, 1 (1), 27.

Queens College. Unpublished English E01 syllabus, Spring 1965.

Robinson, H. A. A note on the evaluation of college remedial reading courses. *J. educ. Psychol.*, 1950, 41, 83–96.

Shaw, P. Teachers of lower freshmen are specialists. *AAUP Bull.*, 1957, 43, 345–352.

Shaw, P. Integration of reading instruction with 'regular' college offerings. In E. P. Bleismer, & A. J. Kingston (Eds.), *Tenth yearbook of the national reading conference for colleges and adults*. Ft. Worth, Tex.: Tex. Christian Univ., 1961.

Siegel, M. Adult reading improvement: a five-year report. *Read. Teacher*, 1962, 16, 250–252.

Smith, Nila B. Patterns of writing in different subject areas, Part I. *J. Read.*, 1964, 8 (1), 31–37. (a)

Smith, Nila B. Patterns of writing in different subject areas, Part II. *J. Read.*, 1964, 8 (2), 97–102. (b)

Spache, G. Trends in college reading programs. In O. S. Causey (Ed.), *Fourth yearbook of the national reading conference for colleges and adults.* Ft. Worth, Tex.: Tex. Christian Univ., 1955. Pp. 46–47.

Spache, G. Improving reading skills in the subject matter areas. In O. S. Causey (Ed.), *Seventh yearbook of the national reading conference for colleges and adults.* Ft. Worth, Tex.: Tex. Christian Univ., 1958. Pp. 32–33.

Spache, G. Reading improvement as a counseling procedure. In O. S. Causey (Ed.), *Eighth yearbook of the national reading conference for colleges and adults.* Ft. Worth, Tex.: Tex. Christian Univ., 1959.

Townsend, Agatha. How can we help college students develop critical reading of textbooks and resource materials. In W. S. Gray, & Nancy Larrick (Eds.), Better reading for our times. *Int. Read. Assoc. Proc.*, 1956.

Part V

Serving the Student

Chapter 17

The Teacher and The Counselor

MURRAY M. HOROWITZ

The Teacher as Counselor

The boundary between teacher and counselor has never been sharp, nor can it ever be, except if artificially and arbitrarily drawn. At one time in higher education, before the term *counselor* even existed on a campus, the teacher performed both functions without being conscious of his dual role. In most other countries, the independent role of the counselor still does not exist. It makes interesting speculation to wonder what would take place on Mark Hopkins' log, if it were ever brought to reality, with student at one end and professor at the other. One thing is fairly certain, that the situation would be as conducive to counseling as it would be to teaching.

The student will always look up to a good teacher, will respect him, will listen to him with a care sometimes bordering on adulation, and will go so far as to imitate him. As one example, the number of students who choose a major or a career based on their contact with a teacher is considerable. Even if the teacher confines himself completely to his subject matter, therefore, his effect on the student as a person is significant.

Subject matter, however, often spills over into the present and involves both student and teacher. Animated discussions will be held on such themes as the events of the day, or the place of the individual in society, and the teacher does not always restrict himself solely and completely to

Murray M. Horowitz is Associate Dean of the College, Brooklyn College of the City University of New York.

his subject matter. He deals with related fields, he draws parallels, and he may even wander far afield. Further, he confers with his students; if not with all, at least with some. It is here that counseling can and does take place, perhaps starting innocently enough with a question on the assignment, but then branching off in many directions. An example or two will suffice. Why is one student falling behind in his work? To answer this question, the student must perforce bring personal considerations into the conversation. Where shall I go to graduate school? To come up with suggestions properly requires analysis of the student, his strong and weak points, his interests and dislikes, his initiative and abilities, his financial standing, and a variety of other personal considerations (all this without even analyzing the graduate schools).

How many teachers can then say that they never "counsel"? Will not those who vehemently deny that they counsel find themselves in the same position as Molière's *le bourgeois gentilhomme* when that worthy gentleman discovered that he had been speaking prose all of his life? A teacher is perforce a counselor whether wittingly or unwittingly. The good teacher, recognizing this identity, will strive to be a good counselor.

The Teacher-Counselor

Of course, in our age, with the growing complexity of collegiate life, with the increase in size of the institution of higher learning, and with the diminution of the opportunities for close relationship between student and teacher, most colleges have taken steps to institute a formal counseling organization making use of both teachers and counselors. It is most unlikely that this trend can be reversed. The professional counselor with his intensive training in one or two fields will generally concentrate on his specialties. But there are seldom enough professional counselors to cover all of the counseling needs, and even if there were, it would not be advisable or even possible to bar the teacher from counseling. So, at many institutions the teacher is called upon in specific terms to serve as a counselor. The rationalization for this activity is further reinforced if one notes the obvious. The teacher sees his students regularly in the course of the year, he is already familiar with the nature of his own and related courses, and, by experience, he is most likely to understand the academic problems of students.

Once drawn into the formal counseling program, the function of a teacher-counselor will generally include advice concerning the student's program, whether on a short-term or long-range basis. Prior to his registration, the student may make use of the information provided in the college bulletin and supplementary official circulars. Unofficial advice, including that of friends, relatives, and fellow students may also be readily available. Armed with this information which either reinforces his own strong predilections, or leaves him confused and undecided, the student meets with his counselor and seeks to arrive at the decisions which will be best for him. After these decisions are reached, and the student acts upon them, he may return from time to time to his counselor to seek further guidance and advice: Has my choice proven correct? Why can't I understand what my science teacher is saying? Is it really necessary for me to continue the study of this foreign language?—These are questions revolving about course or curriculum choice. But the variety will also encompass situations more personal in nature: I can't study at home because my parents are continually bickering. Will I be able to continue my medical pursuits considering my financial situation? I can't keep my mind on my studies: my mind is on my girl friend.

Orientation and Training

Some of these problems are comparatively simple to deal with. Those which are purely of the informational sort would fall into this category. Others are more complex and, in the extreme, there are some problems to which there are no answers. Obviously, some sort of training is required before the teacher can assume the formal role of counselor. Ideally, this training should begin well in advance of the time that the counseling function begins. A regular orientation program including lectures, demonstrations, opportunity for observation and participation, case studies, question-and-answer sessions, and use of a selected reading list, can be most helpful. The form and content will obviously vary depending on the institution and its program. What is essential is that the orientation of the counselor receive as much or more attention as the orientation of the student who will be his charge.

It should not be implied that the training program will equip the teacher-counselor to stand in for the professional counselor in the latter's specialty. The education and experience of the latter cannot readily be absorbed by the former in the type of orientation program under consideration. The goal here is to develop the skills and interests of the teacher and to furnish him with the knowledge and techniques which will enable him to deal with the general problems of the college student.

As for the other problems, a system of referral to the professional counselor or other agencies must be established. The counselor is successfully trained in this regard if he understands his own limitations, if he recognizes the student's need for specialized and professional assistance, and if he can help the student accept the referral.

Although there can be no single orientation program for counselors which can be transferred intact from one college to another, there must be administrative emphasis on and support for such a program wherever it is located. Without this, it necessarily must remain a lifeless program. The support must be tangible as well as vocal.

A teacher's interests will usually center on his discipline. How can he best be persuaded to expand these interests to include counseling as well? The necessity for this activity and its importance must be continually stressed. The partnership between counseling and teaching must be made evident and real. Even beyond this, recognition for performance in the field of counseling must be given, just as it is in the fields of teaching or research. If the task of counseling requires more than a minimal allocation of time and effort, then the instructor's teaching schedule should be lightened proportionately. A combination of both alternatives is also possible. Similarly, recognition of the position of the professional counselor as on a par with that of the classroom instructor is also called for.

Teacher and Counselor Selection

How should teachers be selected for the counseling program? It is conceivable that all teachers should be asked to participate in some fashion. But it is also fairly evident that some individuals are just not suited, temperamentally or otherwise, for this function. It is incumbent on the director of the counseling program, therefore, to seek out those who are concerned and who have the interest and the attributes most likely to lead to success. Applications from individuals may be invited, and department chairmen and deans should be consulted for the names of prospective candidates. The college administrators, moreover, should throw their weight behind the quest for those best qualified to serve. While the numbers accepted, naturally, will depend upon the size and scope of the program, the choice should never include the individual who is surplus in his field, unless he also has the qualities to make a satisfactory counselor.

Nor is it advisable to transform a teacher into a full-time counselor and have him lose complete contact with the student in the classroom setting.

The converse to this last statement should also be stressed. Just as the teacher who is suited for counseling should be encouraged to do so, so should the counselor who is suited for teaching be given the opportunity to engage in this activity. There is no better way to encourage the mutual understanding of the roles of teacher and counselor than by having the teacher counsel and the counselor teach. Similarly, the teacher who counsels will develop a better understanding of the student as an individual, and of his problems and interests, which understanding can carry over in an improved classroom situation. And the counselor who teaches will better understand the student in counseling by participating himself in the classroom learning situation.

Even if all or most teachers are not drawn into the counseling program, a carefully developed system of rotation of personnel will be of benefit. Teachers may ultimately ask to be relieved of their counseling duties because this assignment may prove too onerous or not what they expected. Others may not be invited to return to their counseling assignments because they have not worked out satisfactorily. In addition to these two categories, the director may follow the policy of rotation after a specified number of years to allow for the introduction of new faces and new ideas, and to spread the experience among more staff members than would otherwise be possible. Drawing as many qualified people as possible into counseling will also develop a substantial core of teachers who can explain the counseling program to their colleagues from their own experience, and defend it against unjustified criticism.

Faculty Relations

It is also essential that a regular and continuing flow of information concerning the philosophy and operation of the counseling program reach the faculty. Suspicion of whatever is new or of what seems to break with tradition is as common on the academic scene as elsewhere. Enlisting faculty members to participate in the process is one way to overcome the doubt. In many institutions, the counseling program is as much subject to the control of the faculty as is the curriculum or the entire educational philosophy of the institution. And this is as it should be, if one conceives counseling to be an integral part of the educational process. Therefore, it is most appropriate to keep the faculty informed of the nature of the counseling program.

At the very least, a directory of counseling services should be made available to all members of the faculty. Certainly, the counselor does not operate with a different clientele than does the teacher. Nor does the student take on a new personality and character when he consults with his adviser or when he recites in the classroom.

The team relationship between counselor and teacher is an essential one in making the institutional environment most conducive to the success of the student and the fulfilment of the goals of the college. Therefore, the teacher must be aware of the resources of his institution in helping the student where he himself cannot. He must know what these can do—and what miracles they cannot perform—and be encouraged to make use of these resources. He is often in a superior position to know when to refer students to the counseling agencies, to bring problems to them, and to seek advice on how best to cope with them. More, he can furnish information to the counselor which he alone has. After all, student-teacher contacts in the classroom are far more frequent in most instances than student-counselor contacts.

Student Records

Student records are an integral part in practically all aspects of the counseling program. It makes sense that in helping a student, the counselor should have the benefit of all relevant information. As far as the teacher is concerned, student records should serve a dual function. Aside from the grade report and other administrative entries, the teacher can contribute significant information to the record to develop better understanding of the student. This can range from copies of letters of recommendation to detailed personality reports. Similarly, the teacher should be made to feel welcome in examining student records where he feels it will enable him to gain a better perspective of his students. Each institution may have developed a system of segregating certain categories of data considered so personal and confidential that it can be released or interpreted only by select individuals. This is not meant to imply that other information should not be treated confidentially, or the purpose and value of a records system will soon be vitiated.

Counselors should be on call to assist the teacher in interpreting the records, especially where the uninitiated would find difficulty. And naturally counselors should be available to consult with teachers about their students—and vice versa—for such a joint working relationship is required.

Teacher-Counselor Consultation

This last aspect, that of consultation between teachers and counselors, needs assiduous attention. To make a general declaration inviting teachers to meet with counselors is fine as a matter of policy, but without a carefully planned follow-up campaign, it is bound to produce sparse results. For example, written communications can be used, but beyond this the counselor should take the lead in asking the teacher to meet with him to discuss the difficulties of an individual student. At times, other consultants may be drawn into the discussions. Another method which often leads to excellent results is to assign a group of students enrolled in one section of a course to one counselor, and then to have the teacher and the counselor meet regularly during the course of the year with the student records at hand for easy reference. These meetings can serve as the occasion for the sharing of information about the students—the joint responsibility of both teacher and counselor.

The guidance worker may have helpful suggestions to make to the teacher based upon his professional training and experience, and his knowledge of the student; the teacher may also be able to fill in gaps so that each can better understand the student. Not only can each then learn more about his students from the different vantage points, but the continuing contacts can serve as a fine opportunity for developing and improving the relationship between teacher and counselor.

Just as the faculty must be kept informed of the nature and activities of the counseling program, so should the counselor familiarize himself with the educational philosophy of the institution and the nature of its curricula and programs so that he can work in harmony with them. If the counseling office is an extension of the classroom, if the counselor is to work in partnership with the teacher, then the counselor cannot live in an artificial world inhabited only by counselor and student. When the student complains about the lack of practicality of his courses, when he criticizes the laboratory procedure of his science course, when he expresses doubt about his choice of major, will the counselor have the information at hand which the student is seeking? Obviously, it is not possible for the counselor, or any one person, to know everything there is to know about the institution, nor is there anything inherently wrong in his confessing ignorance and then either digging up the answer or advising the student how to do so. But there are limits to this, for the counselor is a resource person, and frequently voiced student complaints about inadequacies in informational services can strike a deadly blow at the efficacy of any counseling program.

If in-service training and orientation programs are essential to develop and improve understanding of counseling programs, techniques, and procedures, so also would it be of help for the counselor to learn from faculty members about the institution's instructional programs and related educational techniques and developments. This may be accomplished through seminars, colloquia, or lectures, supplemented by printed material as simple as throw-away notes to those as elaborate as carefully edited manuals. Invitations to sit in on classes, workshops, or demonstrations constitute a supplementary approach. Promising results may also be achieved by the more novel techniques of films and TV tapes.

Teacher-Counselor-Student Communication and Research

Not only is it vital to improve and keep open the avenues of communication between teachers and counselors and to channel them harmoniously in the institutional pattern, so that the individual student may receive the maximum encouragement and assistance to realize his potential, but it is just as significant for both groups to keep abreast of the changing nature and differing needs of the student body. Even the casual observer of the college scene must be struck by the dynamic character of student life and action on campus and by the sympathetic ripples—sometimes angry waves—which spread from one campus to another. Here, the counselor usually has a better opportunity than the teacher to work with the student individually and in groups, and to develop an understanding of his background and culture.

Counselors must also accept the responsibility of going further; they must seek out the facts, perform the research, and propose the solutions to cope with the range of problems from the restlessness of some to the indifference of others. There is no doubt that this represents a formidable mission. Consider the dimensions of just one area, that of the changing characteristics of the student as he progresses from freshman to graduate, including those changes fostered (or hampered) by the college environment in all of its aspects. Merely developing methods of gathering and classifying the data is a task requiring a high degree of skill and sophistication, but it should not be shirked by counselors. The project assumes ever more complex dimensions when the job of translating the mass of data into concrete proposals is undertaken. The findings and recommendations of the research workers must be shared with all, and if those counselors who have performed this task have done it well, their position on the college scene will assume new and far more significant dimensions.

In 1965, the annual meeting of the American Council on Education had as its theme "The Student in Higher Education." The questions raised were these: "Who are these young men and women? Why did they go to college? Where are they heading? How can higher education serve their needs and help them in their search for answers to such questions and help them toward their goals?" These are questions of importance to all in the field of higher education, but they are of especial significance to the counselor, whether the professional counselor or the teacher-counselor. Here are vital contributions which they can assist in making, or at the very least, they can join in the search for the answers.

Review and Evaluation

Finally, any program of counseling, whether it involves the faculty in great measure or not, should be subjected to regular review and evaluation. Lachs, (1965) puts it this way in a much broader context:

> Educational policy, more than anything else, is in need of rational justification. Such constant reassessment of aims and procedures is so much a part of any living educational process and institution that it is impossible for a person to claim to be an educator if he denies its legitimacy. (p. 121)

The educational policy of counseling is as subject to the process of reassessment as any other. The counselor should be in the forefront in this regard, and should consider this one of his obligations. Furthermore, he should also encourage and welcome outside evaluation to avoid the implication that only self-analysis is possible or required. A counseling program director who accepts this philosophy will be able to strengthen his program and make it as integral a part of the institution's framework as any other of its educational programs.

REFERENCES

Arbuckle, D. S., & Kauffman, J. F. Student personnel services in liberal arts colleges. *Personnel Guid. J.*, 1959, 38, 296–299.

Bergstresser, J. L. Issues in faculty counseling. In E. G. Williamson (Ed.), *Trends in student personnel work.* Minneapolis: Univ. of Minn. Press, 1949. Pp. 312–319.

Brower, P. J. *Student personnel services in general education.* Washington: Amer. Council on Educ., 1949.

Carpenter, Marjorie, Hopkins, E. H., & Hilton, M. Eunice. College guidance, whose job is it? *NEA J.*, 1953, 42, 272–274.

Davis, J. A. The college teacher as counselor. *J. teach. Educ.*, 1955, 6, 281–285.

Feder, D. D. Selection and training of faculty counselors. In E. G. Williamson (Ed.), *Trends in student personnel work.* Minneapolis: Univ. of Minn. Press, 1949. Pp. 288–300.

Gilbert, W. M. Training faculty members at the University of Illinois. In E. G. Williamson (Ed.), *Trends in student personnel work.* Minneapolis: Univ. of Minn. Press, 1949. Pp. 300–308.

Hardee, Melvene D. Coordinating the work of teachers, counselors, and administrators. In Melvene D. Hardee (Ed.), *Counseling and guidance in general education.* Yonkers, N.Y.: World, 1955. Pp. 306–331.

Hardee, Melvene D. *The faculty in college counseling.* New York: McGraw-Hill, 1959.

Kelso, P. C., & Hardee, Melvene D. Cooperative learning experiences of the faculty. In Melvene D. Hardee (Ed.), *Counseling and guidance in general education.* Yonkers, N.Y.: World, 1955. Pp. 287–305.

Koile, E. A. Faculty counseling in colleges and universities. *Teach. Coll. Rec.*, 1954, 55, 384–389.

Koile, E. A. Characteristics of college teachers interested in faculty counseling activities. *J. counsel. Psychol.*, 1955, 2, 32–34.

Lachs, J. Graduate programs in the undergraduate college. *J. higher Educ.*, 1965, 36, 121–130.

Mueller, Kate H. *Student personnel work in higher education.* Boston: Houghton Mifflin, 1961.

Nelson, A. G. The college teacher as a counselor. *Educ. Forum*, 1954, 18, 349–357.

Shank, D. J. *The teacher as counselor.* Washington: Amer. Council on Educ., 1948.

Shank, D. J. Some questions about faculty counseling. In E. G. Williamson (Ed.), *Trends in student personnel work.* Minneapolis: Univ. of Minn. Press, 1949. Pp. 309–312.

Shepard, E. L. The role of the faculty counselor in general education. In Melvene D. Hardee (Ed.), *Counseling and guidance in general education.* Yonkers, N.Y.: World, 1955. Pp. 161–178.

Stroup, H. The college teacher as counselor. *Sch. & Soc.*, 1957, 85, 120–122.

Tead, O. Integrating personnel and teaching functions in college. *Educ. Forum*, 1953, 17, 401–411.

Tinsley, Mary A. The faculty adviser in the liberal arts college. *Personnel Guid. J.*, 1955, 34, 219–220.

Chapter 18

Society and Values: Students and Citizens

HERBERT STROUP

The World of College Counseling

College counseling is never a solitary or isolated experience. Always it is found in a social context: the interpersonal relationship between the student and his counselor, the office within the college through which the counseling is made available, the college itself as a social system, the larger community of which the college is a part, and beyond that, the world. The primary focus of the counseling relationship may at a given point in time appear to consist of two persons only, but this is an appearance. Group counseling, moreover, apparently on the increase, belies the exclusivity of private relationship.

But in college counseling the nature of the college itself is of high significance. The college sets the stage for whatever activities go on within it. Without an understanding of the college, the nature of college counseling cannot be understood. The college is a social institution, one among many within the community which exist to satisfy basic human needs. Anthropologically, following the suggestions of Bronislaw Malinowski (1939), a social institution constitutes one phase of culture. Malinowski taught that culture is composed of the dynamic inter-relationships between three factors: (1) human needs; (2) social institutions; and (3) "synthetic imperatives."

The human being possesses certain fundamental, physiological needs.

Herbert Stroup is Dean of Students; Chairman, Department of Student Services, Brooklyn College of the City University of New York.

These require organized, collective responses from society. Among these needs are food, shelter, safety, relaxation, movement, growth, and reproduction. The organized responses to these basic imperatives account for the social organization of society. The family, for example, exists for the satisfaction of affectional and reproductive needs. The needs of man for food, shelter, dress, and other material comforts constitute the basis for the economic system which is concerned with production, processing, and exchange. According to this view, no aspect of the social organization of society exists for a self-justifying purpose. All institutions of society are based upon the validity and urgency of human needs.

The needs of human individuals constitute the foundation of the social institutions. All institutions are responsive primarily to the persistent needs of men. All of them—economic, political, legal, educational, familial, social, and the rest—exist for the satisfaction of human needs. Insofar as the social institutions are effective in their ability to satisfy human needs, they flourish. Some social institutions or some parts of them may exist for periods of time in a moribund condition. Ultimately, however, a social institution cannot continue to exist without in some measure satisfying human needs.

Less directly related to the basic, physiological needs of men is the third order of social existence, the synthetic imperatives. These are represented by such social systems as science, magic, myth, religion, and art. The capacity of man whereby he translates his basic needs into abstract systems based upon accumulated experience reveals both the grandeur and the misery of man. Man is able to create systems of knowledge, such as science, whereby he organizes and integrates his human activities. Through such systems a degree of meaningfulness is created by which man is able to evaluate new experience. On the other hand, the discontinuities in man's knowledge and understanding create hesitation and anxiety. Man is a tragic hero. By the synthetic imperatives he is able to order his experience, yet he seemingly must rely upon magic, myth, religion, and art to secure that measure of orderliness of mind and action that satisfies him as a sentient creature.

The whole system of functionalism is for present purposes a theory whose validity need not be discussed here. It has been outlined in a superficially summarized manner from Malinowski's contributions only to create a background for the understanding of the college as a social institution. In this connection it is interesting to note that the German existentialist philosopher Karl Jaspers (1959) also conceives of the university as a social institution, atlhough he seems not to be aware of the details of the structural-functional theory; thus his discussion is more general.

The college as a social institution rests ultimately upon its ability to satisfy certain basic, physiological needs which stand between the more concrete needs of human beings and the highly developed realms of the synthetic imperatives. The relationships of the human needs and the synthetic imperatives and the college as a social institution bear consideration beyond the confines of this discussion. The Christian faith, for example, in Malinowski's view, is a highly important human sentiment. It provides supernatural and public sanction for the beliefs, attitudes, and values which comprise a social morality. Religion makes social cohesion possible. It affirms and reinforces the beliefs and actions which social morality requires. In this sense, religion (and to a lesser degree, magic) constitutes the very foundation of culture. The precise relationship of religion to the college as a social institution and to the problems of freedom and order within the college, however, has never been fully described by the functional anthropologist.

The College as a Social Institution

The college, then, from the perspective of functionalism is a social institution. A social institution (Parsons, 1951) is a system of concerted activities carried on by an organized and specifically designated group of persons who operate under a charter in accordance with definite rules and by means of a material apparatus. In accordance with this definition, each of the component parts of the college as a social institution will be analyzed briefly.

A System of Concerted Activities

The concerted activities of a college are manifold, differentiated, and complex. They derive mainly from the formally stated goals of the college. Obviously, the formally stated goals of colleges differ greatly among themselves, but the activities of a college are, by definition, distinctive to the college rather than to some social institution in society. The college as a social institution is related to the other social institutions in society, but it clearly has its own sphere of accepted and expected activity.

A Specially Designated Group

A social institution also consists of a specially designated group of people who maintain the institution's activities. Commonly there is a variety of people who supply many and discrete contributions to the totality of the college. In the main, the personnel of the college consists of faculty, students, student personnel workers, and administrators. These, working as a team, conduct the activities by which the philosophy of the institution is enforced.

So far as the college's activities are concerned, the responsibility for them rests in part upon specialists and in part upon the general activities of the specialists. In a sense, everyone in the college is a specialist: professor, business manager, counselor, group leader, president, and clerk. Each is valuable to the college because of his specialty. But, in another sense, each also is professionally responsible for certain general functions. The counselor must be concerned with and have knowledge of the work of the professor—otherwise he cannot be an effective counselor. The business manager must have an interest in and a knowledge of the educational opportunities of the college. Otherwise, he may hinder rather than help the college in the attainment of its primary goals. The professor, it is further assumed, must have sympathy with and a wide range of understanding of the whole set of activities that comprise the college. Students are similarly involved.

According to the definition of a social institution previously supplied, a college consists of a system of concerted activities carried on by an organized and specifically designated group of persons. A social institution also involves a charter and a material apparatus.

A Charter

The charter by which a college is maintained is fairly complex, consisting of several planes of expressed responsibility. On the highest level the laws of the federal, state, and local governments provide the basic sanctioning of the college, including all of its programs. These laws are of two general kinds. First, there are those laws that pertain to all individuals and organizations regardless of their status as educational institutions. Second, there are those laws that pertain directly to the organization and conduct of institutions of education.

In addition, it is customary for a college to have its own written charter or bylaws by which it specifically declares its intentions to be itself. Such a charter usually defines the auspices of the college, its chosen philosophy, and such matters as the ways in which the students and staff are secured, advanced, dismissed. Such a charter stands in relation to the college as does a constitution to a republican form of government. It is the alternate basis of appeal. It provides the necessary law by which in open fashion every person attached to the college knows the nature of its administration.

There are also other rules and regulations which comprise the basic charter of the college. The faculty commonly legislates on various academic matters. These rulings are as the following: prescribed courses for all students, the requirement for departmental majors, residence and citizenship regulations, and eligibility for honors programs. Such legislation becomes an important part of the institution's charter. Students also may contribute to the charter of the college. The constitutions of student groups, the constitution and bylaws of the student government, informal requirements for social conduct (such as the freshman tipping his hat to a senior), and other customs and practices comprise a part of the institution's charter.

Without a charter the college can offer no genuine freedom, only unlicensed confusion. The charter at its best is the track upon which the educational train may most expeditiously make its way to its desired destination. Yet, as is obvious, the charter also restricts. The train cannot run in every direction. The authentic need for a carefully worked out charter in a large and complex institution is hopefully self-evident.

A Material Apparatus

The college as a social institution, finally, also requires and possesses a material apparatus. This material apparatus consists of such commonly recognized features as campus, buildings, classrooms, athletic equipment, stages, blackboards, computing machinery, desks, chalk, interview rooms, test booklets, files, and student lounges. These facilities are not at all points distinctive of higher education. Most large-scale or bureaucratic organizations employ much the same sort of apparatus. For example, the college may employ electronic computers to analyze the composition of its student body, but such an instrument is also utilized by other kinds of organizations.

This Malinowskian-functionalist interpretation of the college provides a significant set of interpretations of the nature of the college as a social institution. The college is perceived as a large, complex, but coherent social system. From the standpoint of functional theory, therefore, a number of practical interpretations and consequences for freedom and order within the college may be drawn.

Inherent Limits

The four component parts of the college as a social institution—a system of concerted activities, a specially designated group of people, a charter, a material apparatus—are unequally related to the understanding of the institutional limitations on individual freedom.

Specialization

The specially designated group of people characteristic of the college does not in itself comprise an imposed limitation on individual freedom. Yet those who maintain the social institution's activities possess a built-in limitation upon individual freedom by reason of their specialization or expertness. Thus, the regular activities of the personnel of a social institution are distributed as fixed duties. The division of labor is clearly defined in considerable detail. Each worker has a well-designed subfunction of the total function to perform. He knows what his capabilities and limitations are; he responds to self-imposed limitations, for no normal person in the bureaucratically organized social institution wishes regularly to exceed the estimates of others regarding his specialized competence. His work is distinctively his own and he takes considerable pride in the knowledge that the entire organization rests to some degree upon him for its efficiency. Thus, he limits himself in terms of his specialization.

The limitations imposed upon the personnel of a social institution are organized in scalar fashion. Specialization provides for gradations in the recognition of competence. The person of lower status is presumably (often not in his own eyes) less qualified by some status standard than the person of higher rank. It may be that technical qualifications (degrees from academic institutions, service in the hinterland, relations of a personal nature to the bureaucracy's leadership, production rate, and so on) determine the history and nature of a person's status. But, at its best, the college, like other bureaucracies, has stated standards by which persons qualify at the start and by which they proceed from the lower into the higher positions.

The worker in a social institution is a participant in a career. He thinks of himself as fitting into a personnel system of promotions and achievement. This is the mark of the civil service, but it is also established in the nongovernmental bureaucracies. The officeholder tends to identify his interests with the success of the organizations; therefore, he is willing to work hard at what he has been assigned. Because he expects to win a lifetime of recognition and emolument from the social institution, he is willing to defend it against attack from the outside and under a variety of conditions also from the inside. Loyalty—obviously comprising a limitation on freedom—to the organization is a keynote of the successful bureaucrat. In this connection all of the personnel of the college, including the students, are bureaucratically defined.

Authority

The status system places each person or group in a commonly well-defined position in relation to authority or responsibility. Authority is graduated; each lower office is under the control of a higher one. Thus, freedom to act is confined by status position. The bureaucrat is responsible for his own action (and those of his subordinates) to the person who by definition is above him in the organization. Authority in a bureaucratic social institution means that the higher rank has the right to issue directives and that the lower rank has the duty to obey.

All authority in a bureaucracy, however, is limited. It is limited formally by the authority which exists above it at a given point in the hierarchy. The authority above cannot be capricious; it must be responsible. It must follow the abstract and secondary rules which are binding upon all. Furthermore, it must follow those aspects of the rules and procedures that are especially pertinent to the particular rank exercising the authority.

Informally, too, there are restraints upon the employment of authority. The higher officeholder usually cannot fail to be aware of what he is able to get away with in the issuing of directives. The lower officeholder may not debate the authority of the order, but may on other grounds feel unprepared to act upon it. In extreme cases there may be a disagreement between the higher and the lower officeholders as to the wisdom or efficiency of the directive. Higher authorities learn what directives may and may not be issued. Experience teaches them not what their rights are, but what the lower order is willing to accept gracefully and effectively. Authority, then, may be said to reside in the attitude of the lower toward the higher order; it resides in what will be accepted, both formally and informally, rather than on a quality or an ability of the higher order. Thus, the specially designated group of people involved in the college as a social institution comprise in themselves a set of limitations on individual freedom.

Material Apparatus

The presence of a material apparatus—another component in the functionalist's definition of a social institution—appears to present no significant limitation on individual freedom. At least, the limitations which the material apparatus imposes upon individuals is only indirectly of a human or social character. The availability or lack of availability of a computer, for example, will obviously limit the freedom of an individual who is qualified and wishes to use a computer. Similarly the availability or lack of availability of financial resources within the college to provide programmed instruction by machines constitutes a possible limitation upon individual freedom.

Such limitations, however, seem to be a consequence of the availability or lack of availability of material resources and only indirectly constitute a limitation on individual freedom derived from legal or institutional policy considerations. Yet on occasion the lack of availability of a particular material apparatus may impose severe limitations upon the freedom of certain members of the college organization.

Activities and Charter

The major institutional limitations on individual freedom appear to derive from the two remaining components of the college as a social institution: a system of concerted activities and a charter. The theoretical nature of these has been previously described. Taken together these major limitations derive from the fact that social institutions are created by society in an effort to meet fundamental interests or needs of human beings. These forces or needs are operative in all human beings and as a result institutions come into being to satisfy them as well as to regulate and control them.

Some sociologists, for example, have concluded that there are essentially four major interests and their resulting social institutions in all societies. There are the economic and governmental systems (concerned with the food supply, property, class, and law systems); the family (concerned with courtship, marriage and divorce, training of the young, and treatment of the aged); aesthetic and intellectual expressions and recreational needs (which find outlet in dancing, acting, poetry, art, science, philosophy, social activities, games, and entertainment); and religion with its accompanying beliefs and practices.

Other sociologists, however, have concluded that the social institutions as well as the basic needs from which they are derived are more numerous. Hertzler (1946), for example, classified the social institutions into nine major categories. No matter how the social institutions may be classified, however, their distinctiveness rests upon the assumption that each possesses a relatively unique set of functions or activities by which they are characterized and differentiated from other social institutions. Implicit in the very nature of each social institution is a system of concerted activities by which the coherence and quasi-autonomy of the social institution is asserted and maintained.

From this standpoint the charter of a social institution is the formalized process by which the distinctiveness of the concerted activities of the social institution is defined and protected. Activities and charter are part of a united effort by society to maintain specialized functions on the part of social institutions that are directed toward the satisfaction and regulation of basic human needs. From the standpoint of the functional definition of the social institution, therefore, the college as a social institution exists for the maintenance of a limited set of societally sanctioned activities. These activities are given their mandate publicly by a charter. These activities and their supporting charter enable the college by its very nature to differ from any other social institution in society. Similarly other institutions, whether they be families, labor unions, or churches, do not possess in their activities or charter the distinctive functions of the college as a social institution. Thus, the system of concerted activities and the supporting charter of the college comprise in the final analysis the most significant set of institutional limitations on individual freedom (and institutional freedom as well).

The precise and comprehensive manner in which the concerted activities of the college and the supporting charter places institutional limitations upon individual freedom cannot be adequately discussed within the confines of the present effort. The outreach of these features affects every aspect of the corporate life of the college. Detailed accounts could be provided, for example, of the curricular or academic aspects of the college as well as others. In this limited discussion, however, the activities and charter of the college as a social institution will be related to a few selected aspects of the cocurricular facets of the college. In this regard, the assumption is not made that all or even most of the cocurricular features of the institutional limitations on individual freedom within the college are included. Also, there is no assumption that the discussion will go beyond the providing of illustrations of the full complexity of the subject. The illustrations, moreover, will be presented in relatively simple form. The detailed ambiguities surrounding each one are readily admitted, although the ambiguities will not be explored in detail. Obviously, differences of opinion—at times quite broad and very intense—surround each of the illustrations and their consequences for the themes of the institutional limitations on individual freedom.

Institutional Limitations on Individual Freedom

The institutional limitations on individual freedom, considered from the viewpoint of the college as a social institution, will be discussed in the light of three basic categories: (1) the ordered legal life of the college as a social institution; (2) the ordered social life of the college as a social institution; and (3) the ordered moral life of the college as a social institution.

The Ordered Legal Life of the College

The concerted set of activities that characterize the college as a social institution is based not merely upon private or voluntaristic assumptions by colleges themselves. All social institutions are legally based in society. The laws of a society are categorically organized in terms of the commonality and disparity among the functioning of the several social institutions. So there are laws pertaining to the regulation of family life, the maintenance of economic activities, and the functioning of religious organizations. Similarly colleges do not, every academic year, elect in a voluntaristic and autonomous manner to set limits upon their functioning. Limitations are provided by society in the legal ordering of the life of the college. College law is not ephemeral, but is indeed complex, extensive, and quite specific. Blackwell (1961) has compiled a handbook on college law to give college administrators a better understanding of the legal aspects of operating a college. This handbook defines several basic legal concepts such as: common law, civil law, statutory law, administrative law, due process of the law, and torts. Bakken (1961) has written a monograph the purpose of which is to provide general legal information and guidance for those working in college student personnel services. The second chapter of this monograph discusses particularly the derivation of authority for student personnel work.

Two illustrations will be provided of the ordered legal life of the college as a social institution: (1) in loco parentis; and (2) due process.

IN LOCO PARENTIS

The view that the college relates to its students as a parent does to his child has had a long and checkered career in the courts. It is probably safe to say, despite variations in interpretations of the law, that the college is granted the responsibility of acting as a parent in relation to its students in a wide variety of college activities: the so-called rights of students, student dismissal proceedings, rights and responsibilities of student organizations, student political activity on and off the campus, and the fraternities and sororities. The history of the development and the contemporary implications of the legal theory have been outlined by leading educators in a publication edited by Johnston (1962).

In general the law maintains that the officers of a college may lawfully exert power to restrict and to control the action of its students to the same extent that a parent can. The basic expression of the law was formulated in 1913 in a case involving Berea College. In this case the owners of a public restaurant in the community of Berea, Kentucky, sought an injunction to compel the College to rescind a regulation prohibiting its students from entering public eating houses in the community. The owners of the restaurant were chiefly dependent upon student patronage for their economic success. The court, however, refused the petition and sustained the right of the College to control its students. According to the judgment of the court:

> College authorities stand in loco parentis concerning the physical and moral welfare and mental training of pupils. For the purpose of this case, the school, its officers and students are a legal entity, as much so as any family, and like a father may direct his children, those in charge of boarding schools are well within their rights and powers when they direct their students what to eat and where they may get it; where they may go and what forms of amusements are forbidden. (Dott 3)

The legal principle of in loco parentis apparently pertains to practically all aspects of the life of the college and the student, including the seemingly private spheres of student life, such as the right of the college to entry into student dormitory rooms and lockers, as is outlined by Parker (1961).

In recent years, however, especially with the rise in numbers of nonresidential students, the legal basis for the doctrine of in loco parentis at times has been called into question. Yet there are those who think that the life of the student, at least insofar as it is confined to the campus, is appropriately regulated by the doctrine. Austin MacCormick (1956), for example, a Professor of Criminology at the University of California at Berkeley, has discussed some of the disciplinary functions that deans must exercise. These fall into two main categories: (1) those that involve standards of scholarship, and (2) those involving standards of conduct. He claims that the college properly is to be considered as being in loco parentis, at least with respect to freshmen and sophomores who are chronologically and psychologically immature, who are often bewildered and befuddled by the complexities and wonders of the campus world, and who are suddenly facing problems on which they seriously need guidance.

But, no matter what one's private view may be regarding the desirability of the legal doctrine in loco parentis, or its applicability on or off the campus, the fact is that the law exists and colleges can scarcely deny the obligation to abide by the ordered legal life of the college as prescribed by the laws and courts of the community.

DUE PROCESS

Due process comprises another illustration of the manner in which the ordered legal life of the college as a social institution places limitations on individual freedom. Due process in general discussions of the subject possesses an undeniable concreteness. For example, some authorities seem to take it for granted that the provision of a hearing constitutes an appropriate satisfaction of the requirement of due process. Thus, Ralph F. Lesemann (1961) states that a hearing is desirable and even required in cases involving charges sufficiently serious to justify a student's suspension or expulsion from college. He says:

> Evidence for and against the student [should] be given full, careful, and conscientious consideration to the end that the decision as to whether he is guilty or innocent with respect to the charges, and the action taken against him, if found guilty, will be fair and reasonable and will be supported by the evidence. . . . When a court is convinced that the foregoing requirements have been met, it will not substitute its judgment for that of the university authorities.

This view by the Legal Counsel of the University of Illinois was supported by the United States Court of Appeals which in 1961 indicated that due process required notice and some opportunity for a hearing before a student at a tax-supported college is expelled for misconduct.

On the other hand, many decisions of the court have asserted the right and responsibility of a college to expel a student without due process. Blackwell (1961a) for example, discusses three incidents of student expulsion from state institutions of higher education, reporting that in each case the court upheld the institution's right to expel a student without due process.

The right of a college to dismiss a student without any semblance of due process has often been upheld by the courts. A female student of Syracuse University, for example, was peremptorily dismissed in 1926 after three years of attendance. The University gave no grounds of dismissal and the student was not granted a hearing. The University indicated when suit was brought that it was acting upon the following statement published in its Bulletin and specifically referred to in its registration form which was signed by each student:

> The University, in order to safeguard its scholarship and its moral atmosphere, reserves the right to request the withdrawal of any student whose presence is deemed detrimental. Specific charges may or may not accompany a request for withdrawal.

The New York Supreme Court, following a hearing, directed the University to reinstate the student. The presiding judge stated that the right to one's life, to develop one's character, to have one's reputation free from smirching by the axe of others, is inherent in one of the most valuable of rights; that no institution, by its own act, can endow itself with the power to impair, by indirection, by innuendo, or by implication, the reputation of an individual . . . that regulation, as operative in the instant case, creates an intolerable and unconscionable situation, and that the action of the university is arbitrary, unreasonable, and in a high degree, contrary to a true conception of sound public policy.

The matter, however, did not rest with this declaration. The student was reversed on appeal and the reversal was justified on the grounds that the University need not accept as a student one desiring to become such. It may, therefore, limit the effect of such acceptance by express agreement, and thus, retain the position of contractual freedom in which it stood before the student's course was entered upon. The judge could discover no reason why a student may not agree to grant to the institution an optional right to terminate the relations between them.

The case of a student who had been dismissed without a hearing from the University of Montana, which came before the Supreme Court of Montana in 1927, is of singular importance due to the fact that the court rejected her petition for reinstatement after a careful review of virtually all the important cases on the issue of due process. The Montana Court, in sum, stated that the president of the university has no authority to compel the attendance of witnesses at a hearing or to compel them to testify if they were present. To hold that the power of suspension could only be exercised after a hearing had been held . . . would be to hold that the power was practically ineffective. (Blackwell, 1961a)

The United States Supreme Court denied the request of the student to review the question of her constitutional right of due process of law.

The seemingly dominant interpretation of the courts regarding due process in its legal and technical substance, does not, of course, regulate the local and elective procedures of a particular college. A college may well wish to provide a form of due process appropriate to its own concepts and traditions without involving itself in the technicalities of genuinely legal requirements. It is in this sense that Seavey (1957) suggests that the fiduciary obligation of a college to its students should lead it not only to make its sources of information regarding the misconduct of students available to the students involved, but should afford the students every means of rehabilitation.

In another review of the subject, Richard E. O'Leary, Assistant Dean of Men at the University of Illinois and John J. Templin, Assistant Legal Counsel at the University of Illinois, draw certain conclusions from a review and discussion of a number of court cases. They conclude as follows:

1. The university has powers of discretion in the disposition of disciplinary problems.

2. The courts are expressly unwilling to substitute their judgment for that of the university.

3. The court will be moved to intervene only when the record discloses a fundamental lack of fairness in the disciplinary process.

4. To provide this fundamental fairness, the processes will have provided the student with a fair opportunity to show his innocence, which in turn requires that he be informed of the nature of the charges against him.

5. The necessity of providing the rudiments of formal judicial proceedings is expressly denied as destructive to the educational system.

6. In all aspects of the situation, the university must not have been arbitrary in its actions (O'Leary & Templin).

The seemingly predominant view of the courts that an institution is fulfilling its proper legal responsibilities by limiting individual freedom so far as due process is concerned provides a second illustration of the way in which the ordered legal life of the college as a social institution enforces obvious limitations upon the freedom of the individual. The illustrations of in loco parentis and due process comprise only two examples of the manner in which the freedom of the individual within the college, viewing the college as a social institution, is clearly limited. These limitations obviously do not derive simply from the autonomously expressed wishes of the college as a social institution, but comprise limitations placed upon the college by the community at large in much the same way that the community sees fit to limit the freedom of individuals in their participation in the whole range of social institutions.

The Ordered Social Life of the College

Aside from the legal requirement for the ordered life of the college as a special institution, there are other limitations which are placed upon the freedom of individuals within the college as a consequence of the fact that the college also enjoys an ordered social life. This social or organizational life is necessary to the efficient conduct of the college. Although in part it may derive from legal bases and at times be supported with the force of law, essentially, it is based upon the intrinsic requirements of organized social existence.

RULES

The rules and regulations by which the college possesses its form and the expression of its activities may be viewed in part (by those who think negatively about such matters) as red tape. By this is popularly meant the senseless employment of paper requirements for conducting the social functions of the college. Yet this negative view is what it is—negative.

No matter how one may view rules and regulations, they are part and parcel of any social organization. Rules and regulations are necessary in order that a college be organized for *this* rather than *that*. They help to define the appropriate activities pertinent to the declared social functioning of the college. They give force to the commonly accepted requirement of the community that each social institution be organized in a somewhat distinctive way to maintain its own set of concerted activities.

The social organization of the college is governed primarily by abstract rules. These rules may be formulated by the owning, policy-making, top-authority person or group within the organization. They are generally not too precise or detailed. If they were so, they would not be serviceable. They constitute, rather, so-called first principles, that body of generalization that establishes the ethos of the organization, its basic philosophy, the patina of "holiness" about it. These abstract rules may be expressed in the papers of incorporation, in bylaws, in policy statements by the founder, in systematic memoranda by the chief policy authority, or in other ways, singly or together. They delineate which social functions the college is seeking to fulfill and what means it will use to those ends. They may describe the fundamental structure of the organization or set limits on its vision of its responsibilities.

Next to the abstract rules in depth stand the secondary rules. These are derived assumedly from the more primary principles. They may be direct and specific rationalizations of the primary principles. On the other hand, they may arise as middle-level generalizations, applications of the abstract rules to a variety of practical situations. Thus, there is a kind of common-law inheritance that a college possesses.

The purpose of this system of rules and regulations is that of providing consistency, rationality, and sensibility to the operations of the college. By the rules, every person on the staff of the organization, and even those who are not officially attached to it, know exactly what the college is up to, what its limits are, what its established procedures are for meeting special cases, what the responsibilities are of individual participants in the organization. The coordination of a large number of seemingly disparate and unconnected actions on the part of individual members of the college is thereby obtained. Operation by rule is the keystone in the edifice of all social institutions.

Everyone within a social institution is bound by the regulations, from the top administrator to those who are served. Theoretically, no one is able to make exceptions. Exceptions are the bane of any social organization. The college is devoted to the application of "law," even though some persons are unhappy and unwilling to accept living the law when applied to themselves. The social institution in its bureaucratic features behaves like justice herself—it is blind to individuality. A social institution seeks the achievement of a certain kind of justice, one which eliminates arbitrariness and individualization.

Differentiation must be made between the formal and legal responsibility for the ordered social life of the college and the expressed organizational means by which the social life is maintained and modified. Clearly, the responsibility that the college have an ordered social life is placed upon the legally constituted trustees of the college and their appointed administrators. Thus, an ultimate difference of opinion regarding the desirable ways by which the ordered social life of a college should be expressed resolves itself into a question for administrative policy and action by the governing board. For example, basic power in a college is reserved not to intermediate units of the college organization, or even to individuals within it, but to the "authorities" of the college.

Blackwell (1959) illustrates this point in connection with a former student of the University of Texas who was ordered by the Dean of Student Life to leave the campus. The student refused and was arrested by the University police and confined in the courthouse jail. He brought suit against the University, its Dean and Assistant Dean of Student Life, the Director of the Student Health Center, a member of its medical staff, and the judge of Travis County for punitive and exemplary damages for "false imprisonment, false arrest, libel, violation of civil rights, and being falsely debarred from readmission to the University of Texas." The Court of Civil Appeals of Texas dismissed the suit, declaring that the University officials have inherent power to maintain proper order and decorum on the campus and to exclude therefrom those who are detrimental to its well-being.

PATTERNS OF SOCIAL ORGANIZATION

The college, however, in fact may distribute its responsibilities to any degree and in any manner with which it finds satisfaction. A variety of philosophies and practices illustrate this phenomenon, a few of which may be mentioned. Falvey (1952) has studied the status and emergent trends of student participation in college administration and concludes that student participation in college administration is on the increase.

In the 1950's Bluffton College in Ohio revised its policy concerning organizational relationships between the faculty and the student body. Under the new plan (Lehman, 1953):

> Students were to become full-fledged members of all standing committees, including the administrative committee. In turn, to the student council were added two faculty members, with full voting power. Students on the committees do not merely sit in on meetings but have all the privileges of discussion, of initiating resolutions, and of voting. Faculty members on the student council are not merely advisory but are bona fide members of the council.

Similarly, W. W. Ludeman (1957), the President of Southern State Teachers College, Springfield, South Dakota, has described the plan practiced on his campus, "for the past four years with tremendous success," whereby student representation is used on college standing committees. Again, McGuire (1960) reported on some of the available research on areas in higher education in which students have been able to participate and in which they prefer to participate. He includes: academic standards, admissions, curriculum-planning, discipline, finance, public relations, faculty selection and evaluation, and student activities.

The situation of a new college, one not encumbered by traditional modes of social organization, also has been described in the case of Brandeis University, founded in October 1948. A fresh challenge was presented to its members to build patterns of social organization that would be appropriate to a growing university. The administration and students of Brandeis, in keeping a realistic balance between student freedom and responsibility consistent with student and faculty growth in the democratic process, have shared to a significant degree the problems of establishing a viable campus tradition. The ways in which the new university met the problems of the patterns of control regarding the hazing of freshmen, the editorial policy of the student newspaper, dress regulations, and the student board of review that deals with minor behavioral infractions, have been described by Berman (1955).

The pattern of administration, faculty, and student responsibility in the formulation of the social organization of the college has been developed in recent years at the University of Minnesota where the Student Association adopted a new constitution in 1960. This constitution created a new form of student government that rejected the traditional autonomous-structured student government and created a structure that combines leaders, staff, and faculty members in a coparticipant relationship quite different from the customary student-advisor relationship (Bloland, 1961).

EXTENSION OF RESPONSIBILITY

At times the distribution of responsibility within the social institution of the college seems to be quite extended. In some instances faculty and students may cooperate within a college body with a majority of the membership given to the students. Thus, the Student-Faculty Council of Drake University in Iowa is composed of eight students and seven faculty members. Seven committees stem from the Council: the campus chest, convocations, special events, promotions, social, student union, and mixed recreation committees. All of these committees are predominantly student in makeup, but each has some faculty membership (Kamm, 1954).

Other college bodies have extended the membership of their social organization even beyond the confines of the campus. Thus, the University of California at Berkeley features a Campus-City Coordinating Council for Student Affairs. The Council is composed of city officials, university officers, and key students. It operates not only to control student mass behavior, but to promote better understanding between the campus and the surrounding community. Dean Hurford E. Stone (1959) says of the Council,

> The success which the Coordinating Council has achieved in the city of Berkeley leads us to believe that, in its organization and functioning, it sets a useful pattern for other college or university communities where town-and-gown relationships are of continuing interest and concern. The influence of such a council can and should extend far beyond the realm of preventing disorders. It should serve as a continuing

> resource for better communication and increase co-operation between students of the college and citizens of the community. (pp. 258–259)

It is clear, however, that not all colleges believe that the distribution of responsibility for the ordered social life of the college as a social institution can be efficiently achieved through the extension of membership in controlling bodies of the college. Kerins (1959), for example, believes that conflict between students and administrators in college affairs is not only inevitable but also desirable. He thinks that students are obviously not capable of complete autonomy and that limits upon them are necessary by non-student agencies and persons within the college. He opposes "pseudo-participation" by students in decision-making and advocates that administrators should make clear the actual scope of student autonomy and should do so with neither apology nor deception.

Similarly, the president of West Virginia University, Irvin Stewart (1950), in an address at a Conference on Student Government at Duke University, December 1, 1949, outlined a philosophy of college administration that clearly separates the student government from other centers of control for the college as a whole. He asserted that the best student government is one "which vests in the student body the greatest amount of authority and responsibility which the students are prepared to exercise properly at any given time. The administration should stand ready with advice and assistance as needed to make that government a success."

Mueller (1961, pp. 307–394) also appears to draw back from the complete extension of college responsibility to students when she indicates that there are three principal difficulties encountered in student participation in policy-making. These are: (1) the distrust that both students and administration have of each other; (2) the failure of students to distinguish between freedom and license; and (3) the failure to differentiate policy from the decision-making which flows from it.

Others are more clearly opposed to student participation in the administration of the college. They tend to look upon students as the customers of the college who by definition are not part owners of the organization. Rather, the students are in the position of learners and the college has the responsibility of providing for the college whatever form of social organization meets the requirements of the faculty and the administration for good education.

Gildersleeve (1956) apparently takes this point of view when she states that the function of the faculty and the administration is to decide what measure of self-government or student government is conducive to good education. If the faculty thinks that a stern disciplinary regime would be most effective educationally for the good of the students, then it is the duty of the faculty to impose such a system. If the faculty, however, believes that a considerable measure of self-government, especially in the cocurricular sphere, gives experience of genuine educational value to students, then it is the duty of the faculty to provide the largest possible measure of self-government, freedom of speech, and freedom of the student press conducive to these educational ends. Miss Gildersleeve sharply denies that student participation in the life of a college is a consequence of the rights of students as citizens in a political unit and under a democratic form of government. She believes that such privileges may be desirable solely because they are good for the development of the minds and characters of the undergraduates.

The report of Lunn (1957) on student participation in college administration, prepared for the American Council on Education's Commission on Student Personnel, provides both a historical and philosophical review of the subject and a definition of the barriers between the potential contributions that could be made by students in college administration and the actual achievements in the field. He provides a suitable summary for the foregoing discussion on the variety of institutional formulations by which the ordered social life of the institution is maintained and modified by listing four main problem areas: (1) establishment of avenues for student participation; (2) definition of scope and degree of student participation; (3) development of effective student participation; and (4) overcoming of traditional thinking and procedures as well as the development of adequate interpersonal relationships.

In summary, the fact is that at present there is no unanimity regarding a desirable mode for the ordering of the social life of the college as a social institution. There are only widely differing views on the subject and a need for further study of local policies and practices leading to the formation of more dependable generalizations regarding the advantages and disadvantages of particular forms of the social organization of the college. But, so far as institutional limitations on individual freedom are concerned, there seems to be no form of social organization, beyond that enjoined by certain legal requirements, which of itself provides unlimited freedom to any person or group in the college. All forms of social organization by definition are restrictive. Each establishes a system of social relationships that guide the individual, whether administration, faculty, or students, in his effective collegiate behavior. The forms are nowhere absolute or unchanging; everywhere they are dynamic and adaptive.

There are some individuals in almost every social organization who are basically anarchistic. That is, they are opposed to whatever social organization happens to exist. The Spanish philosopher Miguel de Unamuno apparently was such a person. Addressing the clergy, he praised heretics. Speaking to Communists, he ostentatiously crossed himself, shouting "Christ be praised!" He challenged all parties and creeds and was never worried about contradicting himself. "If someone should organize an Unamuno party," he said, "I would be the first 'anti-Unamunista'." Fortunately, most people are able to accept to some degree whatever social organization in which they happen to find themselves, accepting many features of it as being valid for themselves and others, and working to improve those aspects of it that seem to be unproductive, inhuman, or ineffective.

The various forms of the social organization of the college call for study and interpretation. Until this is done little can be made of "student value studies." These often have been conducted as though values rested ultimately upon either vague and tenuous qualities, unattached to environments, or facets of the personality of the teacher or student, without an embodiment within the social organization of the college to the extent to which the social organization is the controlling set of circumstances. Allen Barton (1964), Director of the Columbia University Bureau of Applied Social Research, says on this subject,

> the study of the particular effects of a college on its students, or of particular aspects of the college environment, can best be understood if we also study the college as a social institution, looking at all its parts and the process which determine its activities. Research on narrowly defined problems will simply reach a dead end if it is not located in a broader program.

The Ordered Moral Life of the College

Despite inherent ambiguities, the ordered legal life of the college as a social institution is highly objective and relatively easily accepted by all. The ordered social life of the college is less authoritative in its nature and in its impact upon individual and collective behavior in the college. But the ordered moral life of the college as a social institution, the last of the three themes that illustrate the institutional limits on individual freedom, appears to be the least obvious, firm, and undebatable aspect of the total life of the college. Indeed, any discussion of it must necessarily involve some participation in the uncertainties themselves. In this sphere the greatest misunderstanding is possible, because there is the least consensus regarding its existence or desirability as a feature of college life. Almost anyone who makes an assertion in the moral sphere, as it pertains to college life, is apt to be misunderstood and as a consequence may find himself being criticized sharply.

The dilemma of the administrator in ethical matters is illustrated by two deans of the University of California at Los Angeles who collaborated in a historical analysis of student drinking and methods of control. They say (Atkinson and Brugger, 1959),

> There is no question that extreme differences in policy and policing exist, but do they have any real effect? The traditional problem of the administrator is that, if lenient, he will get his lumps from the community; if flexible, he will receive the same lumps from the student body, and he may also find that his policy approaches reality about as closely as do the inane hyperboles of the typical college fight song. If he follows a middle-of-the-road policy, he is sure not only to draw fire from both sides but also to be accused by everyone within sight or hearing of being a contemptible, temporizing compromiser. (p. 311)

Yet, no matter how vaguely or even contradictorily formulated, every social institution necessarily possesses some limitations, both written and unwritten, of a moral character that are assumed and acted upon for the welfare of the institution. A college is no exception. A college cannot be completely permissive in morality any more than it can fail to abide by its legal and social ordering.

Students and others within the college necessarily become involved in activities which express for themselves and for the college an estimate or even a conviction regarding moral desirabilities. Thus, when the students at the University of California at Berkeley received national attention for their stands on capital punishment, the House Un-American Activities Committee Hearings, compulsory R.O.T.C. and peace, the University as well as the students was deeply involved in ethical considerations of high significance. Or, when the president of Randolph-Macon Women's College (Quillian, 1961) explained the College's position regarding the sit-in demonstrations in the city of Lynchburg, Virginia, by saying that he believed them to be unwise because: (1) they are a violation of existing laws; (2) they show inadequate consideration for existing organizations set up to deal with the problem; and (3) they create situations of pressure and criticism harmful to the institution; he was deeply involved in moral considerations.

When, fictionally speaking, Francis Prescott's life is narrated by his former students in Louis Auchincloss' (1946) novel, he is shown to be a ferocious disciplinarian and moralist in order to cover up his own anxieties, being strangely possessed, for example, with homosexuality. He encourages vicious hazing to make the boys "tough." He will not let the boys wander off together in pairs, saying: "I did not think a hundred examples of David and Jonathan were worth one of sodomy." Prescott, for good or ill, is a moralistic administrator who is viewed as going far beyond what some might consider his tacit or official responsibilites.

Finally, when the president of Yale University, Kingman Brewster, Jr. (N.Y. *Times*, Sept. 15, 1964, p. 39) spoke to the freshmen of the class of 1968 he stressed moral elements, stating, "Yale has no business offering its privileges to any student who has demonstrated a willful disregard for the person, dignity or property of others, whether in New Haven or anywhere else."

So there seems to be no escape from ethical issues in the college, whether they relate to the unheralded actions of a routine existence or the much publicized activities involving dramatic issues of undoubtedly great human consequences.

SIGNIFICANT CHANGES

Part of the present dilemma in connection with the ordered moral life of the college as a social institution lies in the almost revolutionary changes that have occurred within the moral life itself. These significant changes are especially apparent in the attitudes of students and others toward love and sex. A physician, Mary S. Calderone (1964), makes this point in a talk to Vassar College freshmen contrasting the situation at Vassar in 1921 and its "annual notorious 'sex' lecture" with the situation today. Vassar College graduate Calderone says,

> The need for panel discussions on sex and lectures such as this one was not then apparent. Problems such as those faced by young people today existed, of course, but they were not as general or as obvious. With little or no access to cars, very limited week ends, and no parties without chaperones, a college girl almost automatically led a protected life, and indeed had to exercise considerable ingenuity to get into a situation which could lead to pregnancy. . . . My oldest daughter graduated from Vassar in 1948, and I also have a twenty-year-old and a seventeen-year-old daughter, but as a mother and physician I am deeply impressed by the fact that the customs and behavior patterns of young people have changed far more in the fifteen years since my oldest daughter's graduation than they did in the twenty-five years between my graduation and hers. (p. 39)

In the face of such basic changes in morality, the college as a social institution is properly perplexed and unsettled.

The recent years have seen a heightened development of individualism in morality. In this connection it is interesting to note that *The Crimson,* the Harvard College undergraduate newspaper, published a series of articles and letters, following publication of a newspaper story on September 24, 1963 (N.Y. *Times,* Nov. 1, 1963, p. 69), that Dr. Robert B. Watson, Dean of Students, would make an intensive study of the visiting rules. The *Crimson*'s editorial position in connection with the charge by one of the deans of Harvard College that a "growing number of students" took the room-visiting privileges as "a license to use the college rooms for wild parties or for sexual intercourse" was that sexual freedom was analogous to freedom of religion and speech, that is, a matter of individuality or of private standards of conduct.

In the same vein, Ann Trabue (1962), Dean of Women at Radford College, Virginia, after an effort to construct the main theories as to why students cheat, concludes that not only is there a "massive increase in cheating in all phases of education," but for her "what is worst the shift in attitude toward cheating." The "shift in attitude" involves the increasing assumption that students look upon individual misbehavior as being of no social consequence, especially "if no one gets hurt."

Colleges in general have been less certain of their ordered moral life than they have been of their ordered legal and social life, and in part this is understandable. Many educators who have relatively clear convictions regarding the legal and social bases for the college are neutral or uncaring regarding the moral life of students and others. Such a perspective is strengthened by comparisons to European higher education in which the private life of the student is relatively unrelated to the academic-institutional demands of the college. Others have been caught up by a philosophy of moral experimentalism in which the admitted educational policy of the college is one that tolerates or even encourages certain trial-and-error activities on the part of the students. Again, the assumption of objectivity, especially as it has been developed in the sciences, mitigates against the assertion of absolute values in the moral sphere.

In some quarters there is disheartenment with the ability of the college to control or modify the values of its students, in part as a consequence of the study by Jacob (1957), who says,

> Evidently colleges in general, or colleges in particular, do not break or alter the mold of values for most students . . . if anything the 'typical' college graduate is a cultural rubber stamp for the social heritage as it

> stands rather than the instigator of new patterns of thought and new standards of conduct. (pp. 12, 38)

But, whatever its pragmatic justification, the proper, planned and conscientious involvement of the college in the ordered moral life of the institution is relatively weak.

On the other hand, every college inescapably possesses moral policies. These policies are not unrelated to the ordinary activities of the college, since morality does not exist in the abstract. Always it is related to the actions of persons as they engage in activities intrinsic to the fulfillment of the whole range of human needs and aspirations. Thus, a college may not consciously wish to increase premarital sexual relations among its students, yet its policy regarding visiting hours in the dormitories inevitably relates to the subject and the practice. Graham B. Blaine, Jr., (N.Y. *Times*, Nov. 1963, p. 43), a psychiatrist on the staff of the Harvard University Health Services, testifies to the direct relationship between college policy and student practice. "The trend in sexuality is due partly to the accessibility of bedrooms in college dormitories and many students fall into sexual relations for which they are not ready. . . . Colleges put themselves in a unique position by allowing girls in boys' bedrooms." A college may have one or another policy pertaining to any aspect of the total range of its responsibilities toward its students and others, but any policy will have direct ethical consequences of a serious import for the persons involved.

In this connection, a national education conference held at Williston Academy in East Hampton, Massachusetts, in October 1963, witnessed several expressions by educators of the need for a more sensitive awareness and a more explicit articulation of the moral requirements of the ordered life of the college. Two expressions or viewpoints may be noted (N.Y. *Times*, Oct. 1963). First, Alma Hull, Assistant Dean of Students at Goucher College in Baltimore, said: "It time for all of us to stop acting as if we think students are always right. I think students want us to say we believe in something." Second, Lieutenant Colonel Robert S. Day, Director of Admissions at West Point, said: "If you set the standards, the students will meet them."

Prior to the conference in East Hampton, Massachusetts, some educators were struck by the firm letter that the President of the University of Notre Dame, the Reverend Theodore M. Hesburgh, sent to his students. President Hesburgh wrote in part,

> Beyond the normal griping, if anyone seriously believes that he cannot become well educated here without a car, or girls in his room, or if one really thinks that his personal freedom is impossibly restricted by

> curfew, or state laws on drinking . . . then I think the only honest reaction is to get free of Notre Dame.

The lack of a sufficiently ordered moral life in the college, however, cannot be remedied simply by a reversion to older moral standards. It cannot be improved by repetitive and dogmatic assertions, any more than the most efficient social organization for the college can be achieved by pronouncements *ex cathedra*. Despite the fact that the current generation of college students has been studied in volume and intensity almost to the point of desperation, progress will probably not be made on the basis of information alone, although everyone wants dependable information. Also improvement in the ethical atmosphere and practice of the college cannot be secured without massive changes in the surrounding and supporting culture in which college and noncollege persons are deeply involved and committed.

SOME TENTATIVE PROPOSALS

But there may be ways open to educators whereby experimental programs that look toward the fearless facing of the moral dimensions of collegiate life may be begun and constructive steps taken toward the establishment of a changed climate. Several of these possibilities may be tentatively indicated.

First, it may well be that student personnel workers need to examine their stance of alleged objectivity. Despite the commendable efforts of counselors and others to refrain from efforts to direct the lives of students, the resulting broad tolerance of even the extremes of community-defined misbehavior may lead the student to assume that neither the counselor nor anyone else has settled views or convictions regarding ethical activity. Williamson (1956) constructively calls for a new emphasis on the part of student personnel workers as they relate themselves to the many kinds of misbehavior by students. He urges them to abandon their "neutrality" roles with respect to the development of the individual. He calls them to help the student grow in moral and social ways which are facilitating of the growth of the students and that of others.

Doris M. Seward (1961), Dean of Women at the University of Connecticut, also is troubled about the implications of educational discipline. She says that so much of our concern currently aroused by the controversial word *discipline* is a result of greater sophistication about human relations, and less certainty about the future in which young people will be involved. She asks that the disciplinarian seek answers to three questions: (1) what do we mean by discipline?; (2) how do our personal beliefs affect what we do in disciplinary situations?; and (3) do the methods we use in discipline reflect the training and knowledge we profess?

Another tentative proposal involves the possibility of making academic experience more authentic and exciting. It is apparent to some, for example, that the practice of student cheating in examinations is directly related to the nature of the examining process in many instances and to the character of the academic experience offered to students. If education is partly the evaluation of "gamesmanship" in which the student and the faculty member are antagonists, and in which the faculty member wittingly or otherwise himself engages in unethical academic practices, then it may well be expected that the student will learn his lessons and utilize undesirable methods.

Such a conclusion is offered by Goldsen (1960, pp. 74–80) and others as a partial explanation of cheating in examinations. A team of sociologists on the faculty of Cornell University polled the opinions of students on 11 selected university campuses in an effort to discover how students see the world in which they live. Thirty-six per cent of the students at all the universities polled were in agreement that "most college students would cheat on an examination, if they were sure of not being caught," while 13 per cent were uncertain how to respond. The study discovered that 51 per cent disagreed with the wording of the statement. The Goldsen study concluded that three value clusters were found to have a direct relationship to cheating: (1) the formal or informal nature of the social control; (2) the tendency to conform to what is perceived as the current practices of one's peer-group; and (3) a general depreciation of the academic experience as such. In connection with the possibility of making the academic experience more authentic and exciting, the third conclusion seems to be relevant.

In support of this suggestion, the study by Trabue (1962) seems to be significant. This author, following a review of the literature, suggests four main theories as to why students cheat: (1) to maintain pressure imposed from outside; (2) because the work is too difficult for them; (3) because the work is too easy and they haven't been challenged to learn; and (4) because the work seems meaningless to them and they have no interest in mastering the material. Again, several of these "main theories" appear to be relevant to the proposal that academic experience in itself may be another basis for the current moral climate or the lack of it of the college.

A third tentative proposal involves a fresh, massive, and responsible concern on the part of all persons in the college for the appropriate ordering of the moral life of the social institution. Probably the claim can go unchallenged that currently colleges fail to devote as much informed and skilled resources to the moral implications of their total life as to the need for improving their social organization. From this standpoint, colleges probably get what they deserve; curricula to which constant and urgent attention is given, while at the same time the moral implications of the curriculum and other aspects of the college lie undisturbed on fallow ground.

Of course there is the tendency on the part of some colleges to assume that the religious organizations associated with the campus as forms of "campus ministry" are fundamentally responsible for the moral climate of the entire college. Increasing conviction is found, however, on the part of those who participate in the campus ministry, as well as others, that such programs, often operating at the periphery rather than the core of the life of the college, constitute an important but not a fundamental platform from which the moral life of the institution can be ordered and developed. No matter how effective the services of campus ministries may be, the basic and undeniable responsibility for the moral life of the college rests upon those who have a total college responsibility for all aspects of the institution's life.

The president of Southern State Teachers College, Springfield, South Dakota (Ludeman, 1962), may be on the right track when he suggests that much more careful attention will have to be given by the college itself to a variety of concerns and activities, if campus behavior problems are to be reduced. The areas in which he suggests the development of a larger share of a college's resources are as follows: (1) more pointed admission screening; (2) dismissal for misconduct; (3) publicizing the policy of the institution on student behavior; (4) student-council leadership; and (5) closer adviser-advisee relations.

By these means, therefore, a strengthening of the ethical life of the college may be at least envisaged.

GROUP BEHAVIOR

Although the need for attention and action to the moral needs of individual students is important, the need for efforts relating to group or mass behavior is also apparent. Unfortunately, there seems to be much more reliable information and concern regarding the misbehavior of individuals than there is on the misconduct of groups and masses of students. There are relatively few dependable studies of the nature of group misbehavior and the ways by which it can be controlled and prevented. This sphere of college life remains an open challenge to everyone concerned with the strengthening of the ordered moral life of the college as a social institution.

It is true that some understanding of group misbehavior is currently available, although its dependability and implications are highly perplexing. For example, the so-called panty raid has been analyzed and suggestions have been proposed for its control and prevention. Allen (1962) has compared the characteristics of mob behavior with descriptions of comparable student behavior evidenced during a campus panty raid. He suggests a plan of action to be followed by university administrators as a preventive approach. He also delineates action to be taken during an "in-progress" student mob formation.

Loucke (1961) has added to available knowledge regarding panty raids by describing in detail a series of three such raids at the Florida State University where he is Dean of Men. He explains how University officials developed techniques for bringing the raids under control. After the first raid, which got out of hand due to the unpreparedness of University officials and the influence of outsiders (such as a local radio station giving a play-by-play description of events from location), University officials took appropriate measures for limiting the activities. In the two following "lace riots," quick, on-the-spot action by University officials, reinforcement and action by security officials, and on-the-scene name-gathering kept the raids and participants to a minimum.

Finally, Michigan State University (Truitt, Burnitt, & Walther, 1959), as a result of campus experience, officially formulated a five-phase plan for the prevention and control of irresponsible student mass behavior. The policy statement involves five divisions: (1) policy and procedures by which the program is oriented; (2) procedures for dispersing the group before it becomes unruly and destructive; (3) procedures for handling the group should it become violent; (4) procedures for handling violators; and (5) methods for transmitting to the public a realistic appraisal of the student disturbance.

Despite the availability of some information regarding one phase of student group and mass misbehavior, this aspect of the corporate life of the college remains relatively unexplored both in terms of its behavioral configurations and its moral import. This and other aspects of group and mass behavior require urgent and skilled attention.

The problems related to the ordered moral life of the college as a social institution are undoubtedly formidable. Yet some kind and degree of moral ordering in the college is necessary and inescapably existent. As a consequence of its existence, institutional limitations on individual freedom exists. No college permits any and all activities. Whatever activity is permitted and prohibited rests upon moral assumptions, even though these may not consciously be known or be rationally defensible.

The moral implications of collegiate life cannot be reduced successfully to other than moral categories, such as the social and legal. They are inextricably bound up with all of the activities of the college, yet they constitute an approach to and a measure of the worthiness of the activities themselves.

The explication of these factors, the study of them from a variety of viewpoints, and the courageous effort to trace out their implications in constructively experimental programs of action may well constitute the most significant challenge to those within higher education who in the forthcoming years seek in reason and in faith to establish the full nature of education.

The unfamiliar is often exciting but threatening, appealing but fearsome, challenging of one's potential but bearing the danger of frustration and even of defeat. It would be strange indeed if going to college did not involve these mixed emotions. The testimony of alumni confirms these assertions. Colleges, too, are well aware of the mixed emotions of their students and strive through a variety of counseling offerings to enable them to overcome their uncertainties.

The view that adolescence is a serenely blissful period in one's life is a badly-told tale by romanticists. Youth, whether in college or not, exist in tension, stress, and conflict. It is not enough to say that every stage of growth has its problems and that youth's problems are superficial and illusory. They are real. They are real to those who possess them. They are real, moreover, in the sense that they take their toll of failure or success in a measure that many adults are unaware of or do not wish to face. Every thought, feeling, action of the college student counts toward his own character development.

The college student who experiences anxieties about being a success in college should know that he is not alone. He has many fellow students who are undergoing to one degree or another the same sorts of questions that run through his mind. Most college students are strong enough psychologically to bear up under these stresses and even to distinguish themselves by many positive accomplishments. A few will require assistance in overcoming their unsettlement.

Fortunately, the majority of college students are able to persist and to survive, eventually receiving a degree. But no more than 60 per cent of all students who enter degree-granting institutions ultimately receive their degrees. About 40 per cent fall by the wayside. The problem of dropouts, by now so familiar for the precollege population, is one of the most vexing and important dilemmas facing everyone involved in higher education. Obviously withdrawals from college cannot be completely eliminated, although they may be significantly reduced. The present rate of college dropouts signifies a loss of important talent to the nation as a whole, retarding the development of a larger professional work force and as a consequence a higher economic and cultural level for the nation.

The college experience is not always a constructive influence. For many it is corrosive of traditional values, leading to deep questioning of the fundamental bases for human life itself. In part such unsettlement is an avowed purpose of higher education insofar as it is liberal education. For, liberal education is an education that liberates the individual from his parochialisms; it is an education that transforms the individual's values from a popularly accepted, uncritical, and unexamined basis to values that are intellectually defensible, in accord with the deepest and most universal experiences of man, and supported by a sense of commitment.

But colleges do not succeed with their lofty purposes for many students. On the contrary, the college experience may neutralize the values of students. The variety of subjects, problems, departments, viewpoints expressed by the faculty, and the generally incoherent organization of the intellectual life, at least on the deeper levels, lead many college students to question themselves and their ability ever to reach a firm ethical and philosophical position. Expecting reason to be united in college, many students find it to be divided into sometimes petty, often competitive, and generally unconnected learning.

Students, moreover, especially those who attend colleges away from home, often come into contact with students from different regional, racial, ethnic, and religious backgrounds. They quickly learn that their own personal and family traditions are not necessarily those held by others. This, too, is unsettling. As a consequence many college students struggle to form their own identities in a world of "vanishing absolutes."

Not all college students, however, are at sea in relation to their ethical and religious beliefs. Some compartmentalize their inherited beliefs and their new-found knowledge, never letting either interfere with the other. Others, who undergo serious examination of their basic values find satisfying solutions in conventional ethics and religion.

In general, however, studies of the faiths and doubts of college students about religion show that the college experience intensifies faith for some and raises doubts for others. Only about a third of college graduates report that the college experience has led to no change in their attitudes toward religion.

College students who are unsettled in their ethical and religious outlook can look to a number of resources within the college itself as aids to the formation of a settled life philosophy. Other students often are potent agents in enabling unsettled students to form their self-identity. The traditional value of "bull sessions" can scarcely be overestimated in this regard. Similarly, the faculty act as models even when they are not active as answerers of questions and counselors of students in private matters. Also, most colleges provide student personnel services which consist of group leaders, counselors of various kinds, and religious advisers (deans of chapels, campus ministers, professional advisers to religious organizations). In addition, many communities provide social-welfare agencies and other forms of community-based assistance for those who undergo severe questioning.

In the final analysis, however, the college student must make up his own mind regarding his own ultimate beliefs. The task of others is one of encouragement and support for the student who seeks to solve his problems for himself. The solutions that are accepted by one person cannot become the authentic possession of another without a search for values that can command the individual's own conviction and obedience. The student who has not "found" himself may govern his actions by such external incentives as grades, money, or prestige. He will not as a consequence be a free or mature individual, for such a person regulates his behavior by the intrinsic satisfactions that he gets from dealing effectively with his world on bases of norms that are genuinely his own. Through counseling the student may be able to face the full range as well as the details of the varied factors that are a part of the development for the student of a mature value system.

Ages ago that prototype of the human race, Abraham, went out from Ur of the Chaldees "not knowing whither he went" to a place he was to receive as an inheritance. So, too, Ulysses, the ancient Greek wanderer, left Ithaca for a life of travel through strange and threatening lands. These heroes of the past point in the present to the situation that faces every young person. Every individual though he may travel little or much, is impelled to leave the safe moorings of a sheltered life within the family to make his way upon the stormy and untried seas of life itself. Going to college is for many the start of that journey. Counseling is a major resource, provided by the college, whereby the student may attain his desired haven of maturity.

REFERENCES

Allen, J. S. Student mob behavior: a sociological approach to its prevention. *J. Coll. Stud. Personnel,* 1962, 3, 119–125.

Anthony v. Syracuse University, 130 Miscellaneous 249, 233 New York Supplement 796, Sup. Ct. 1927.

Anthony v. Syracuse University, 224 Appellate Division 487, 231 New York Supplement 435, 1928.

Atkinson, B. H., & Brugger, A. T. Do college students drink too much? *J. higher Educ.,* 1959, 30, 311.

Auchinloss, L. *The rector of Justin.* Boston: Houghton Mifflin, 1964.

Bakken, C. J. *The legal basis for college student personnel work.* Student Personnel Series No. 2, Amer. Personnel and Guid. Assoc. Washington: Amer. Coll. Personnel Assoc., 1961.

Barton, A. H. *The college as a social institution.* New York: Bur. of Appl. Soc. Res., Columbia Univ., 1964. No. 382.

Berman, Deborah. Evolving patterns of democratic social control at Brandeis University. *J. educ. Sociol.,* 155, 28, 359.

Blackwell, T. E. The maintenance of law and order on the campus. *Coll. Univ. Bus.,* 1959, 27, 24.

Blackwell, T. E. Can a student be expelled without due process? *Coll. Univ. Bus.,* 1961, 31, 58–59 (a)

Blackwell, T. E. *College law: a guide for administrators.* Washington: Amer. Council on Educ., 1961. (b)

Bloland, P. A. A new concept in student government. *J. higher Educ.,* 1961, 32, 94–97.

Calderone, Mary S. A distinguished doctor talks to Vassar college freshmen about love and sex. *Redbook,* 1964, 122 (4), 39.

Dixon v. Alabama State Board of Education, 294 Federal Reporter, 2nd series, No. 18641, U.S. Ct. of Appeals, Circuit 5, 1961, 150–165.

Dott 3. Berea College, 156 Ky. 376, 161 S. W. 204, 1913.

Falvey, Frances E. *Student participation in college administration.* New York: Bur. of Publ., Teach. Coll., Columbia Univ., 1952.

Gildersleeve, Virginia C. The abuse of democracy. *Saturday Rev.,* 1956, 39, 15–16.

Goldsen, Rose K., & Others. *What college students think.* Princeton: D. Van Nostrand, 1960.

Havice, C. (Ed.) *Campus values.* Boston, Mass.: Northeastern Univ., 1966.

Hertzler, Joyce. *Social institutions.* Lincoln: Univ. of Neb. Press, 1946.

Jacob, P. E. *Changing values in college: an exploratory study of the impact of college teaching.* New York: Harper, 1957.

Jaspers, K. *The idea of the university.* Boston: Beacon Press, 1959.

Johnson, N. (Ed.) *In loco parentis.* Philadelphia: U.S. Nat. Studt. Assoc., 1962.

Kamm, R. B. A student-faculty approach to campus government. *Sch. & Soc.,* 1954, 79, 186–188.

Kerins, Frances J. Student autonomy and administrative control: the fallacy of absolute cooperation between student and administrator. *J. higher Educ.*, 1959, 30, 61–66.

Lehman, C. M. Can students help run a college? *Coll. Univ. Bus.*, 1953, 14, 22–24.

Lesemann, R. F. Due process in student disciplinary proceedings. Speech given at the Nat. Conf. Univ. Attorneys, Ann Arbor, April 17, 1961.

Loucke, D. A triad of lace riots. *J. Coll. Stud. Personnel*, 1961, 34, 13–18.

Ludeman, W. W. We give students a voice in shaping college policies. *Coll. Univ. Bus.*, 1957, 22, 25–26.

Ludeman, W. W. Facing up to student behavior. *Coll. Univ. Bus.*, 1962, 32, 24.

Lunn, H. H. *The student's role in college policy-making*. Washington: Amer. Council of Educ., 1957.

MacCormick, A. The nonconformist in the crew-cut crowd. Paper read at the 38th Anniver. Conf. Nat. Assoc. Stud. Personnel Admin., Berkeley, June 22, 1956.

Malinowski, B. The group and the individual in functional analysis. *Amer. J. Sociol.*, 1939, 44, 939–964.

McGuire, E. C. The role of the student in college policy making. *Personnel Guid. J.*, 1960, 38, 378–384.

Mueller, Kate H. *Student personnel work in higher education*. Boston: Houghton Mifflin, 1961.

O'Leary, R. E., & Templin, J. J. The college student and due process in disciplinary proceedings. *Illinois Law Forum*, in press.

Parker, D. Some legal implications for personnel officers. *J. nat. Assoc. Women Deans Counsel.*, 1961, 24, 198–202.

Parsons, T. *The social system*. New York: Free Press, 1951.

Quillian, W. S., Jr. Statement made to the student body at assembly on January 3, 1961.

Scott, J. F. The changing foundations of the Parsonian action scheme. *Amer. sociol. Rev.*, 1963, 28, 716–735.

Seavey, W. A. Dismissal of students: due process. *Harvard Law Rev.*, 1957, 70, 1406–1410.

Seward, Doris M. Educational discipline. *J. nat. Assoc. Women Deans Counsel.*, 1961, 24, 192–197.

State ex. rel. Ingersoll E. Clapp, 81 Montana 200, 263 Pac. 433, 1927.

Stewart, I. Student government as a university president sees it. *Assoc. Amer. Coll. Bull.*, 1950, 36, 90–97.

Stone, H. E. A project in campus-community cooperation. *J. higher Educ.*, 1959, 30, 255–259.

Trabue, Ann. Classroom cheating—an isolated phenomenon? *Educ. Rec.*, 1962, 43, 309–316.

Truitt, J. W., Burnitt, R. O., & Walther, C. L. The prevention, deterrent and control of irresponsible student mass behavior. *Safety Monogr. Coll. Univ.*, 1959, No. 9.

Williamson, E. G. Preventive aspects of disciplinary counseling. *Educ. psychol. Measmt.*, 1956, 16, 68–81.

Chapter 19

Student Services: Administration and Structure

MAX SIEGEL

Administration in Higher Education

The Association for Higher Education, in its recent publication devoted to "Current Issues in Higher Education" (Smith, 1966), includes seven papers on administration and at least a dozen others which border upon administrative matters. The United States Office of Education, in a recent Bulletin of 229 pages (Ayers, Tripp, & Russell, 1966), recognizes the distinctive purpose and nature of student services and provides data regarding the organization and administration of student services in United States colleges and universities. Signs of the times, these publications reflect the growing recognition of the importance of administrators to college operations. By choice or (more likely) by necessity, most colleges are deeply involved with the explosion in numbers now taking place. The complexity of institutions which have grown from 800 to 8,000 or from 8,000 to 80,000 is almost indescribable. Grants, physical plants, recruitment, and finances generally, have made colleges and universities partners to big business and, as such, dependent upon intricate networks of administration.

Administrators include college presidents, vice-presidents, chancellors, provosts, deans, registrars, department chairmen, insofar as key management roles are concerned. Historically, academicians have tended to regard administrators with disdain, if not with outright contempt. As Campbell

Max Siegel is Professor, Department of Education; Coordinator, School Psychologist Training Program; and formerly, Associate Dean of Students, Brooklyn College of the City University of New York.

(1966, p. 235) points out, "Any professor who becomes a president or a dean has sold his soul. . . . There seems to be a positive correlation between the prestige of an institution and the strength of this contempt." The size and complexity of contemporary college organizations have begun to infiltrate even the academics, who must face the reality that every member of the staff is a potential administrator at one time or another. Administration now goes beyond the lofty perch of the president or dean, and devolves upon coordinators, unit heads, and directors of various kinds. Instructional departments increasingly face the need to establish internal coordination of special programs requiring more and more administrators. It seems clear that administration is here to stay and indeed may even be achieving respectability among academic colleagues. Of course, the professor who does begin to feel that he has sold his soul is always in the position of regaining his essential freedom by renouncing the role in question. The literature in this area provides more detailed data (e.g., Ayers & Russel, 1962; Russel & Ayers, 1964).

Administration in Student Services

Student services in higher education usually include all counseling, testing, and health services; student activities, including all cocurricular and extracurricular programs, student government, and student publications; admissions, discipline, records, and residence arrangements; orientation and foreign student programs, remedial clinics and workshops, and other informal educational services. Administration of student services includes the centralization, coordination, direction, and staffing of all services and programs described above.

In a recent survey (Ayers et al., 1966) of a 50 per cent sample of the universities, liberal arts colleges, teachers colleges, and junior colleges in the United States, 86 per cent of the sample report a student services program under one administrative head classifiable as the chief student services officer. Private institutions do not tend to have such an official more than public agencies, but the great majority of colleges of both kinds delegate administrative responsibility to a person identifiable as the chief student services officer. In exactly half of the institutions reporting, the title used for this officer is Dean of Students or Dean of Student Affairs or Dean of Student Services. Others report the titles Director of Student Personnel Services, Vice-President for Student Services, Dean of Men, and Dean of Women. It seems clear that the title Dean of Students is firmly established as referring to the chief student services officer in higher education. (Ayers, et al., 1966, p. 8)

The Dean of Students

According to the available data, most Deans of Students carry institutional responsibilities beyond those related to student services. These include teaching and other administrative tasks. Men outnumber women in a sample population of 621 in the order of about 4 to 1. More than 70 per cent are under 50 years of age, and about 38 per cent fall into the 40–49 year interval. Noticeably more men over 50 are found in the universities, younger Deans of Students being seen more among liberal arts colleges and private institutions. Comparatively, the male chief student services officer is younger than his female counterpart. The majority of men are in the 40–49 age range, and women, in the 50–59 bracket. The master's degree is the typical one held by these officers, and more than one third of the population have a research doctorate. Public institutions (7 out of 10) employ larger percentages of those with doctorates than private ones (3 out of 10). Most of the Deans of Students have obtained their preparation in the field of education (some 50 per cent), and one fifth coming from the social sciences. The heterogeneous academic backgrounds of these administrators is marked, some 10 per cent being educated in psychology. It seems clear that formal professionalization of their work is still in its infancy and that many officers acquire competency through experience rather than training. (Ayers, et al., 1966, pp. 13–14)

The titles Dean of Men and Dean of Women, respectively, have the broadest currency of any titles of the major student services deans, among those who report to Deans of Students. Associate Deans of Students are the next largest group, with Assistant Deans following. Reporting institutions indicate that the title Director of Counseling is firmly established for the officer who is responsible for counseling services ranging from psychiatric to faculty counseling.

Twenty administrative functions have been identified as the student services most prevalent in American higher education (Ayers, et al., 1966, p. 43): recruitment, admissions, academic records, nonacademic records, counseling, testing, financial aids and awards, foreign student programs, nursing services, medical services, residence hall, married student housing, job placement, student union, other extracurricular problems, intercollegiate athletics, intramural athletics, food services, and religious affairs. Others, statistically much less prevalent, include remedial clinics, veterans affairs, and registrar's duties. The pattern seems clear that in larger institutions the respective function is assigned to a particular director or coordinator, while in smaller colleges, functions are integrated according to size and need. In general, these functions are performed by officials who report to the Dean of Students.

Administrative Channels

In almost three fourths of the institutions surveyed by Ayers, et al. (1966), the chief student services officer reports to the president. In about 10 per cent of the colleges, he reports to the chief academic officer. In a third of the sample the dean of men is directly responsible to the president, and in about a fourth he reports to the chief student services officer. The larger the institution, the less likely is any student services officer to report to anyone other than the chief student services officer (i.e., the dean of students). This applies as well to deans of women.

In half of the institutions reporting, the director of admissions reports to the president; in a fourth, to the chief academic officer; and in about a tenth, to the chief student services officer. The director of athletics tends to report to the president in half the institutions and to the chief academic officer or chief student services officer in a fourth. In about 40 per cent of the colleges, the director of counseling reports directly to the president, and in a fourth, to the chief student services officer or to the chief academic officer. The director of food services tends to be responsible to the business officer, and the registrar tends to be responsible to the president. Directors of health services, housing, financial aids, placement, religious affairs, remedial clinics, student unions, testing, veterans affairs, and foreign students advisement, fall into the pattern of reporting to the chief student services officer when enrollment is above 2,500. The recurrent pattern is that the larger the institution, the more likely it is that the chief student services officer is the responsible official in the functions indicated. (Ayers et al., 1966, pp. 60–69) The academic dean is responsible for academic advisory programs in a sizable portion of all institutions, the faculty as a group ranking second. Again, in larger public institutions and teachers colleges, the chief student services officer exercises responsibility in this area.

Personnel and Budget

Relatively little attention is paid in the literature to such mundane matters as salaries, rank, conditions of employment, and related issues. The national range of variation is clearly great, and consistency of variation is totally lacking. Staff members in departments of student services or in offices of the dean of students vary from clerical-administrative to full-faculty responsibility. In the smaller, particularly in the private, colleges counselors are on a par with clerks, working an 11 month year and a 35 to 40 hour week on salaries considerably below those of the faculty, and without tenure. In the larger colleges and universities (e.g., the City University of New York), members of the department of student services hold regular faculty rank and tenure, including all faculty benefits and responsibilities. Where members of the instructional staff teach on a 12 or 13 hour schedule, for example, staff members in the department of student services counsel on a 26-hour a week schedule during the academic year. As a result, the status and prestige of such staff members are considerably higher than their counterparts in institutions providing no faculty rank. Of course, such counseling staff members are expected in return to maintain scholarly standards, teach, and make serious contributions to their profession. In some institutions, the Dean of Students is chairman of a department which incorporates all student personnel workers. In others, the chairman of such a department may be another faculty member, with responsibility to the chief student services officer. Again, consistency around the country seems to be absent at this time.

Student Records

The American Association of University Professors (AAUP) has for some years given serious thought to the matter of student records, particularly insofar as the academic freedom of students is concerned. The AAUP Committee on Faculty Responsibility for the Academic Freedom of Students published the following tentative statement of policy, approved by the AAUP Council (Committee S, 1965):

> *Student Records*
>
> Institutions should have a carefully considered policy as to the information which should be part of a student's permanent educational record and as to the conditions of its disclosure. To minimize the risk of improper disclosure, academic and disciplinary records should be separate, and the conditions of access to each should be set forth in an explicit

> policy statement. Transcripts of academic records should contain only information about academic status. Data from disciplinary and counseling files should not be available to unauthorized persons on campus or to any person off campus except for the most compelling reasons. No records should be kept which reflect the political activities or beliefs of students. Provision should also be made for periodic routine destruction of noncurrent disciplinary records. Administrative staff and student personnel officers should respect confidential information about students which they acquire in the course of their work. (p. 448)

The guidelines recommended by the AAUP appear to summarize, succinctly, general policy. The statement, however, makes no provision for the handling of information which is nonacademic and nondisciplinary, except in the very general last sentence regarding confidentiality. The scope of the problem can only be touched upon in this limited manner, but its importance cannot be minimized.

Colleges must, of course, maintain records. Student records can be of assistance to the student in connection with future employment, applications to graduate schools, and a variety of related purposes. While the student is in attendance and for at least five years thereafter, these records should be readily available so that reference letters and responses to inquiries from schools, employers, and governmental agencies may be prepared. Needless to say, information regarding students should be disclosed only with the permission of the student, except where the national security is involved.

In the interest of the student, records should be microfilmed at some agreed upon time following graduation or withdrawal from the college. Materials to be microfilmed might include awards and commendations, entrance and other test data, letters of recommendation, latest transcript, medical records, veterans' office records, student activities reports, and significant correspondence. Members of the faculty should have access to student record folders when they consider that such access will be helpful in their relationship with the student. Students should have the right to have the contents of their records interpreted to them by a qualified counselor at any time, upon their own request.

The major area of conflict and controversy is that which touches upon privileged communications and the question of confidentiality. This might include, though not be limited to, personal family information, psychiatric or psychological data, court actions, certain medical reports, financial matters, and any other material which is clearly not public. Some institutions meet the problem by maintaining no records other than those which are clearly academic. Others maintain a separate file of a confidential nature under the personal jurisdiction of the chief student services officer. Still others have a flexible policy which permits the judgment of the college official involved to operate. The growing body of literature relating to the problem of confidentiality attests to its importance, but the absence of consensus attests to its controversiality (see, for example, the extensive bibliographic references at the end of this chapter and at the ends of preceding chapters making reference to records and to problems of confidentiality during the past several years). In the opinion of the writer, no solution to the problem is equitable if it does not protect, completely and inviolately, the right of the student to approve any disclosures that are made which are the product of a counseling relationship. There can be no compromise on this point, or there will be no true counseling relationships.

REFERENCES

Ayers, A. R. & Russel, J. H. *Internal structure: organization and administration of institutions of higher education.* U.S. Dept. of Hlth., Educ. and Welf., Off. of Educ. Washington: Govt. Print. Off., 1962.

Ayers, A. R., Tripp, P. A., & Russel, J. H. *Student services administration in higher education.* U.S. Dept. of Hlth., Educ., and Welf., Off. of Educ. Washington: Govt. Print. Off., 1966.

Campbell, R. F. Evaluation of college administrators. In G. K. Smith (Ed.), *Current issues in higher education: higher education reflects on itself and on the larger society.* Washington: Assoc. for Higher Educ., Nat. Educ. Assoc., 1966.

Clark, M. Confidentiality and the school counselor. *Personnel Guid. J.*, 1965, 43, 482–484.

Committees on Faculty Responsibility for the Academic Freedom of Students. Statement on the academic freedom of students. *AAUP Bull.*, 1965, 52, 447–449.

Jacobson, S. How confidential should counseling be kept? *Coll. Univ. Bus.*, 1963, 35, 42–43.

Lewis, E. C., & Warman, R. E. Confidentiality expectations of college students. *J. Coll. Stud. Personnel*, 1964, 6(1), 7–11, 20.

Magoon, T. Confidentiality of student records. *N.E.A. J.*, 1962, 51, 29–30.

National Education Association. *Opinions of the committee on professional ethics.* Washington: Author, 1964.

Rezny, A. A., & Dorow, E. Confidential information and the guidance program. *J. Educ. Research*, 1961, 54, 243–250.

Russel, J. H., & Ayers, A. R. *Academic administration: case studies in the liberal arts college.* U.S. Dept. of Hlth., Educ., and Welf., Off. of Educ. Washington: Govt Print. Off., 1964.

Schneiders, A. A. Problems of confidentiality in university and college counseling centers. *Personnel Guid. J.*, 1963, 42, 252–254.

Smith, G. K. (Ed.) *Current issues in higher education: higher education re-*

flects on itself and on the larger society. Washington: Assoc. for Higher Educ., Nat. Educ. Assoc., 1966.

Slovenko, R. *Psychotherapy, confidentiality, and privileged communication*. Springfield, Ill.: Charles C Thomas, 1966.

Slovenko, R., & Usdin, G. L. The psychiatrist and privileged communication. *Arch. gen. Psychiat.*, 1961, 4, 431–444.

Vance, F. L. Confidentiality interpreted by professional judgment and staff review. *Personnel Guid. J.*, 1963, 42, 255–257.

Ware, Martha L. (Ed.) *Law of guidance and counseling*. Cincinatti: W. H. Anderson, 1964.

Warman, R. E. Confidentiality interpreted by established agency policy. *Personnel Guid. J.*, 1963, 42, 257–259.

Appendices

Appendix A

Journals Related to Student Personnel Work

The list which follows has been adapted from one prepared in the Office of the Dean of Students at Brooklyn College. Dean Herbert Stroup has graciously granted authorization for the reproduction of this list. The efforts of Mrs. Thelma Abelew, then Fellow in the Department of Student Services, in the preparation of this listing are acknowledged with many thanks.

AAUW JOURNAL (American Association of University Women) (quarterly)
2401 Virginia Avenue N.W.
Washington, D.C., 20037

ACAC NEWSLETTER (Association of College Admissions Counselors)
610 Church Street
Evanston, Illinois 60201

ADMINISTRATIVE SCIENCE QUARTERLY (quarterly)
Graduate School of Business and Public Administration
Cornell University
Ithaca, New York 14850

ADULT LEADERSHIP (monthly)
University of South Carolina
Columbia, South Carolina 29208

AMERICAN ASSOCIATION OF UNIVERSITY PROFESSORS (quarterly)
Editorial Office
1785 Massachusetts Avenue, N.W.
Washington, D.C. 20036

AMERICAN EDUCATION (ten times a year)
U.S. Office of Education
Washington, D.C. 20202

AMERICAN EDUCATIONAL RESEARCH JOURNAL (quarterly)
American Educational Research Association
1201 Sixteenth Street, N.W.
Washington, D.C. 20036

AMERICAN JOURNAL OF ORTHOPSYCHIATRY (five times a year)
Leon Eisenberg, Editor
1790 Broadway
New York, New York 10019

AMERICAN JOURNAL OF SOCIOLOGY (bimonthly)
1130 East 59 Street
University of Chicago
Chicago, Illinois 60637

AMERICAN PSYCHOLOGIST (monthly)
American Psychological Association, Inc.
1200 17th Street, N.W.
Washington, D.C. 20036

AMERICAN SOCIOLOGICAL REVIEW (bimonthly)
206 South Hall
University of California
Berkeley, California 94720

ASSOCIATION OF COLLEGE UNIONS (five times a year)
Bulletin
Wisconsin Union
Madison, Wisconsin 53706

BEHAVIORAL SCIENCE (quarterly)
James G. Miller, Editor
Mental Health Research Institute
University of Michigan
Ann Arbor, Michigan 48104

BRITISH JOURNAL OF SOCIOLOGY (quarterly)
Routledge and Kegan Paul Ltd.
Broadway House
68-74 Carter Lane
London E.C. 4, England

BULLETIN ON INTERNATIONAL EDUCATION (eight times a year)
American Council on Education
1785 Massachusetts Avenue, N.W.
Washington, D.C. 20036

CALIFORNIA JOURNAL OF EDUCATIONAL RESEARCH (five times a year)
1705 Murchison Drive
Burlingame, California 94010

CARNEGIE CORPORATION OF NEW YORK QUARTERLY (quarterly)
New York, New York 10001

CATHOLIC EDUCATIONAL REVIEW (monthly except June, July and August)
Catholic University of America Press
620 Michigan Avenue, N.E.
Washington, D.C. 20017

COLLEGE AND UNIVERSITY (quarterly)
American Association of Collegiate Registrars and Admission Officers
450 Ahnaip Street
Menasha, Wisconsin 54952

COLLEGE AND UNIVERSITY BULLETIN (semi-monthly)
Association for Higher Education
Department of the National Education Association
1201 16th Street, N.W.
Washington, D.C. 20036

COLLEGE AND UNIVERSITY BUSINESS (monthly)
500 Fifth Avenue
New York, New York 10036

COLLEGE BOARD REVIEW (quarterly)
College Entrance Examination Board
475 Riverside Drive
New York, New York 10027

COLLEGE STUDENT PERSONNEL ABSTRACTS (quarterly)
College Student Personnel Institute
165 East 10th Street
Claremont, California 91711

CONTEMPORARY PSYCHOLOGY (monthly)
Fillmore H. Sanford, Editor
New College
Sarasota, Florida 33578

COUNSELOR EDUCATION AND SUPERVISION (quarterly)
Association for Counselor Education and Supervision
1605 New Hampshire Avenue, N.W.
Washington, D.C. 20009

CURRENT ISSUES IN HIGHER EDUCATION (annually)
Association for Higher Education
Department of National Education Association
1201 16th Street, N.W.
Washington, D.C. 20036

DATA PROCESSING FOR EDUCATION
American Data Processing
4th Floor, Book Building
Detroit, Michigan 48226

EDUCATIONAL AND PSYCHOLOGICAL MEASUREMENT (quarterly)
G. Frederic Kuder, Editor
Box 6907
College Station
Durham, North Carolina 27708

EDUCATIONAL DATA PROCESSING NEWSLETTER (bimonthly)
Chicago Teachers College North
5500 North St. Louis Avenue
Chicago, Illinois 60625

THE EDUCATIONAL RECORD (quarterly)
American Council on Education
1785 Massachusetts Avenue, N.W.
Washington, D.C. 20036

EDUCATIONAL THEORY (quarterly)
105 Gregory Hall
University of Illinois
Urbana, Illinois 61822

EXPANDING OPPORTUNITIES (eight times a year)
Committee on Equality of Educational Opportunity
American Council on Education
1785 Massachusetts Avenue, N.W.
Washington, D.C. 20036

FINANCIAL AID NEWS
College Entrance Examination Board
475 Riverside Drive
New York, New York 10027

GENETIC PSYCHOLOGY MONOGRAPHS (semi-annually)
Carl Murchison, Editor
The Journal Press
2 Commercial Street
Provincetown, Massachusetts 02657

HARVARD EDUCATIONAL REVIEW (quarterly)
Longfellow Hall
13 Appian Way
Cambridge, Massachusetts 02138

HUMAN RELATIONS (quarterly)
Secretary, Editorial Committee
Human Relations
The Research Center for Group Dynamics
University of Michigan
Ann Arbor, Michigan 48104

IMPROVING COLLEGE AND UNIVERSITY TEACHING (quarterly)
10 Commerce Hall
Oregon State University
Corvallis, Oregon 97331

INTERNATIONAL ASSOCIATION OF UNIVERSITIES BULLETIN (published irregularly)
19, Avenue Kleber
Paris 16, France

JOURNAL OF COMMUNICATION (quarterly)
George Borden, Editor
Pennsylvania State Union
University Park, Pennsylvania 16802

JOURNAL OF APPLIED BEHAVIORAL SCIENCE (quarterly)
Goodwin Watson, Editor
Kirby Lane North
Rye, New York 10580

JOURNAL OF APPLIED PSYCHOLOGY (bimonthly)
Kenneth E. Clark, Editor
College of Arts and Sciences
302 Morey Hall
University of Rochester
Rochester, New York 14627

JOURNAL OF COLLEGE PLACEMENT (quarterly)
Warren E. Kauffman, Editor
College Placement Council
35 East Elizabeth Avenue
Bethlehem, Pennsylvania 18018

JOURNAL OF COLLEGE STUDENT PERSONNEL (quarterly)
Robert Callis, Editor
220 Parker Hall
University of Missouri
Columbia, Missouri 65202

JOURNAL OF CONSULTING PSYCHOLOGY (bimonthly)
Jules D. Holzberg, Editor
Department of Psychology
Wesleyan University
Middletown, Connecticut 06457

JOURNAL OF COUNSELING PSYCHOLOGY (quarterly)
Francis P. Robinson, Editor
The Ohio State University
1945 North High Street
Columbus, Ohio 43210

JOURNAL OF EDUCATIONAL MEASUREMENT
Michigan State University
East Lansing, Michigan 48824

JOURNAL OF EDUCATIONAL PSYCHOLOGY (bimonthly)
Raymond G. Kuhlen, Editor
Department of Psychology
Syracuse University
123 College Place
Syracuse, New York 13210

JOURNAL OF EDUCATIONAL RESEARCH (ten times a year)
Wilson B. Thiede, Editor
Dembar Educational Research Services
P.O. Box 1148
Madison, Wisconsin 53701

JOURNAL OF EXPERIMENTAL EDUCATION (quarterly)
John Schmid, Editor
College of Education
University of Arkansas
Fayetteville, Arkansas 72701

THE JOURNAL OF GENERAL EDUCATION (January, April, July, and October)
B. Euwema, Editor
The Pennsylvania State University Press
University Park, Pennsylvania 16802

JOURNAL OF GENETIC PSYCHOLOGY (quarterly)
The Journal Press
2 Commercial Street
Provincetown, Massachusetts 02657

THE JOURNAL OF HIGHER EDUCATION (monthly except July, August, and September)
F. J. Pegues, Editor
Ohio State University Press
Columbus, Ohio 43210

JOURNAL OF HUMAN RELATIONS (quarterly)
Central State College
Wilberforce, Ohio 45384

JOURNAL OF HUMANISTIC PSYCHOLOGY (semi-annually)
Anthony J. Sutich, Editor
2637 Marshall Drive
Palo Alto, California 94303

JOURNAL OF THE NATIONAL ASSOCIATION OF WOMEN DEANS AND COUNSELORS (quarterly)
National Association of Women Deans and Counselors
National Education Association
1201 16th Street, N.W.
Washington, D.C. 20036

JOURNAL OF NEGRO EDUCATION (quarterly)
Howard University
Washington, D.C. 20001

JOURNAL OF PERSONALITY (quarterly)
Department of Psychology
Duke University
Durham, North Carolina 27706

JOURNAL OF PERSONALITY AND SOCIAL PSYCHOLOGY
Daniel Katz, Editor
American Psychological Association
1200 Seventeenth Street, N.W.
Washington, D.C. 20036

JOURNAL OF PSYCHOLOGY (six times a year)
The Journal Press
2 Commercial Street
Provincetown, Massachusetts 02657

JOURNAL OF SOCIAL ISSUES (quarterly)
Robert Chin, Editor
Society for the Psychological Study of Social Issues
P.O. Box 1248
Ann Arbor, Michigan 48106

JOURNAL OF SOCIAL PSYCHOLOGY (bimonthly)
The Journal Press
2 Commercial Street
Provincetown, Massachusetts 02657

JUNIOR COLLEGE JOURNAL
American Association of Junior Colleges
1777 Massachusetts Avenue, N.W.
Washington, D.C. 20036

LIBERAL EDUCATION (quarterly)
Association of American Colleges
1818 R Street, N.W.
Washington, D.C. 20009

MERRILL-PALMER QUARTERLY OF BEHAVIOR AND DEVELOPMENT (quarterly)
Merrill-Palmer Quarterly
71 East Ferry Avenue
Detroit, Michigan 48202

MILBANK MEMORIAL FUND QUARTERLY (quarterly)
Robin F. Badgley, Editor
40 Wall Street
New York, New York 10005

NAFSA (National Association of Foreign Student Advisers)
NAFSA Studies and Papers
500 Riverside Drive
New York, New York 10027

NASPA (National Association of Student Personnel Administrators
Richard A. Siggelkow, Editor
210 Harriman Library
State University of N.Y. at Buffalo
Buffalo, New York 14214

NORTH CENTRAL ASSOCIATION QUARTERLY
5454 South Shore Drive
Chicago, Illinois 60615

OCCUPATIONAL PSYCHOLOGY (quarterly)
National Institute of Industrial Psychology
14 Welbeck Street
London, W. 1, England

PEABODY JOURNAL OF EDUCATION (bimonthly)
George Peabody College for Teachers
Nashville, Tennessee 37203

THE PERSONNEL AND GUIDANCE JOURNAL (monthly)
The Personnel and Guidance Journal
1605 New Hampshire Avenue, N.W.
Washington, D.C. 20009

PERSONNEL JOURNAL (monthly)
100 Park Avenue
Swarthmore, Pennsylvania 19081

PERSONNEL PSYCHOLOGY (quarterly)
Personnel Psychology, Inc.
P.O. Box 6965
College Station
Durham, North Carolina 27708

PHI DELTA KAPPAN (monthly, September through June)
Eighth Street and Union Avenue
Bloomington, Indiana 47401

PSYCHOLOGY IN THE SCHOOLS (quarterly)
W. A. Hunt, Editor
Department of Psychology
Northwestern University
Evanston, Illinois 60201

PSYCHOLOGICAL ISSUES (quarterly)
George Klein, Editor
International Universities Press Inc.
227 West 13 Street
New York, New York 10011

PUBLIC OPINION QUARTERLY (quarterly)
F. F. Stephan, Editor
Princeton University Press
Box 231
Princeton, New Jersey 08541

REHABILITATION COUNSELING BULLETIN (quarterly)
American Personnel and Guidance Association
1605 New Hampshire Avenue, N.W.
Washington, D.C. 20009

REHABILITATION COUNSELING BULLETIN (or BULLETIN OF REHABILITATION COUNSELING)
Division of Rehabilitation Counseling
American Personnel and Guidance Association
1605 New Hampshire Avenue, N.W.
Washington, D.C. 20009

REVIEW OF EDUCATIONAL RESEARCH (five times a year)
American Educational Research Association
1201 Sixteenth Street, N.W.
Washington, D.C. 20036

SCHOOL COUNSELOR (quarterly)
American School Counselor Association
1605 New Hampshire Avenue, N.W.
Washington, D.C. 20009

SCHOOL REVIEW (quarterly)
School Review
5835 Kimbark Avenue
Chicago, Illinois 60637

SCHOOL AND SOCIETY (biweekly)
William W. Brickman, Editor
1834 Broadway
New York, New York 10023

SCIENCE (weekly)
American Association for the Advancement of Science
1515 Massachusetts Avenue N.W.
Washington, D.C. 20005

SOCIAL FORCES (quarterly)
G. B. Johnson and R. B. Vance, Editors
Williams and Wilkins
428 East Preston Street
Baltimore, Maryland 21202

SOCIAL PROBLEMS (quarterly)
Howard S. Becker, Editor
Adelphi University
Garden City, New York 11530

SOCIOLOGY OF EDUCATION (or JOURNAL OF EDUCATIONAL SOCIOLOGY (quarterly)
Danish National Institute of Social Research
Borgergade 28
Copenhagen K, Denmark

SOCIOLOGY OF EDUCATION (quarterly)
Machmer Hall
University of Massachusetts
Amherst, Massachusetts 01003

SOCIOMETRY (quarterly)
Department of Sociology
University of California
Los Angeles, California 90024

STUDENT GOVERNMENT BULLETIN (quarterly)
U.S. National Student Association
3457 Chestnut Street
Philadelphia, Pennsylvania 19104

SUPERIOR STUDENT (monthly)
Inter-University Committee on the Superior Student
924 Broadway
University of Colorado
Boulder, Colorado 80304

TEACHERS COLLEGE RECORD (monthly October through May)
Teachers College
Columbia University
525 West 120 Street
New York, New York 10027

UNIVERSITIES QUARTERLY (quarterly)
10 Great Turnstile
London W.C. 1, England

VOCATIONAL GUIDANCE QUARTERLY (quarterly)
National Vocational Guidance Association
1605 New Hampshire Avenue, N.W.
Washington, D.C. 20009

JOURNAL OF THE AMERICAN COLLEGE HEALTH ASSOCIATION (quarterly)
R. W. Alexander, Editor
Gannett Medical Clinic
Ithaca, New York 14850

Appendix B

Audio-Visual Aids Relating to The Counseling of College Students

AN ANNOTATED LISTING[1]

I. Admissions and Selection of College

College for Me?
Educational Audio-Visual Inc.
29 Marble Avenue
Pleasantville, New York 10570

Film strip on choosing the right college, advantages of college, financing a college education.

Getting into College Today (40 minutes)
Guidance Associates
Box 5
Pleasantville, New York 10570

Admissions officers and guidance counselors discuss range of modern college admissions problems and practices.

Getting Ready for College (34 frames)
Guidance Information, Basic College Preparation Film Strip Service
Campbell Films
Academy Avenue
Saxtons River, Vermont 05154

Preparing for selecting a college for collegebound high school students.

1. Time in minutes indicates a motion-picture film; frames indicate a film strip. The assistance of Mrs. Thelma Abelew, then Department Fellow is gratefully acknowledged in the preparation of this listing.

How to Choose a College (34 frames)
Campbell Films
Academy Avenue
Saxtons River, Vermont 05154

Plan for high school student to use in selecting right college for himself. Importance of such a plan.

So You're Going to College
Educational Audio Visual Inc.
29 Marble Avenue
Pleasantville, New York 10570

Film strip on study habits, curricula, extracurricular activities, college as an opportunity, approach to exams.

The Urban University (15 minutes)
Guidance Associates
Box 5
Pleasantville, New York 10570

Forces and attractions leading college freshmen to urban universities. Types of students doing well or poorly there. Differences between public and private urban universities.

Who should go to an Urban University? (color filmstrip and record)
Guidance Associates
Pleasantville, New York 10570

Conveys to students the experience of attending an urban university.

II. Counseling—Freshmen

The College Dropout—six out of every ten (2 color filmstrips; 2 records)
Guidance Associates
Pleasantville, New York 10570

Personal accounts by several dropouts acquaint collegebound students with many of the factors leading to the common freshman-year question, "What am I doing here?" Explores many of the freshman-year pressures, probes the "identity crisis," "Sophomore Slump," etc.

College Perspectives (28½ minutes)
College Entrance Examination Board
375 Riverside Drive
New York, New York 10027

Unrehearsed interviews with college students who discuss life on a college campus. Opportunities for college students today.

Developing Effective College Study Practices (2 color filmstrips; 2 records)
Guidance Associates
Pleasantville, New York 10570

Distinguishes between high school study techniques and those required at the college level.

Freshman Year at College (color filmstrip and record)
Guidance Associates
Pleasantville, New York 10570

Prepares students for the emotional and physical adjustments they must make in their transition from high school to college. Covers areas such as handling the increased study load, joining extracurricular activities, etc.

I Wish I'd Known that Before I Went to College (2 color filmstrips; 2 records)
Guidance Associates
Pleasantville, New York 10570

Explores nineteen stumbling blocks which confront most college freshmen—misconceptions about the college, the abrupt transition from the warmth of orientation week to the business of the fall term, sororities and fraternities, etc.

III. Counseling—General, Disciplinary, Personal

The Case of Jim (42 minute record)
Educational Test Bureau
2106 Pierce Avenue
Nashville, Tennessee 37212

The case of Jim illustrates the nondirective approach to counseling as a means of personality reorientation. Jim, in his early twenties, has a speech handicap that interferes with his individual and social adjustments. The record reproduces characteristic sessions over a period of two years of counseling.

Case Problems in Guidance
Wayne State University
Detroit, Michigan 48202

3 records, 6 sides: 1–2, Developing group responsibility; 3–4, Disorder—then what?; 5–6, Jim is truant.

Challenge of Change: The Case for Counseling (30 minutes)
Indiana University
Audio-Visual Center
Bloomington, Indiana 47401

Process of counseling in school and involvement of various individuals in process.

Counseling Discipline Cases (20 minutes)
Pennsylvania State University
Audio-Visual Aids Library
University Park, Pennsylvania 16802

A student, often absent from school, has a forged excuse. The counselor explores reasons for absences—economic, social, academic, family and vocational—and works with the student toward a solution of the problem.

Counseling Forecast
American Personnel & Guidance Assn.
1605 New Hampshire Avenue N.W.
Washington, D.C. 20009

Based on Dr. Gilbert Wrenn's study, "The Counselor in a Changing World." Discusses the complex role of the school counselor.

Counseling Upset Students (31 minutes)
Pennsylvania State University
Audio-Visual Aids Library
University Park, Pennsylvania 16802

A senior high school student is troubled about her future because the present neither interests nor satisfies her. An expert counselor helps her toward fuller insight.

A *Counselor's Day* (12 minutes)
New York University Film Library
26 Washington Place
New York, New York 10003

A counselor's day is a busy one with appointments, consultations, teaching classes, extracurricular activities and professional writing. Shows the counselor's working relationship with the school staff and students.

Diagnosis and Planning Adjustments in Counseling (18 minutes)
New York University Film Library
26 Washington Place
New York, New York 10003

After a brief review of information accumulated in *Using Analytical Tools,* this film outlines the techniques for diagnosing the case and then illustrates methods employed by the counselor to help the student work out his own personal adjustments.

Emotional Health (20 minutes, sound, 1947)
McGraw-Hill, Inc.
330 W. 42 Street
New York, New York 10036

Three primary objects: 1. To convince young people of college age that emotional upsets are common; 2. To show that, if an emotional disturbance is prolonged, the need for professional counsel and care is just as important and normal as with any physical illness; and 3. To explain in simplified language some of the basic techniques of psychiatric treatment and thereby allay some of the stigma attached to the necessity for treatment.

Return (38 minutes)
Pennsylvania State University
Audio-Visual Aids Library
University Park, Pennsylvania 16802

The therapists role, equipment and methods, important facets of rehabilitation psychology.

Role Playing in Guidance (14 minutes)
University of Michigan
Audio-Visual Center
Education Center
Frieze Building
Ann Arbor, Michigan 48104

How role-playing was used in a problem situation involving a high school boy; how it was introduced and conducted. Some techniques useful in varying the effectiveness of the training.

IV. Interviewing

Counseling—Its Tools and Techniques (22 minutes)
New York University Film Library
26 Washington Place
New York, New York 10003

One of a series on vocational guidance, this film describes the techniques involved in counseling, specifically the interview. Elements of counseling illustrated by an interview between a counselor and a high school boy who is having difficulties in his classroom and is in need of guidance.

Improving Interviewing (33 minutes)
Pennsylvania State University
Audio-Visual Aids Library
University Park, Pennsylvania 16802

Excerpts from hundreds of real interviews presented with "real-life" illustrations. Viewers' guide should be distributed before film is shown.

Interviewing Principles and Techniques (17 minutes)
Pennsylvania State University
Audio-Visual Aids Library
University Park, Pennsylvania 16802

Preparing for Interviews (30 minutes)
Pennsylvania State University
Audio-Visual Aids Library
University Park, Pennsylvania 16802

Tess—experienced counselor seeks help from a colleague in synthesizing information about a student in preparation for an interview.

V. Placement and Career Counseling

Aptitudes and Occupations (16 minutes)
Coronet Instructional Films
65 E. South Water Street
Chicago, Illinois 60601

Shows six fundamental human abilities—mechanical, clerical, social, musical, artistic and scholastic—and how these can be determined. Indicates broad fields in which certain combinations of abilities are required.

Career and Vocational Guidance Programs (6 filmstrips with records)
Guidance Associates
Pleasantville, New York 10570

Intended as aid to college guidance counselors and students seeking career advice. The units offer help in selection: "Your Future in Elementary Education"; "Retailing"; "Nursing"; "Professional Home Economics"; "Engineering and Applied Science"; and "Engineering Technology."

Career Choice Counseling (18 minutes)
Pennsylvania State University
Audio-Visual Aids Library
University Park, Pennsylvania 16802

Counselor helps student, in the top tenth of his class in grades and abilities, further define his occupational goals.

Careers for Girls (18 minutes)
New York University Film Library
26 Washington Place
New York, New York 10003

Shows wide variety of fields now open to women and suggests that proper guidance and self-knowledge is a key to success.

Choosing Your Career (11 minutes)
Coronet Films
65 E. South Water Street
Chicago, Illinois 60601

Self-appraisal, occupational possibilities, preparation requirements, guidance facilities.

Doctor (10 minutes)
Michigan State University
Auido-Visual Center
East Lansing, Michigan 48823

The work of the doctor, including a health examination, preventive medicine, home calls, emergency hospital calls, and hospital rounds.

Dropping Out—Road to Nowhere (4 filmstrips, 2 records)
Guidance Associates
Pleasantville, New York 10570

Factual, well-organized material for presenting to teenagers the reactions of students who have actually dropped out of high school. Also provides good basic counseling material for sessions devoted to career guidance, job counseling, and preparation for placement interviews.

Employment Interview (11 minutes)
Michigan State University
Audio-Visual Center
East Lansing, Michigan 48823

Importance of the employment interview in getting the right man on the job.

Engineering: A Career for Tomorrow (25 minutes)
Michigan State University
Audio-Visual Center
East Lansing, Michigan 48823

Engineering field is illustrated for prospective engineering students at high school Career Day.

Engineers in the Making (20 minutes)
General Motors Corp.
3044 W. Grand Boulevard
Detroit, Michigan 48202

Describes the General Motors Institute cooperative education program.

Finding the Right Job (11 minutes)
Michigan State University
Audio-Visual Center
East Lansing, Michigan 48823

Essentials of locating the right job. Knowing the type of job wanted, developing leads, writing letters of application, importance of interviews, and interview techniques. How to evaluate job offers.

Finding Your Life Work (22 minutes)
Pennsylvania State University
Audio-Visual Aids Library
University Park, Pennsylvania 16802

General orientation on vocational guidance; should be used before films on specific vocations. Suggestions for obtaining information about different occupations and the practical value of various school subjects.

Going our Way (30 minutes, color)
Parke, Davis & Co.
Joseph Campon Avenue at the River
Detroit, Michigan 48232

Centers around a young physician beginning his career. Opportunities of related professions are also described.

How You can study Occupations (14½ minutes, phonotape)
University of Colorado
National Tape Repository
Bureau of Audio-Visual Instruction
Boulder, Colorado 80302

Information and sources of information on occupations.

Idea with a Future (30 minutes)
ANA—KLN Film Service
10 Columbus Circle
New York, New York 10019

The Associate Degree of Nursing program is presented.

Insuring Our Investment in Youth
University of Michigan
Audio-Visual Education Center
Frieze Building
720 East Huron
Ann Arbor, Michigan 48104

Need for adequate vocational guidance service in our schools, satisfactory guidance program in operation, waste through lack of personalized course planning and false vocational starts.

Journey into Medicine (39 minutes)
New York University Film Library
26 Washington Place
New York, New York 10003

The medical career of a young man who enters Columbia University medical school and a description of experiences culminating in his desire to enter public health work.

More Power for the Job (19 minutes, color)
International Film Bureau
332 S. Michigan Avenue
Chicago, Illinois 60604

Illustrates points available to those students who consult the school Vocational Guidance Counselor, in order to establish career goals and plan educational and training programs.

New Career Opportunities (41 frames)
McGraw-Hill Textfilms
330 W. 42nd Street
New York, New York 10036

Discusses new career opportunities created by this modern age.

Pick Your Tomorrow (20 minutes)
Michigan State University
Audio-Visual Center
East Lansing, Michigan 48823

Finding the right job through a combination of self analysis and analysis of job possibilities, revealed in interview situations.

The Tower Evaluators (30 minutes)
Institute for the Crippled & Disabled
400 First Avenue
New York, New York 10010

Shows the training of vocational evaluators in the use of the TOWER System (Testing, Orientation, and Work Evaluation in Rehabilitation).

Time for Tomorrow (20 minutes)
University of Michigan
Audio-Visual Education Center
Frieze Building
720 East Huron
Ann Arbor, Michigan 48104

How a pharmacy student spends his time in laboratory, classroom, and after school hours.

What Greater Challenge (8 minutes)
Copley Productions
P.O. Box 1530
La Jolla, California 92037

Presents the various jobs performed in the production of a newspaper.

Where do I go from Here? (25 minutes, color)
College Placement Council Inc.
35 E. Elizabeth Avenue
Bethlehem, Pennsylvania 18018

In addition to telling the story of college placement, the film stresses the desirability of career planning—beginning early in the student's academic life and climaxed by an intelligent employee search.

Your Career in Elementary Teaching (27 minutes)
Modern Learning Aids
3 E. 54 Street
New York, New York 10022

The ability to know and understand people is the most important aptitude, beyond ability to learn, for the prospective elementary school teacher.

Your Future in Elementary School Teaching (13 minutes)
Guidance Associates
P.O. Box 5
Pleasantville, New York 10570

Presents the preparation, desirable qualities, and responsibilities of the elementary school teacher.

VI. Student Activities

Choice and Challenge (26 minutes)
Brooklyn College Television Center
Bedford Avenue & Avenue H
Brooklyn, New York 11210

This instructional television program recorded on video tape describes activities of students in clubs, House Plan, student government, freshman orientation, student adviser leadership training, country fair, and social affairs board, as part of total Student Activities Program.

Extra Curricular (15 minute phonotape)
Purdue University
Audio-Visual Center
Lafayette, Indiana 47907

What is more important: high grades or participation in activities?

Fraternity (19 minutes)
State University of Iowa
Bureau of Audio-Visual Instruction
East Hall, Iowa City, Iowa 52240

Presents what the Inter-Fraternity council believes are the beneficial aspects of fraternity life. Explains the philosophy behind fraternities and shows prospective members what the fraternity has to offer.

The Fraternity Idea (22 minutes)
Indiana University
Audio-Visual Center
Bloomington, Indiana 47401

Fraternity activities before, during, after pledging. Emphasizes pleasure and responsibilities of fraternity life.

Particulars on Extra-Curriculars (14 minute phonotape)
University of Colorado
National Tape Repository
Bureau of Audio-Visual Instruction
Boulder, Colorado 80302

Importance of extracurricular activities in developing a well-rounded individual.

UCLA (44 minutes)
Pennsylvania State University
Audio-Visual Aids Library
University Park, Pennsylvania 16802

Student life, student government, athletics, social events, classroom activities, and academic opportunities in American colleges and universities.

VII. Testing

Administering a Testing Program (13 minutes)
Educational Testing Service
Cooperative Test Division
Princeton, New Jersey 08540

Six points of the testing program: planning, handling of material, preparing students, training sessions, scoring, administering tests.

College Entrance Examinations (181 frames)
Educational Filmstrips
Box 289
Huntsville, Texas 77340

Three filmstrips on college entrance examinations: Part I, Reasons colleges require examinations; Part II, Types of questions; Part III, Recognized national examinations.

The Meaning of Test Scores (28 minutes)
North Dakota State University
Fargo, North Dakota 58102

Presents facts about standardized test score interpretation.

The Public Relations of Testing (11 minutes)
Educational Testing Service
Cooperative Test Division
Princeton, New Jersey 08540

How to achieve good public relations with students, teachers, parents, and community at large, in regard to test data.

Using Analytical Tools (15 minutes)
New York University Film Library
26 Washington Place
New York, New York 10003

Shows how a counselor goes about the task of analyzing a counseling case. The student presented is a representative type of high school boy in high schools today.

Using Test Results (19 minutes)
Educational Testing Service
Cooperative Test Division
Princeton, New Jersey 08540

How test results can benefit instruction, through test problem analysis and guidance, and through expectancy charts, to advise students in course selection, administration, etc.

You and Your College Boards, parts 1 and 2 (35 minutes)
Guidance Associates
P.O. Box 5
Pleasantville, New York 10570
Attn: Jack L. Goodman

Operations of test making, score processing, and distribution of College Entrance Examination Boards. Value of scores and place in college admissions decisions.

You and Your College Entrance Examinations (2 full-color filmstrips; 2 records)
Guidance Associates
P.O. Box 5
Pleasantville, New York 10570

Places the major entrance examinations in perspective: Material will help student understand: 1. What the tests measure; 2. How they are evaluated by college admissions officers; 3. Their use as a guidance device; 4. How Verbal, Math and Achievement scores are interpreted.

Indexes

Name Index

Subject Index